General of the Army George Catlett Marshall

Biennial Reports

OF THE

CHIEF OF STAFF OF THE

UNITED STATES ARMY

TO THE

SECRETARY OF WAR

1 July 1939-30 June 1945

CENTER OF MILITARY HISTORY

UNITED STATES ARMY

WASHINGTON, D.C., 1996

Library of Congress Cataloging-in-Publication Data

United States. War Dept. General Staff.
    Biennial reports of the Chief of Staff of the United States Army
to the Secretary of War : 1 July 1939-30 June 1945.
      p. cm.
    Reports made by George C. Marshall.
    Originally published as three separate vols.: Washington, DC :
G.P.O., 1941-1945. With new introductory material.
    1. World War, 1939-1945—Campaigns—Sources. 2. World War,
1939-1945—United States—Sources. 3. United States. Army—
History—World War, 1939-1945—Sources. I. Marshall, George C.
(George Catlett), 1880-1959. II. United States. War Dept.
III. Title.
D735.B47 1996
940.54'00973—dc20   96-14075
                                                           CIP

Editors' Note

    This book reproduces in one volume the three biennial reports of General George C. Marshall, Chief of Staff of the United States Army, to the Secretary of War for the period 1 July 1939-30 June 1945. The Table of Contents has been reworked, and the text, maps, and charts have been renumbered consecutively to eliminate duplication or confusion. Within the text, obvious typographical errors have been corrected, but the punctuation, capitalization, grammar, and usage are those found in the original editions.

CMH Pub 70-57

For sale by the U.S. Government Printing Office
Superintendent of Documents, Mail Stop: SSOP, Washington, DC 20402-9328
ISBN 0-16-048657-2

FOREWORD

One president called him "the greatest living American," and another told him, "I feel I could not sleep at night with you out of the country." Sir Winston Churchill found him to be not only "a rugged soldier and magnificent organiser" but also "a statesman with a penetrating and commanding view of the whole scene"; to Britain's great wartime leader, he was "the noblest Roman of them all." Perhaps the most moving tribute came from his wartime boss, at a small, evening ceremony in the Pentagon, the day Nazi Germany surrendered. Secretary of War Henry L. Stimson, whose own experience with the Army reached back almost to the turn of the century, told his close associate and confidant, "I have seen a great many soldiers in my lifetime, and you, sir, are the finest soldier I have ever known."

Acclaimed by his colleagues and duly praised by historians of World War II, General of the Army George C. Marshall nevertheless has been overshadowed in popular acceptance by other leaders. In part, the lack of widespread public recognition of Marshall stems from his role as the Army's Chief of Staff, creating the armies that others led to glory. In part, it can be traced to his personality. Austere and sometimes aloof, modest and self-effacing, he lacked MacArthur's flair for publicity and Eisenhower's common touch. As a superb staff officer in World War I and the interwar Army, he was accustomed to working behind the scenes. Still, he remembered that soldiers are human beings, not cogs in a machine, and he possessed an unusual appreciation for the citizen-soldier based on his extensive experience with reserve forces. Associates were struck by his relentless perfectionism and impatience with military dogma. Most of all, however, they were impressed by his strength of character: the integrity, self-discipline, sense of duty, lack of political ambition, and presence which conveyed firmness, intensity, and calm. Perhaps it was these qualities that led President Franklin D. Roosevelt, in September 1939, to bypass thirty-four generals senior to Marshall and appoint him Chief of Staff.

For the feat of transforming the miniscule interwar Army to the great force that defeated the Axis in Africa, Europe, the Pacific, and Asia, no one could claim more credit than Marshall. When he took office, the 174,000-man U.S. Army ranked nineteenth in size in the world, behind Portugal and only slightly ahead of Bulgaria. Its half-strength divisions were scattered among numerous posts, its equipment obsolete, its reliance on the horse increasingly anachronistic. Given the strength of isolationist sentiment and apathy toward a distant war in Europe, prospects for improvement were anything but promising. To Marshall fell the thankless task of preaching preparedness, of pointing out the need for the United States to "put our house in order" before the sparks from the European conflagration could reach it. The passage of the nation's first peacetime conscription act in the summer of 1940 was largely due to the shock from the fall of France, but it also owed much to Marshall's skillful relations with Congress, which came to trust implicitly his judgment and integrity. As the country mobilized its manpower, Marshall faced the enormous tasks of organizing and training the new recruits, finding competent leaders, and weighing the critical needs of his own forces for new equipment against the Allies' desperate pleas. In six years, he presided over the growth of the Army to a force of over eight million men, backed by an economic and logistical base of unprecedented proportions.

If Marshall had done nothing else, his guiding role in creating the Army that won World War II would have been enough to ensure his place in history; in fact, he did much more. As a global strategist, he achieved a position of preeminence among the Allied military chiefs, not through bluster or deception, but through a strength and generosity of character which commanded respect among his peers. In his relations with officers from other services and nationalities, from the Navy's crusty Fleet Admiral Ernest J. King to the condescending Field Marshal Sir Alan Brooke, he displayed a genius for cooperation. He insisted on the same spirit in subordinates assigned to high-level theater positions.

Finally, Marshall's strategy carried the Allies to victory over Nazi Germany. From the first days of American intervention in the war, he advocated the earliest possible cross-Channel attack to come to grips with German forces near the heart of Axis power on the Continent. He encountered near-constant opposition from the British and even at times from his president and colleagues on the Joint Chiefs of Staff but, in the end, won them over to the Normandy invasion which sounded the death knell of the Third Reich.

Fifty years after the close of World War II, the U.S. Army Center of Military History takes pleasure in bringing together for the first time all three installments of Marshall's wartime reports. Published at two-year intervals, these reports provide a comprehensive picture of global war as seen from the perspective of the Chief of Staff. The first report describes the race to mobilize an unprepared country and Marshall's appeal on the eve of war for the renewal of Selective Service, a reminder of how far the U.S. Army had to come to meet the Axis challenge. The second recounts the initial defeats after Pearl Harbor and the ultimately successful efforts of the United States and its Allies to turn the tide. The final report describes the drive to victory and outlines Marshall's analysis of the reasons for the Allied triumph. Summaries give an overall view of the progress of the war, but the scholar and military professional will find most interesting Marshall's comments on such topics as technology, the "90-division gamble," the replacement system, troop morale and the citizen-soldier, and demobilization. These comments and the other material presented in the reports provide not only a fresh perspective on the myriad problems of conducting a global war at the highest levels but also renewed appreciation for the man whom Churchill appropriately called "the organiser of victory."

Washington, D.C.
12 February 1996

JOHN W. MOUNTCASTLE
Brigadier General, USA
Chief of Military History

CONTENTS

July 1, 1943, to June 30, 1945

Charts

Maps

Biennial Report

OF THE

CHIEF OF STAFF
OF THE
UNITED STATES ARMY

July 1, 1939, to June 30, 1941

TO THE

SECRETARY OF WAR

DEAR MR. SECRETARY:

With the Nation in a state of unlimited emergency, the undersigned submits the attached report covering the period from his assignment as Chief of Staff on September 1, 1939, to July 1, 1941.

In reviewing the events of the past 2 years, the extent of this Nation's military preparation may roughly be divided into two distinct phases, each coincident with decisive events in the European war. The first phase, commencing with the beginning of the current conflict and extending until the late spring of 1940, was a period of uncertainty as to its influence on the United States. The General Staff, aware of the possibilities of the situation, particularly with regard to the time factor, directed its attention to the urgency of creating and equipping an Army capable of operating under the exacting conditions of modern warfare. Upon the part of the American people this period was marked by a slow awakening to the necessity of augmenting our armed forces.

In a democracy such as ours the War Department is limited in its actions by the appropriations approved by the President and provided by the Congress. These agencies are in turn motivated by the will of the people. Consequently the outstanding characteristic of the first phase was an increasing interest in national defense, but an interest still insufficient to prevent reductions in military appropriations which the War Department had requested as necessary to carry out certain objectives. This phase terminated with the decisive successes of the German Army in Western Europe in May 1940.

The second phase, which covers approximately the fiscal year 1941, was marked by a growing national consciousness of the seriousness of the international situation, and by the ready appropriation of billions of dollars for national defense. It witnessed the peacetime mobilization of a citizen Army upon a wartime scale, and the establishment of scores of great military camps in large training areas. It required the reorientation of national industry to an unprecedented peacetime production rate. It involved, in effect, a great experiment in democracy, a test of the ability of a Government such as ours to prepare itself in time of peace against the ruthless and arbitrary action of other governments whose leaders take such measures as they see fit, and strike when and where they will with sudden and terrific violence.

THE FIRST PHASE

State of the Armed Forces, July 1, 1939

The undersigned became Acting Chief of Staff on July 1, 1939, and Chief of Staff September 1, 1939. On July 1 the active Army of the United States consisted of approximately 174,000 enlisted men scattered over 130 posts, camps, and stations. A schematic view of the organization of the active Army at this time is given by chart 1.

Within the United States we had no field army. There existed the mere framework of about 3½ square divisions approximately 50 percent complete as to personnel and scattered among a number of Army posts. There was such a shortage in motor transportation that divisional training was impracticable. There were virtually no corps troops, almost no Army troops or GHQ special troop units, which are necessary for the functioning of the larger tactical units. The Air Corps consisted of but 62 tactical squadrons. The funds which were authorized for training were less than 5 percent of the annual War Department appropriations. As an army we were ineffective. Our equipment, modern at the conclusion of the World War, was now in a large measure obsolescent. In fact, during the post-war period, continuous paring of appropriations had reduced the Army virtually to the status of that of a third-rate power.

In February 1939, while Deputy Chief of Staff, my statement to the Senate Military Affairs Committee included this summary of the situation, that it was of vital importance that we have modern equipment for the Regular Army and National Guard; that we modernize our artillery; that we replace our 34-year-old rifles with more modern weapons; that we have the antitank and antiaircraft matériel in the actual hands of the troops; that we have the necessary reserves of ammunition; and that these matters be emphatically regarded as fundamental to the entire proposition of national defense. During the post-war period the encouraging moves in national-defense preparations had been the augmentation of the Air Corps to an authorized 5,500-plane program, including an increase on July 1, 1939, of the strength of the Army from 174,000 to 210,000 men, and an appropriation of $116,000,000 for matériel and seacoast defenses. The increase in manpower was entirely devoted to the garrison in Panama and to the increase of the Air Corps.

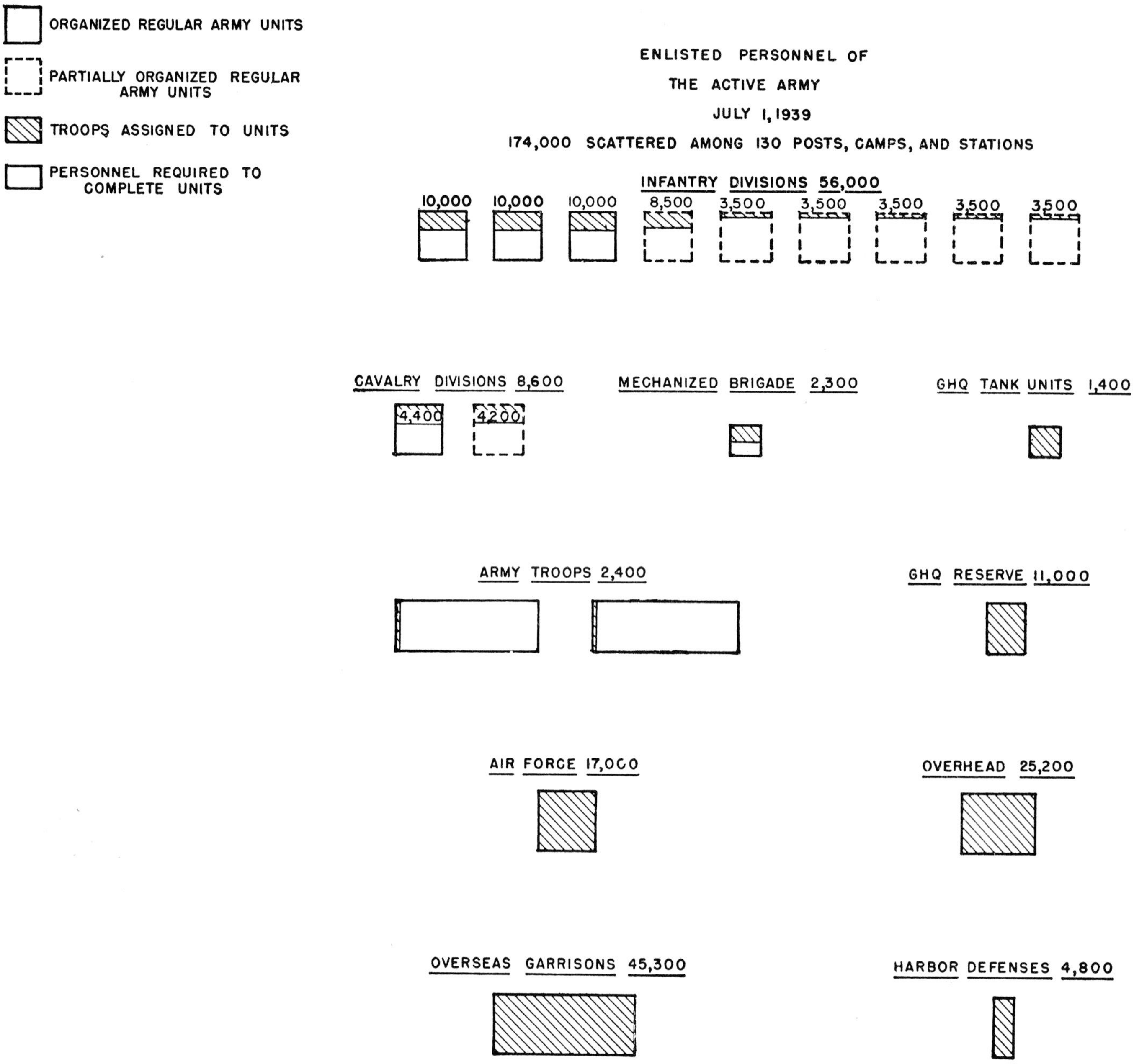

ORGANIZED REGULAR ARMY UNITS

PARTIALLY ORGANIZED REGULAR
ARMY UNITS

TROOPS ASSIGNED TO UNITS

PERSONNEL REQUIRED TO
COMPLETE UNITS

ENLISTED PERSONNEL OF
THE ACTIVE ARMY
JULY 1, 1939
174,000 SCATTERED AMONG 130 POSTS, CAMPS, AND STATIONS

INFANTRY DIVISIONS 56,000
10,000 10,000 10,000 8,500 3,500 3,500 3,500 3,500 3,500

CAVALRY DIVISIONS 8,600   MECHANIZED BRIGADE 2,300   GHQ TANK UNITS 1,400
4,400   4,200

ARMY TROOPS 2,400   GHQ RESERVE 11,000

AIR FORCE 17,000   OVERHEAD 25,200

OVERSEAS GARRISONS 45,300   HARBOR DEFENSES 4,800

The President's Emergency Proclamation September 8, 1939

At the outbreak of the European war the President issued a limited emergency proclamation, in which he authorized an expansion of the active army from 210,000 to 227,000 men, and an increase of the National Guard to 235,000 men. The War Department was also authorized to create certain deficiencies, including the purchase of approximately twelve million dollars' worth of motor transportation. This small increase of 17,000 men to the Regular Army permitted the reorganization of our pathetically incomplete square divisions into five new type triangular divisions, and also permitted the assembly of those divisions, along with other units, in the field for the winter. It enabled us to establish the peace complement of corps troops for one army corps. The limited emergency permitted the number of armory drills of the National Guard to be increased from 48 to 60 per year and an additional week of field training to be conducted that fall supplementary to the 2 weeks of summer camp and to provide for the training of the recently recruited men.

The urgent necessity for Army maneuvers involving large units was manifest. For the past 5 years field training had been limited to the assembly of the four paper organizations, called field armies, once every 4 years, and then only for a 2-week period, of which about 5 days could be devoted to very limited action due to lack of motor transportation and the unseasoned state of the National Guard personnel. This system, together with a general lack of corps troops, heavy artillery, engineers, medical regiments, signal battalions, quartermaster truck trains, and a complete lack of corps headquarters and experienced higher

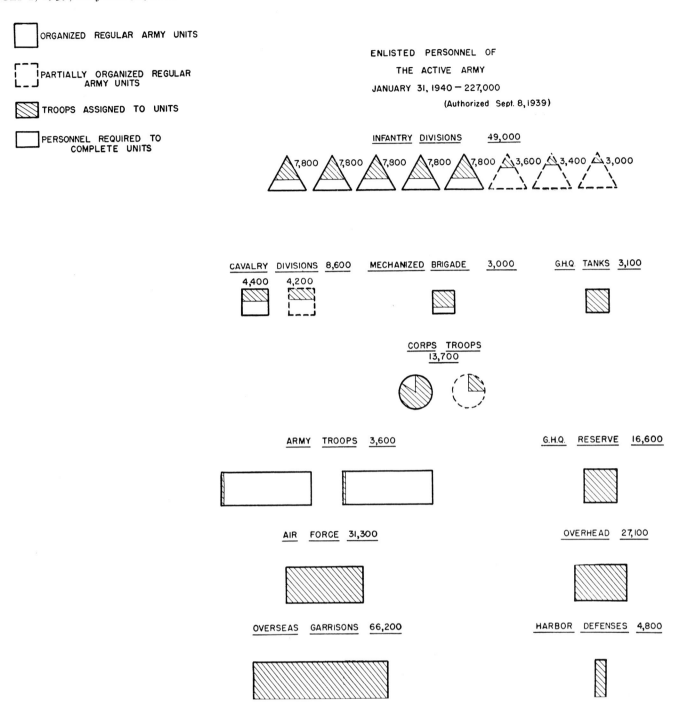

commanders, made it virtually impossible for the mobile combat troops of the Regular Army to be prepared as an immediately available combat force, experienced in the technique of large-scale field operations. It was essential that the higher commanders and staffs be given opportunities for training in the technique, tactics, and teamwork involved; that the troops be accustomed to operating in large groups. The authorized deficiencies and later appropriations for this purpose permitted the assembly, in the late spring of 1940, of some 70,000 Regular Army troops for the frst genuine corps and army maneuvers in the history of this Nation.

The organization of the Army on January 31, 1940, as a result of these changes, may be seen by referring to chart 2.

During this period the war in Europe was in a quiescent state. Poland had been conquered, but the situation in Western Europe was to all intents stabilized. There was a feeling by many that the field fortifcations established in France and Belgium furnished ample security to those nations. Requests for further increases in the armed forces of the United States were regarded in many quarters as mere warmongering. On February 23, 1940, I stated to the Appropriations Committee of the House of Representatives that if Europe blazed in the late spring or summer we must put our house in order before the sparks reached the Western Hemisphere. It was urged that definite measures should be taken step by step to prepare the Nation against the possibility of chaotic world conditions. Opposed to plunging into a sudden expansion of personnel in such a manner that our small nucleus of trained troops would be fatally diluted, but yet conscious of the importance of the time factor, the General Staff was equally opposed to the policy of waiting until the last moment and then attempting the impossible. With respect to the time factor, a grave feature was the matter of critical munitions which required a long time to produce, and it was felt that there could be no longer delay in obtaining the deficiencies in equipment for the initial issue to the Regular Army and the National Guard. The Army was almost completely lacking in clothing for prospective increases of the Regular Army or the National Guard from a small peace strength organization status to full strength. The fundamental obstacle at the time was the fact that the American people were unable to visualize the dangerous possibilities of the situation. For example, as late as March of 1940 War Department estimates for a small number of replacement airplanes were cut by the House of Representatives to 57 planes. An estimate of $12,000,000 for the development of a defensive force in Alaska was refused.

During May and June of 1940 the German avalanche completely upset the equilibrium of the European continent. France was eliminated as a world power and the British Army lost most of its heavy equipment. To many the invasion of Great Britain appeared imminent. The precariousness of the situation and its threat to the security of the United States became suddenly apparent to our people, and the pendulum of public opinion reversed itself, swinging violently to the other extreme, in an urgent demand for enormous and immediate increases in modern equipment and of the armed forces. It was at this time that the second phase of the period of the current emergency commenced.

THE SECOND PHASE

The President's Messages of May 16 and May 31, 1940

On May 16, 1940, in a special message to Congress, the President recommended the appropriation of approximately $1,000,000,000, of which $732,000,000 was for equipment and to increase the Army by 28,000 men, including 13,000 for the Air Corps. On May 31 in a second defense message to Congress the President recommended an additional appropriation of approximately $1,000,000,000.

Supplementary to the amounts recommended by the President in his messages of May 16 and May 31, two additions made by committees of Congress were of inestimable assistance to the War Department in carrying out its program. On May 20, 4 days following the President's message of May 16, the Senate Appropriations Committee inserted into the bill under consideration an additional appropriation of $50,000,000 for a further personnel increase of 25,000 men, bringing the Army to an authorized strength of 255,000 men. A few days following the President's message of May 31, the House Appropriations Committee added $322,000,000 to the bill under consideration which permitted an increase in strength of the Army of 95,000 men, bringing it to a total authorized strength of 375,000. Although these sums of money and increases in personnel, which the committees of Congress added, do not seem especially significant today in the light of the billions recently appropriated, they enabled the War Department to take a preliminary step of vast importance to the great expansion soon to come. Skeleton units could be organized and manufacturers started to work on clothing and equipment which had to be available by October. It was largely for this reason that the induction of the National Guard and the first of the selectees was made possible.

Further authorizations included in the legislation at this time consisted of a substantial increase in the number of aircraft and funds for additional pilot training together with the inclusion of civilian schools to assist in this training; additional money for field exercises, an increase in seacoast defenses, funds for modernization of existing planes, establishment of ordnance munitions plants and the additional purchase of critical items of equipment. The Air Corps was authorized to be increased to 54 combat groups, and funds for the organization of an armored force were included. The tangible influence of these events on the organization of the Army is indicated in chart 3.

At this time the President referred to the desirability of authorizing him to call out the National Guard. Although sadly lacking in modern equipment and at less than 40 percent of its full strength, the Guard represented one of the few organized defense assets, and its federalization therefore became a matter of pressing importance. Another significant development of the phase which we were entering was the changing attitude of our industrialists regarding their production capacities and rates of deliveries with respect to airplane engines and other items of heavy ordnance. As the crisis abroad developed, they grew increasingly willing to undertake production schedules that had previously been regarded as out of the question.

The expansion of the Army during the summer of 1940 in general followed the long-standing protective mobilization plan, but the violent change in the international situation as to the French fleet and the peril of England necessitated an immediate reorientation regarding the means at our disposal. The possible loss of the British Navy introduced a new time factor for our defensive preparations, and immediately imposed an urgent and tremendous demand for the manufacture of time-consuming critical items of equipment.

In weighing the problems of the time factor against the possibilities of the situation, two aspects of the

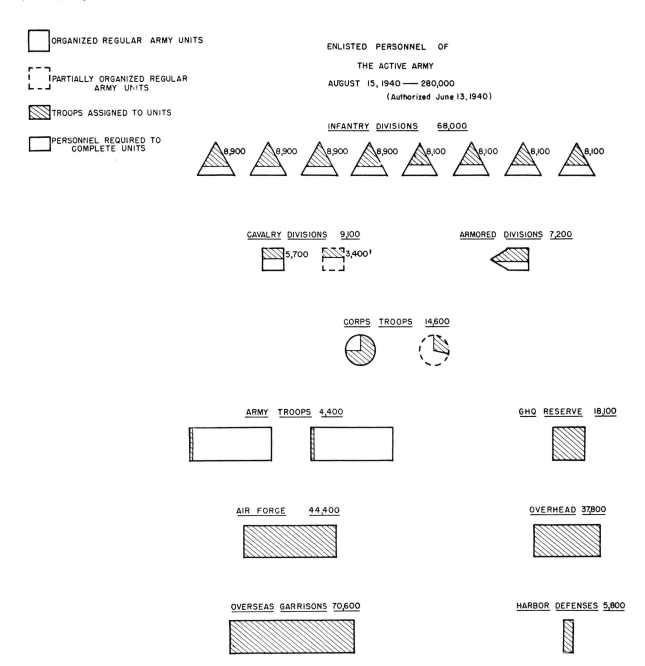

matter had to be considered. One related to the possible dangers of the situation within the next 6 months. The other related to what should be done over a period of years. It was considered that for the time being the first issue was of dominant importance. Ordnance, ammunition, and other critical items of equipment could not be produced overnight, but the other requisite for an armed force, that is, personnel, was available and could be conditioned, disciplined, and trained with the old World War material available and the new matériel then under manufacture. It was not believed that the men necessary to form an Army of the size required to meet the contingencies of the situation could be obtained by voluntary enlistment. The alternative was a selective service system which would furnish sufficient personnel to bring the National Guard and the Regular Army to full strength in the shortest possible time, and to do this in a controlled and therefore

efficient manner, in contrast to the piecemeal, unbalanced basis of voluntary enlistments. It was suggested by members of Congress that the Regular Army be tremendously increased. However, this would have been a futile procedure unless the necessary equipment could be made available, and this could have been arranged only by subverting the National Guard and making a fundamental change in the existing military policy of the Government. The decision was made to call the National Guard into the Federal service and utilize its personnel and equipment with that of the Regular Army to train the first contingent of the thousands of men necessary for the defense of the country.

The federalization of the National Guard and the speedy enactment of selective-service legislation at once became matters of urgent importance to the War Department in the summer of 1940. The original request for the federalization of the National Guard occurred in May with the purpose of utilizing summer camps while preparing the cantonments for the expanded Army, so that when cold weather set in, the necessary semipermanent preparations would have been completed for the first increment and construction well under way for the remainder. The democratic processes of legislation resulted in a prolonged debate on these two measures, which continued throughout the summer.

In my testimony before the Senate Appropriations Committee on August 5, the following statements were made:

> Shelter is a serious problem at the present moment. We thought that Congress would settle the question of authority to order out the National Guard, and the matter of compulsory training by the first of August. On that basis, the Guard was to be brought into the Federal service during September and the first induction of men under the Selective Service Act during October. What has happened is that the weeks have been passing and we have no authority to enter into contracts to provide the additional shelter required.
>
> We have been trying to find some manner, some means for getting started. We want to proceed in an orderly and businesslike manner. We know exactly what we want to do and exactly where we want to do it, but we have neither the authority nor the funds and time is fleeting. So far as construction is concerned the winter is upon us, because it requires from 3 to 4 months to provide proper shelter. We had hopes at first to gain time by providing a progressive mobilization of the National Guard during the summer. We planned to put troops in tent camps, while better shelter was being prepared in the climates that demand special protection against the winter. However, weeks have come and have gone and we have been unable to make a start. The present uncertainties make a businesslike procedure almost impossible. We must make a start toward getting water lines laid; a start on the sewage-disposal systems; a start on the temporary roads and certainly the walks to keep our people out of the mud; and we must get under way the start of construction of temporary hospital facilities. These are fundamental necessities and take time to develop.

One factor of assistance in this dilemma was the $29,500,000 which the President authorized from his emergency fund on August 2, 1940. The availability of this sum permitted the initiation of construction of basic utilities, hospitals, and warehouses in twelve National Guard camps and also a divisional cantonment at Fort Dix, N. J.

The problems of funds were further complicated by the concurrent consideration of authority to call the National Guard and selective-service legislation. Authorization for the National Guard to be called into Federal service was finally given on August 27, 1940, but the $128,000,000 necessary for initial construction was not appropriated until September 9. The first Guard units were inducted on September 16, the same day that the Selective Service Act was signed by the President. Incidentally, the department would have preferred to delay these inductions for about a month or at least for 2 weeks in order to put the money just appropriated to work. This action was precluded by the advice that the announcement of such plans would probably defeat the passage of the Selective Service Act. Money for selective service construction became available September 24, as the leaves were beginning to fall.

Progress During the Winter of 1940-41

The expansion of our armed forces from 172,000 to approximately one and one-half million men in a relatively short time imposed a tremendous responsibility on the War Department. A basic requirement was the establishment of shelter, hospital facilities, and training areas in strategic and favorable training localities throughout the United States. With winter upon us, the problems of construction incident to unusually bad weather—snow, rain, and mud—added further complications. It was highly important to provide recreational facilities and to make suitable provisions for the spiritual welfare of our citizen soldiers. The problems of acquiring land were complicated by the fact that in some areas selected as camp sites the local population viewed the projects with disfavor. In other instances the War Department was bombarded with requests from local business bureaus and political delegations. Errors were made in the tremendous program which the Army undertook during the winter of 1940-41, but viewed in the light of the actual achievement, it would appear that the task was creditably performed.

The passage of the Selective Service Act in effect authorized the Army of the United States to consist of 1,400,000 men, of which 500,000 were to be in the Regular Army, 270,000 in the National Guard, and 630,000 selectees. A graphical picture of the active army on June 30, 1941, is indicated by chart 4, and its tactical organization by chart 5.

Special Problems Incident to the Expansion

The training of this large force required a tremendous broadening of our Regular Army activities. The continuous formation of training cadres, for new units or schools, resulted in a succession of drafts on the rapidly expanding Regular Army units for experienced officers and noncommissioned officers. This was a disheartening process for the commanders concerned, air and ground, who, while struggling to merge large increments of untrained men into efficient combat teams, were called upon time after time to give up their best leaders in all grades, and compelled by circumstances to drive ahead in their training program while developing new leaders and training new recruits to replace the losses. The National Guard units were spared this demoralizing process in order to give them the fullest opportunity to perfect their

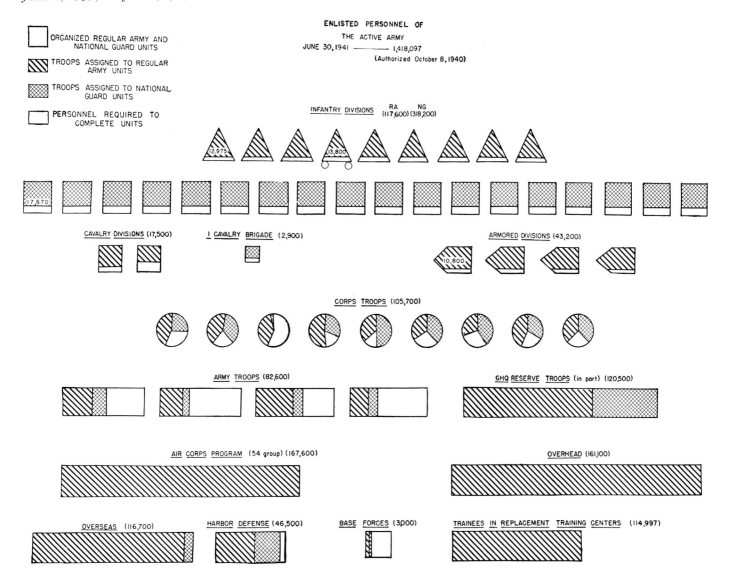

ENLISTED PERSONNEL OF
THE ACTIVE ARMY
JUNE 30, 1941 ———————— 1,418,097
(Authorized October 8, 1940)

ORGANIZED REGULAR ARMY AND NATIONAL GUARD UNITS
TROOPS ASSIGNED TO REGULAR ARMY UNITS
TROOPS ASSIGNED TO NATIONAL GUARD UNITS
PERSONNEL REQUIRED TO COMPLETE UNITS

INFANTRY DIVISIONS   RA   NG
(117,600) (318,200)

CAVALRY DIVISIONS (17,500)   I CAVALRY BRIGADE (2,900)   ARMORED DIVISIONS (43,200)

CORPS TROOPS (105,700)

ARMY TROOPS (82,600)   GHQ RESERVE TROOPS (in part) (120,500)

AIR CORPS PROGRAM (54 group) (167,600)   OVERHEAD (161,100)

OVERSEAS (116,700)   HARBOR DEFENSE (46,500)   BASE FORCES (3,000)   TRAINEES IN REPLACEMENT TRAINING CENTERS (114,997)

organization. Profiting from events in the European war, new organizations, new methods of employment, and new types of equipment became a constant matter of reexamination and experiment. The tempo of the school system was rapidly increased, and courses were quickly established to graduate about 600 officers every 5 weeks.

The procurement of suitable officer personnel was fortunately solved by the fact that during the lean, post-war years over 100,000 Reserve officers had been continuously trained, largely the product of the Reserve Officers' Training Corps. These Reserve officers constituted the principal available asset which we possessed at this time. Without their assistance the program could not have been carried out except in a superficial manner, as is evidenced by the fact that today they constitute 75 to 90 percent of the officer strength with Regular Army units.

For the induction of selectees, we established 29 large reception centers throughout the United States, where thousands of men could be classified, uniformed, and routed to the replacement training centers where they would receive their basic training. The locations and capacities of the reception centers are indicated by chart 6.

For the basic training of recruits, 21 replacement training centers were established where each arm and service of the Army could give individualized basic training in the fundamentals of a soldier. Each soldier entering the Army receives 13 weeks of basic training, after which he is assigned to a tactical unit ready to participate in the tactical training of those units. These establishments were constructed and placed into operation during the winter and spring of 1940–41, despite seriously adverse weather conditions, bottlenecks of material, and shortage of facilities. Their location and capacities are indicated on chart 7.

The establishment of these centers marked our arrival at a normal method of maintaining an Army, and yet they constituted a fundamental departure from past practices. No phase of the development of the present field Army has been so gratifying and impressive as the product of the training centers, both in quality of selectees and in the amazing amount of instruction they have absorbed in the short period of 13 weeks. From now on our regiments and divisions can steadily advance with their combat training, unburdened by the necessity of training recruits or delaying their work in order to conduct individual instruction in weapons or similar matters.

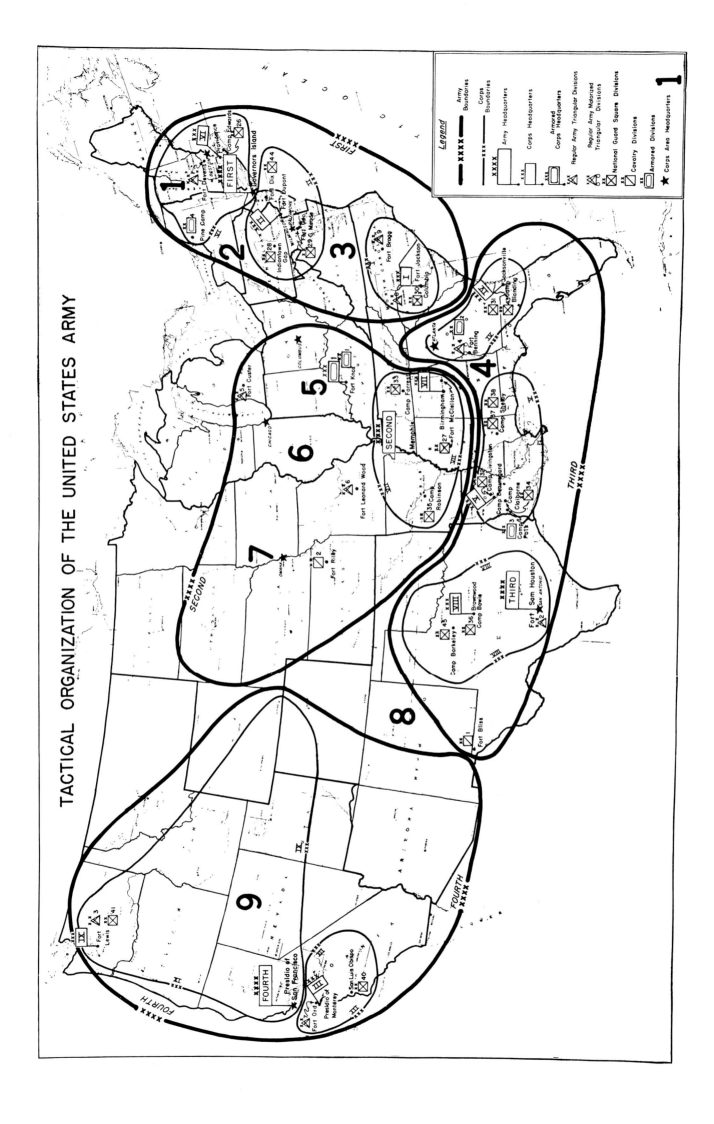

TACTICAL ORGANIZATION OF THE UNITED STATES ARMY

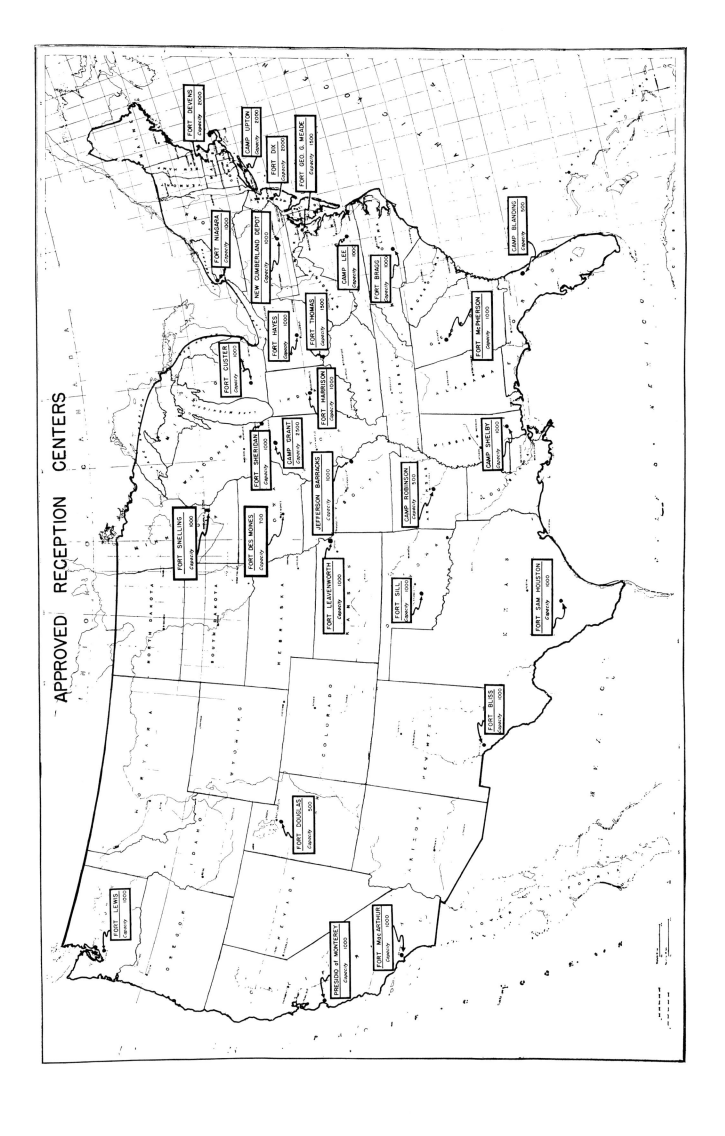

APPROVED RECEPTION CENTERS

FORT DEVENS
Capacity 2000

CAMP UPTON
Capacity 2000

FORT DIX
Capacity 2000

FORT GEO. G. MEADE
Capacity 1500

CAMP BLANDING
Capacity 500

FORT NIAGARA
Capacity 1000

NEW CUMBERLAND DEPOT
Capacity 1000

CAMP LEE
Capacity 1000

FORT BRAGG
Capacity 1000

FORT HAYES
Capacity 1000

FORT THOMAS
Capacity 1500

FORT McPHERSON
Capacity 1000

FORT CUSTER
Capacity 1000

FORT HARRISON
Capacity 1000

CAMP SHELBY
Capacity 1000

FORT SHERIDAN
Capacity 1000

CAMP GRANT
Capacity 2500

JEFFERSON BARRACKS
Capacity 1000

CAMP ROBINSON
Capacity 500

FORT SNELLING
Capacity 1000

FORT DES MOINES
Capacity 700

FORT LEAVENWORTH
Capacity 1000

FORT SILL
Capacity 1000

FORT SAM HOUSTON
Capacity 1000

FORT BLISS
Capacity 1000

FORT DOUGLAS
Capacity 500

FORT LEWIS
Capacity 1000

PRESIDIO of MONTEREY
Capacity 1000

FORT MacARTHUR
Capacity 1000

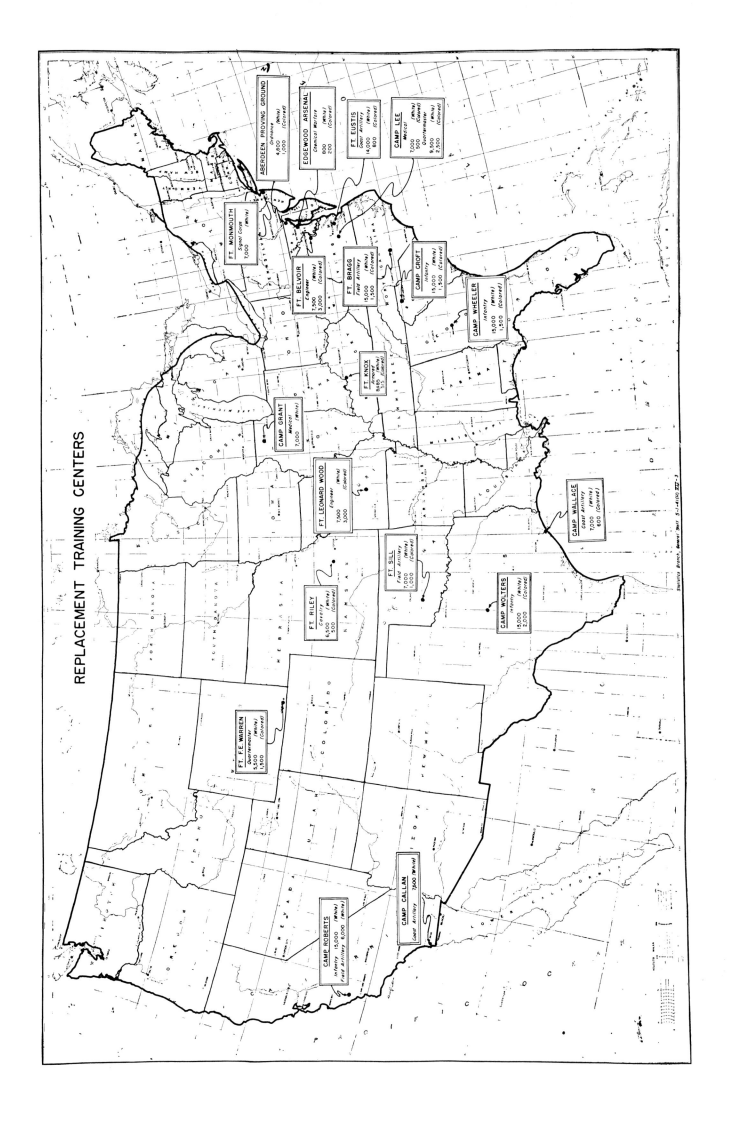

REPLACEMENT TRAINING CENTERS

ABERDEEN PROVING GROUND
Ordnance
4,800 (White)
1,000 (Colored)

EDGEWOOD ARSENAL
Chemical Warfare
800 (White)
200 (Colored)

FT. EUSTIS
(White)
14,000 (White)
800 (Colored)

CAMP LEE
Medical
7,000 (White)
500 (Colored)
Quartermaster
9,500 (White)
2,500 (Colored)

FT. MONMOUTH
Signal Corps (White)
7,000

FT. BELVOIR
Engineer (White)
7,500 (White)
3,000 (Colored)

FT. BRAGG
Field Artillery
15,000 (White)
1,500 (Colored)

CAMP CROFT
Infantry
15,000 (White)
1,500 (Colored)

CAMP WHEELER
Infantry
15,000 (White)
1,500 (Colored)

FT. KNOX
Armored
8,485 (White)
515 (Colored)

CAMP GRANT
Medical (White)
7,000

FT. LEONARD WOOD
Engineer (White)
7,500 (White)
3,000 (Colored)

CAMP WALLACE
Coast Artillery
7,000 (White)
600 (Colored)

FT. SILL
Field Artillery
(White)
7,000 (White)
1,000 (Colored)

CAMP WOLTERS
Infantry
15,000 (White)
2,000 (Colored)

FT. RILEY
Cavalry
6,500 (White)
500 (Colored)

FT. F.E. WARREN
Quartermaster
(White)
5,500 (White)
1,500 (Colored)

CAMP ROBERTS
Infantry 15,000 (White)
Field Artillery 6,000 (White)

CAMP CALLAN
Coast Artillery
7,500 (White)

Statistics Branch, General Staff 5-1-41(R) XII-3

During the spring of 1941, the program of expansion continued. In March, further increases in the Air Corps were authorized and plans undertaken to train 30,000 pilots and 100,000 mechanics annually. Steps were taken toward the occupation of the new bases in the Atlantic leased from the British Government. The augmentation of the garrisons in our foreign possessions and in Alaska continued. Closely interrelated with the problems of procurement incident to a colossal expansion of our defense forces were national commitments to furnish great quantities of critical munitions to sister democracies. Though short of equipment ourselves, the international situation demanded that we furnish equipment to others. This situation introduces the most difficult problem of coordination and direction imposed on the War Department in the present emergency. It represents a complete reversal of the situation in 1917–18 when our Allies provided us with practically all of our munitions. The passage of the Lease-Loan bill in March 1941 permitted the coordination of the entire matter of placing contracts, the types of matériel to be manufactured, and the inspection service to be carried on during this period of production. Increased production due to the authorization of the necessary funds should add to our own strength rather than diminish our resources.

To provide additional officer personnel, to offer a fair opportunity to the man in the ranks, and most important of all, to utilize a rare opportunity for securing outstanding leaders, the War Department has established a series of officers' candidate schools, the students for which are selected from enlisted men of the Army who have given positive evidence of marked capacity as leaders. In a series of 3-month courses these schools will produce a minimum of 10,000 officers a year and are capable of rapid expansion if the situation demands. The location and type of training given at the various officers' candidate schools are indicated on chart 8.

Reorganization of Command and Staff

In the gradual merging of the Army from a peacetime basis into an organization for possible action, the following additional changes have taken place:

General Headquarters of the field forces was set up at the Army War College last July to direct and supervise the training of the troops. More recently it was placed on an operating basis by the addition of a portion of the War Plans Division of the War Department General Staff. By this arrangement, General Headquarters not only supervises training throughout the Army but is being prepared to perform its normal theater of operations functions if required.

To enable the field forces to concentrate on training, the zone of interior functions pertaining to administration and supply have been taken over by the nine corps areas distributed geographically over the United States. Under these corps areas, service commands have been established and are performing the necessary overhead duties, freeing the field forces from obligations of this nature.

For purposes of air defense, the United States has been divided into four air-defense areas where the coordination of aviation, antiaircraft, aircraft warning, and balloon barrage defense has been placed in the hands of the respective Air Force commanders, under the commander of the GHQ Air Force, now the Air Force Combat Command.

To insure unity of command in the entire Caribbean area, Puerto Rico, Panama, and all the newly acquired leased bases in that region have been organized into the Caribbean Defense Command and placed under one commander. The strategic location of Newfoundland has required the development and occupation of this base by air and ground forces, all of which have been placed under the command of an Air Force officer.

The port of embarkation facilities in New York, Charleston, New Orleans, San Francisco, and Seattle have been expanded tremendously throughout the emergency incident to the movements of troops and supplies to oversea garrisons, and the reception and redistribution of certain supplies in continental United States. For some time the New York base alone has been handling a volume of tonnage comparable to that handled during the World War.

Incident to the tremendous amount of business handled by the General Staff during this current expansion, it has been found necessary to increase the number of Deputy Chiefs of Staff from one to three. One of these Deputies is charged solely with all matters pertaining to the Air Force. Another is charged with matters pertaining to supply, equipment, construction, and the Armored Force. The other Deputy handles all other matters incident to General Staff business.

State of the Armed Forces, July 1, 1941

Today the Army has been increased eightfold and consists of approximately 1,400,000 men. The ground forces in the continental United States form four armies of nine army corps and twenty-nine divisions, and an Armored Force of four divisions, soon to be increased to six. The Air Force includes 54 combat groups, and the initial equipment requirements of these forces will be met with the stocks now on hand and under manufacture, plus those to be produced from funds set up in current estimates.

OFFICERS' CANDIDATE SCHOOLS

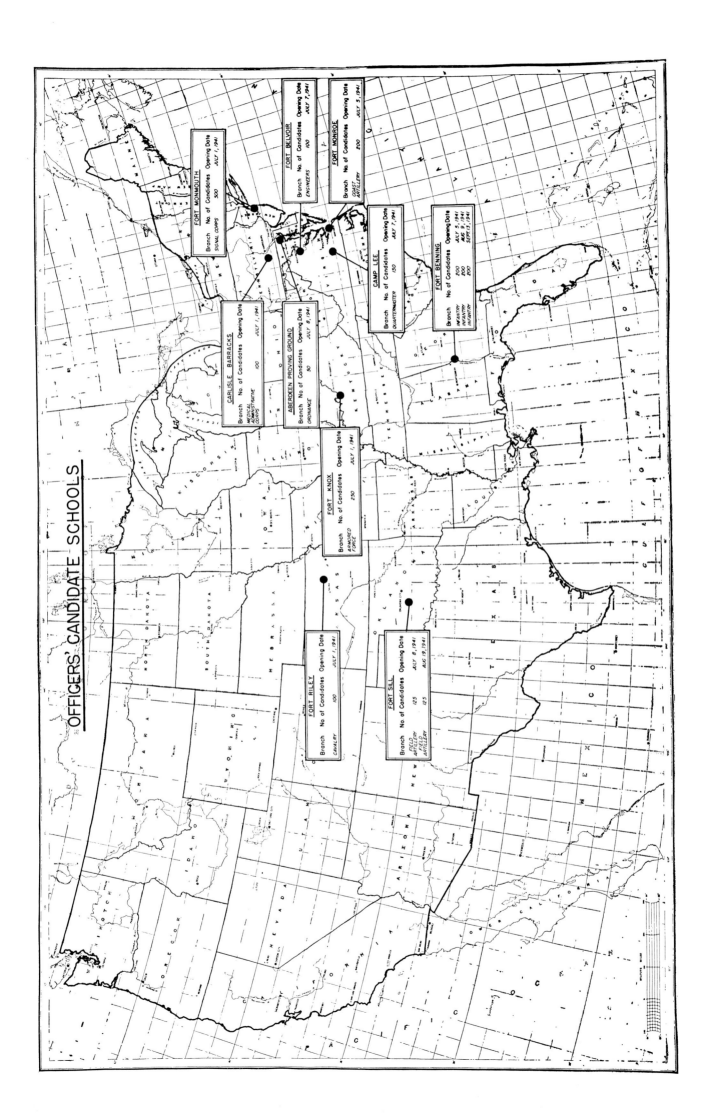

FORT MONMOUTH | Opening Date JULY 1, 1941
Branch | No. of Candidates
SIGNAL CORPS | 500

FORT BELVOIR | Opening Date JULY 7, 1941
Branch | No. of Candidates
ENGINEERS | 100

FORT MONROE | Opening Date JULY 5, 1941
Branch | No. of Candidates
COAST ARTILLERY | 200

CAMP LEE | Opening Date JULY 7, 1941
Branch | No. of Candidates
QUARTERMASTER | 150

FORT BENNING | Opening Date JULY 5, 1941 / AUG. 9, 1941 / SEPT. 13, 1941
Branch | No. of Candidates
INFANTRY | 200
INFANTRY | 200
INFANTRY | 200

CARLISLE BARRACKS | Opening Date JULY 1, 1941
Branch | No. of Candidates
MEDICAL ADMINISTRATIVE CORPS | 100

ABERDEEN PROVING GROUND | Opening Date JULY 8, 1941
Branch | No. of Candidates
ORDNANCE | 50

FORT KNOX | Opening Date JULY 1, 1941
Branch | No. of Candidates
ARMORED FORCE | 250

FORT RILEY | Opening Date JULY 1, 1941
Branch | No. of Candidates
CAVALRY | 100

FORT SILL | Opening Date JULY 8, 1941 / AUG. 19, 1941
Branch | No. of Candidates
FIELD ARTILLERY | 125
FIELD ARTILLERY | 125

The strength of the Army is now allocated approximately as follows: 456,000 men to the 29 divisions of the field armies; 43,000 men to the Armored Force; 308,000 men to some 215 regiments or similar units of field and antiaircraft artillery, engineers, signal troops, etc., who form the corps, army, and GHQ troops to support the divisions; 167,000 men in the Air Corps; 46,000 men manning our harbor defenses; 120,000 men in oversea garrisons including Alaska and Newfoundland; and 160,000 men who provide the overhead to maintain and operate some 550 posts or stations, the supply depots, and the ports of embarkation; and finally from 100,000 to 200,000 selectees under recruit training in the replacement training centers. Our long coast lines and numerous oversea bases involve the employment of a large number of men not related to the field forces now being developed in continental United States.

The organization of the Air Force has been revised to insure its most efficient employment for the welfare of the Nation. Among the units formed or expanded, as necessity dictated, are armored divisions, parachute troops, ski troops, antitank units, antiaircraft units, mountain troops, motorized units, and a great number of service maintenance units essential to the existence of a modern army which must be prepared to operate in any one of a varied number of climates or terrains. The members of our armed forces have passed through a winter of rigorous training and are in splendid physical condition. The training and welfare agencies have produced a gratifying state of morale. Although sufficient equipment exists for training purposes, the necessary amount of critical items is still far short of requirements, and only a small portion of the field Army is at present equipped for extended active operations under conditions of modern warfare. However, quantity production has been getting under way for an increasing number of items, and the next 4 months should greatly improve the situation.

Small as it was, the Regular Army personnel has been the invaluable leaven of the present forces without which developments to date would have been impossible except in rather superficial results to be measured principally in numbers. The progress made has proved the soundness of the plans laboriously prepared throughout the years by the General Staff, despite the lack of opportunity to work with large bodies of troops or, for that matter, with a complete organization of any kind in continental United States. The elaborate school system of the Army maintained since 1920 has declared a huge dividend. Our experienced officers and noncommissioned officers have been ready in technical knowledge, in skill as instructors and ability as leaders to unify the various elements of our professional and citizen soldiers into a great Army of the United States.

Recommendations for the Elimination of Certain Legal Limitations and Restrictions

The foregoing has been largely a recital of problems and progress during the past 2 years. An effort has been made to indicate some of the complications involved in the rapid creation of a large Army under peacetime conditions. As this report is submitted the possibilities of a year ago have become dangerously near probabilities today, and it is vital to the security of the Nation that the hazards of the present crisis be fully recognized.

What has happened is history. Of grave concern today are the contingencies of the present and the future. There are legal restrictions on the use of the armed forces which should be removed without delay. Events of the past 2 months are convincing proof of the terrific striking power possessed by a nation administered purely on a military basis. Events of the past few days are even more forcible indications of the suddenness with which armed conflict can spread to areas hitherto considered free from attack.

It is, therefore, urgently recommended that the War Department be given authority to extend the period of service of the selective-service men, the officers of the Reserve Corps, and the units of the National Guard.

It is the purpose of the War Department to proceed with the military training of annual increments of selectees, replacing those now in active service as soon as the situation permits, especially the older men. In general, the same intention pertains to the Reserve officers whom we wish gradually to replace with others who have not yet been brought into active service. However, a fixed rule cannot be applied at this time, in our opinion. Some are in Hawaii, some in the Aleutian Islands, others in units to be dispatched to oversea bases, and still others are in organizations to be trained as task forces for possible special operations.

In the light of the situation it is believed that our interests are imperiled and that a grave national emergency exists. Whatever we do for the national defense should be done in the most efficient manner. Differences of views regarding national policy should not, it seems to me, be permitted to obscure the facts relating to the preparation of the armed forces for service, which has been the purpose of our vast program of the past 12 months. When and where these forces are to serve are questions to be determined by their Commander in Chief and the Congress, and should not be confused with the problem of their readiness for service. All, it is believed, will admit that the time factor has been of dominant importance in the march of events since September 1939, in the availability of matériel, in the effect of the complete readiness of huge, highly trained units for employment in chosen theaters. The matériel phase of our task is generally understood. The personnel phase is not, and it is here that legal limitations, acceptable at the time of their passage, now hamstring the development of the Army into a force immediately available for whatever defensive measures may be necessary.

To illustrate: In accordance with plans of long standing we have reached the point of availability of troops and matériel, where we now can and urgently should organize and train certain task forces against the possibility of the necessity arising for their use. What is the status of these troops? The Regular Army divisions contain from 75 to 90 percent Reserve officers whose term of service is legally limited to 12 months. In other words, some 600 officers in a division under the law would soon be entitled to drop their present duties and return to their homes. The 12 months' service period of many, if not most of the officers in the first priority divisions, is now nearly completed. Must we replace most of the trained officer personnel of a division—the leaders—at the moment of departure for strategic localities? In two of the Regular divisions we have restricted the enlisted personnel to 3-year men, but in the others, of necessity, the number of selectees varies from 25 to 50 percent. The problem here is the same as for the Reserve officer personnel. The National Guard units involve three distinct limitations as to personnel—that for the National Guard unit, that for the 10 percent Reserve officers in their regiments and now being increased, and that pertaining to selectees who comprise more than 50 percent of the men in the ranks. Furthermore, a task force involves all components. While we may select regular units as the divisional components for task forces, we must utilize National Guard organizations for the special supporting units—antiaircraft, heavy artillery, engineers, etc. So we have become involved in a complete confusion of restrictive details regarding personnel. Add to this problem the fact that plans for large units must cover every conceivable contingency, based on the means available; that time is required to prepare such a force; and that under present conditions we must submit these plans to the time-consuming business of public investigation and debate—along with the advertisement of such plans to the world at large, and I submit that the limitations referred to should be removed as quickly as possible if we are to have a fair opportunity to protect ourselves against the coldly calculated, secret, and sudden action that might be directed against us. Incidentally, our history includes some unfortunate incidents resulting from quite similar legal difficulties, which risked a battle or possibly a campaign. In the present crisis the risks to the Nation are far more serious.

A year ago last July the Army was confronted with a problem very similar to that of this July so far as the time factor and an efficient basis for procedure are concerned. Then we desired authority to put the first increment of the National Guard into summer camps to commence its training, and we wished to be given the money so that we could proceed immediately under favorable weather conditions with the construction of cantonments suitable for occupancy in the winter season. The summer had passed before we were able to proceed in this matter.

Another limitation at the present time involves leadership. There has been submitted to the Congress within the past few days the draft of a joint resolution designed to vitalize the leadership in the Army.

The purpose of this legislation is to remove from the active list a few officers who slow down the development of our emergency Army through lack of qualities of vigor, and intelligent, aggressive leadership. Under existing law the commissions of officers of the Reserve Corps may be revoked at the discretion of the President, and the Federal recognition of officers of the National Guard may be withdrawn upon the recommendation of a board of officers appointed by the Secretary of War. In the case of officers of the Regular Army, however, the law governing their removal from the active list requires a procedure so cumbersome as to make it totally ineffective during a national emergency. In brief, the War Department desires authority to correct deficiencies in the Regular Army as it is now able to do for the National Guard and the Officers' Reserve Corps.

So far as temporary promotions are concerned, the War Department has recently established a mechanism to improve leadership. A system of promotion by selection to the grade of colonel has been instituted, and to date 286 lieutenant colonels have been selected for advancement. It is intended that this procedure will be carried progressively into the lower grades. In all these matters the interests of the soldier and the Nation, rather than that of the individual officer, have governed.

These proposals which the War Department recommends for action by Congress have but one purpose: the security of the American people; to permit the development of the national defense on the orderly and businesslike basis necessary if the dangers of the present situation are to be met. Such a purpose does not admit of delay.

General Comments

While all branches of the service have had to carry a rapidly increasing burden in the expansion program, I do not think the public generally appreciates the vastness of the undertaking which has been imposed upon the Air Corps in both personnel and matériel, the Ordnance Department in production of arms and ammunition, the Quartermaster Corps in construction, supplies, and motor transportation, and the Corps of Engineers in the organization of new units and the sudden undertaking of a construction program for the Air Corps and for the leased bases. The creation and development of the Armored Force has been an enormous task, and is being accomplished with the utmost speed and with remarkable efficiency.

The merging of the three components of our Military Establishment into a unified Army of the United States has been accomplished with high morale and a generous spirit of cooperation throughout. The men in the ranks have worked hard and uncomplainingly in good weather and bad and throughout a difficult winter. Probably the most gratifying feature of the past year has been the quality and the attitude of the men drawn into the Army under the Selective Service Act. They have been a fine example of men cheerfully and earnestly performing the duties to which they have been called as citizens for the security of their Government. This particularly applies to the older men for whom this service has imposed the greatest sacrifice and the heaviest physical ordeal.

The dealings of the War Department with the Bureau of the Budget and with the Committees of Congress during the past year have been without precedent in the evident desire of those officials to lend every possible aid to the Department in meeting the situation.

In closing this report it should be stated that the progress achieved during the past 2 years could not have been made without the highly efficient cooperation of the War Department staff and the commanders and staffs in the field. Their cheerful acceptance of the tremendous burdens of responsibility has furnished a reassurance which cannot be measured in words of thanks.

G. C. MARSHALL,
General, United States Army,
Chief of Staff.

WASHINGTON, D. C., July 1, 1941.

APPENDIX

ORGANIZATION

Military operations abroad constitute a great laboratory and proving ground for the development and testing of organization and matériel. These operations have been characterized by increasing use and importance of armored, motorized, and other specialized divisions and by concurrent effort for development of means to counter armored (tank) divisions operating in close coordination with air and motorized units from mobile striking forces of great speed and power which so far have been uniformly successful in their operations. We have given careful consideration to foreign military developments and, as a result, our own organization is undergoing constant change and development. We do not minimize the enormous power of armored units used in conjunction with accompanying air power; but we do not overlook the fact that the Army of the United States differs in one important characteristic from the armies of Europe. Ours must be an all-purpose Army as we are in an entirely different position from a European nation which knows its traditional or potential enemies and the terrain over which it will have to fight. We must be prepared to operate in the Arctic or in the Tropics, in deserts or mountains, and the elements of our ground forces must be properly balanced to meet any contingencies. Our organization must be a balanced one with armored, air, and foot elements in proper proportion to provide the maximum flexibility.

After 3 years of careful study and tests an organization for a triangular infantry division was approved and placed in effect in the Regular Army during the fiscal year 1940. The square division, adopted during the World War and modifed several times since, has been retained in the National Guard.

The organization of the horse cavalry regiment was revised as a first step in the reorganization of the horse cavalry division. New organizations adopted included the horse-mechanized cavalry regiment designed as the reconnaissance unit of a corps, the antitank battalion, and the corps topographic company. In addition, approximately 100 Tables of Organization for other units were reviewed and brought up to date without any essential changes in organization.

Six Regular Army infantry divisions and two sets of corps troops were formed during the report period, partly by consolidations or conversions of existing units and partly by utilization of increased personnel made available by augmentations to the Army. In addition to these large units, a number of small units were organized. These were used to complete battalions and regiments and to provide service elements, previously lacking. The organization of these units not only materially increased the field efficiency of the Army, but greatly facilitated the greater expansion soon to come. The new organizations were tested in division, corps, and army maneuvers in the winter and spring of 1939-1940. These maneuvers formed a sound basis for future planning, revision, and further tests.

Continuing study is given our own and foreign organizations to take full advantage of developments in weapons, transportation, equipment, and technique. In general, our organizations are sound and well balanced and fully adaptable to modern warfare. Because we have no definite theater of operations, most divisions are necessarily general in purpose and are not specialized. A new type motorized division organization which is intended primarily to complement armored units has been approved. Current study is being given to the organization of a division designed primarily for operation in mountainous country; and of other special units which have only a restricted use.

There are 33 divisions now in active service as follows:

> 26 infantry divisions, including 18 National Guard (square) and 8 Regular Army (triangular);
> 1 motorized division (triangular);
> 4 armored divisions;
> 2 horse cavalry divisions, one partly complete.

There are also enough service and reinforcing troops to complete a balanced field force to two armies, totaling four army corps. The two remaining armies, totaling five army corps, are incomplete.

Present trends in organization are in the direction of increasing the proportion of armored, motorized, and antimechanized units.

ARMORED FORCE

A War Department directive dated July 10, 1940, created for service test an Armored Force to include all armored corps and GHQ reserve tank units. It also prescribed the duties of the Chief of the Armored Force, combining the command functions of a commander of a large tactical unit and many of the responsibilities of the chief of a combatant arm. This included the development of tactical and training doctrines for all units of the Armored Force and research and advisory functions pertaining to development and procurement of all special transportation, armament, and equipment used primarily by armored units.

Regular Army personnel, consisting of the 7th Cavalry Brigade (mechanized), the 66th Infantry (light tanks), and a few scattered infantry tank units, were the nucleus for the initial organization of the Armored Force. This organization consisted of the 1st Armored Corps, the 1st and 2d Armored Divisions, one GHQ reserve tank battalion (70th), and the Armored Force Board. The station of the 1st Corps, the 1st Armored Division, and the Board was at Fort Knox, Kentucky. The 2d Armored Division was organized at Fort Benning, and the 70th Tank Battalion at Fort Meade, Maryland.

In November 1940 the Armored Force School was activated at Fort Knox, Kentucky. The overhead for this unit consisted of about 182 officers and 1,847 enlisted men. This school has a capacity of over 6,000 students at any one time or a graduating capacity of about 26,000 students per year.

During the months of November and December 1940 and January 1941, four National Guard reserve tank battalions were activated and brought into the Federal service. These were the 191st at Fort Meade, Md., the 192d at Fort Knox, Ky., the 193d at Fort Benning, Ga., and the 194th at Fort Lewis, Wash.

In February 1941 the 1st GHQ Reserve Tank Group Headquarters was activated at Fort Knox, Ky. All GHQ reserve tank battalions in existence at that time were placed under this headquarters.

Early in March the Armored Force Replacement Center was activated with an overhead of 240 officers and 1,241 enlisted men. The capacity of the replacement center was 9,000. It was filled up with selectees in March; these selectees were used later for newly activated Armored Force units.

On April 15, 1941, the 3d Armored Division was activated at Camp Beauregard, La., and the 4th Armored Division was activated at Pine Camp, N. Y.

The Armored Force Headquarters and Headquarters Company was activated in May 1941 with headquarters at Fort Knox, Ky.

In early June, five light and five medium GHQ reserve tank battalions were activated. The cadres for this activation came from the 1st and 2d Armored Divisions, and the fillers came from the replacement training center.

Critical and controlled items of equipment have been available in sufficient quantities for minimum training only. This condition will continue until about September 1941.

Training tests of armored units have indicated that these units have met their training requirement. Due, however, to the tremendous expansion involved, armored units have not reached their ultimate efficiency.

TRAINING

Trained, disciplined manpower is the fundamental requirement of any army. Our training program has been designed to build a seasoned body of men who have the basic knowledge and skill to handle any job that may be assigned to them. Its purpose is to build soldiers and leaders—men who, when they have completed their basic training, can take their places in planes or in tanks or behind guns or in the operation of technical equipment with only the final detailed instruction necessary to cover the mechanism which they are to use. Regardless of other matériel shortages, we have the equipment to give this basic training, and our purpose has been to complete it while the production of modern weapons is catching up with our development of modern manpower. The soldier of today has devoted only 20 hours to close order drill out of a total of 572 hours of his basic training period. He has spent his time in learning the things that make a man efficient in combat; that cause him to act intelligently in an emergency; and that toughen him physically to withstand the rigors of modern warfare. Basic training culminates in field maneuvers designed to weld individuals into seasoned, efficient combat teams and to develop the command leadership and staff technique necessary for the handling of large units on the modern battlefield. The comprehensive training program carried out during the fiscal year 1940 was made possible through the appropriation for additional special field exercises as a result of the unlimited emergency and the increasing importance of national defense.

By early September 1939 the following had been completed: the First Army maneuvers in New York and Virginia, training about 100,000 officers and men of the Regular Army, National Guard, and Organized Reserves; the Fourth Army command post exercise, held at the Presidio of San Francisco and training about 700 officers of all components.

Further intensive training for all individuals and units of the Regular Army was initiated in September and October 1939 and continued throughout the year. Armory drills for National Guard units were increased by twelve, and seven additional days of field training away from home armories were given all units. Five complete Regular Army infantry divisions and one cavalry division were assembled in divisional camps or cantonments for intensive training as divisions in the field. Corps area commanders assembled their nondivisional troops for intensive field training. Troops of the oversea garrisons conducted special field training and field exercises pertinent to their assigned missions.

The training of pilots and mechanics for the augmented Air Corps was successfully expanded by use of civilian schools in addition to full capacity of expanded Air Corps training agencies. Procurement of missing equipment was pushed to the utmost in order to provide a sufficient amount for best training results. Several thousand Reserve officers were ordered to active duty for varying periods to assist in and benefit from the intensified training.

The 3d Division assembled at Fort Lewis, Wash., and underwent preliminary training there. In January 1940 it moved by transport to join the Fleet in the Pacific and to participate in landing exercises in the vicinity of Monterey, Calif. After these exercises, the division was given intensive field training at Fort Ord, Calif.

The assembly and divisional training of the 1st, 5th, and 6th Division, together with Fourth Corps troops and nondivisional units culminated in April 1940 with 3 weeks of corps maneuvers at Fort Benning, Ga. During this time the 2d Division and 1st Cavalry Division and corps troops maneuvered in eastern Texas. This was followed by 3 weeks of corps versus corps maneuvers between these two forces, plus the 7th Cavalry Mechanized Brigade, in the Sabine area of Louisiana.

During major divisional and corps field exercises, the division commander and staff of each National Guard division was given a 3-day period of training in actual command and handling of one of the Regular Army divisions. During the large maneuvers in the Sabine area, any National Guard State adjutant general and any National Guard division commander who had not participated as a division commander in a corps exercise was invited to attend the maneuvers as observer.

Throughout the fiscal year 1940, practical training in the field for officers of all grades was stressed. Courses at the Command and General Staff School and the special service schools of the arms and services were suspended February 1, 1940, and officers on duty there were sent to units of the Army undergoing field training.

In order to disseminate to officers and men of the Army the lessons gained from the current war in Europe, steps were taken to facilitate the revision of our training literature and revision of all mobilization training programs. Increased appropriations by Congress for this purpose have made this possible.

During the fiscal year 1941, the Army extended its training activity on a scale never before attempted in peacetime. The primary training objective was the preparation of units to take the field on short notice at existing strength ready to function effectively in combat.

Taking advantage of the lessons learned in the exercises conducted by Regular Army units during the preceding winter and spring, all four armies carried out maneuvers in the summer and fall of 1940, involving all continental Regular Army and National Guard mobile forces. Progress attained was marked, but the exercises demonstrated the necessity of continuing intensive training.

To assist the Chief of Staff in his capacity as Commanding General of the Field Forces, a nucleus of General Headquarters was created and charged initially with the direction of training of all harbor defense and mobile troops within the continental United States and General Headquarters aviation.

The passage of the Selective Service Act, the induction of the National Guard into Federal service for a period of 1 year, and the expansion of the Regular Army created a training problem of vast proportions which necessitated adjustment in the program.

The War Department instituted its planned mobilization training program, modified to meet these new conditions. Troop units generally were stationed at large posts and camps to facilitate training and to develop teamwork. Most of the large posts are in localities which permit year-round training, although enough are in other parts of the country to insure training and experimentation in all types of terrain and in various climates. The year of training prescribed was divided into three 4-month periods; the first devoted to individual and small unit training; the second to progressive combined arms training; and the third to corps and army training including field maneuvers. The climax of this period will come during the summer and fall of 1941 when the four armies, the General Headquarters Air Force, the Armored Force, and parachute troops will participate in maneuvers involving more than half a million men.

To provide means for the training of selectees, those inducted early were assigned to Regular Army and National Guard units. The replacement training center program of the Army mobilization plan was initiated, and as fast as construction was completed, 21 centers were opened. The majority began operating in March and April, and by June were functioning at maximum capacity receiving selectees from reception centers. At replacement training centers, selectees and recruits are given basic training in their arm or service for a period of 13 weeks and then are assigned to units. The maximum trainee capacity of these centers is now approximately 182,500. This system is greatly facilitating the training of the entire Army.

Training in special operations was conducted by selected units. Two divisions trained in landing operations, two combat teams participated in joint exercises with the Navy in the Caribbean area, and units stationed in the snow belt specialized in winter warfare training and tests of special equipment.

Special attention has been given to air training. Tactical squadrons in continental United States and oversea stations have increased 500 percent from the 1939 total. This has required additional flying personnel, likewise has accounted for the original three schools operating in 1939, expanding to a total of 40 schools, 28 of which are conducted through civilian contract arrangement. Additional flying training schools are authorized and likely by the end of the present calendar year will be in full operation. Twelve of the flying schools have been designated for the training of R. A. F. flying cadets.

Pilot training has been increased 700 percent from the output of graduates in 1939. It is estimated that at the close of the present fiscal year the production of pilots for this period will be approximately 3,400. Enlisted personnel has kept pace in the development, for its strength has increased six times over that existing in 1939. The present figure of 132,000 has been augmented by nearly 10,000 flying cadets, together with personnel from former National Guard squadrons now inducted into Federal service. To assure that sufficient technicians are available for combat crews and ground crews, the technical schools have stepped up their production of trained graduates 16 times over the output of 1939. The close of the current fiscal year will see 20,000 graduates return to squadrons where their services will be largely instrumental in the success of the Air Corps expansion program.

Evaluation of lessons learned from current operations abroad and numerous changes in our organization and equipment have necessitated a wide revision of training literature for the Army. Sixty Field Manuals and one hundred sixty Technical Manuals were prepared and printed during the fiscal year. Complete revision of Army extension courses is in progress.

Supplemented by the facilities of the motion-picture industry, the Signal Corps is engaged in a comprehensive training film–production program. Some eighty training films, and ninety film strip subjects have already been completed and distributed throughout the service. These visual aids are proving of great value in the training of the new Army.

PERSONNEL

Regular Army

Officers.—The authorized commissioned strength of the Regular Army at the close of the fiscal year 1940 was 13,637, and at the close of the fiscal year 1941 it was 14,016. Under the provisions of the act of April 3, 1939, the commissioned strength will increase to 14,490 in the fiscal year 1942, and continue to increase annually by approximately equal increments until the strength of 16,719 is reached on June 30, 1949. Present plans do not contemplate any additional increase in the Regular Army commissioned strength beyond that now authorized. Increased demands for commissioned personnel will continue to be met by bringing Reserve officers to extended active duty.

During the past fiscal year there has been a redistribution of Regular Army officers in an effort to maintain the greatest possible number on duty with the field forces and in the oversea garrisons. As new units have been activated and new installations have been created it has been necessary to reassign Regular Army officers so as to provide a nucleus of experienced officer personnel with these new units and installations. The additional positions created throughout the Military Establishment which could not be filled by Regular Army officers have been filled by calling Reserve officers to extended active duty.

Enlisted men.—At the beginning of the fiscal year 1940 the Regular Army was in the process of expanding from 174,000 to 210,000 enlisted men, in order to provide for the increased strength authorized for the Air Corps and for augmentation of the Panama garrison.

In the limited emergency proclamation of September 8, 1939, the President ordered that the enlisted strength of the Regular Army be increased to 227,000 enlisted men as rapidly as possible by means of voluntary enlistment. After an intensive recruiting drive this objective was reached in February 1940.

Rapid expansion was still being effected at the outset of the fiscal year 1941. The annual appropriation act provided for an increase to the authorized strength of 280,000, which permitted the activation of three additional triangular divisions, certain coast-defense units, mechanized units, and certain corps, army, and GHQ troops. The First Supplemental National Defense Appropriation Act, 1941, furnished funds for increasing these forces by 95,000, bringing the strength for which appropriations had been made to 375,000. This augmentation permitted the activation of two armored divisions, certain increases in triangular divisions previously authorized, as well as the implementation of organizations in the zone of the interior, such as reception centers. The Third Supplemental National Defense Appropriation Act, 1941, provided a total enlisted strength for the Regular Army and the National Guard, including selective-service trainees, of 1,418,000 by the end of fiscal year 1941.

Regular Army Reserve

In the beginning of fiscal year 1941 the strength of the Regular Army Reserve was 28,099. In February 1941 this component was ordered to active duty under the authority of Public Resolution No. 96, Seventy-sixth Congress. Discharges for dependency, in accordance with the above-mentioned resolution reduced the available number of Regular Army Reservists to 12,260.

Enlisted Reserve

The strength of the Enlisted Reserve Corps at the beginning of the fiscal year 1941 was 3,233. By March 31, 1941, this strength had increased to 4,658, of which number 34 were on active duty. Enlistments in the Enlisted Reserve Corps were suspended except in case of men who had served 2 years in the Regular Army, and of members of the Air Corps Enlisted Reserve over selective-service age.

Selective Service

The Selective Training and Service Act, approved September 16, 1940, prescribed the registration of male citizens and aliens between the ages of 21 and 36, and authorized the call of not more than 900,000 registrants in any one year for a period of 12 consecutive months' training and service. Each such man, after the completion of his period of training, is to be transferred to a reserve component of the Army of the United States. Until he attains the age of 45 or until the expiration of a period of 10 years after such transfer, he is to be a member of such reserve component and shall be subject to such training and service as may be prescribed by law.

CONSTRUCTION AND HOUSING

Appropriations authorized by the Seventy-sixth Congress and allotments from the WPA made available approximately $127,000,000 for permanent and temporary construction during the fiscal year 1940. The larger part of this sum was used for increasing the operating facilities at established air fields and for establishing two air bases and two air depots in the continental United States, one air base in Puerto Rico, one air base in Panama, and an air station at Fairbanks, Alaska.

In addition, three new posts were established in the Panama Canal Department. These provide accommodations for an increase of about 5,800 enlisted men of the coast artillery.

Temporary housing was provided at all posts, camps, and stations where garrisons were increased as a result of the Army's expansion to 227,000 enlisted men.

For the fiscal year 1941, funds in the amount of $1,633,133,355 have been appropriated by the Seventy-sixth Congress for construction necessary to accommodate the Army, as authorized by the Selective Service Act and the act calling the National Guard into Federal service for a period of 1 year.

Quartermaster Corps construction.—This legislation imposed upon the Quartermaster Corps the tremendous task of housing approximately 1,400,000 men. As time was a major factor, construction was pushed vigorously throughout the winter of 1940–41. Progress was hampered by excep-

tionally unfavorable climatic conditions and shortages of labor and materials. However, construction necessary to house the above number of men has now been accomplished, and some 45 communities with populations ranging from 10,000 to 63,000 have been constructed. More than one-half of these communities have been erected at new camp sites, where initiation of construction was dependent upon land acquisition.

The development of the necessary services in a great many cases called for the installation of basic utilities at some distances from the centers of population. The established policy provided for tent camps for National Guard units in those sections where climatic conditions permitted such housing for the period of National Guard service, and for mobilization-type cantonment construction in other cases. The housing for well over half a million men at new camps is approximately evenly divided between temporary cantonments and tent-camp construction. Housing constructed during the emergency at established, permanent Regular Army posts consists mostly of cantonment construction. Existing permanent facilities have been utilized wherever possible, and no new permanent housing has been authorized.

Hospitalization has been provided at the posts and camps by enlarging existing hospitals, converting permanent barracks into hospitals, or by the erection of new cantonment hospitals. The capacity of general hospitals has been increased approximately 10,000 beds by the construction of nine new general hospitals and by additions to existing hospitals.

In addition to the housing and hospitalization necessary to accommodate an army of 1,400,000 men, recreation facilities, chapels, service clubs, hostess houses, railroad facilities necessary for their convenience and comfort have been provided.

Corps of Engineer construction.—In order to distribute the load of construction and to assist in expediting the Air Corps construction program, the transfer from the Quartermaster Corps to the Corps of Engineers of all construction at Air Corps station, Panama excepted, and all construction in Alaska, was authorized on November 20, 1940. The authority for this transfer is contained in Section 102, Public, No. 781, Seventy-sixth Congress, approved September 9, 1940. Seventy-two projects were transferred during the period December 1, 1940–March 1, 1941, and 15 additional projects were assigned directly to the Corps of Engineers.

During the early part of the fourth quarter of the fiscal year 1941, the Corps of Engineers was responsible for Air Corps construction work in the total amount of $624,465,000. The Corps of Engineers has been able to assume this additional construction load by making use of its decentralized organization of 11 divisions and 50 districts covering the entire continental United States, Alaska, and the insular possessions. In those projects which were taken over from the Quartermaster Corps, the continued orderly progress of the work during the transition period was assured by absorbing in the organization of the Corps of Engineers a large part of the local personnel of the Quartermaster Corps.

Defense housing.—As a result of appropriations made by the Seventy-sixth Congress in Public, Nos. 671, 781, and 849, the President has approved the construction of 21,893 units of defense housing for the families of noncommissioned officers of the first three grades and permanently employed civilians of the War Department. This program is well along toward completion.

WPA projects.—Under the terms of the "Emergency Relief Appropriations Act, fiscal year 1941," WPA projects totaling approximately $70,000,000 have been approved by the President for construction or improvement at War Department posts, camps, and stations.

ARMAMENT AND EQUIPAGE

Troop bases for a protective mobilization plan of approximately 1,400,000 men and an augmented force representing a ground Army of about 2,200,000 men, plus an air force and replacements, have been established. Funds provided during fiscal year 1941, plus stocks on hand or under procurement, will, with some exceptions, provide modern equipment for the over-all requirements in critical and essential items for the protective mobilization plan and initial allowances in critical items for the augmented force. The exceptions mentioned comprise largely ammunition, combat maintenance in motor vehicles, completion of the modernized seacoast defense program, some chemical munitions, and combat reserve stocks of clothing and equipage. Financing of these shortages should be provided in subsequent estimates.

a. Mechanization.—The mounting experience and lessons learned from the present European conflict dictate a greater proportion of mechanized units in our Army. This has been accomplished by the provision in the protective mobilization plan and the augmented force of 6 and 8 armored divisions, 9 light-tank battalions, 6 and 16 medium-tank battalions to be equipped with heavy tanks in these respective forces. From the appropriations provided during fiscal year 1941, procurement has been initiated to cover the various types of combat vehicles, such as light and medium tanks, scout cars, and cross-country personnel carriers, in quantities to meet the needs of our protective mobilization plan and, with minor exceptions, sufficient to supply the initial requirements of the augmented force. Development is well along on a new heavy tank. In addition, scout cars will be available to meet the needs of 2 cavalry divisions, the initial requirements of 27 triangular infantry divisions, and 11 mechanized cavalry regiments.

b. Antiaircraft.—Considerable progress has been made in providing for critical items of modern antiaircraft equipment. Funds made available by appropriations for the fiscal year 1941, together with items previously provided for, will generally provide guns and automatic weapons, as well as the necessary searchlights and fire-control instruments for the 88 antiaircraft regiments, mobile and semimobile, and the 16 separate antiaircraft battalions included in the expanded force.

The only items of this type remaining to be financed to complete the requirements of the force of approximately 2,200,000 men are some caliber, .50 machine guns and mounts, 37-mm automatic guns, the necessary fire-control equipment for these weapons, and some searchlight trucks.

The 90-mm antiaircraft gun has been standardized, and a large number of these guns are in production.

c. Seacoast defense.—A modernization program was initiated in fiscal year 1941 to replace outmoded armament with equipment of the most modern type for all harbor defenses in the continental United States. The programs for augmentation of the seacoast defenses of Hawaii and the Panama Canal were substantially advanced in fiscal year 1941.

Funds made available by appropriations for the fiscal year 1941 will provide essential fire-control elements and some ordnance matériel for existing armament and installations. Shortages in equipment for the modernization program initiated in fiscal year 1941 must be financed by subsequent appropriation as construction on the various projects progresses.

d. Miscellaneous equipment.—Modern small arms and artillery weapons have been financed by appropriations for the fiscal year 1941 in quantities sufficient to meet, with but few exceptions, the over-all requirements of the protective mobilization plan and the initial requirements of the augmented force. These modern weapons include 60-mm and 81-mm mortars, machine guns of various types, semiautomatic rifles, 37-mm tank and antitank guns, 105-mm howitzers, and heavy artillery comprising 155-mm and 8-inch guns and 240-mm howitzers. About 900,000 semiautomatic rifles will have been provided upon the completion of the present program, which represents the approximate over-all requirements of the protective mobilization plans as well as the initial requirements of the augmented force.

Procurement of sufficient 105-mm howitzers for the initial needs of the augmented force has been initiated for the purpose of replacing the 75-mm gun in the divisional light-artillery regiments. Upon completion of the program for the fiscal year 1941, there will be sufficient 155-mm guns, comprising modernized (high-speed) and new M1 types, to cover the initial requirement of the expanded force. Further procurement of these weapons to meet requirements to cover maintenance has been held in abeyance pending conclusions on tests now in process relating to the adoption of a new 155-mm howitzer and 4.5-inch gun. These latter weapons are mounted on identical carriages. They present no production difficulties and appear to offer great promise. Special ordnance maintenance vehicles have been financed to meet the over-all requirements of the protective mobilization plan and, with but few exceptions, the needs of this force in signal, chemical, quartermaster, engineer, and medical items are being provided.

e. Motorization.—Funds provided for procurement of motor vehicles during the fiscal year 1941, from both regular and supplemental appropriations, were adequate to complete the initial requirements of the protective mobilization plan and provided a limited amount for normal training replacement.

Tactical organizations are being completely equipped with new equipment, model 1939 and later, and the replaced vehicles made available for administrative use. Approximately 50 percent of the above requirements in motor vehicles will be filled by July 1, 1941, by actual deliveries of vehicles now under procurement. The delivery of 100 percent of the above requirements will be accomplished by about March 1942, provided none of the vehicles under procurement are diverted to other uses.

A marked improvement in cross-country mobility of tactical vehicles has resulted from development of the all-wheel drive.

f. Distribution.—All Regular Army and National Guard organizations have been arranged on one priority list for the distribution of the more important items of equipment which are essential to combat or training. Individual National Guard and Regular Army units are placed on this list according to their probable employment in the event of an emergency and according to their training needs. All equipment and ammunition resources, whether procured from National Guard, Regular Army funds, or funds not specifically appropriated to either, have been pooled, and distribution is being made to both components in such a manner as best to meet the problems of the present emergency. The Chief of the National Guard Bureau has cooperated in every way in the establishment of policies affecting the diversion of equipment or funds to or from the National Guard.

Shortages of equipment exist in most organizations and, with but few exceptions, are being rapidly overcome. These shortages are primarily due to—

    (1) The rapid, far-reaching expansion of the Army.
    (2) The time lag between the availability of funds and delivery of supplies.
    (3) Lack of modern or modernized depot stocks.
    (4) Time required for overhaul or modernization of old equipment which has been stored since 1918.

g. Airplane procurement.—A substantial number of airplanes of the most modern combat and training types are being provided from appropriations for the fiscal year 1941. These, along with present available resources, will provide the 54 combat and 6 transport groups of the Air Corps program with initial requirements and ample reserves. Some equipment for service units under the program has been deferred to the fiscal year 1942. Material progress has been made in the development and acquisition of combat aircraft which are equal or superior in performance and adaptability to any military planes in the world today.

Manufacturing plant space has been expanded 130 percent to facilitate production of aircraft and aircraft accessories. Actual production meanwhile was three times greater in the fiscal year 1941 than in the fiscal year 1939.

NATIONAL GUARD

The National Guard has made more substantial gains in training, personnel, and equipment during the fiscal years 1940 and 1941 than during any similar peacetime period in its history. Upon induction it provided 20,006 officers, 216 warrant officers, and 282,805 enlisted men. The following comparative figures illustrate the steady increase in the total strength of the actual Guard:

    June 30, 1939----------------------------- 199,491
    June 30, 1940----------------------------- 241,612
    June 30, 1941----------------------------- 303,027

For the fiscal year 1940, armory drill periods were increased from 48 hours to 60 hours, and 7 days were added to the normal period of field training at or near home stations. A resulting improvement in the combat efficiency of the Guard was noted during the maneuvers of the First Army in August 1939.

Plans had long been established for the entrance of the National Guard into the active military service of the United States in the event of a national emergency declared by Congress. Pressure of international events made it apparent that the National Guard would be used even though the specific emergency should not exist as legally contemplated.

Joint Resolution No. 96, approved August 27, 1940, authorized the President to order the National Guard into service for 12 consecutive months. Executive orders designated units to be inducted in successive increments commencing on September 16, 1940, with 4 infantry divisions, 18 coast artillery units, and 4 Air Corps squadrons, and continuing until the last division entered active service on March 5, 1941, and

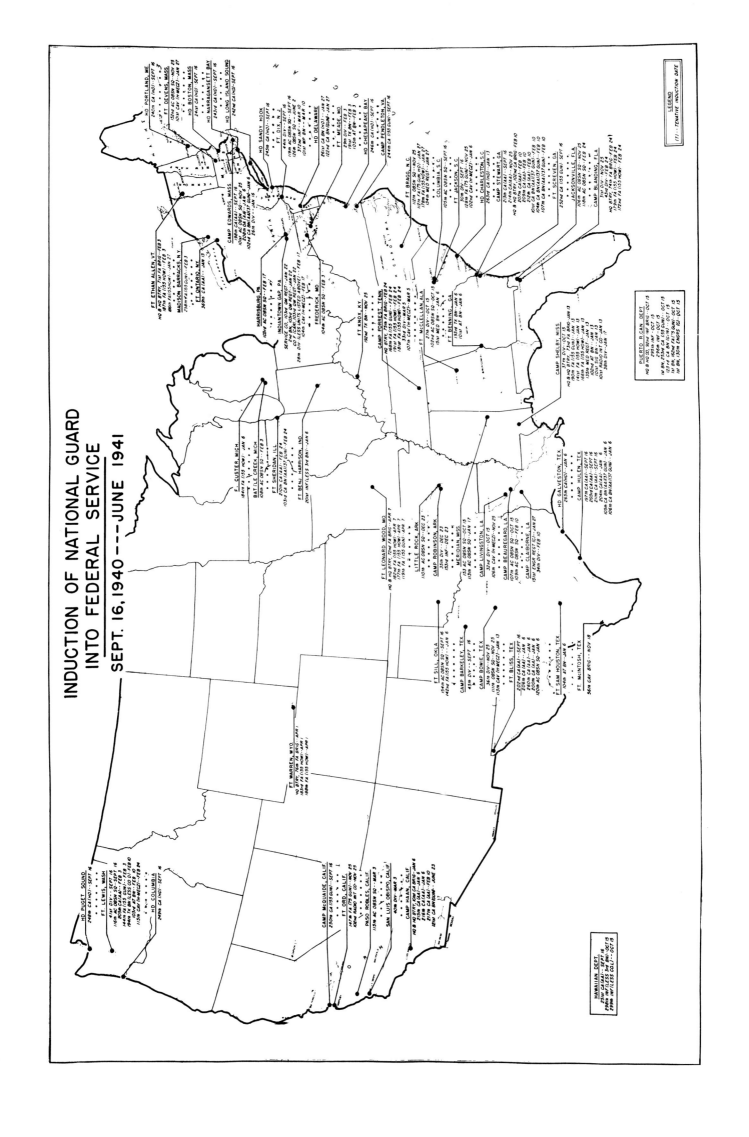

INDUCTION OF NATIONAL GUARD INTO FEDERAL SERVICE
SEPT. 16, 1940 --- JUNE 1941

the last unit on June 23, 1941. By the end of the fiscal year, all of the National Guard was in active service except for 1 new infantry battalion and 8 newly organized observation squadrons. The induction dates and stations of National Guard units are indicated on chart 9.

While this induction was being planned and put into effect, other activities were initiated and continued to perfect the training and organization of the Guard for prospective tasks. Training was intensified. There was an attendance of 802 officers and 261 enlisted men at Army service schools and 733 officers and 402 enlisted men at temporary schools and camps of instruction. This attendance, which was approximately four times the normal quota, utilized the facilities at the various schools to capacity. For the fiscal year 1941 the annual field-training period was again increased from 15 to 21 days, and an additional period of 7 days was authorized; the number of armory drills was again increased; there was Nation-wide participation in the maneuvers held by all four field armies during the summer of 1940.

To make the character of our forces conform to the new demands of modern war, many reorganizations, conversions, and increases were made prior to Federal induction. Four National Guard cavalry divisions were broken up. Seventeen cavalry regiments were converted into 7 horse-mechanized cavalry regiments, 7 field artillery regiments, 7 coast artillery regiments and separate battalions, and 1 antitank battalion. Eight infantry regiments were converted into 4 field artillery regiments, 8 coast artillery regiments, 1 antitank battalion, and 1 military police battalion. Tank companies were withdrawn from infantry divisions and formed into tank battalions. Antitank units were expanded and increased in number. Nine new observation squadrons were organized.

Officer allotments were increased from maintenance strength to equal Regular Army peace strength. The increase in strength authorized by Executive Order of September 6, 1939, was virtually complete at the beginning of the fiscal year.

As a result of increases in officer strength, conversion of units, and officer losses for physical and other reasons, a great many appointments and promotions were made in the National Guard throughout the country. This necessitated examination and formal procedure for Federal recognition, and the magnitude of the task is indicated by the fact that the National Guard Bureau completed action on cases as follows:

July 1940-- 1089	November---- 1553	March ----- 3090
August----- 1281	December---- 1314	April------- 1404
September 1500	January 1941- 3521	May-------- 573
October--- 1870	February ----- 3142	June ------- 415

Because there was no legislative provision for money allowances to dependents of enlisted men in Federal service, and because it was understood that draft boards would defer draftees with dependents, instructions were issued on July 23, 1940, that upon request, discharge would be granted enlisted men with persons dependent solely upon them for support. This process was initiated early in all units regardless of prospective induction dates, in order to give opportunity for filling vacancies by local enlistments. From the date of these instructions on June 30, 1941, it was reported that 51,501 enlisted men had been discharged on account of dependency. This loss would appear large, but it made the Guard conform in personnel to the other elements of the Army and it was rapidly remedied by enlistments.

Induction of the National Guard left the States without their normal forces for suppressing local disturbances. By act of Congress, approved October 21, 1940, a State is authorized to organize and maintain local defense forces so long as any part of its National Guard is in active Federal service. Under this authority, and by virtue of existing and new State legislation, these forces were created under such designations as State Guard, Defense Force, Reserve Militia, Active Militia, Reserve Military Force, Home Guards, Protective Force, Home Defense Force, Defense Guard, State Defense Corps, Reserve Defense Corps. More than three-fourths of the States have raised such forces.

Rifles and bayonets have been made available for issue in quantities equal to 50 percent of the normal National Guard allotment to each State, and training literature has been issued. Ammunition, cartridge belts, mess kits, and other items of field equipment have been made available for sale to the States, while procurement of uniforms has been left to the States alone. By June 30, 1941, units had been organized with a total strength of 85,587.

ORGANIZED RESERVES

The activities of this component show a marked increase throughout the 2 years covered by this report. Never before has the Officers' Reserve Corps been afforded such splendid opportunities for training in peacetime.

During the fiscal year 1940, appropriations made possible the training of a greater number of officers for 14-day periods than previously. The number of students taking 3-month courses at service schools was three times greater than it had been the year before. In addition, about 2,500 officers were trained for 28-day periods with units of the Third Army during the spring of 1940.

During 1939–1940, opportunities for extended active duty for periods of 6 months or more with the Air Corps and other Regular Army units—including opportunities offered under the Thomason Act—were expanded during the last half of the fiscal year, and on June 30, 1940, more than 2,700 Reserve officers were on such duty.

Even greater strides were made during the fiscal year 1941. The passage of Public Resolution No. 96, Seventy-sixth Congress, which became effective August 27, 1940, permitted the ordering of Reserve officers to extended active duty, with or without their consent, for a period of 12 consecutive months. Pursuant to this authority the number of Reserve officers on active duty has steadily increased, and on June 30, 1941, approximately 55,000 Reserve officers, or about 55 percent of those eligible, were on active duty. These officers have been used to meet the need for additional officers in carrying out the current military expansion and wherever possible have been assigned as replacements, thereby making additional Regular Army officers available for troop duty.

Fourteen-day training was discontinued, except in isolated cases, as the opportunities for bringing Reserve officers to duty for extended periods eliminated the need for this type of training.

Although the eligible strength showed no material increase during either of the fiscal years, greater effectiveness of the Officers' Reserve Corps has been attained through improved training opportunities and physical standards. An increase of approximately 10 percent over previous years in original appointments from the Reserve Officers' Training Corps was a contributing factor. This increase was offset by a corresponding decrease of appointments from civil life as a result of a general suspension of appointments from this source imposed at the close of the calendar year 1939. In addition, a classification system, which was set up during the past year, has made readily available detailed information pertaining to the Officers' Reserve Corps along such lines as civil pursuits of the individual, progress of training, and other statistical data.

Voluntary training performed through the pursuit of courses of instruction of the Army extension courses and attendance at troop schools was increased, resulting in a better preparation of the individual for entering upon a tour of extended active duty. Improvement in all phases was satisfactory with possibilities of further progress as the available facilities are augmented.

UNITED STATES MILITARY ACADEMY

Legislation for the fiscal years 1937 and 1938 appropriated funds for the acquisition of approximately 6,068 acres of land. Of this amount, the War Department has acquired title to 2,533 acres. At the end of the fiscal year 1941, the remaining land—approximately 3,535 acres—was in process of acquisition by condemnation proceedings through the Department of Justice, and it was expected that the greater part of this land would be secured before January 1, 1942.

RESERVE OFFICERS' TRAINING CORPS

The applications for new R. O. T. C. units in both the junior and senior divisions were extensive during the fiscal year 1940. Estimates indicated that if the applications for junior units were approved, the enrollment would be increased by 200,000. Because of the requirements of the Army itself and the consequent lack of suitable personnel for the proper operation of new R. O. T. C. units, however, none has been established since August 1937.

During the school year 1939-1940, approximately 7,623 Reserve officers were commissioned from the R. O. T. C. The 9,000 Reserve officers which it is planned to produce annually in the future are expected to meet anticipated requirements without the establishment of additional units.

Strength at the end of the fiscal year 1940 was as follows:

Senior division (226 units):
Advanced course ------------ 17,387
Basic course ----------------- 86,431

Total -------------------- 103,818
Junior division (139 units) --------- 66,134
55c units (35) -------------------- 10,268

During the fiscal year 1941, for the first time since the establishment of the R. O. T. C., large numbers of Reserve officers have been called to extended active duty. By the end of the fiscal year the figure had reached approximately 56,000, mostly officers of company grade, a large percentage of whom are recent graduates of R. O T. C. units. This has afforded the first real opportunity to make a practical appraisal of its product. The success already attained by these officers indicates the importance of the role of the R. O. T. C., especially the senior division, in our national defense. Without these officers the successful rapid expansion of our Army during the past year would have been impossible. Reserve officer production from R. O. T. C. has met immediate requirements from that source. Nearly 8,500 graduates were commissioned in June and ordered to active duty.

Demands for expanding R. O. T. C. training have continued. An increase of 1,000 enrollments in the advanced course was authorized for the school year 1940-41. In order to meet special requirements three new units have been established as follows: University of Alaska, Tuskegee Institute (colored), and the Harvard School of Business Administration. The number of active Regular Army officers on R. O. T. C. duty has been reduced by approximately two-thirds. Officers thus relieved have been replaced by retired and Reserve officers with very satisfactory results. Other than for the foregoing, the R. O. T. C. establishment has, in general, remained unchanged.

Training programs have been revised to bring text references in line with the latest Training Manuals. Since students are to be ordered to active duty shortly after graduation, greater emphasis has been placed on practical training, including methods of instruction, in order to prepare the graduate for the immediate command and instruction of small units.

CITIZENS' MILITARY TRAINING CAMPS

62,587 applications for this training were received; 37,152 were enrolled; and 36,151 completed the month of training offered during the fiscal year 1941. These totals are approximately the same as for the previous year.

In order to concentrate all available means and facilities on the vitally important and immediate task of training the combatant forces, C. M. T. Camps have been suspended for the fiscal year 1942.

CIVILIAN CONSERVATION CORPS

During the period covered by this report, the War Department continued to carry on its assigned missions pertaining to the administration and supply of the Civilian Conservation Corps. These diversified activities have been accomplished promptly and efficiently.

The authorized enrolled strength of the Corps was 300,000, composed of 272,800 juniors and 27,200 veterans. These enrollees were allocated among 1,500 companies, 1,364 of which were made up of juniors and 136 of veterans. The 1,500 camps, each having a capacity of 200 enrollees, were distributed throughout the United States, with some located in every State as well as in the District of Columbia; in addition, two companies were assigned to Annette Island, Alaska.

The Civilian Conservation Corps has been assisting in the expanding national defense program. CCC companies have been allocated to military reservations for the purpose of clearing and developing maneuver and training areas.

MORALE

The problems incident to the maintenance of a high state of morale in our expanded Army have been of primary importance during the past 2 fiscal years. The introduction of selective service, the induction of the National Guard, and the calling to active duty of a large number of Reserve officers have brought many diverse elements into the Army. This rapid expansion, coupled with the difficulties encountered in housing, clothing, feeding, and training the new Army produced many new problems in the field of morale. These special problems were recognized early in the expansion, and steps were taken immediately to solve them. As a result of these timely measures, it can be reported that a high state of morale is now clearly evident throughout our Army.

One of the outstanding indications of improvement in morale has been the continuous diminution of court-martial rates. During the fiscal year 1940, the general court-martial rate per thousand enlisted men fell from 11 to 9; the special court-martial rate, from 23 to 21; and the summary court-martial rate, from 56 to 48.

A growing consciousness of the importance of morale activities led to the creation, on March 14, 1941, of a separate branch for military morale with a general officer as chief of branch. The functions previously exercised by the Morale Division of the A. G. O. were transferred to the Morale Branch, which thereafter functioned under the supervision and control of the Chief of Staff.

A new impetus was imparted to morale activity both on the part of the War Department and of commanders in the field. The Chief of the Morale Branch was charged with the development of methods and procedures to enable him at all times to know the state of morale of the Army. There was no disturbance of the conception that morale and leadership are inseparable. That conception was strengthened by increased latitude permitted to regional and tactical commanders by the grant of authority to conduct conferences of morale officers and the authorization of a special staff officer, without additional duty, for morale purposes.

The appointment by the President of the Federal Security Administrator as Coordinator of Health, Welfare, Recreation, Education, Nutrition, and all other activities related to the defense program permitted a normal division of responsibility for morale activities. Under this arrangement, the War Department assumes full responsibility for morale activity within the borders of military reservations, and other Federal agencies assume the responsibility for morale work outside military boundaries.

Within the borders of a military reservation, the commander is held accountable for the state of morale. The Morale Branch exists to coordinate, stimulate, and influence morale activities and to act as consultants and advisers on morale. Athletic equipment has been made available by reasonable allotments of funds for that purpose, and inclement weather problems are being solved by the erection of field houses which permit continuity of athletic programs in winter months. The primary source of entertainment has been, and will continue to be, motion-picture programs. To date 185 posts and camps have been provided with facilities for showing pictures to approximately 214,000 men at a single showing. Amateur theatricals have been encouraged and have proved highly successful. A system of mobile units has been inaugurated to provide entertainment with volunteer professional talent. The social life within military camps has been the subject of extensive thought and preparation. The outstanding need of a place to gather, to read, to hold dances and entertain friends has been met by the construction of 113 service clubs, the great majority with a library and a cafeteria. Provision in the form of 97 guest houses has been made to furnish simple overnight accommodations to families and friends who may visit the soldier in camp. Due recognition has been given the need of feminine influence in the guidance of morale activities by the employment of 297 hostesses and 96 librarians.

A new problem arose with camps far removed from communities of sufficient size to meet the recreation needs of a large military population. A solution has been found by the construction of tent camps in the nearest sizable communities where recreational facilities are already in existence. Currently 26 such camps have been authorized which will accommodate 15,000 men each weekend. The basic consideration in the establishment of a recreational camp has been to provide soldiers at nominal cost with a place to spend a full weekend in enjoying the normal pleasures available in an average American community.

Another important step in our morale program was the establishment in December 1940 of a civilian committee which subsequently became known as the Joint Army and Navy Committee on Recreation and Welfare. The function of this committee is to coordinate welfare activities between the War Department and other Government departments and to develop closer relationship between civilian communities and military garrisons in order to provide a wholesome, leisure-time atmosphere for the enlisted men. The work of the committee has been of great value in developing public morale and in directing civilian effort into channels which will best serve to increase the morale of the Army.

Because of the intimate relationship to morale, the supervision of the post-exchange system has been charged to the Chief of the Morale Branch. Modernization of post-exchange methods is in process and within a short time a centralized Army Exchange Service will be announced.

While the physical comforts and recreational needs will remain in the spotlight of attention, it is recognized that everything physical and psychological affects human conduct. The Morale Branch is constantly engaged in the study of all factors which contribute and adversely affect morale and the advance planning for morale work in the event of a movement to theaters of operation.

Biennial Report

OF THE

CHIEF OF STAFF

OF THE

UNITED STATES ARMY

July 1, 1941, to June 30, 1943

TO THE

SECRETARY OF WAR

This report summarizes the important events affecting the United States Army between July 1, 1941, and June 30, 1943. It is a record of what was done and why it was done, and is submitted while America is at war to permit a better understanding of the great offensive operations now in progress.

Formal reports of operations in the Philippines, North Africa, and the Southwest Pacific have not yet been received. This report is based on messages, current reports, and official records of the War Department which are sufficiently complete to form an accurate picture.

DEAR MR. SECRETARY:

With the Nation at war I submit a biennial report covering the period from July 1, 1941, to June 30, 1943.

In my first report, which covered the period between July 1, 1939, to June 30, 1941, the events were treated in two phases. The first phase included the fall of France and covered the period of national uncertainty as to the influence of the war upon the United States. The second phase, commencing with the Battle of Britain and terminating with the German declaration of war against Russia, was conspicuous for a growing national appreciation of the seriousness of the international situation and was marked by a limited peacetime mobilization of the citizen army, large appropriations by Congress of funds to develop the Military Establishment, and the orientation of industry to speed up the peacetime production rate of munitions of war.

The initial period covered by this report constitutes a third phase which was brought to an abrupt conclusion by the Japanese attacks of December 7, 1941. With war upon us we entered a fourth phase which covered the complete mobilization of the power of the United States and its coordination with that of our allies.

During the fourth phase the United States and the United Nations were forced to assume a defensive role while mobilizing their strength for a global fight to the finish. Efforts during this period were devoted to the rapid deployment of men and resources to check the momentum of the Axis assaults, while establishing protected lines of communication around the world, and at the same time initiating a vast expansion of our Military and Naval Establishments (chart 10).

Democratic governments devote their resources primarily to improving the standard of living of their people. Therefore, when attacked by nations which have concentrated on preparations for a war of conquest, the initial successes inevitably will go to the aggressors. This was the case with the democracies of Western Europe and later on was found true in the case of the United States. Approximately 8 months were required by this country, acting in collaboration with its allies, to accumulate the munitions, train the initial forces, and then to transport them to theaters of operations where they could be employed in offensive action against the enemy. This phase of the great emergency ended in August 1942 with the successful assault on the Japanese positions at Guadalcanal and Tulagi in the Solomon Islands (map 1).

The fifth phase, in which we are now engaged, involves the launching of Allied military power against our enemies in a series of constantly increasing offensive blows until they are beaten into complete submission.

THE THIRD PHASE

On July 1, 1941, the international situation was extremely critical. The full power of the German Army, overwhelmingly successful in all its previous conquests, had just been loosed against Russia, and the momentum of its first drive had overrun vast areas of Russian territory. Sizable concentrations of German troops remained deployed along the English Channel, a constant menace to the security of Great Britain; and German activities in both the North and South Atlantic threatened the security of the Western Hemisphere.* Strong Italian forces meanwhile were massing in Africa. In the Pacifc the menacing preparations of Japan were regarded as a possible preface to attacks upon British and Dutch possessions in the Far East and upon the Philippines, Malaysia, Hawaii, and the Panama Canal. Aggression in Indo-China gave unmistakable evidence of Japan's plan to enlarge her empire at the expense of weaker countries.

Extension of Service

In this grave situation in the summer of 1941 the War Department was faced with the disintegration of the Army, which had reached a strength of more than 1,500,000 men, unless legislative action intervened to save the situation. Under the terms of the Selective Training and Service Act, selectees could only be retained in the service for a period of 1 year unless a national emergency existed. Also, National Guard units and Reserve officers must be returned to an inactive status after 1 year of service. The critical international situation demanded the retention of

* In August 1940, following the fall of France and the critical situation resulting with regard to the security of the British Isles, the United States and Canada had formed a Permanent Joint Board on Defense. This Board consists of 6 members from each country. Mayor F. H. LaGuardia, of New York City, is presently the chairman of the American section of the Board. Vice Admiral A. W. Johnson is the senior United States Navy member and Maj. Gen. Guy V. Henry, the senior Army member.

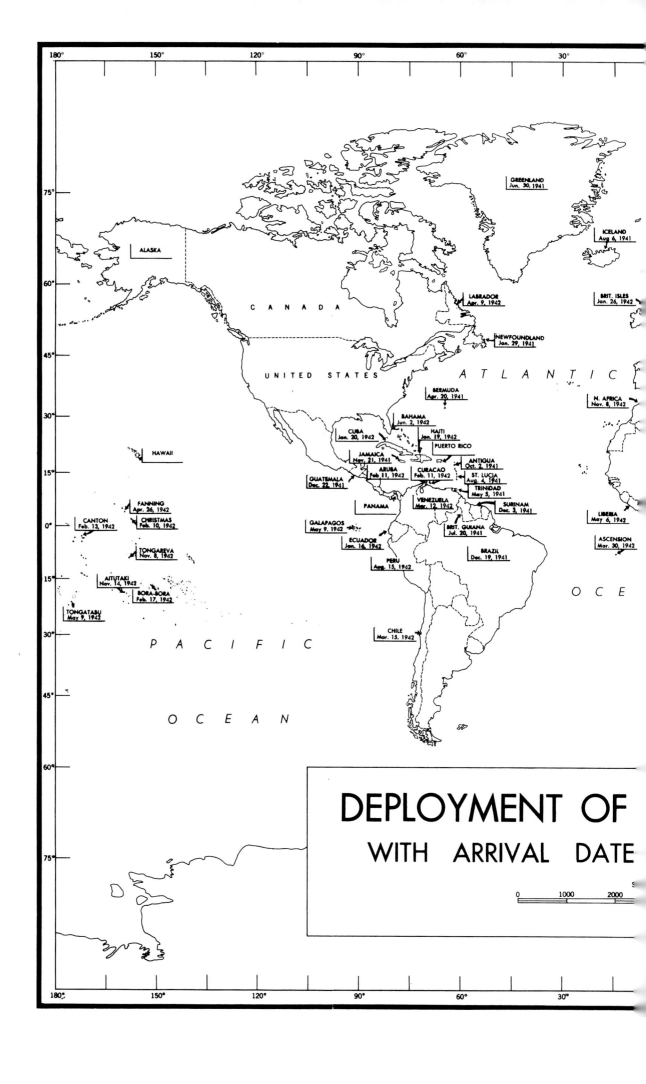

DEPLOYMENT OF

WITH ARRIVAL DATE

Map labels (west to east, north to south):

ALASKA

GREENLAND
Jun. 30, 1941

ICELAND
Aug 6, 1941

C A N A D A

LABRADOR
Apr. 9, 1942

BRIT. ISLES
Jan. 26, 1942

NEWFOUNDLAND
Jan. 29, 1941

UNITED STATES

A T L A N T I C

BERMUDA
Apr. 20, 1941

N. AFRICA
Nov. 8, 1942

BAHAMA
Jun. 2, 1942

CUBA
Jan. 20, 1942

HAITI
Jan. 19, 1942

PUERTO RICO

HAWAII

JAMAICA
Nov. 21, 1941

ANTIGUA
Oct. 2, 1941

ARUBA
Feb. 11, 1942

CURACAO
Feb. 11, 1942

ST. LUCIA
Aug. 4, 1941

GUATEMALA
Dec. 22, 1941

TRINIDAD
May 5, 1941

FANNING
Apr. 26, 1942

PANAMA

VENEZUELA
Mar. 12, 1942

SURINAM
Dec. 3, 1941

CANTON
Feb. 13, 1942

CHRISTMAS
Feb. 10, 1942

GALAPAGOS
May 9, 1942

BRIT. GUIANA
Jul. 20, 1941

LIBERIA
May 6, 1942

ECUADOR
Jan. 16, 1942

ASCENSION
Mar. 30, 1942

TONGAREVA
Nov. 8, 1942

BRAZIL
Dec. 19, 1941

AITUTAKI
Nov. 14, 1942

PERU
Aug. 15, 1942

BORA-BORA
Feb. 17, 1942

TONGATABU
May 9, 1942

O C E A

CHILE
Mar. 15, 1942

P A C I F I C

O C E A N

0   1000   2000

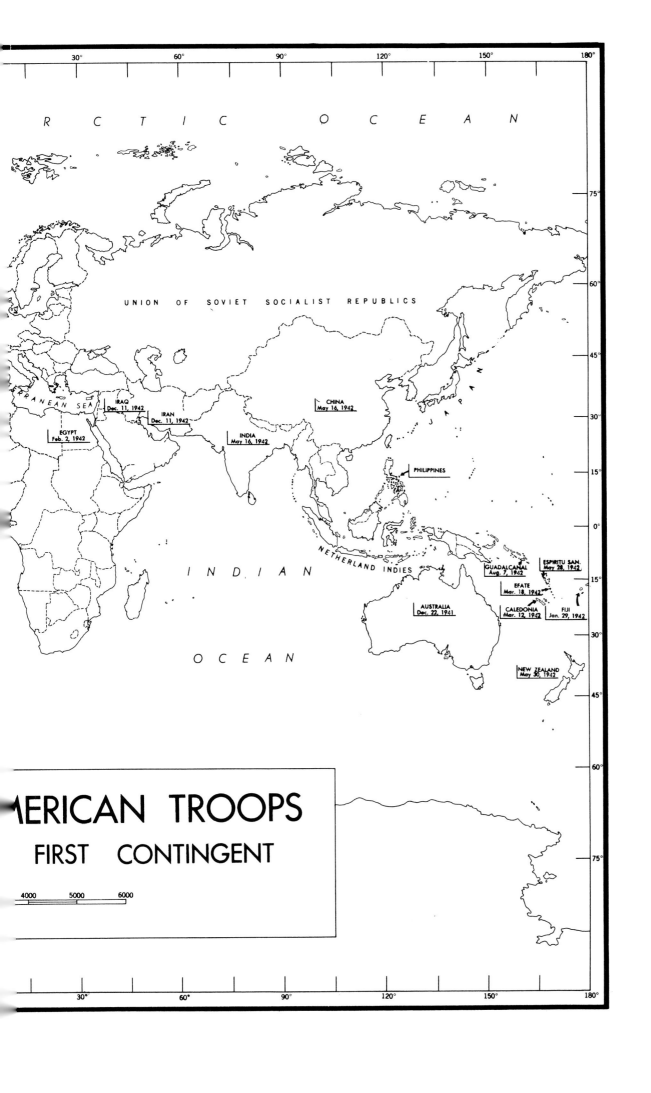

ARCTIC OCEAN

UNION OF SOVIET SOCIALIST REPUBLICS

MEDITERRANEAN SEA

IRAQ
Dec. 11, 1942

IRAN
Dec. 11, 1942

EGYPT
Feb. 2, 1942

CHINA
May 16, 1942

INDIA
May 16, 1942

PHILIPPINES

JAPAN

NETHERLAND INDIES

INDIAN

OCEAN

GUADALCANAL
Aug. 7, 1942

ESPIRITU SAN.
May 28, 1942

EFATE
Mar. 18, 1942

AUSTRALIA
Dec. 22, 1941

CALEDONIA
Mar. 12, 1942

FIJI
Jan. 29, 1942

NEW ZEALAND
May 30, 1942

MERICAN TROOPS
FIRST CONTINGENT

4000   5000   6000

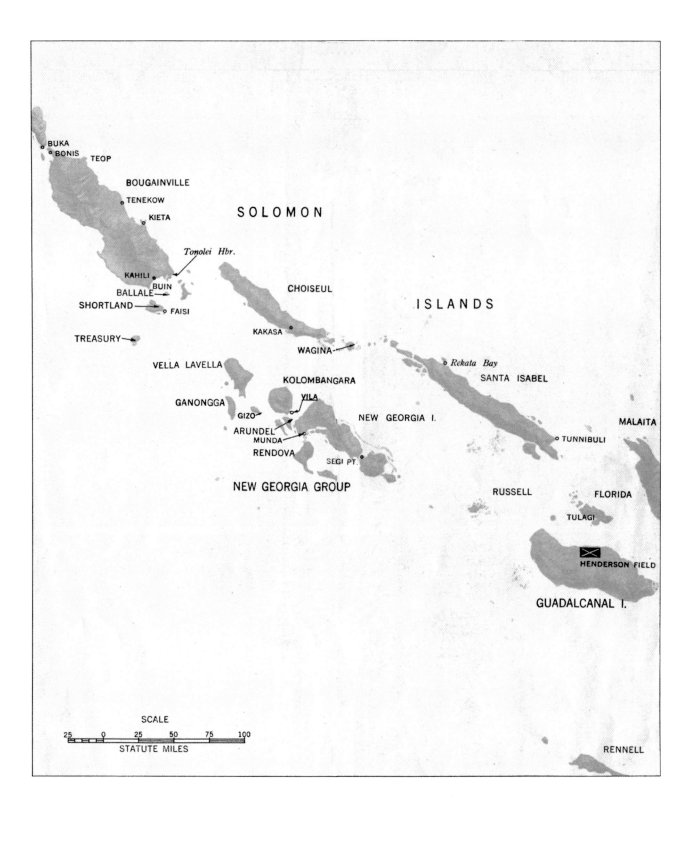

BUKA
BONIS
TEOP
BOUGAINVILLE
TENEKOW
KIETA

SOLOMON

Tonolei Hbr.

KAHILI
BUIN
BALLALE
SHORTLAND
FAISI

CHOISEUL

ISLANDS

KAKASA

WAGINA

Rekata Bay
SANTA ISABEL

TREASURY

VELLA LAVELLA

KOLOMBANGARA

VILA

GANONGGA

GIZO

NEW GEORGIA I.

MALAITA

ARUNDEL
MUNDA
RENDOVA

SEGI PT.

TUNNIBULI

NEW GEORGIA GROUP

RUSSELL

FLORIDA

TULAGI

HENDERSON FIELD

GUADALCANAL I.

SCALE

25   0   25   50   75   100

STATUTE MILES

RENNELL

these men and organizations if the security of the Western Hemisphere was to be assured, and such a recommendation was made to the Congress by the President early in July. The Selective Service Extension Act of 1941 was approved the latter part of August, 4 months before the attack on Pearl Harbor.

Development of the Army

At this time the Army of the United States consisted of a partially equipped force of 28 Infantry divisions, a newly created armored force of four divisions, two Cavalry divisions, the harbor defenses of the United States, and an air force of 209 incomplete squadrons. There was in existence a number of establishments such as induction stations, replacement training centers, and officer candidate and specialists schools, which provided the necessary basis and experience for a rapid expansion of the Army in the event of war (chart 11).

During the summer of 1941, large battle rehearsals continued which included maneuvers in August, September, and November of some 900,000 troops.[1] The organization and training of the necessary nondivisional units (heavy artillery, engineers, etc.) to support our divisions were expedited, while special attention was directed to the development and training of the armored force and antiaircraft organizations which were faced with the prospect of enormous expansions. Selected units were given specialized training in mountain and jungle warfare and amphibious operations, and a Tank Destroyer Center was created. Supply and administrative units and installations were activated and trained to meet the greatly increased logistical demands of combat forces, but we were never able to provide them in sufficient numbers to meet service requirements for the active employment of the tactical units. During this period, port installations were expanded to support possible overseas operations.[2]

Reinforcements for Overseas Garrisons

Lack of modern matériel, especially in airplanes and antiaircraft guns, as well as lack of trained units embarrassed the War Department during this period both in the training of troops (including air units) and in the preparation of our overseas establishments to meet possible attacks in both oceans. Since 1935 the Hawaiian Islands, having been given first priority, had been provided with more complete troop garrisons and munitions than any other overseas garrison. It now became imperative that the defenses of the Panama Canal and Alaska be given immediate priority. Also, the uncertainty of the European situation involv-

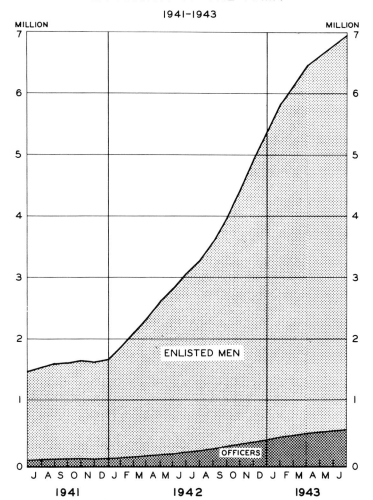

EXPANSION OF THE ARMY
1941–1943

ing the peril of the British Isles* and the British Fleet made it urgently necessary for us to secure the defenses of the Western Hemisphere by establishing air bases and defensive garrisons throughout the Caribbean and in Newfoundland. With our limited means the situation developed into a problem of priorities in attempting to meet these requirements, and it was not until February 1941 that additional aircraft, antiaircraft, and other items of modern equipment could be shipped to the Hawaiian Islands. A little later

---

*(The substance of the following paragraph for secrecy reasons could not be included in my biennial report of June 30, 1941.)

Immediately after Dunkirk in 1940, the British Isles were in effect defenseless so far as organized and equipped ground forces were concerned. Practically all their field army equipment had been lost and an immediate invasion was threatened. In this situation, Lee Enfield rifles, Browning automatic rifles and machine guns, 75 mm. artillery, with limited ammunition and TNT of the World War stock were hurriedly released to the British in return for immediate contracts to be let in the United States for modern matériel. For the United States the military issue immediately at stake was the security of the British Fleet to dominate the Atlantic. These releases left us with World War stocks of matériel of the types mentioned sufficient to equip 1,800,000 men, with quantity production to be underway in time to meet additional troop requirements. Incidentally, at this time great lend-lease shipments to Great Britain, Russia, China, and our other allies were unforeseen.

the first shipments of modern aircraft were made to the Philippines and the Philippine Scout organization was doubled in strength, drawing the necessary personnel from the trained cadres of the new Philippine Army. The fighter planes secured for these purposes were largely obtained by stripping the limited number of squadrons then in training in the United States.

In July 1941 the development of quantity production made it possible for the first time to assign modern matériel in sizable lots to the Philippines. On August 28 the first flights of Flying Fortresses were started across the Pacific via Midway and Wake Islands and thence south through Rabaul, Port Moresby, or Port Darwin, and north to the Philippines. By the first week in November some 35 Fortresses had completed this trip. A gap in airplane deliveries from the factory combined with adverse winds between San Francisco and Hawaii prevented the ferrying of an additional 48 Fortresses prior to the attack on Pearl Harbor.

In view of the potentialities of the situation in the Philippines, orders were issued in February 1941 to evacuate the dependents of Army personnel stationed there. The decision was also taken to retain in the islands most of the Regular Army personnel beyond the 2-year tour of service.

July 26, Gen. Douglas MacArthur was recalled from duty with the Philippine Commonwealth, placed on active duty, and designated as commander of United States Army Forces in the Far East. Intimately familiar with the situation in the Philippines, he at once proceeded to expedite preparations for defense within the limits of the available munitions and trained manpower.

(During the late summer of 1941, arrangements were made for the improvement of the landing strips at Rabaul, Port Moresby, and Port Darwin,[3] and the commanding general of the Philippines was directed to deliver gasoline and bombs to these points and to Balikpapan in Borneo and Singapore in Malaysia. Deliveries to all but the last two points had been completed when the Japanese took the offensive, December 7.)

National Guard antiaircraft and tank units which had progressed sufficiently in training and for which the necessary modern equipment could be provided were dispatched to the Philippines during this period of preparation. Some 100 light tanks and the first 50 self-propelled artillery weapons delivered by our arsenals were shipped to the Philippines and arrived prior to the outbreak of war.

In August, President Roosevelt issued a proclamation mobilizing the Philippine National Army and steps were taken to furnish these partially trained forces with whatever equipment could be made available from the United States, in addition to that held in reserve in the Philippines. Referring to this

mobilization of the Philippine forces and the shipments from the United States of troops, planes, and other munitions already effected or in progress, General MacArthur in a letter to the Chief of Staff on August 30 made the following comment:

I wish to express my personal appreciation for the splendid support that you and the entire War Department have given me along every line since the formation of this command. With such backing the development of a completely adequate defense force will be rapid.

In early September the War Department recommended to Congress that the Philippine Independence Act of 1934 be amended so as to authorize the expenditure of certain sugar excise tax funds and currency devaluation funds accruing in the Treasury of the United States for defensive purposes in the islands. These funds amounting to approximately $52,000,000 were wanted primarily for the extension of airfields. While awaiting legislative action the War Department obtained $10,000,000 from the emergency fund for the President to be utilized for Philippine defenses. This, plus another $10,000,000 from Army Air Forces funds, was quickly exhausted and an additional $5,000,000 was obtained from the emergency fund for the President while the debate was in progress in Congress. Still later when the sugar excise tax legislation did not receive favorable action the War Department included in the Third Supplemental National Defense Appropriation Act, 1942, $269,000,000 for the Army of the Philippines, but this did not become available until the act was approved on December 17, 1941.

By October 1941 it had been found possible to assemble 500,000 tons of supplies and 20,000 fully equipped and fairly well-trained troops as reinforcements for the Philippine Islands. Few troop transports were available, but with hasty conversion of passenger ships to troop carriers, 11 troop ships were scheduled to sail between November 21 and December 9. Twelve cargo vessels were to sail between November 21 and January 6. Six of the troop ships and nine cargo vessels were at sea when word of the Pearl Harbor attack was received. Orders were flashed to all of these vessels to proceed to the nearest friendly port and to observe radio silence. Four of the troop ships returned to San Francisco. The other two, which were well out from Honolulu with 4,500 troops aboard, made Brisbane, Australia, after 15 days of silence and uncertainty. All but one of the cargo vessels reached friendly ports. The exception was presumed captured after having reported on January 1 from 600 miles south of Tahiti that an unidentifed airplane had ordered her to halt but that she was proceeding to New Zealand. Another vessel whose cargo included P–40 fighters, motor vehicles, rifles, ammunition, and gasoline, was at Christmas Island at the time the Japanese struck. It immediately put to sea and no word was heard from it until the 23d of December when it sailed into Los Angeles harbor with its cargo intact.

Further deliveries to the Far Eastern area were hampered by the loss of Wake Island which necessitated the immediate development of an alternate trans-Pacific route via Christmas Island, Canton Island, Fiji, and New Caledonia. The new route was opened to traffic during January 1942. In the interim all heavy bomber air movements were immediately undertaken from Miami, Fla., via Brazil, equatorial Africa, and India through Sumatra to Java and Australia. The loss of Sumatra in February terminated deliveries by this route. While this sudden reversal of a movement half way around the earth demonstrated the mobility of the airplane, it also demonstrated the lack of mobility of air forces until a lengthy process of building up ground service forces and supplies (mechanics, ordnance and radio technicians, signal personnel, radar warning detachments, antiaircraft, medical, and quartermaster units, as well as the troops to capture air fields and defend them against land attack, and the accumulation of repair machinery, gasoline, bombs, and ammunition) had been laboriously completed by transport plane, passenger and cargo ship—the last two largely being slow-moving means of transportation. The planes flew to Australia in 10 days. The ground units and matériel to service the planes and keep them flying required approximately 2½ months or longer for the transfer.

Time Factor

Our greatest problem during this period was the recognized urgency of the situation as opposed by the fact that we were just in the process of obtaining ammunition, arms, and equipment as a result of appropriations made from a year to 2 years previously and of having available only partially trained troops as a result of the recent mobilization and expansion to war strength of the National Guard and the few Regular Army units, and the passage of the Selective Service Act the previous fall. Our first obligation had been to see that the troops assembled in this country possessed enough equipment (about 30 to 50 percent per division)[4] to permit them to be trained for employment wherever the defenses of the Western Hemisphere might require, and to make certain that we had in the Panama Canal Zone, Hawaii, and Alaska sufficient garrisons and armament to prevent a hostile landing. All this took time, and time was what we lacked.

Deficiencies in arms and equipment especially in ammunition and airplanes required for the immediate defense of the Western Hemisphere,* the Panama Canal Zone, Alaska, and for the Regular Army and National Guard with supporting troops, were so serious that adequate reinforcements for the Philippines at this time would have left the United States in a position of great peril should there be a break in the defenses of Great Britain. It was not until new troops had been trained and equipped and Flying Fortresses, fighter planes, tanks, guns, and small-arms ammunition began to come off assembly lines on a partial quantity production basis in the late summer of 1941 that reinforcements for our most distant outpost could be provided without jeopardy to continental United States.

As an example of the degree of our shortages, the necessity for disapproving the requests of the Government of the Netherlands East Indies is cited. After urgent requests through the various channels the representatives of that Government finally called on me personally in the latter part of August 1941 and made a moving appeal for, among other things, an initial allotment of 25,000,000 rounds of small-arms caliber .30 ammunition. They stated that they feared the disintegration of their ground forces unless at least a small amount of ammunition was promptly issued. We had an extremely critical situation here in the United States but the dilemma of these fine people was so tragic in the face of the Japanese threat that it was finally decided to accept the hazard of reducing the ammunition reserve for the troops in movement to Iceland to an extent which would permit 7,000,000 rounds being turned over to the Dutch. Four million of these rounds were to be made quickly available by shipment from Manila, replacement shipments being started from San Francisco immediately. (Incidentally, 7,000,000 rounds was to be the daily delivery of a plant which was due to get into production in early October, but that was to be too late for the gathering storm in the Far East.)

On all the fighting fronts the Allies were in a desperate situation due to lack of adequate matériel while facing an enemy who possessed an abundance of the most modern equipment conceived at that time. The trying problem of the War Department was to meet the urgent necessities of critical fronts with-

---

*Vitally important in the strategic defense of the United States is Brazil which offers the nearest point of approach to this continent from the east. It is also vital to the security of the Panama Canal that the various avenues of approach through Brazilian territory be in friendly hands and adequately guarded. The traditional friendship between Brazil and the United States and complete agreement between the two peoples on matters of interest to the Western Hemisphere have had an important bearing on our defense preparations. Close cooperation between the United States and Brazil was crystallized through the formation of a Joint Brazil–United States Defense Commission in May 1942. This Commission has since been working on mutual defense plans and matters related to our common war effort.

out jeopardy to the security of continental United States. Money in large appropriations had been made available but not available was the time in which to convert this money into munitions ready for issue.

The Lend-Lease Act was passed in March 1941, but it was not until the latter part of that year that it began to be effective in its results. An agreement for aid to Russia in cooperation with the British was implemented in October and was just becoming effective when we entered the war as a belligerent. In spite of our situation, it was vital that we help both Russia and the United Kingdom for our own security. This matter was considered so important that lend-lease aid continued throughout the crisis of our entrance into the war without notable interruptions except in the case of a few critical items.[5]

Changing Situation

In connection with the foregoing and with what follows, it is difficult to keep in mind the constant changes in the international situation and in the development of trained troops and munitions which dictated the succession of decisions and actions. For example, in the light of the situation today, the summer of 1943, we are not justified in maintaining large air and ground installations in the Caribbean from Trinidad north to Cuba and even in the Panama Canal Zone itself so far as mobile ground forces are concerned. The original program was undertaken in view of the possibility that a great tragedy suddenly might befall the United Kingdom with the consequent complete reversal of the naval situation in the North and South Atlantic. Then as well as much later our military developments in the Caribbean had to be measured by the constant threat of a German occupation of Morocco and Dakar and fifth column activities throughout Latin America.* As these possibilities, at times seeming probabilities, were wiped from the slate, the requirements in the Caribbean were altered materially and construction of installations was canceled and large portions of the garrisons withdrawn.

Our deployments were made in the light of limited resources in troops and equipment at the time and a continuing lack of sufficient ocean tonnage or landing craft, or both, and were influenced also by the length of turn-around required of ocean ship-

ping and the limited docking facilities at many ports. As these conditions changed our strategical approach to the war was altered accordingly. The recent opening of the Mediterranean to convoys, for instance, has profoundly affected the logistical possibilities in this world-wide war.[6]

THE FOURTH PHASE

War Is Declared

The Japanese attack on Pearl Harbor on December 7, 1941, galvanized the entire military organization of our Nation into the immediate tasks of protecting the United States, Alaska, and the Panama Canal Zone against surprise attack and sabotage. It also precipitated the movement of additional men and matériel to guard our extended naval and air lines of communications from the United States to active and prospective theaters of operations, and to replace losses in Hawaii. Plans which had been formulated in preparation for a possible state of war were put into effect according to the demands of the actual situation.

Since the Japanese attacks on the Pacific Fleet in Hawaii had uncovered the entire west coast of North America, the reinforcement of garrisons along the west coast, Panama, Hawaii, and in Alaska was given first priority. The movement of air forces and antiaircraft units was initiated immediately by flight and fast freight specials. The movement of an army corps of two Infantry divisions and corps troops to the west coast started on December 14, 1941, and was completed a few days later. By December 17 the critical areas on both the Pacific and Atlantic coasts had been provided with a reasonable degree of protection against air and sea attack.* Additional antiaircraft units were sent by sea, and air reinforcements were flown to the Panama Canal. In the first 5 weeks of the war these deployments in conjunction with the forces en route to Hawaii, Alaska, and other bases involved a rail movement of approximately 600,000 troops with their vehicular transportation, guns, and equipment. The railroads of the Nation handled this sudden and tremendous volume of traffic in personnel and matériel in an extremely efficient manner, thanks in part to the previous elaborate organization in depth of coastal ports of embarkation with their intermediate storage depots and regulating stations

---

*In March 1942 the Inter-American Defense Board was created composed of military and naval technicians appointed by the governments concerned to consider measures necessary for the defense of the continent. Lt. Gen. Stanley D. Embick is presently Chairman of the Board and is senior United States member. All of the Latin American countries are represented. The charter of this board is contained in the resolutions of the Third Conference of Foreign Ministers held at Rio de Janeiro in January 1932.

---

*In February 1942, the Joint Mexican-United States Defense Commission was established to consider problems relating to the common defense of the United States and Mexico. The cooperation between the two Governments in these matters has been complete.

extending as far inland as Phoenix, Ariz., Ogden, Utah, and Harrisburg, Pa.*

A first necessity was to make good the damage in Hawaii and to strengthen its defenses and those at Midway, to establish a succession of island bases to guard the Pacific lines of communication with Australia and New Zealand and to permit the transport of bombers and transport planes and the servicing of naval aircraft and shipping. Ships in the Pacific coast harbors were immediately requisitioned, reloaded, and sent westward with combat and service personnel, aircraft equipment, and other matériel. Two fast convoys were organized, loaded and left San Francisco for Hawaii during the first 10 days of the war. A convoy en route to the Philippines was diverted to Australia.

Troops were sent to relieve the Marines and British forces in Iceland and, at the same time, the first echelon of troops was sent overseas to Northern Ireland to assist in the protection of the British Isles and to pave the way for future American activities in Europe.

The outposts of the Panama Canal defenses were rapidly extended by the establishment of air bases in South and Central America[7] and by the provision of small coast artillery detachments with 155-mm. guns to defend the critical points along the South American coast as far as Chile.

To meet the situation in the United States the areas contiguous to the east and west coasts were organized into the Eastern and Western Defense Commands respectively and placed under the command of Lt. Gen. Hugh A. Drum and Lt. Gen. John L. DeWitt. Integrated into this command set-up was the operational control of interceptor aircraft assigned to protect our coast lines. In addition, General DeWitt retained control over the Alaskan Defense Command and General Drum over the United States troops in Newfoundland and Bermuda (chart 12).

Work on the Alaska Military Highway was accelerated and the road was opened to traffic on October 29, 1942, despite the difficulties of weather and terrain.[8]

Strategy and Control

On December 23, 1941, Winston Churchill, Prime Minister of Great Britain, accompanied by the British Chiefs of Staff, arrived in Washington to confer with the President and the American Chiefs of Staff. Out of the series of discussions which then followed resulted an agreement, not only regarding the immediate strategy for our combined conduct of the war, but also for the organization of a method for the strategical command and control of British and American military resources. Probably no other Allied action, in the field or otherwise, has exerted as powerful an

effect on the conduct of this war as the prompt establishment of a prescribed procedure for achieving unity of effort through the medium of the combined Chiefs of Staff acting under the direction of the leaders of their respective governments. There has been a gradual expansion of the system to include most of the activities involved in the war effort and we have been able to solve our problems and settle our differences in an orderly and effective manner. The control of military intelligence, of secrecy, the requirements in manpower, troop types and munitions, the allocation of organizations, matériel and shipping, the coordination of communications, the intricate civil administration to be established under the military government of newly occupied or captured regions, all these and other factors involved in the conduct of a global war have been resolved through the orderly channels of the adopted system.[9]

During this first meeting between the British and American military authorities, which terminated January 14, 1942, steps were taken to insure unified direction of the war effort in the Far East to meet the rapidly spreading attacks of the Japanese in that area. Gen. Sir Archibald Wavell, commander in chief in India, who was in Chungking, China, at the time with Maj. Gen. (now Lt. Gen.) George H. Brett, of the United States Army, was designated supreme commander for American, British, Dutch, and Australian forces, with General Brett as his deputy, and although the strong, carefully prepared tide of the Japanese advance overran the Philippines, the Netherlands East Indies, the Malay Peninsula, and Burma, the cooperative results obtained in this desperate emergency by the creation of a united command established a firm basis for future combined operations.

Global War

The attack by Japan and the declaration of war by Germany and Italy immediately involved the United States and Great Britain in a war of global proportions unique in the history of the world. It was not merely war on two fronts but in several theaters, with lines of communication encircling the earth and extending over 56,000 miles (chart 13).

For both Great Britain and the United States, military operations in the Pacific area and the Far East created unprecedented logistical problems with respect to shipping. Time and space factors dictated our strategy to a considerable degree. To land and maintain American forces in Australia required more than twice the ship tonnage necessary for similar American forces in Europe or North Africa. In this critical period, however, it was necessary to establish without delay large supply bases in Australia both for air and ground troops and especially for the purpose of giving logistical support to our forces in the Philippines.

---

*The rail tonnage concentrated on the Brooklyn Army Base in the fall of 1941 exceeded that of 1918 on the port of New York.

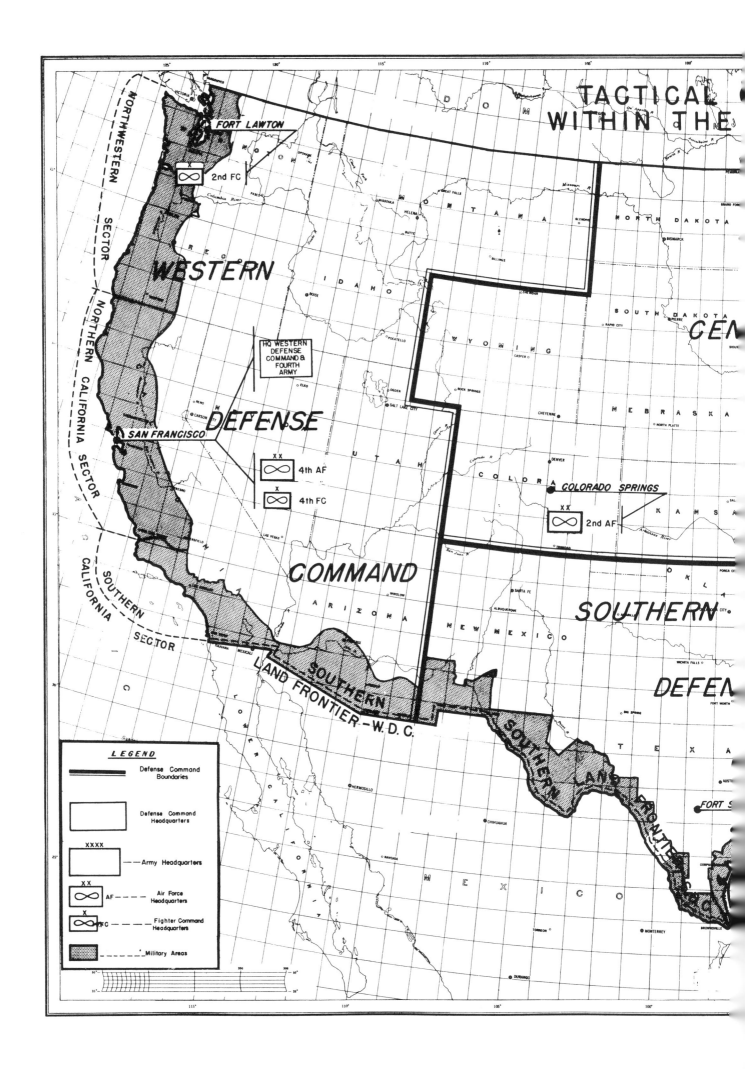

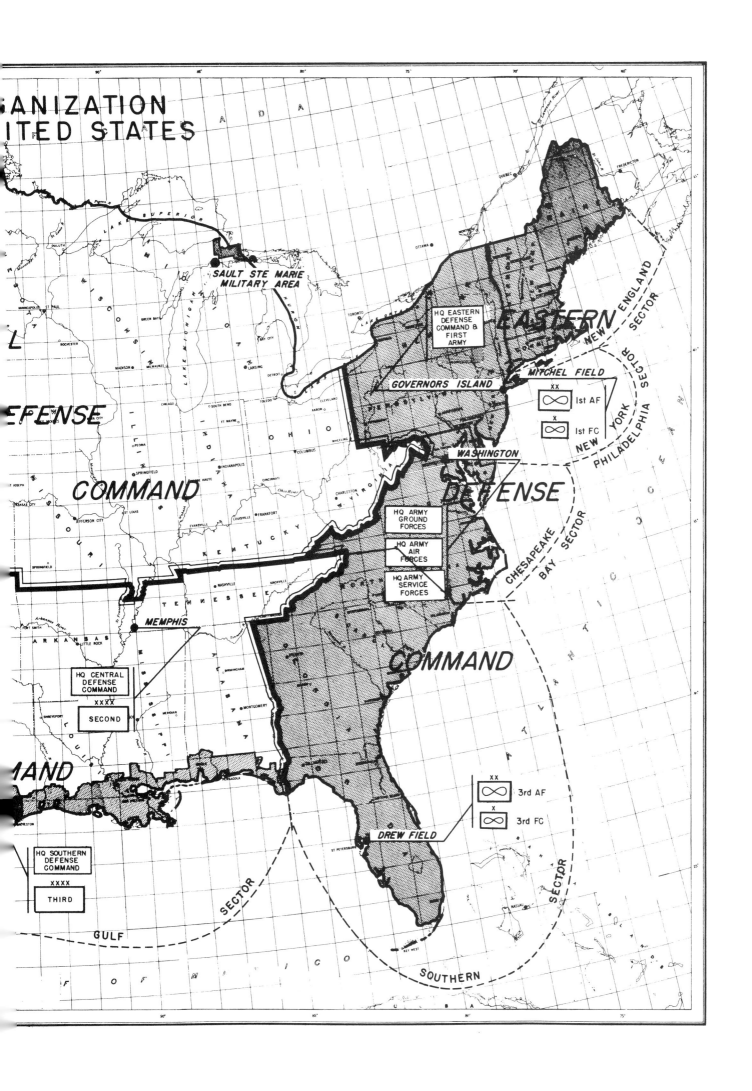

ANIZATION
ITED STATES

EASTERN

DEFENSE

COMMAND

SAULT STE MARIE
MILITARY AREA

HQ EASTERN
DEFENSE
COMMAND &
FIRST
ARMY

GOVERNORS ISLAND

MITCHEL FIELD

1st AF

1st FC

WASHINGTON

HQ ARMY
GROUND
FORCES

HQ ARMY
AIR
FORCES

HQ ARMY
SERVICE
FORCES

MEMPHIS

HQ CENTRAL
DEFENSE
COMMAND

XXXX

SECOND

MAND

HQ SOUTHERN
DEFENSE
COMMAND

XXXX

THIRD

GULF

SECTOR

3rd AF

3rd FC

DREW FIELD

SOUTHERN

SECTOR

NEW ENGLAND SECTOR

NEW YORK SECTOR

PHILADELPHIA SECTOR

CHESAPEAKE BAY SECTOR

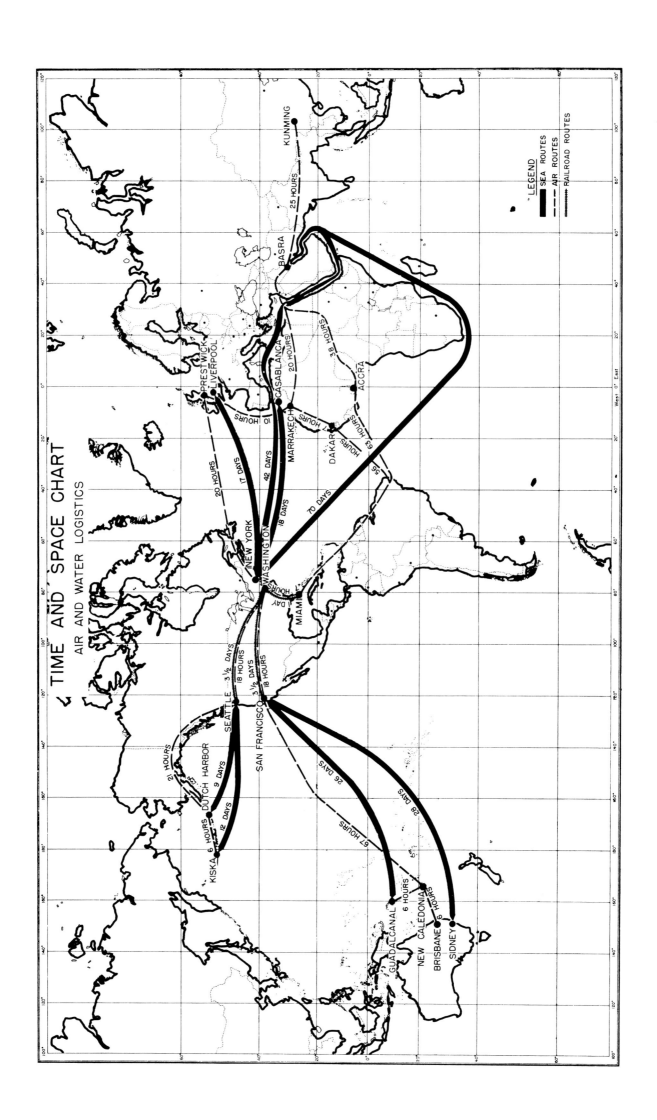

TIME AND SPACE CHART
AIR AND WATER LOGISTICS

LEGEND
━━━━ SEA ROUTES
━ ━ ━ AIR ROUTES
wwwww RAILROAD ROUTES

KUNMING
25 HOURS
BASRA
CASABLANCA 20 HOURS
38 HOURS
ACCRA
MARRAKECH 17 HOURS
DAKAR 36 HOURS
10 HOURS
17 DAYS
42 DAYS
LIVERPOOL
PRESTWICK
20 HOURS
18 DAYS
70 DAYS
56
NEW YORK
WASHINGTON
7 HOURS
MIAMI 1 DAY
18 HOURS
3½ DAYS
SEATTLE 3½ DAYS
18 HOURS
SAN FRANCISCO
21 HOURS
DUTCH HARBOR 9 DAYS
KISKA 6 HOURS 12 DAYS
26 DAYS
28 DAYS
67 HOURS
GUADALCANAL 6 HOURS
NEW CALEDONIA 6 HOURS
BRISBANE 6 HOURS
SIDNEY

By June 1942, 150,000 Army troops as well as Marine and Navy ground echelons had been established in the South and Southwest Pacific areas.* The peculiar topography and character of the Australian continent made the task there one of extreme difficulty. Australian distances are tremendous, the communications—road, rail, and electric wire—were limited and complicated by the absence of standardization, and the frontier for 4,500 miles was exposed to possible Japanese landings.

Japan struck at Hawaii, the Philippines, Malaya, and strategic islands in the central Pacific. With the advantage of a long period of preparation, including numerous initial moves in China and IndoChina to establish advance air and other bases, and, capitalizing upon surprise action, the Japanese launched their thrust to prevent the concentration or reinforcement of Allied forces to halt the drive south toward Australia and Burma.[10]

Struggle for the Philippines

The left wing of the southward advance of the Japanese was concentrated on the reduction of the Philippines. Our strength in the islands at that time consisted of 19,000 United States Army troops, 12,000 Philippine Scouts, and approximately 100,000 men of the newly mobilized and but partially trained and equipped Philippine Army. Included in these forces were some 8,000 Army Air Forces personnel equipped with some 250 aircraft, of which 35 were Flying Fortresses and 107 were P-40 fighters.

The enemy led off with systematic bombing of airfields and key points in Luzon which resulted in the destruction of a large number of our planes due to limited dispersal fields and lack of sufficient radar warning equipment, antiaircraft guns, and other matériel.

On December 10 and 22, Japanese landings were made in northwestern Luzon. Outnumbered and incompletely equipped, lacking air support, and utilizing troops but recently mobilized and organized for the first time into regimental groups, General MacArthur was left no alternative but that of a delaying action. His action was further complicated by another Japanese landing, in force, on the eastern coast of Luzon. Under great difficulties an orderly withdrawal was effected into the Bataan Peninsula for a final defensive stand, protected and supported by the fortress of Corregidor. The remaining bomb-

ing planes were sent to Mindanao (later to Australia) with the mission of securing bases from which to support the operations on Bataan. The enemy rapidly concentrated his forces ashore and launched heavy attacks against the Bataan garrison, which heroically contested every foot of ground.

(By the end of January, Japanese troops had seized the important oil center of Tarakan on the northeast coast of Borneo, captured Rabaul and Kavieng in the Bismarck Archipelago and Kieta on Bougainville Island in the Solomons, were rapidly approaching Singapore* from the north, and controlled the sea and air routes to the Philippines. They stood along a 4,000-mile frontier of the Dutch East Indies and the Melanesian Barrier with their forces in position to threaten the remaining Dutch possessions, Australia, and the islands to its north and east.)

The difficulties of the supply situation on Bataan, under the Japanese blockade, were greatly aggravated by the fact that thousands of civilians accompanied the army into the Bataan Peninsula. The number of people to be supplied quickly forced a reduction of the entire command to half rations. Efforts were immediately initiated to organize blockade running from the Netherlands East Indies and Australia and to carry medicines, special fuses, and other critical munitions by submarine. The blockade running, financed from the funds placed at the disposal of the Chief of Staff by Congress, involved many difficulties; for example, it was found that the small shipowners and crew members approached in Java, Timor, and New Guinea would not accept checks on our Federal funds deposited in Melbourne, but demanded cash. Therefore the actual money had to be flown across Africa and India by plane for delivery in Java. A complete report of these perilous operations has never been received. Of seven ships dispatched from Australia only three arrived at Cebu. Attempts to transship these supplies from Cebu to Corregidor failed because of the rigid enemy blockade. At least 15 of these blockade runners, totaling 40,000 tons, were sunk or captured by the enemy while attempting to get supplies through to Bataan. Several over-age destroyers were also fitted out as blockade runners but none of these succeeded in reaching the Philippines prior to the fall of Corregidor. Deliveries of supplies and the evacuation of certain personnel by submarine continued at intervals throughout the siege.

The difficulty of penetrating the Japanese blockade and getting supplies to Corregidor and Bataan caused the military situation to deteriorate. The half rations issued since January 11, 1942, had been further reduced by the end of March, and horses and mules were being slaughtered for food.

---

*American units were also landed in New Zealand. The Government of New Zealand and the local municipal governments have cooperated in every practicable manner to provide facilities, services, and buildings required by our forces. New Zealand troops now are operating with American forces in complete cooperation in carrying out assigned missions.

---

*Singapore fell to the Japanese on February 15, 1942.

In view of the enemy's capabilities throughout the Pacific and our untenable position in the Philippines, the major efforts of the United States were directed toward a rapid concentration of defense forces along our route to Australia, the creation of an effective striking force on that continent, and the dispatch of material aid to the forces of our allies in the East Indies.[11] Accordingly, Hawaii was strengthened, additional islands along the South Pacific air-ferry route were garrisoned, and a large force was provided for the defense of New Caledonia. The components of a balanced air force were shipped to Australia, the heavy bombers being flown in via Hawaii or India. Shipping limitations precluded the early dispatch of large bodies of ground troops.

In February 1942 General MacArthur was instructed by the War Department to proceed to Australia to assume command of the newly designated Southwest Pacific area. His directive from the Combined Chiefs of Staff included the missions of holding Australia, checking the enemy's advance along the Melanesian Barriers, protecting land, sea, and air communications with the Southwest Pacific and maintaining our position in the Philippines. Lt. Gen. Jonathan M. Wainwright, succeeding General MacArthur as commander of the forces in the Philippine Islands, continued the gallant defense which has become an epic in American history.

On March 31 the Japanese initiated the anticipated general assault on the Bataan position, an attack relentlessly maintained during the next 7 days. As our lines were finally penetrated and field hospitals were shelled by Japanese artillery, it became apparent that the courageous but exhausted defenders could no longer avoid disaster.

On April 9 the following radio was received from General Wainwright on Corregidor:

> Shortly after flag of truce passed through the front line this morning hostilities ceased for the most part in Bataan. At about 10 o'clock this morning General King was sent for, to confer with the Japanese commander. He has not returned, as of 7 o'clock p.m., nor has result of conference been disclosed. Since the fall of Bataan the hostile air force has renewed its attack on Corregidor. This island was heavily bombed this afternoon but has suffered no damage of military consequence.

Despite Bataan's loss, Corregidor, Fort Drum, and Fort Hughes (all island fortifications) continued to resist enemy attacks with counterbattery and antiaircraft fire for nearly a month. On April 13 and 14 a squadron of American bombers from the south successfully attacked Japanese installations and shipping in the Philippine area.

On May 5, after a week of intensive bombardment which buried many of the shore defenses under landslides, the enemy made a landing on North Point of Corregidor. The shattered defenses were unable to dam the Japanese tide. The following day the exhausted and depleted forces were overwhelmed and finally surrendered.

The final spirit of General Wainwright's heroic command is indicated by the extract from a letter written by him just before Corregidor fell:

> As I write this we are subjected to terrific air and artillery bombardment and it is unreasonable to expect that we can hold out for long. We have done our best, both here and on Bataan, and although beaten we are still unashamed.

Concurrently with the campaign to reduce the Philippines, the enemy had exploited his successes on the Malayan Peninsula to bring the entire Netherlands East Indies under his domination. Concentration of Japanese forces there and in the Bismarck Archipelago and Solomon Islands constituted a direct threat to our lines of communication in the Pacific and to the north coast of Australia.

These initial Japanese successes were due to Allied lack of military means, especially in aircraft and its supporting warning and maintenance services, to oppose an adversary whose preliminary strategic deployments permitted successive concentrations of overwhelming superiority in land, sea, and air forces on selected objectives.

The effects of the desperate resistance offered by the Philippine Army and United States forces on Bataan, holding as they did a sizeable portion of Japanese strength, were now being felt. During the delay thus gained men and materials were dispatched to Australia, New Caledonia, and other Pacific islands. The growth of power of the United Nations in the southwest Pacific was presaged by our air forces which were now performing long-range bombing missions against Japan's newly acquired bases in the Bismarcks and New Guinea, and were also making Japanese attempts to bomb Port Moresby and northern Australia increasingly costly. The bombing of Japan by our planes commanded by Lt. Col. (now Maj. Gen.) James H. Doolittle was a heartening event in a generally somber picture. Despite heavy losses in men and materials sustained by the Allies in Malaya, the Netherlands East Indies, and the Philippines, the military balance was approaching an equilibrium. The initiative was no longer completely in enemy hands.

Coral Sea—High Tide of Aggression

That Japan intended to exploit her victories to the limit was indicated by preparations for an offensive toward Australia based on the Bismarcks and the upper Solomons. On May 4, 1942, this new adventure was signalized by the seizure of the port of Tulagi in the central Solomons (*see* map 1). Between May 7 and 11, however, a heavy column of enemy naval vessels and transports moving southward in the Coral

Sea was decisively defeated by Allied naval and air forces off the Louisiade Archipelago. Suffering heavy losses the enemy retired toward bases in the Mandated Islands. Army aircraft supported this action by repeated attacks on Japanese bases at Lae, Salamaua, Rabaul, Kieta, and the Shortland areas in southern Bougainville, where concentrations of enemy shipping provided lucrative targets (map 2).

The Coral Sea action marked the high tide of Japanese conquest in the southwest Pacific. The possibility that the enemy would shift his strength northward to attack Midway or Hawaii prompted a regrouping of our naval units and a further reinforcement of the air and ground units at Hawaii, Midway, and other island outposts. Midway-based long-range bombing and patrol aircraft were assigned offensive reconnaissance missions over extensive ocean areas. On the morning of June 3 a naval plane sighted an enemy force with transports some 470 miles to the westward. Next day, when another force with a heavy carrier concentration

was located about 180 miles to the north of Midway, it became evident that the largest concentration of enemy naval strength yet assembled for Pacific operations was headed eastward with the capture of Midway as its preliminary objective. All available Navy carrier and land-based Army and Navy air forces were concentrated against the enemy. In the historic 2-day battle which followed, heavy losses in ships and airplanes were inflicted on the Japanese who retired at once.

The battles of the Coral Sea and Midway restored the balance of sea power in the Pacific to the United States and lessened a grave threat to our Pacific possessions. Midway climaxed our first half year of war and marked the opening of a new phase of operations in the Pacific. The enemy offensive had definitely been checked; the United Nations firmly held chains of island bases extending from the United States to Australia; our forces had begun to deliver staggering blows; and our commanders were now free to prepare for offensive operations.

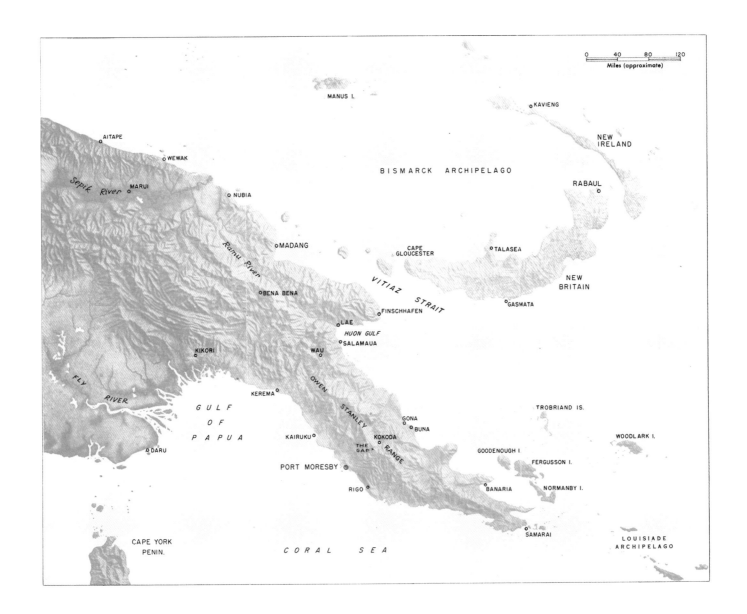

THE FIFTH PHASE

The Solomons

The operation against Guadalcanal inaugurated a series of offensive moves in the Pacific which have continued to the present date. The enemy occupation of the Solomon Islands permitted him the use of advance air and naval bases from which to attack our long Pacific supply line and the north coast of Australia. On August 7, 1942, therefore, United States Navy and Marine forces seized beachheads on Guadalcanal and Florida Island and occupied Tulagi. The highly prized airfield on Guadalcanal was held by the Marines against a long series of heavy air, sea, and ground assaults by the enemy. The resolute defense of these Marines under Maj. Gen. (now Lt. Gen.) Alexander A. Vandegrift and the desperate gallantry of our naval task forces marked the turning point in the Pacific.

Army ground units commenced reinforcements of the Marines on October 13. On December 9, command in the Guadalcanal-Tulagi area passed to the Army under Maj. Gen. Alexander M. Patch. Early in 1943, a series of well-executed and vigorous operations by Army divisions and one Marine regiment in conjunction with air offensive, defensive, and support operations compressed and then destroyed all enemy resistance on the island.

Papua

While strongly contesting our offensive in the Solomons during the summer and fall of 1942, the enemy's determination to exploit his previous gains was indicated by persistent reports of activities in the Bismarcks, upper Solomons, and New Guinea. These proved to be preparations for an overland push from Buna through the Owen Stanley Mountains with Port Moresby, our advance base on the south coast of New Guinea, as the immediate objective.

By September 12, the Japanese had forced Allied ground forces back to within 30 miles of Port Moresby in an advance which demonstrated great skill in jungle and mountain fighting; however, reinforcement of Allied ground troops coupled with effective air support finally turned back this threat. By the end of November, converging attacks by American and Australian troops had confined the enemy to pockets along the northeast coast. In the final stages of the Allied drive, the Army Air Forces under Lt. Gen. George C. Kenney, while destroying the enemy shipping employed in attempts to supply his troops, flew a complete striking force—troops, equipment, and food—from Port Moresby over the Owen Stanley Range to the Buna area, utilizing bombers as well as transport planes.[12]

Our air offensive ultimately forced the now desperate Japanese to use parachutes and submarines to supply their forces which were resisting our ground pressure with fanatical tenacity. Early in 1943, the northeast coast of New Guinea was finally cleared of the enemy by American and Australian troops under the command of Lt. Gen. Robert L. Eichelberger, as far north as Buna, but only after he had been systematically rooted out of his fox-holes along the beaches and destroyed by the determined assaults of our men. Success in this campaign is all the more remarkable in view of the fact that throughout General MacArthur's operations he was handicapped by a serious lack of small vessels, transport planes, and special jungle equipment in a climate deleterious to white races.

The United Nations in the Pacific theater now possessed more secure positions from which to counter Japanese offensive ventures; also, commanders and troops had secured valuable experience in battle. Unified command arrangements were welding sea, air, and ground forces into efficient fighting teams. Air superiority was demonstrated by a loss ratio of four to one in our favor (chart 14); and a more complete control of the sea was made possible by the "skip-bombing" tactics perfected in the southwest Pacific by General Kenney's airmen. In a single instance, a convoy proceeding through Vitiaz Strait into Huon Gulf was completely destroyed by this type of attack. In this Battle of the Bismarck Sea, Allied losses were 1 bomber and 3 pursuit planes, with a casualty list of 13 men, compared to a known Japanese loss of 61 planes and 22 ships, and an estimated loss of an entire division of 15,000 men.

Rapidly increasing military resources in the Pacific now afford us considerable freedom of action. The characteristics of the theater, predominantly oceanic, demand precise and efficient teamwork on the part of our naval, air, and ground forces. There are no shortcuts in the accomplishment of the arduous task. Successes thus far in piercing the enemy's protective screen of island citadels prove the soundness of combining surface and submarine attacks on hostile sea routes of communication, strategic employment of our long-range bombers against the enemy's staging and supply bases, and coordinated assaults by all elements upon successive objectives.[13]

European Theater

Prior to our entry into the war, the United States, through lend-lease operations, had supported British war economy and had included measures to insure safe delivery of these supplies and materials. When we were precipitated into active participation in the

COMPARISON OF U.S. & ENEMY PLANE LOSSES
IN SOUTHWEST PACIFIC & NORTH AFRICAN THEATERS

EXCLUDING KNOWN NON-COMBAT LOSSES
(NOVEMBER 1942 thru MAY 1943)

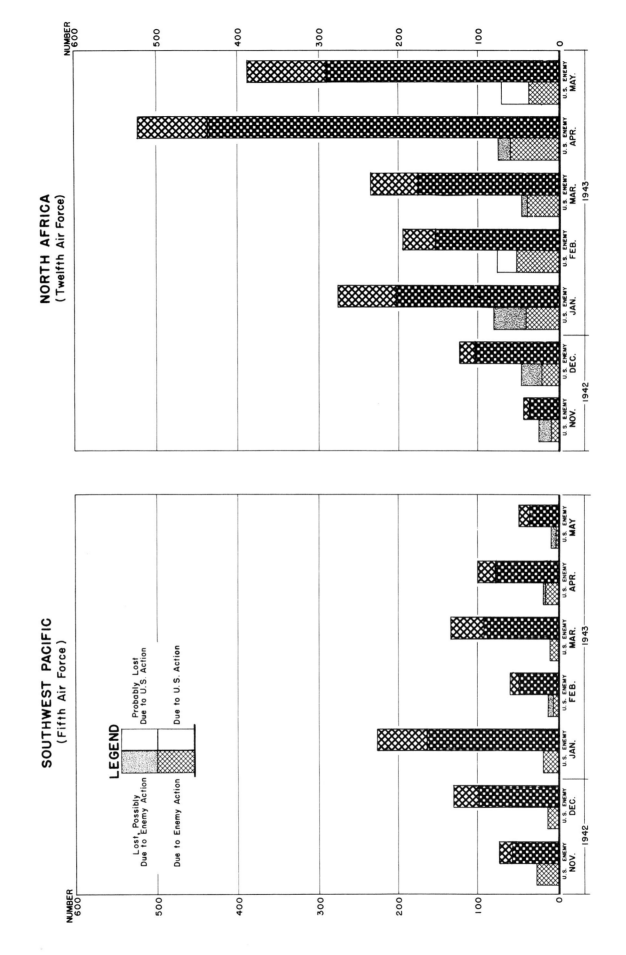

NORTH AFRICA
(Twelfth Air Force)

SOUTHWEST PACIFIC
(Fifth Air Force)

LEGEND

Lost Possibly Due to Enemy Action

Probably Lost Due to U.S. Action

Due to Enemy Action

Due to U.S. Action

struggle, the necessity for the protection and control of the trans-Atlantic sea routes became both urgent and vital. Initial preparatory measures on our part therefore included the strengthening of both sea and air communication routes and this in turn involved the further development of bases in Newfoundland, Greenland, Iceland, and the United Kingdom.

When we entered the war, Germany, although committed on the eastern front, had sufficient divisions in northwestern Europe to threaten a cross-Channel invasion or a possible thrust to seize Iceland on the flank of the sea lanes from the United States to the United Kingdom and Russia. American forces, in sufficient strength to discourage such a venture, previously had been dispatched to augment the British garrison in Iceland. The latter was relieved in its entirety by the summer of 1942.

United States Troops Move to United Kingdom

Despite the fact that the initiative at this time lay wholly in the hands of the Axis our preliminary movements were based on future aggressive action. The time factor now became increasingly important, time in which to train the new armies, to procure the shipping and munitions, and to organize the long lines of communications, while holding the enemy at bay. Detailed planning for specifc future offensive operations was already under way in line with the basic strategy which had been previously determined.

Upon our entry into the war it became urgently desirable to move United States troops into the United Kingdom as early as possible to bolster the defenses there which had been seriously weakened by the dispatch of troops to the Middle and the Far East, and for the psychological effect on the British people. At that moment, however, the threat to Australia was so serious that most of the shipping immediately available in the Atlantic in January had to be hurriedly employed for the movement of 25,000 troops to the southwest Pacific, largely to garrison New Caledonia. It therefore was not possible to send more than a single division to Ireland until the following summer.

Steps were immediately taken to build up in the United Kingdom a strong American air force, notably precision bombers. These units would afford additional protection to the British Isles against any invasion attempt.

The movement of United States troops to the United Kingdom utilized our shortest line of communications overseas and effected a concentration of British, Canadian, and American forces which, with the support of the powerful metropolitan Royal Air Force, forced the enemy to employ additional troops in northwestern France, thereby reducing the strength he could employ elsewhere.

In the latter part of January 1942, the first convoy of our troops arrived in Northern Ireland. The complicated transportation, construction, and administrative problems were solved with the close cooperation of all the British agencies concerned.

By June the gathering strength of United States forces in the United Kingdom made it necessary to establish a headquarters and organization for a European theater of operations, and Maj. Gen. (now Gen.) Dwight D. Eisenhower was placed in command.

The United States Army Air Forces assault on the continent of Europe was launched on July 4, 1942, when six American aircraft and crews participated in a Royal Air Force attack on targets in Holland. The combined American-British bomber offensive against the continent of Europe today gives promise of being a decisive factor in the ultimate destruction of the German citadel. It has for its objectives the reduction of German air combat strength to a virtual impotence; the disruption of vital elements of the enemy's lines of communications; the progressive destruction and dislocation of the German military, industrial, and economic system; and by the resultant psychological impact on the German people, the undermining of their morale and their willingness to continue to support the war effort. Thus the objective of the combined bomber offensive is the elimination of both the German ability and will to continue to wage war.

Aerial Assault on Fortress of Europe

The British heavy bomber command was developed for the purpose of carrying out night missions, while the American Flying Fortresses and Liberators were developed for daylight operations. In the British planes, speed and armament were limited in favor of long range and heavy bomb loads. This type plane is especially effective for night operations over industrial areas where a high degree of precision in bombing is not vitally necessary. On the other hand the American bomber design tends toward a fast, very heavily armed and armored high-altitude plane. Its more limited bomb capacity is compensated for by the perfection of the precision bombsight which permits small specific targets to be singled out for destruction. The violence of the German fighter plane reaction to our daylight attacks is convincing evidence of the deadly effect of precision bombing. The enemy must find a counter to this technique or accept the emasculation of his industries and his fighter command.

Allied operations to cope with German submarine activities furnish an excellent example of British and American cooperation, coordinated to achieve maximum results. There are three possible types of offensive action against submarines; that is, to sink them at sea, to destroy the factories which build and equip them, and to attack the bases from which they operate. Factories and bases may be rendered inoperative either by a night mass attack to effect general destruction on the area or by daylight precision attacks against vital utilities such as power plants, fuel supply installations, or special repair facilities.

Reports during the past months have mentioned with increasing frequency air attacks against Lorient, St. Nazaire, Brest, and La Pallice, all U-boat bases on the west coast of France. The precision attacks have been aimed against critical points, the destruction of which render the general installations ineffective, a particularly important procedure where the docks and other vital installations have been protected by heavy concrete overhead cover. The night bombing attacks carried out by the British have involved loads of over 1,000 tons dropped in a single operation with the effect of devastating general service facilities and of shattering the morale and working efficiency of the personnel operating the submarine bases. At the same time heavy attacks have been made day and night against the submarine shipyards at Vegesack (near Bremen) and Wilhelmshaven, and against the Essen, Dusseldorf, Mannheim, Karlsruhe, and other industrial areas producing component parts for submarines.

These bombing operations, together with the action of the AntiSubmarine Command and Allied destroyers and escort vessels, appear to be in process of driving the submarine from the seas.

Experience over the European continent has demonstrated the soundness of the tactical doctrines of our air forces and of the basic design of their aircraft. Notable early examples were raids against Vegesack and Wilhelmshaven during March 1943, in which 180 of our heavy bombers destroyed over 80 German fighters with a loss of but 5 of our own planes. These raids effectively put out of action for a period of many months the Vegesack plant and administered crippling damage to the naval installations at Wilhelmshaven.

Our air assaults on Germany and northwestern Europe have grown heavier and heavier with the constantly increasing strength of the Eighth Air Force operating out of the United Kingdom. More recently it has been possible to coordinate these attacks closely with operations using bases in North Africa. The enforced concentration of the Germans' most experienced fighter pilots in northwestern Europe had an important bearing on air operations during the final battle in Tunisia and on the situation in Russia.[14]

The build-up of depots, airfields, and administrative services for our operations in the United Kingdom has involved a tremendous program of shipping, construction, and the organization of an extensive service command. These vital factors in modern war are time-consuming in preparation and impose a heavy burden on our air and ocean transportation facilities, but they provide the solid foundation which is an imperative requirement in conducting the specialized and technical warfare of the present day.[15]

On May 10, 1943, following the unfortunate airplane accident which resulted in the death of Lt. Gen. Frank M. Andrews, command of the European theater of operations was assumed by Lt. Gen. Jacob L. Devers.

North African Theater

In January 1942, when the Prime Minister and his chiefs of staff were in Washington, operations in northwest Africa, in Morocco and Algiers, were discussed in detail. Our limited means at the time made it impracticable to mount such an expedition. There were further discussions at the time of the Prime Minister's visit to Washington the following June and the final decision was taken in July to launch an expedition into northwest Africa in conjunction with the preparations for the advance westward of the British Eighth Army then reorganizing on the El Alamein line. The opening of the Mediterranean would facilitate Allied global operations, and the removal of the constant threat of German activities in western Morocco and at Dakar would add immeasurably to the security of the Allied position while gathering strength to administer the final punishing blows. Furthermore, if our occupation of North Africa could be carried out without fatally embittering the French troops and authorities in that region it would provide a setting for the reconstitution of the French Army in preparation for its return in force to the homeland. The psychological effect of the conquest of North Africa would be tremendous.

The adopted plans provided that task forces from both the United Kingdom and the United States should strike simultaneously at Algiers, Oran, and Casablanca (map 3). It was urgently desired to make initial landings to the east of Algiers at Bone, Philippeville, and possibly Tunis, but the lack of shipping and of landing boats and aircraft carriers at the time made this procedure impracticable. It was desired to carry out the operation early in the fall but it was necessary to delay until November in order to receive a large number of craft from the shipyards and provide and train the crews for the operation of these vessels. Some of the larger vessels did not become available until a week before the convoys sailed.

The success of the operation depended on the efficient handling of a mass of details as well as on the training and fighting qualities of the troops, and

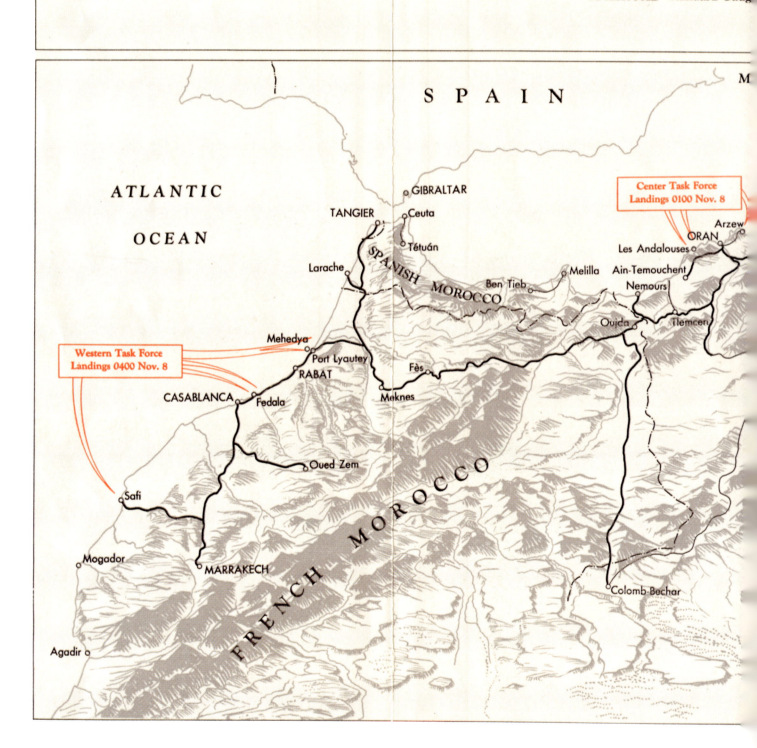

FRENCH NORT

RAILROAD Standard Gaug

SPAIN

M

ATLANTIC

OCEAN

GIBRALTAR

TANGIER
Ceuta

Tétuán

Larache

SPANISH MOROCCO

Ben Tieb
Melilla

Center Task Force
Landings 0100 Nov. 8

Arzew
ORAN
Les Andalouses
Ain-Temouchent
Nemours

Oujda
Tlemcen

Mehedya

Western Task Force
Landings 0400 Nov. 8

Port Lyautey
RABAT
CASABLANCA
Fedala

Fès
Meknes

Oued Zem

FRENCH MOROCCO

Safi

Mogador

MARRAKECH

Colomb-Bechar

Agadir

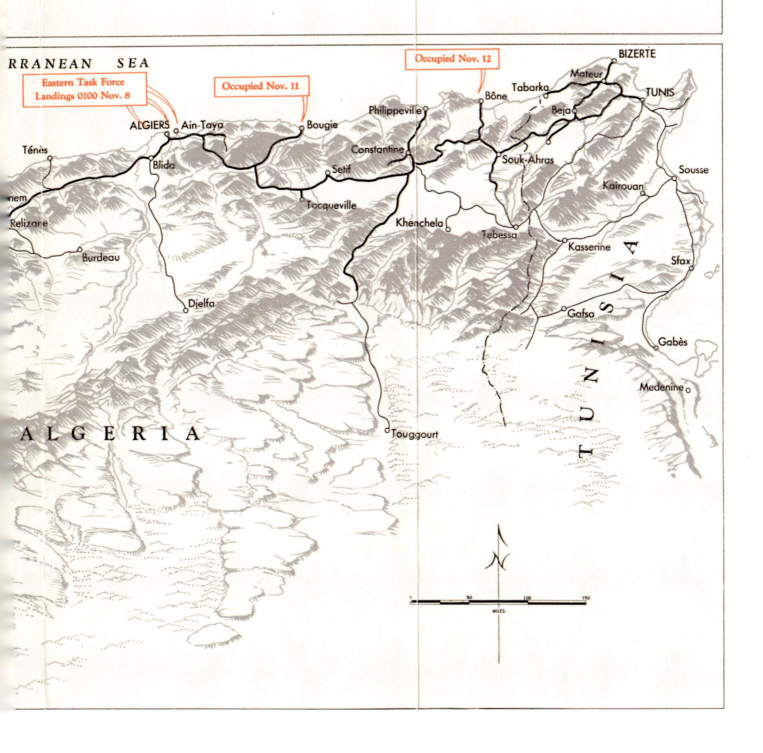

VEST AFRICA

—— RAILROAD Narrow Gauge

RRANEAN SEA

Eastern Task Force
Landings 0100 Nov. 8

Occupied Nov. 11

Occupied Nov. 12

BIZERTE

Mateur

Tabarka

TUNIS

Bône

Beja

Philippeville

Ténès

ALGIERS Ain-Taya

Bougie

Blida

Constantine

Souk-Ahras

nem

Setif

Sousse

Relizare

Tacqueville

Kairouan

Burdeau

Khenchela

Tebessa

Kasserine

Sfax

Djelfa

Gafsa

Gabès

TUNISIA

Medenine

ALGERIA

Touggourt

N

| 5 | 50 | 100 | 150 |

MILES

above all, upon the secrecy with which this vast undertaking had to be prepared.

General Eisenhower, who was designated to command the Allied forces involved, organized a combined staff in London and directed the planning. Three task forces were formed: one entirely American sailed directly from the United States and carried out the landings along the west coast of Morocco, another of American troops escorted by the British Navy sailed from Great Britain and landed in the vicinity of Oran, the third, a combined British-American ground force escorted by the British Navy, sailed from the British Isles and landed at Algiers. There were naval covering forces, both British and American. The combined air forces, other than carrier-borne and a few transports and heavy bombers, had to be funneled through the single restricted field at Gibraltar which could have been put out of action in less than an hour. There was no choice but to accept this hazard.

The problem of how to avoid fighting with the French forces in Africa was difficult of approach. In the first place, and most important of all, the hazard to the secrecy with which the operation must be prepared and launched presented an extremely delicate balance in the choice of methods to be followed. Should an approach be made to a single Frenchman who proved unsympathetic to our purpose we risked the slaughter of soldiers on the beaches of North Africa as well as decisive losses in shipping. The psychological impact from such a defeat, at that particular moment in the war would have been little short of catastrophic in its possible consequences. To a certain degree, however, this risk had to be accepted. Even so, the discussions regarding such an expedition had to be conducted on a more or less indefinite basis as to timing. Not until 4 days before the convoys would deploy off the beaches at Algiers, Oran, and Casablanca were the few Frenchmen we had contacted informed of the actual date for the operation. This of course made it extremely difficult, in cases impossible, for these French officials to take all the steps necessary to facilitate our landings. The consequences of disclosure of our purpose to the enemy, however, involved too great a peril to justify earlier notification.

The singular relationship existing between the Vichy government and Berlin, and with the French provinces in North Africa, together with the differences of religion and race and the deep-rooted hatreds of the heterogeneous populations of Algiers and Morocco, imposed a political problem of maximum complexity on General Eisenhower. At the moment his energies and direction had to be concentrated on the successful penetration of an 800-mile coastline and a vast hinterland by a force of but 107,000 men. To further complicate the situation he must be on guard against the possibility of an Axis stroke through Spain to sever our communications through the Straits of Gibraltar and interrupt by aerial bombardment the single railroad line from Casablanca through Fez to Oran.

Concurrently with the preparation in the United Kingdom of two task forces, one of Americans to land at Oran and the other a mixed force to land at Algiers, a third task force composed of the 3rd Infantry and 2nd Armored Divisions, the major part of the 9th Infantry Division, and reinforced with supporting arms and services, was organized in the United States under Maj. Gen. (now Lt. Gen.) George S. Patton, Jr. His headquarters were temporarily established in the Operations Division of the General Staff in Washington which became the coordinating medium between General Eisenhower and General Patton. Rear Admiral (now Vice Admiral) H. K. Hewitt, who commanded the expedition until its disembarkation in Africa, assembled the force at sea on October 24 and sailed for Casablanca. This task force was to effect a junction with the force under Maj. Gen. (now Lt. Gen.) Lloyd Fredendall which was to land in the vicinity of Oran.

General Fredendall's troops consisted of the 1st Infantry Division and one-half of the 1st Armored Division, reinforced by corps troops. In addition to seizing Oran and the adjacent airfields and making contact with General Patton's force in the vicinity of Fez, this expedition was also charged with the mission of effecting a juncture with the Eastern Task Force which had the mission of capturing Algiers. The latter force under Lt. Gen. K. A. N. Anderson of the British Army, consisted of British commando and infantry units together with two United States regimental combat teams, one from the 9th and one from the 34th Infantry Divisions, and a Ranger battalion. The first landing was to be effected under the direction of Maj. Gen. Charles W. Ryder of the American Army. General Anderson took over command after the American troops had been established ashore.

The two task forces sailed from the British Isles on October 25 under British naval escort. All three task forces were provided the protection of three naval covering forces, one American.

To facilitate the capture of the airfields near Oran a 1,500-mile flight was undertaken by our troop-carrier command with United States parachute troops.

November 8 was designated as D-day on which the three task forces were to strike simultaneously. Three days previously General Eisenhower opened his command post at Gibraltar, and apropos of Allied unity of purpose in this war it is interesting to report that for the time being he commanded the fortress of Gibraltar. Just prior to his departure from London, General Eisenhower radioed me the following message:

I cannot leave the United Kingdom without expressing to you once more, and to all of your assistants in the War Department my lasting appreciation for the perfect assistance and support you have provided us. If you deem it appropriate, and a convenient occasion will occur, I should like you to pay my respects to the President and the Secretary of War and to say to them that all of us are determined to make this operation a real success.

The Landings

Despite the negotiations which had been carried on with a few French officials the amount of resistance which the landing forces would encounter remained problematical. General Eisenhower broadcast a proclamation of our friendly intentions toward French North Africa and instructed the French forces to display certain signals to indicate their nonresistance. However, each task force proceeded on the assumption that determined resistance must be expected. They were under orders not to fire until fired upon. A code signal, "Play ball," was to be broadcast to the entire force at the first hostile act on the part of the French in any sector, as a warning to initiate vigorous offensive action.

At the moment the landings in Algeria began, at 1 o'clock on the morning of November 8, President Roosevelt assured the French people by short-wave radio that the Allies sought no territory and asked for French cooperation. The Spanish Government was also informed at this time that the occupation was in no way directed against Spanish Morocco or other Spanish possessions in Africa.

The landings were carried out in accordance with plans and with a boldness and efficiency which secured the initial objectives, the major airfields and ports in North Africa, within a period of 48 hours.

Diplomatic Negotiations

These military operations were staged against a background of diplomatic negotiations through which speedy cessations of French resistance was sought. Both Gen. Charles de Gaulle, leader of the Fighting French, and Gen. Henri Giraud, who had escaped from Germany to France and then from France to Gibraltar, broadcast pleas for French cooperation when our operations started.

General Eisenhower had announced that General Giraud would be responsible for civil and military affairs in North Africa, but the French military officials on the ground were found to be loyal to Marshal Petain's government. President Roosevelt's note to the French Chief of State had assured Marshal Petain of our desire for a liberated France but the Vichy answer was disappointing. Our ambassador was handed his passports on November 9 and orders were dispatched from Vichy to French African units to resist our forces which by then had already accomplished their missions except on the Casablanca front.

Unexpectedly, Admiral Jean Darlan, Petain's designated successor, and commander in chief of all French forces, was found to be in Algiers visiting a sick son when our forces landed. He was taken into protective custody and when it was found that the French leaders stood loyal to the Vichy government, a series of conferences immediately followed with the purpose of calling a halt to the French resistance against General Patton's task force in the vicinity of Casablanca. When, on the morning of November 11, the Germans invaded unoccupied France, Darlan rejected the pseudo-independent Vichy government, assumed authority in North Africa in the name of Marshal Petain, and promulgated an order to all French commanders in North Africa to cease hostilities. This order reached Casablanca a few minutes before the assault on that city was to be launched on the early morning of November 11.

The North African government was reoriented and brought into close collaboration with the United Nations under a provisional government headed by Admiral Darlan with General Giraud as commander in chief of the French ground and air units. Subsequently French West Africa under Gov.-Gen. Pierre Boisson announced its adherence to the Darlan regime, bringing to the Allied cause additional naval power and trained ground units and making immediately possible a short air route from the United States to the North African battle fronts. Cordial relations were quickly established with the Sultan of Morocco. Later it was possible to convince General Orgaz, High Commissioner of Spanish Morocco, that the American forces contemplated no action against Spanish territory.

Upon the cessation of hostilites General Eisenhower's forces were faced with numerous and pressing problems. Harbors had to be cleared of sunken ships, wharfs and docks repaired, neglected and slender lines of rail communication had to be developed to carry heavy traffic, antisubmarine patrols organized to protect our sea routes in the Mediterranean, the civil population had to be provided for and its economy started on the road to reconstruction,[16] French troops in North Africa had to be equipped,[17] our forces had to be disposed to prevent a successful Axis thrust through Spain, and finally, and most important of all, our forces had to close with the enemy in Tunisia to effect his destruction in North Africa.

Race for Tunisia

The rapid extension of the offensive eastward was facilitated by the expeditious landing at Algiers resulting from French cooperation. Our forces had suffered comparatively few casualties in this particular landing and as quickly as logistical support could be prepared they were headed toward Tunisia.

It was apparent that a strategical surprise had been effected. Tunisia was lightly garrisoned by the French. Far to the east the German Afrika Korps and the accompanying Italian forces had been hurled back from the El Alamein position by Gen. Sir Bernard Montgomery's Eighth Army a few days prior to the landings.

Despite the manifest difficulties of supply, the immediate occupation of Tunisia appeared mandatory. As soon as French collaboration was assured, the leading elements of the British First Army, including a few of the American units which had landed at Algiers, reembarked for a movement eastward to Bougie where they landed on November 11. An overland march immediately followed and Bone was occupied the following day by two companies of British parachutists and a commando unit which arrived by sea. On November 15 orders were issued for the movement of French troops then at Algiers and Constantine to protect the southern flank of the American and British units which were now advancing into Tunisia along the coastal corridors crossing the frontier. The French units were reinforced with American troops, including tank destroyer units, and one of their assigned missions was the protection of advance airfields in the Tebessa-Gafsa area. Meanwhile, our air units had moved into eastern Algeria and were rendering support to our columns from inadequate or improvised airfields despite shortages in gasoline and the great difficulty of supply.

Immediately following the landings in North Africa, Axis forces were rushed into Tunisia by sea and air. As early as November 16 our advancing troops encountered German patrols 60 miles west of Tunis. The leading units of the British First Army, with American reinforcements, reached Medjez-el-Bab, 30 miles southwest of Tunis, on November 25 and took possession of the airfields at Djedeida on November 28. Farther to the south, Allied units reached Pont du Fahs and American parachute troops were operating in the Sbeitla-Gafsa area. Axis resistance steadily increased, with intensified mechanized and artillery activity. Our advance on the Station de Jefna, 32 miles southwest of Bizerte, was repulsed on November 30. Strong Axis counterattacks with tanks forced Allied withdrawals from Tebourba, but similar enemy aggressive action directed against Medjez-el-Bab was successfully resisted. The short and easily maintained air and sea lines of communication between Sicily and Tunisia permitted the rapid build-up of the Axis forces. The nearest ports of Allied entry at Bone and Phillippeville were of very limited capacity. The enemy's greatest advantage, however, lay in the possession of all-weather airfields, as the devel-

opment of the rainy season for a time rendered fighter-plane support of our advance troops impossible. Difficulties of supply became so serious that active operations were practically suspended in early December. Meanwhile the enemy rapidly reinforced his positions which assumed the character of a bridgehead protecting the Bizerte-Tunis area and extending southward to cover the bases into the coastal plain leading to Sousse, Sfax, and Gabes. Medjez-el-Bab remained the key point of the Allied position.

In the midst of this campaign, the assassination of Admiral Darlan created a political crisis which was met by the action of the French North African governors in designating General Giraud as Darlan's successor.

Fall of Tunisia

The new year opened with the opponents in Tunisia testing each other's strength along the partially stabilized line and matching each other's bids for air supremacy, both forces concentrating against ports and lines of communication.

In Libya, Rommel's Afrika Korps with its complement of Italians abandoned a succession of defensive positions, withdrawing finally into Tripolitania. By February his troops were established on the Mareth Line in southeast Tunisia.

Meanwhile, General Eisenhower's troops were being regrouped on the Tunisian front preparatory to renewing the offensive against the Axis positions. The troops were under the operational command of General Anderson, commanding the British First Army. So far as was practicable, American units were concentrated and the French units organized into a combat corps. German thrusts at weakly held French positions, however, necessitated a further intermingling of Allied units.[18]

Throughout the African operation up to this time, General Eisenhower had retained control of the United States Army forces in the British Isles, ground and air. This arrangement had been continued in order to afford him a free hand in drawing on such resources as we had established in the United Kingdom. Plans had been made before the launching of the African enterprise to effect a separation in February, and this was actually carried out on February 4 when General Andrews, a highly specialized air officer who had been sent to the Middle East for experience in combat and in contacts with our allies, was appointed commander of the United States forces in the European theater of operations with headquarters in London. This order was paralleled by the creation of a North African theater of operations, under General Eisenhower.

Upon the arrival of the British Eighth Army on the Mareth Line, it came under the direction of General

Eisenhower. General Sir Harold Alexander, of the British Army, was appointed his deputy and given direct command of the Eighteenth Army Group, which consisted of the British First Army, the British Eighth Army, the United States II Corps, and the French units on the Tunisian front. North African air units were organized into the Mediterranean Air Command under Air Chief Marshal Sir Arthur Tedder, with Maj. Gen. (now Lt. Gen.) Carl Spaatz, of the United States Army, as commander of the Northwest African Air Force. All heavy bombers, together with fighter support, were organized by General Spaatz into the Strategic Air Force under General Doolittle. Action was initiated at this time by General Spaatz to unify command of light and medium bombers and fighter support into a force known as the Tactical Air Force to lend close support to land and naval operations. Admiral of the fleet, Sir Andrew Cunningham, became naval commander in chief in the Mediterranean under General Eisenhower's direction. These Allied command arrangements led directly to the victories which soon followed (Battle of Tunisia and conquest of Sicily).

The junction of the veteran Afrika Korps with Von Arnim's command in Tunisia permitted the enemy to launch offensive strokes against the lightly held portions of the long Allied line. On February 14, hostile armored units reinforced by artillery and infantry and supported by dive bombers struck westward from Faid and broke through the Kasserine Pass (map 4). By the afternoon of February 21 the Axis forces had advanced a three-pronged armored thrust 21 miles beyond the pass, threatening the Allied position in central Tunisia. Of this operation General Eisenhower radioed the following comments :

Our present tactical difficulties resulted from my attempt to do possibly too much, coupled with the deterioration of resistance in the central mountainous area which began about January 17. That deterioration has absorbed the bulk of the United States 1st and 34th Divisions which formations had originally been pushed forward to provide general reserves and to permit us to attack from the line which we were then holding.

You would have been impressed could you have seen the magnificent display everywhere by the American enlisted men. I assure you that the troops that come out of this campaign are going to be battlewise and tactically efficient.

There were considerable tank losses on both sides. The enemy was able to maintain himself in his forward position for only 2 days before he recoiled under a concentrated attack by our ground forces powerfully assisted by the entire Allied air force in North Africa. Even the heavy bombers were used against their retreating columns. During this withdrawal, the enemy endeavored to capitalize upon possible Allied reinforcing moves to the south, delivering heavy attacks in the Medjez-el-Bab area, but these were held or checked after small gains. These thrusts were the last offensive efforts of the enemy

in Tunisia. The rains had ceased, the roads had been improved; the railroad had been vitalized with American methods and matériel, and more than 10 gasoline pipe lines, the two most important being from Bone to Ferriana and from Philippeville to Ouled Bamoun, had been built. These increased facilities permitted the movement into Tunisia of additional American troops. The time had come for a coordinated Allied effort which would free the African continent of Axis forces. The development of the plan is succinctly stated in the following paragraph of a radio from General Eisenhower on March 11th:

Our own plans contemplate a rising scale of offensive operations and it will be the role of the II Corps to draw all possible strength (enemy) from the south so as to help General Montgomery's Eighth Army through the Mareth Gap. Once we have the Eighth Army through that bottleneck, this campaign is going to assume rapidly a very definite form with constant pressure and drive kept up against the enemy throughout the region.

The last phase of the Battle of Tunisia opened on the evening of March 20 when the Western Desert Air Force in rear of the British Eighth Army (including the Ninth United States Air Force under General Brereton) launched an air offensive with continuous 24-hour bombing of the Axis positions and installations in the Mareth area, surpassing the intensity of any previous preparations since the capture of the El Alamein position. The Eighth Army attacked and secured a bridgehead through the minefields in the north, while the New Zealand Corps flanked the Mareth Line to the south. Coordinated pressure by the British First Army, the French, and the American II Corps under General Patton against the Axis bridgehead served to divert the enemy effort from the south. His position gradually crumpled and finally on April 7 patrols of the 9th Division, advancing southeast from Gafsa, made contact with units of the Eighth Army 20 miles inland from the coast.

Sfax was captured on April 10 by General Montgomery's forces. Rommel's columns were unable to make a stand at Sousse because of an Allied breakthrough at Fondouk, with the resulting capture of Kairouan and Pichon. He therefore fell back to a prepared and final position through Enfidaville.

Enemy Air Power Shattered

The air attacks of this period provided a classic example of strategic and tactical use of air power. Allied air forces over a long period of time had studied every aspect of the enemy air transport activity across the Sicilian Straits. They awaited the moment to catch a maximum concentration of transport aircraft on the Tunisian or Sicilian fields and to strike when the enemy was in greatest need of this air transport service. On April 5 the opportunity developed and air attacks of consistent intensity were

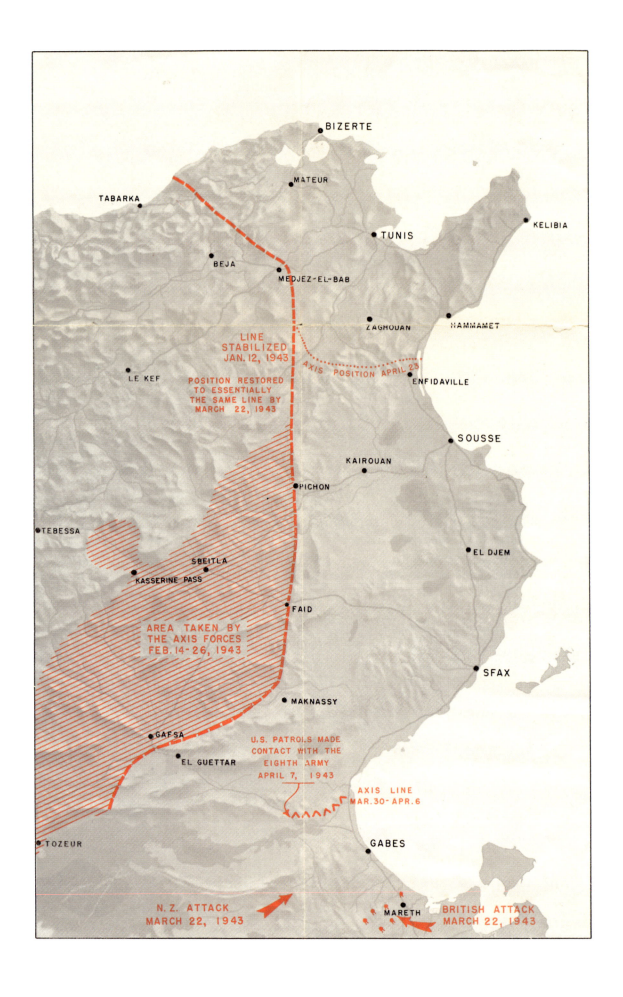

BIZERTE

MATEUR

TABARKA

TUNIS

KELIBIA

BEJA

MEDJEZ-EL-BAB

ZAGHOUAN

HAMMAMET

LINE
STABILIZED
JAN. 12, 1943

AXIS POSITION APRIL 23

LE KEF

POSITION RESTORED
TO ESSENTIALLY
THE SAME LINE BY
MARCH 22, 1943

ENFIDAVILLE

SOUSSE

KAIROUAN

PICHON

TEBESSA

EL DJEM

SBEITLA

KASSERINE PASS

FAID

AREA TAKEN BY
THE AXIS FORCES
FEB. 14-26, 1943

MAKNASSY

SFAX

GAFSA

EL GUETTAR

U.S. PATROLS MADE
CONTACT WITH THE
EIGHTH ARMY
APRIL 7, 1943

AXIS LINE
MAR. 30- APR. 6

TOZEUR

GABES

N. Z. ATTACK
MARCH 22, 1943

MARETH

BRITISH ATTACK
MARCH 22, 1943

launched on the airdromes of Sicily and Tunisia, resulting in the destruction of over 150 enemy airplanes on the ground and 50 more shot down in the air; Axis ports and shipping were also heavily attacked. In all, during a period of 14 days, 147 transport planes and 31 vessels, large and small, were damaged or destroyed. The suddenness of this complete and violent rupture of Axis communications with their Tunisian forces undoubtedly came as a surprise, upset their plans for delaying actions and the defense of the Cape Bon Peninsula, and precipitated the collapse of the German and Italian forces.

The advance of the British Eighth Army up the coast pinched out the II Corps which was withdrawn and started on an extremely difficult movement across the rear of the British First Army to reappear on the left flank of the Allied forces. General Patton, who had commanded the corps during the operation concerned with the breaking of the Mareth Line, was withdrawn in order to go ahead with the plans for the expedition to Sicily, and Maj. Gen. (now Lt. Gen.) Omar N. Bradley, who had been his deputy, assumed command.

Recognizing the weakness of the broad river valleys within the bridgehead, Von Arnim heavily mined all possible avenues of mechanized approach. By the 20th of April the II Corps was attacking across the mountainous terrain north of Medjez-el-Bab, clearing the way for an armored thrust into the Tine River Valley which resulted in the fracture of the Axis position. On May 3 the 1st Armored Division broke through in a powerful thrust that carried it into Mateur, only 20 miles in an air line from Bizerte. The time was ripe for the final blow.

General Eisenhower on May 5 reported:

Tomorrow morning we start the big drive which we hope and believe will see us in Tunis in a day or so. I believe we can clear up the Bizerte angle very quickly but the Bon Peninsula may be a difficult matter.

British armored units had concentrated between Medjez-el-Bab and Pont du Fahs in preparation for the drive down the Medjerda Corridor. After 2 days of bitter infantry fighting this armored force on May 7 under cover of an unprecedented concentration of air units, struck through the gaps secured by the British infantry and artillery and drove without check into the outskirts of Tunis (map 5). Once cracked, the Axis defense ring collapsed. The II Corps exploited its initial gains, advancing north into Bizerte on May 7 and surrounding the Axis forces north of Garaet-Achkel and Lac de Bizerte. Troops of the corps then turned east to block the threat to the north of the Axis lines on the Medjerda plain.

Meanwhile British forces poured through their initial gap, widening the split between the Axis forces defending the Cape Bon Peninsula and those trapped between Tunis and Bizerte. The latter force surrendered on May 9. Other hostile troops to the south had been withdrawn to the dangerous refuge of Cape Bon under heavy pressure from the British Eighth Army, and the French XIX Corps under Gen. Louis Marie Koeltz. Two British armored divisions brushed aside the remnants of Axis armor south of Tunis and drove directly against the base of the Cape Bon Peninsula on May 10, shattering the last resistance of the enemy.

During this period the naval action under Admiral Cunningham, and the complete destruction of German air transport approaches to Tunisia, had isolated the enemy, cut off his supplies, and made impossible the escape of even the enemy high command. Directly connected with the Allied domination of the air had been the punishing defeats of German fighter forces administered by our precision bombers in their daylight attacks on northwestern Europe. The enemy had found it impossible to concentrate on the African front either enough aircraft or enough skilled pilots to dent the overwhelming surge of British and American planes.

Some 252,415 German and Italian troops and a large amount of equipment were surrendered (chart 15). This completed the conquest of the African continent and placed the United Nations in a position to launch more direct attacks on the southern face of the European fortress.* But this was only one result of the victory. The Mediterranean was again open to Allied shipping which, by shortening the turn-around of vessels, in effect meant an immediate increase of shipping equivalent to some 240 vessels. A French Army had been reborn, celebrating its birthday by the capture of 48,719 prisoners following a deep penetration of the enemy's position. American troops had demonstrated their battle efficiency and had gained a wealth of experience which could be disseminated throughout the Army. Allied air forces had successfully demonstrated a technique involving effective coordination with ground forces and the strategic application of air power. Unity of Allied effort, command, and staff, had been demonstrated to the world in a most convincing manner, as evidence of the growing concentration of power which will sweep the enemy out of control of the European continent.[19]

Middle East

Under the lend-lease program large quantities of American equipment were being sent to the Middle East in the month immediately preceding the Pearl Harbor attack. Technical personnel, largely civilian, for servicing American planes, truck, and tanks, was pro-

---

*The decision to capture Sicily was made at the Casablanca conference in January 1943.

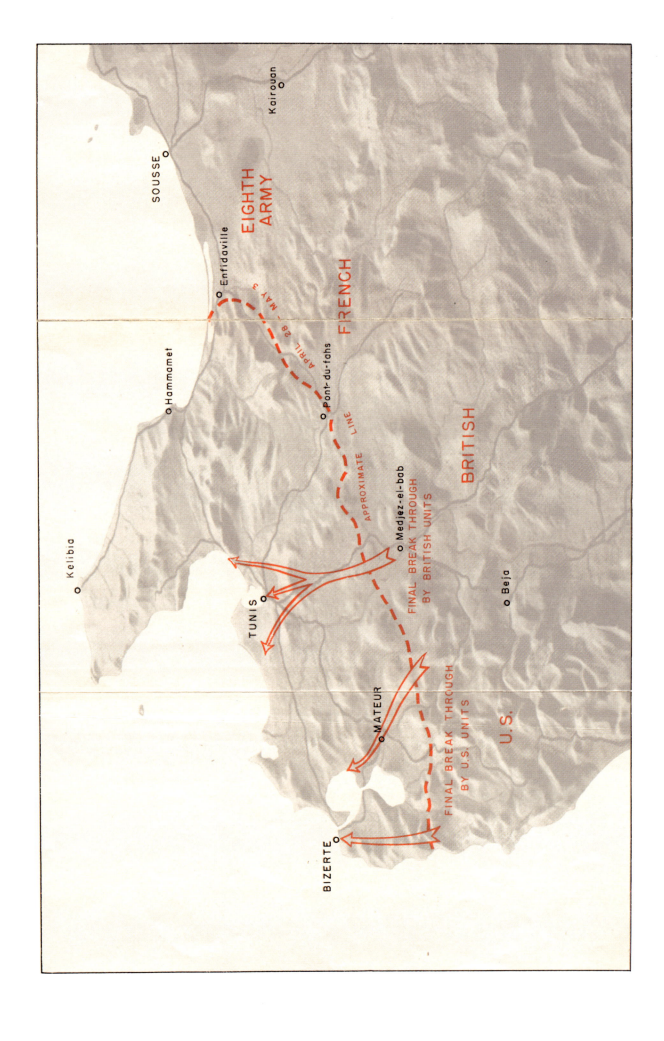

vided by us to assist the British in maintaining the efficiency of the American equipment in their hands.[20] American missions were established in Egypt and in Iran to coordinate and supervise lend-lease activities and to establish the necessary air-ferry routes over which American aircraft could be dispatched to the Middle East, to Russia, to India, and to China.

Upon our entry into war, the missions previously referred to, composed largely of civilian technicians, were gradually transferred to military control. In June 1942 it became necessary to designate a commander for the United States Army forces in the Middle East with responsibility not only for the North African and Iranian missions but also for military personnel in the area.[21] At the same time a similar command was formed for the control of United States Army forces across equatorial Africa, which unified air transport command activities along the trans-African air routes.

The crisis which developed in June 1942 with the withdrawal of the British Eighth Army to the El Alamein line threatened not only the Suez Canal but also our air transport routes to Russia and to Asia. Therefore, such aircraft as could be spared from other operations were concentrated in the Middle East to operate against the communications of the Afrika Korps in Libya and across the Mediterranean. Medium tanks and 105 mm. guns on self-propelled mounts were rushed by train and ship to the British Eighth Army and every possible measure consistent with the military situation in other parts of the world was taken to assist the Eighth Army in maintaining its position while it was refitted and prepared for its triumphant march westward through Libya.

In subsequent months our heavy bombers extended their operations over the Mediterranean in attacks against Axis ports along the southern European coast. Such heavy shipping losses were inflicted on the enemy that he was compelled to provide a heavy escort for his convoys, thereby considerably reducing the volume of cargo which he could move. American medium bombers for the Middle East were ferried across Africa from the United States and fighter aircraft in large numbers were delivered in Cairo, some by "flyaway" from aircraft carriers shuttling across the Atlantic and others, delivered in crates to Takoradi on the West Coast of Africa, were assembled there and flown to their destinations.

By October, General Montgomery's improved situation in troops, equipment, and logistical arrangements enabled him to crash through the El Alamein line and pursue the enemy 1,500 miles into Tunisia. Our aircraft, heavy and medium bombers and fighters, organized into the Ninth Air Force under General Brereton, participated in the preparation that preceded the attack on the enemy's positions at El Alamein and made important contributions to the subsequent pursuit. Planes from this air force struck heavy blows against German transport flights across the Sicilian Straits in the last phases of the Battle of Tunisia. Thereafter, the Ninth Air Force was occupied in the bombing operations against Axis Mediterranean positions including Pantelleria and Sicily, and in destructive raids against Naples, Messina, Reggio, and other points in Italy, all of which provided an important contribution to the shattering of Italian morale.[*]

Asiatic Theater

In January 1941, the Curtiss plant, completing a British contract for the manufacture of P-40 fighter planes, announced that if an order could be placed within 10 days it would be possible to produce 300 additional P-40's by June of that year. Under the British contract the United States Army controlled the allotments of additional planes. The Chinese were in grave distress for lack of fighter aircraft. I proposed, therefore, that if the British would immediately turn over 50 P-40's to the Chinese government from their existing contracts followed by 25 in February and 25 in March, the United States Government would permit the allocation of the 300 planes, referred to above, for delivery in June to the British. This arrangement was accepted and the 100 planes reached China in the early summer of 1941, providing the equipment for the famous "Flying Tigers" organization piloted by volunteers under the leadership of Col. (now Maj. Gen.) Claire Chennault, a former United States Army officer, then in the service of the Chinese Government.

Through the medium of lend-lease, material of various types and character had been reaching China by way of the Burma Road (map 6). With Japan's entry into the war China's position grew increasingly critical because of the possibility that Chinese airfields might become bases for bombing operations against Japan proper. In view of the gravity of the situation in that region, Maj. Gen. (now Lt. Gen.) Joseph W. Stilwell was selected to represent the United States in the manifold activities relating to our military interests as to pilots, planes, air transport service, matériel for Chinese ground forces and their technical and tactical instruction.

By January 1942, Japan's drive into Malaysia had spread into southern Burma. With the fall of Singapore in February the Japanese were able to launch a successful offensive against the British

---

[*]On August 1 the heavy bombers of the Eighth and Ninth Air Forces struck a devastating blow at the lubricating oil and gasoline resources of the Germans by destroying in a single raid possibly 75 percent of the Ploesti refineries in Rumania. The length of flight, the astonishing accuracy of the bombing, and the daring of the enterprise present a conspicuous example of the quality of the American flyers and their planes.

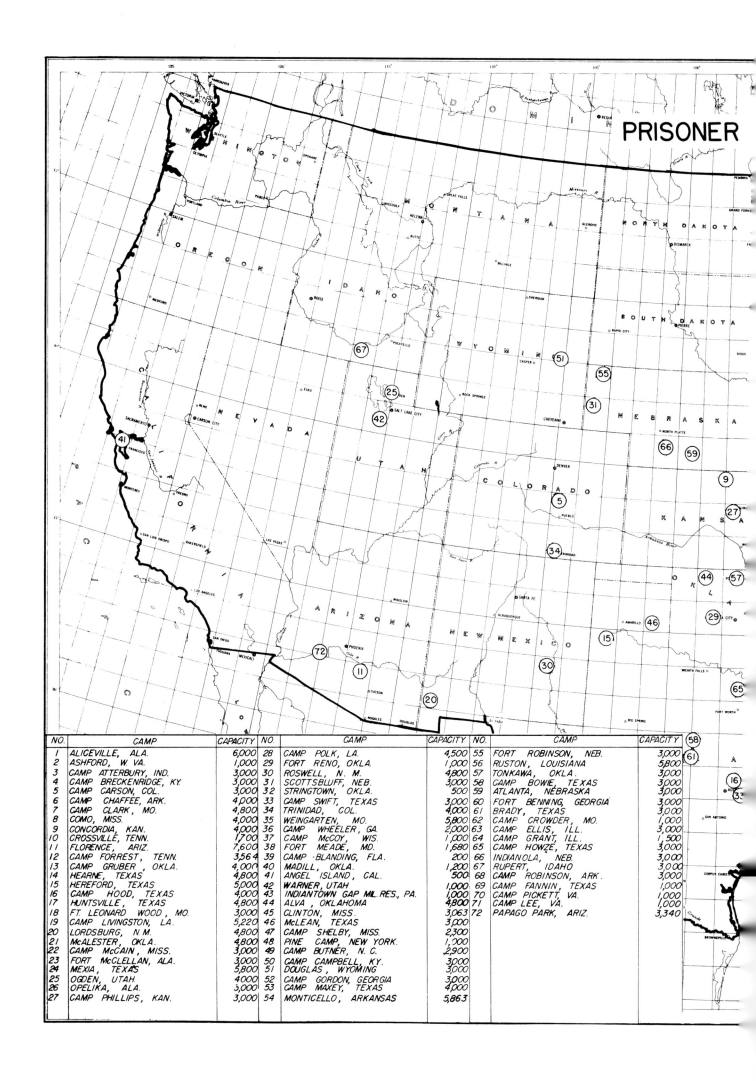

PRISONER

NO.	CAMP	CAPACITY	NO.	CAMP	CAPACITY	NO.	CAMP	CAPACITY
1	ALICEVILLE, ALA.	6,000	28	CAMP POLK, LA.	4,500	55	FORT ROBINSON, NEB.	3,000
2	ASHFORD, W. VA.	1,000	29	FORT RENO, OKLA.	1,000	56	RUSTON, LOUISIANA	5,800
3	CAMP ATTERBURY, IND.	3,000	30	ROSWELL, N. M.	4,800	57	TONKAWA, OKLA.	3,000
4	CAMP BRECKENRIDGE, KY.	3,000	31	SCOTTSBLUFF, NEB.	3,000	58	CAMP BOWIE, TEXAS	3,000
5	CAMP CARSON, COL.	3,000	32	STRINGTOWN, OKLA.	500	59	ATLANTA, NEBRASKA	3,000
6	CAMP CHAFFEE, ARK.	4,000	33	CAMP SWIFT, TEXAS	3,000	60	FORT BENNING, GEORGIA	3,000
7	CAMP CLARK, MO.	4,800	34	TRINIDAD, COL.	4,000	61	BRADY, TEXAS	3,000
8	COMO, MISS.	4,000	35	WEINGARTEN, MO.	5,800	62	CAMP CROWDER, MO.	1,000
9	CONCORDIA, KAN.	4,000	36	CAMP WHEELER, GA.	2,000	63	CAMP ELLIS, ILL.	3,000
10	CROSSVILLE, TENN.	1,700	37	CAMP McCOY, WIS.	1,000	64	CAMP GRANT, ILL.	1,500
11	FLORENCE, ARIZ.	7,600	38	FORT MEADE, MD.	1,680	65	CAMP HOWZE, TEXAS	3,000
12	CAMP FORREST, TENN.	3,564	39	CAMP BLANDING, FLA.	200	66	INDIANOLA, NEB.	3,000
13	CAMP GRUBER, OKLA.	4,000	40	MADILL, OKLA.	1,200	67	RUPERT, IDAHO	3,000
14	HEARNE, TEXAS	4,800	41	ANGEL ISLAND, CAL.	500	68	CAMP ROBINSON, ARK.	3,000
15	HEREFORD, TEXAS	5,000	42	WARNER, UTAH	1,000	69	CAMP FANNIN, TEXAS	1,000
16	CAMP HOOD, TEXAS	4,000	43	INDIANTOWN GAP MIL. RES., PA.	1,000	70	CAMP PICKETT, VA.	1,000
17	HUNTSVILLE, TEXAS	4,800	44	ALVA, OKLAHOMA	4,800	71	CAMP LEE, VA.	1,000
18	FT. LEONARD WOOD, MO.	3,000	45	CLINTON, MISS.	3,063	72	PAPAGO PARK, ARIZ.	3,340
19	CAMP LIVINGSTON, LA.	5,220	46	McLEAN, TEXAS	3,000			
20	LORDSBURG, N.M.	4,800	47	CAMP SHELBY, MISS.	2,300			
21	McALESTER, OKLA.	4,800	48	PINE CAMP, NEW YORK.	1,000			
22	CAMP McCAIN, MISS.	3,000	49	CAMP BUTNER, N. C.	2,900			
23	FORT McCLELLAN, ALA.	3,000	50	CAMP CAMPBELL, KY.	3,000			
24	MEXIA, TEXAS	5,800	51	DOUGLAS, WYOMING	3,000			
25	OGDEN, UTAH.	4,000	52	CAMP GORDON, GEORGIA	3,000			
26	OPELIKA, ALA.	3,000	53	CAMP MAXEY, TEXAS	4,000			
27	CAMP PHILLIPS, KAN.	3,000	54	MONTICELLO, ARKANSAS	5,863			

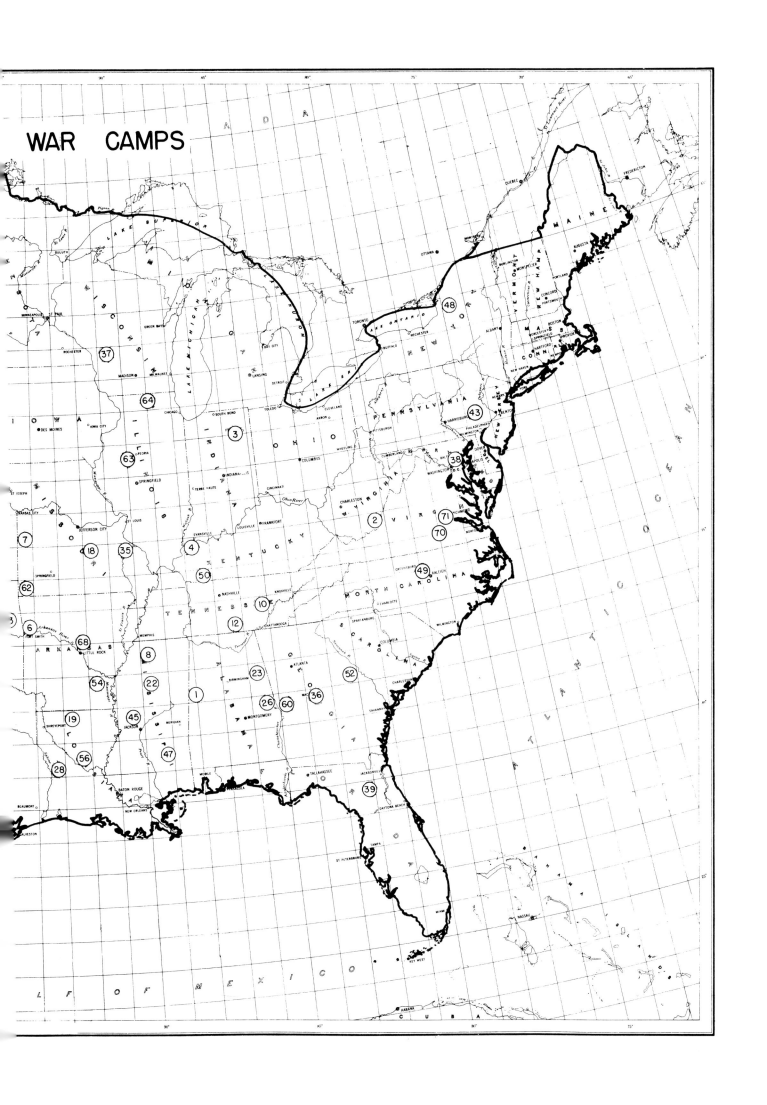

WAR CAMPS

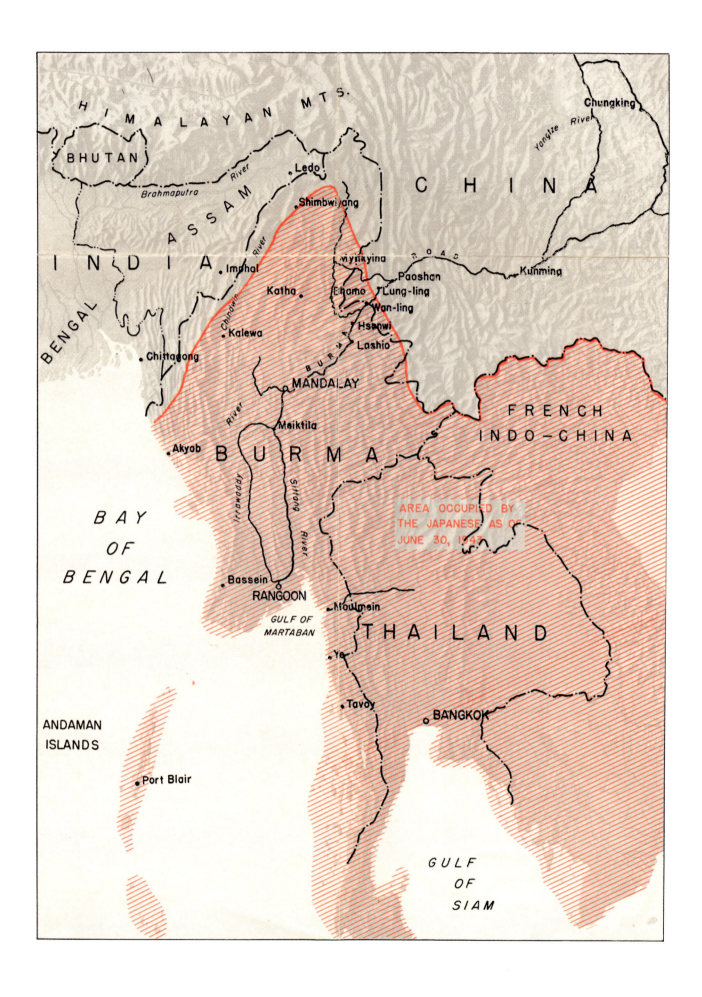

HIMALAYAN MTS.

BHUTAN

BRAHMAPUTRA River

Ledo

ASSAM

INDIA

Shimbwiyang

CHINA

Yangtze River

Chungking

Imphal

Katha

Myitkyina

ROAD

Kunming

Paoshan

Bhamo

Lung-ling

Wan-ling

BENGAL

Chindwin River

Kalewa

Hsenwi

Lashio

BURMA ROAD

Chittagong

MANDALAY

Irrawaddy River

Meiktila

FRENCH
INDO-CHINA

Akyab

BURMA

Sittang River

BAY
OF
BENGAL

AREA OCCUPIED BY
THE JAPANESE AS OF
JUNE 30, 1943

Bassein

RANGOON

Moulmein

GULF OF
MARTABAN

THAILAND

Ye

ANDAMAN
ISLANDS

Tavoy

BANGKOK

Port Blair

GULF
OF
SIAM

and the reinforcing Chinese troops in Burma, a success which was rapidly followed up by the capture of Lashio, the western terminus of the Burma Road. In this unsuccessful Allied operation General Stilwell commanded two small Chinese armies whose willingness to fight was greatly hampered by an almost complete lack of air, artillery, and adequate logistic support.

Following the cutting of the Burma Road, General Stilwell immediately initiated plans for an air-ferry service route over the Himalayas, utilizing Army personnel and equipment, together with a small combat air force. The nucleus of the latter was provided by bombardment and pursuit planes and service units sent from Australia to India late in February.

The development of American air power in India to meet the hostile challenge across the Bay of Bengal permitted offensive bombing operations to be initiated on April 2 against enemy fleet units in the Andaman Islands. The first flight of the Air Ferry Command into China over the Himalayas was completed 6 days later. Moving personnel, equipment, gasoline, and other supplies over the mountains into China following its transportation by sea and air halfway around the globe, imposed an unparalleled logistical problem. The operations of our air forces in India, Burma, and in China held in that region Japanese airplanes which might have been employed elsewhere; losses were inflicted on the enemy's air force, depots, and communications; and, most important of all, Chinese morale was greatly stimulated by this evidence of America's intention to support China in every way possible.

There have gradually developed since the summer of 1942 increasingly destructive bomber attacks over Burma and out of China with targets from Hopei to French Indo-China, including Hainan Island.* The enemy's retaliatory attacks usually have been repulsed with astonishingly heavy losses to his flyers. Day by day the power of our air offensive in these regions is growing, and forcing a dispersion of Japanese means along their southern front, extending from Burma, 5,500 miles to the Solomon Islands, to meet our attacks which are involving them in losses so destructive as to threaten the maintenance of their air power and the efficiency of their sea forces.[22]

By the summer of 1942 a large amount of equipment had accumulated in India which could not be transported into China under the limiting conditions of air traffic. It was therefore decided to move the Chinese troops to the equipment rather than follow the usual procedure of delivering equipment to the troops. A considerable Chinese force had retired into India on withdrawing from Burma and this was the nucleus around which General Stilwell developed a highly modern training center for infantry, artillery, and the supporting arms and services. This project has developed with most gratifying results, providing complete tactical units thoroughly indoctrinated as to technique and tactics in the use of weapons with which they are equipped, and furnishing cadres for the training of Chinese divisions beyond the mountains in China proper.

A somewhat similar project has been carried out for the training of Chinese air cadets in the United States and with our Tenth Air Force in India.

Operations in Alaska

The threat to the security of our Pacific Coast region reached its peak in June 1942 when the large Japanese task force approached Midway and another force approached the Aleutians. Both were turned back after suffering punishing losses. Dutch Harbor in the Aleutians appeared to be the immediate objective of the Japanese. Hostile reconnaissance planes had appeared over the western Aleutians, submarines had been reported in the vicinity of Umnak and Unalaska, and our Intelligence had reported the presence of a naval task force proceeding toward Alaskan waters.

On June 4, following an enemy bomber attack on Dutch Harbor the preceding day, our Army and Navy flyers located an enemy fleet consisting of at least two carriers, two cruisers and eight destroyers, 165 miles to the southwest. Despite fog, rain, and most unfavorable weather, our aircraft, attacking repeatedly, sank one enemy cruiser, damaged another and forced the enemy to withdraw. Ten days later a hostile task force of cruisers and transports was discovered at Kiska Island, suggesting the probability that the enemy, having retired out of range of our aircraft, had occupied Kiska with troops initially destined for an assault on Dutch Harbor. Attu Island and Agattu Island were also discovered to have been occupied by the enemy.

Strategically the occupation of these barren islands was of comparatively small importance except for the possibility of infiltrations along the island chain which might eventually permit the enemy to operate against our sea routes along the southwestern coast of Alaska. Psychologically this hostile occupation was productive of serious repercussions in our Pacific Northwest. It was decided, however, in view of our almost fatal limitations in ships, planes, and trained troops at this time to main-

---

*The fortitude of the Chinese people under the leadership of Generalissimo Chiang Kai-shek has been an inspiration to the United Nations. For 6 years these brave people have resisted the assaults of the enemy despite the lack of arms and equipment and without protection against the enemy's fighters and bombing planes.

tain the situation in the central, south, and southwest Pacific, no immediate action would be undertaken to recapture Kiska and Attu. Measures were taken, however, to bring these islands within effective air range of our combat craft. Advanced airfields were developed by troops landed on Adak August 31, 1942, from which the first mass raid against Kiska was launched on September 14. The Japanese air forces in the Kiska region were soon destroyed and his attempts to reinforce the garrison were rendered relatively ineffective by the destruction of his shipping en route to Kiska.

Bases still farther west were required to strengthen our air position in the Aleutians. Consequently in January 1943, an American task force landed unopposed on Amchitka, 69 miles east of Kiska. In less than a month the fighter strip had been developed and our aircraft was operating from this advanced base against Kiska and Attu.

In the late spring shipping and matériel, though limited, at last became available to launch a formal challenge to the enemy's occupation of the Aleutians. A task force composed of a portion of the 7th Infantry Division, reinforced, landed on Attu Island, the outermost island of the Aleutian chain, on the morning of May 11, heavily supported by its naval escort. Heavy fogs limited air action. Despite the mountainous character of the country, deep snow, and the absence of roads, the troops, strongly supported by our Navy and by the air forces so far as the weather permitted, fought their way across the island to encircle the Japanese troops defending Chichagof Harbor. There on May 31 the operation was successfully terminated after a loss of 512 American soldiers against the annihilation of 2,350 Japanese.

The capture of Attu evidently came as a complete surprise to the enemy who had anticipated an assault on Kiska which now lay trapped by our planes and naval craft operating from Amchitka and from Attu, a fighter strip having been completed in 12 days on the latter island.*

SUMMARY

Reviewing briefly the military situation as we find it on July 1, 1943, it will be remembered that our entry into war was marked by a succession of serious reverses, at Pearl Harbor, in the Philippines, and through the Malaysian Archipelago. It was a time for calm courage and stout resolution on the part of the people of the United States. With our Pacific fleet crippled and the Philippines overwhelmed at the outset, we were forced to watch the enemy progressively engulf our resistance to his advances. One year ago the German offensive in Russia was sweeping through the Donetz Basin, jeopardizing the whole of south Russia and the Caucasus and ominously menacing the Allied positions in the Middle East, particularly the oil supply at Abadan on which the naval forces in the eastern Mediterranean, the Indian Ocean, and Australia depended, in addition to the air and ground motor requirements in those theaters. Rommel's Afrika Korps with selected Italian troops had the British with their backs to Cairo, threatening the lifeline of the British Empire. Our successes in the Coral Sea and at Midway and the repulse of the Japanese forces in the Aleutians had not prevented the Japanese from carving out a vast empire from which they threatened India, Australia, and our position in the Pacific. Just a year ago also the ability of the United States to transport its power in supplies, munitions, and troops across the Atlantic was being challenged by submarines which in a single month had sunk 700,000 gross tons of shipping.

July 1, 1943, finds the United States Army and Navy united against the Axis powers in purpose and in operation, a unity shared when the occasion demands by the British Commonwealth of Nations, the Chinese, Dutch, French, and other fighting elements among our friends and supporters. Across the Atlantic the enemy has been driven from North Africa, and Europe has been encircled by a constantly growing military power. The Russian Army, engaging two-thirds of the German ground forces and one-third of the German air fleet in deadly and exhausting combat, has dispelled the legend of the invincibility of the German Panzer divisions.[23]

The British Isles are stronger than ever before and a new France is arising from the ashes of 1940. Strategically the enemy in Europe has been reduced to the defensive and the blockade is complete. In the Pacific the Japanese are being steadily ejected or rather eliminated from their conquered territory. The Aleutians are about to be cleared of all tracks and traces of the enemy. In the south and southwest Pacific two facts are plainly evident to the Japanese command as well as to the world at large: Our progress may seem slow but it is steady and determined, and it has been accompanied by a terrific destruction of enemy planes and surface vessels. This attrition must present an appalling problem for the enemy high command. Whatever satisfaction they may draw from the fanatical sacrifice of their soldiers with whom our forces come in contact, the destruction of their air power and shipping continues on an increasing and truly remarkable scale.

In brief, the strength of the enemy is steadily declining while the combined power of the United Nations is rapidly increasing, more rapidly with each

---

*With the occupation of Attu by our forces, the enemy position on Kiska became untenable. On August 15 a landing force was put ashore at Quisling Cove on the western coast of Kiska, which met no opposition, the enemy having evacuated the garrison to avoid further losses.

succeeding month. There can be but one result and every resource we possess is being employed to hasten the hour of victory without undue sacrifice of the lives of our men.

CONCLUSION

Organization

During the past 2 years the enlisted strength of the Army has been increased by 5,000,000 men;[24] the officer corps has grown from 93,000 to 521,000[25] (chart 16). Included in these figures is the development of an air force of 182,000 officers and 1,906,000 men. Expansion as to time and numbers, having in mind the technical requirements of modern warfare, has been without precedent. For example, the expansion of the service units for the Army Air Forces has been approximately 12,000 percent, and that of the air forces proper about 3,500 percent. The Corps of Engineers has been increased by 4,000 percent.[26]

This tremendous expansion required a fundamental reorientation of the conduct of the War Department and its methods of doing business;[27] it required that the various services and supply agencies be integrated into a command organization which would not only insure the efficient assembling of the means of war within the United States, but also would provide for their transportation and distribution to combat units overseas; it required that the air arm be granted the fullest exercise of initiative in developing and producing modern types of combat aircraft and in creating the most powerful air force in the world; it required that the training installations of the ground forces of the Army be centralized into one authority which would provide orderly processes in building a huge citizen army and would insure maximum effectiveness of our troops on their first entry into battle.

Early in 1942, after a period of exhaustive study extending over a year, and paralleled by a number of preliminary moves or readjustments, a committee headed by Maj. Gen. (now Lt. Gen.) Joseph T. McNarney completed the plan which established three great commands under the direct supervision of the Chief of Staff—the Army Air Forces, the Army Ground Forces, and the Services of Supply (later designated as the Army Service Forces) (chart 17). The proposed reorganization was approved by the President and the Secretary of War and made effective March 9, 1942. Later, on his appointment as Deputy Chief of Staff, it fell to General McNarney to supervise the procedure of reorganization and integration. Decentralization of authority was an imperative requirement for the tremendous war expansion, which could not otherwise have been achieved without confusion, inefficiency and the delays inherent in the transformation from a small peacetime army to the present vast organization. The fact that this complete reorganization of the machinery of the War Department and the Army at large was quietly carried out during the most perplexing period of our war effort, without confusion and with the best of good will by those concerned, was a tribute to the singleness of purpose of the senior officers and also to the manner in which the plans were developed and launched.

Logistics

The Army Service Forces are charged primarily with logistical matters which include the supply, equipping, and movement of troops at home and overseas; food, clothing, equipment, ammunition, medical service;[28] motor, rail, and ship transportation; records of personnel, and mail service. Under the present War Department organization many matters pertaining to morale, such as movies, educational programs, and newspapers, are also included within the supervision of this command.[29] In addition, the coordination of production requirements for military munitions in the United States, the actual issue of weapons and equipment, considerations pertaining to efficient maintenance of this equipment, and the provision of a steady stream of supplies practically on an automatic basis to the various theaters of war, are functions concerned with logistical requirements (chart 18). Global war has introduced lines of communication encircling the earth (a rough check indicates that present protected supply lines extend over 56,000 miles). It has made necessary harbor improvements with depots and railroad management, as in the Persian Gulf for the transportation of supplies to Russia, and in the region of the Suez Canal and the Red Sea. It has required construction of bases in Australia and throughout the Pacific and bases at Karachi and Calcutta on the west and east coasts of India; pipe lines and pumping plants to facilitate movement of gasoline, and a multiplicity of requirements to support our fighting forces and permit them to devote their undivided attention to the enemy. All these matters are involved in the logistical problem for the Army in this war. The continual flow of trained replacements, many of them specialists, must be maintained (chart 19). Each new venture usually involves new convoy routes with the additional naval escorts required. It imposes a continuing burden of supply of men and matériel which must be taken into account when new operations are considered which inevitably impose additional and continuing supply burdens.

Along with this goes the problem of providing munitions and other supplies to our Allies, and in most cases transporting them overseas to points of

OFFICER STRENGTH
UNITED STATES ARMY

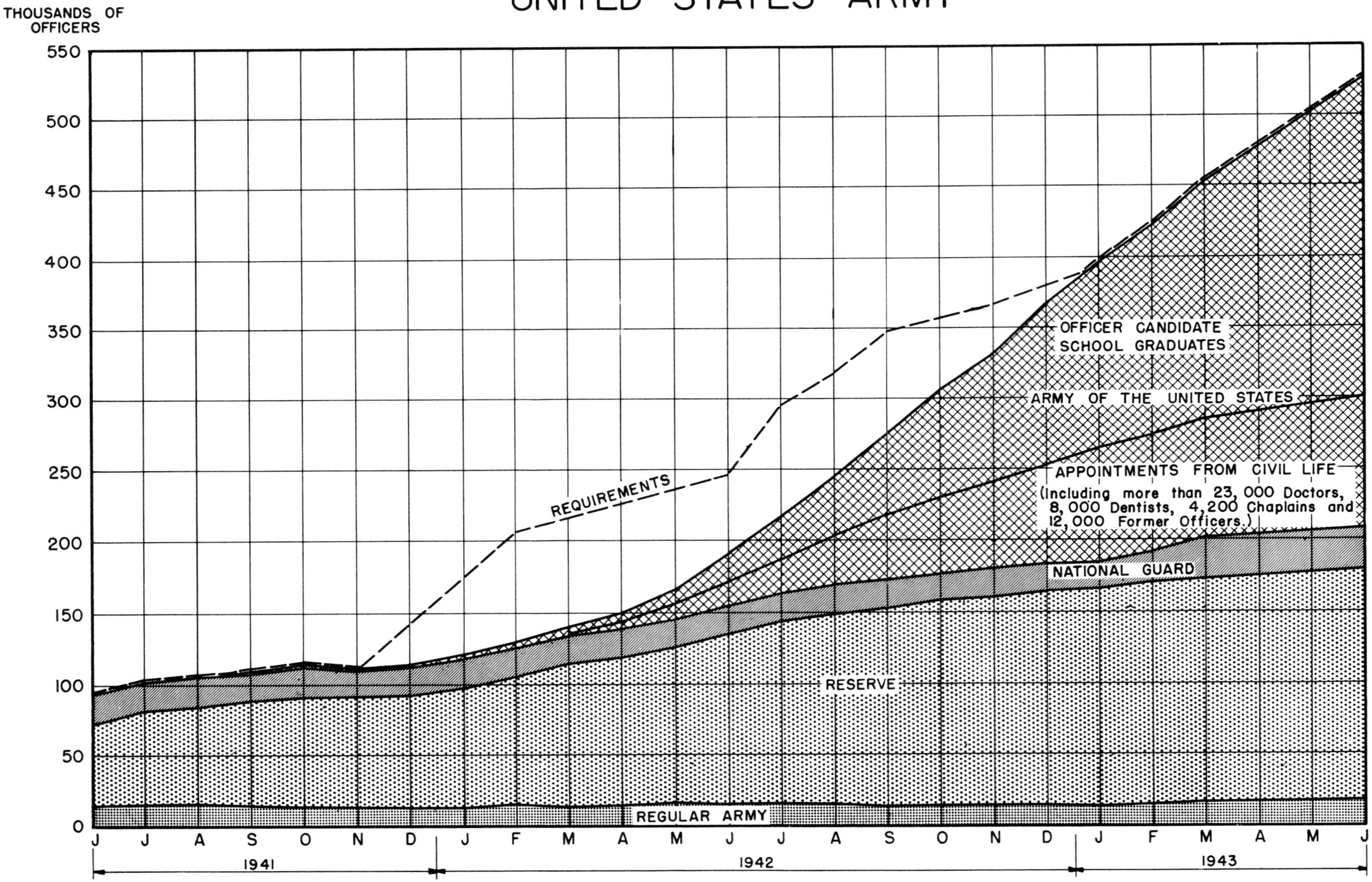

THOUSANDS OF OFFICERS

OFFICER CANDIDATE SCHOOL GRADUATES

ARMY OF THE UNITED STATES

APPOINTMENTS FROM CIVIL LIFE
(Including more than 23,000 Doctors, 8,000 Dentists, 4,200 Chaplains and 12,000 Former Officers.)

REQUIREMENTS

NATIONAL GUARD

RESERVE

REGULAR ARMY

550
500
450
400
350
300
250
200
150
100
50
0

J A S O N D J F M A M J J A S O N D J F M A M J

1941   1942   1943

ORGANIZATION OF THE ARMY

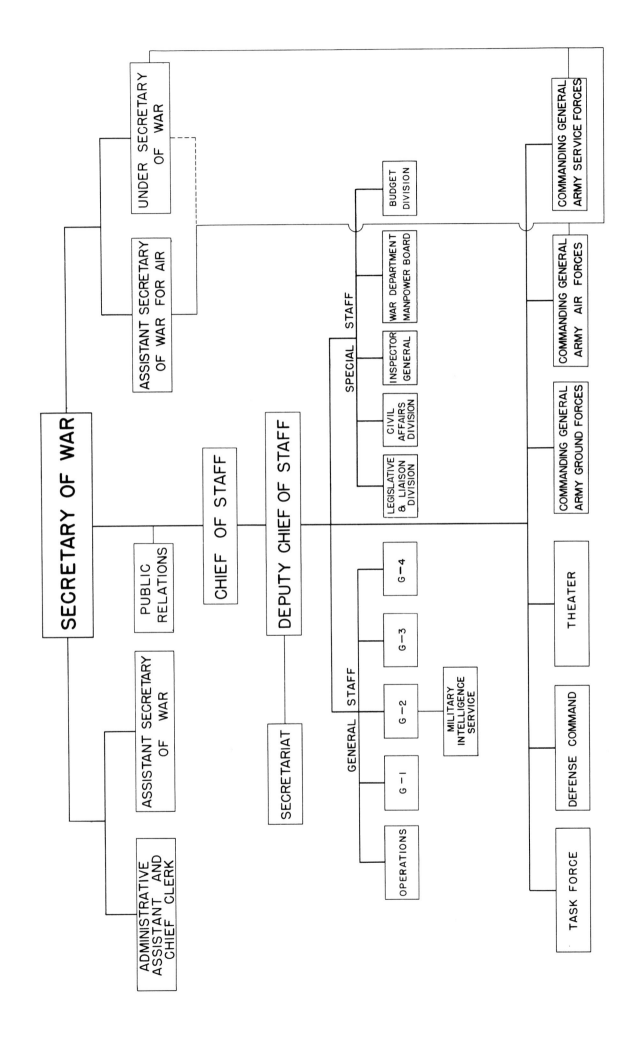

COMMA
ARMY
CHIE

DEPUTY
FOR SE
E

STA

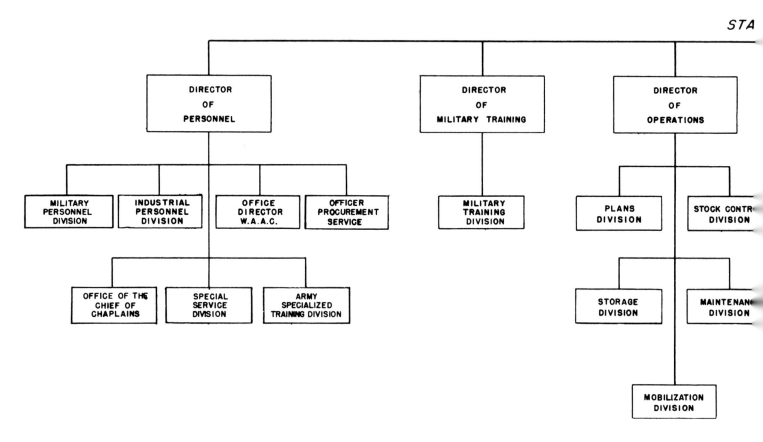

| DIRECTOR OF PERSONNEL | DIRECTOR OF MILITARY TRAINING | DIRECTOR OF OPERATIONS |

- MILITARY PERSONNEL DIVISION
- INDUSTRIAL PERSONNEL DIVISION
- OFFICE DIRECTOR W.A.A.C.
- OFFICER PROCUREMENT SERVICE
- MILITARY TRAINING DIVISION
- PLANS DIVISION
- STOCK CONTR DIVISION

- OFFICE OF THE CHIEF OF CHAPLAINS
- SPECIAL SERVICE DIVISION
- ARMY SPECIALIZED TRAINING DIVISION
- STORAGE DIVISION
- MAINTENANC DIVISION

- MOBILIZATION DIVISION

TECHNIC

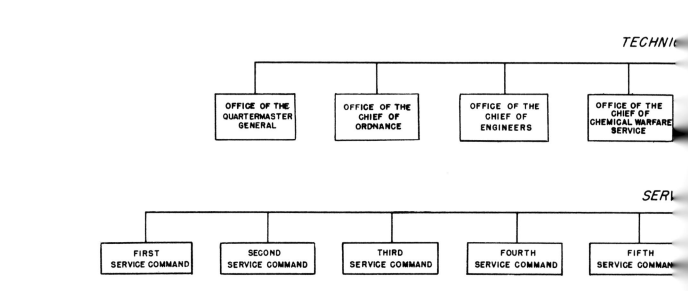

- OFFICE OF THE QUARTERMASTER GENERAL
- OFFICE OF THE CHIEF OF ORDNANCE
- OFFICE OF THE CHIEF OF ENGINEERS
- OFFICE OF THE CHIEF OF CHEMICAL WARFARE SERVICE

SER

- FIRST SERVICE COMMAND
- SECOND SERVICE COMMAND
- THIRD SERVICE COMMAND
- FOURTH SERVICE COMMAND
- FIFTH SERVICE COMMAN

ARMY SERVICE FORCES

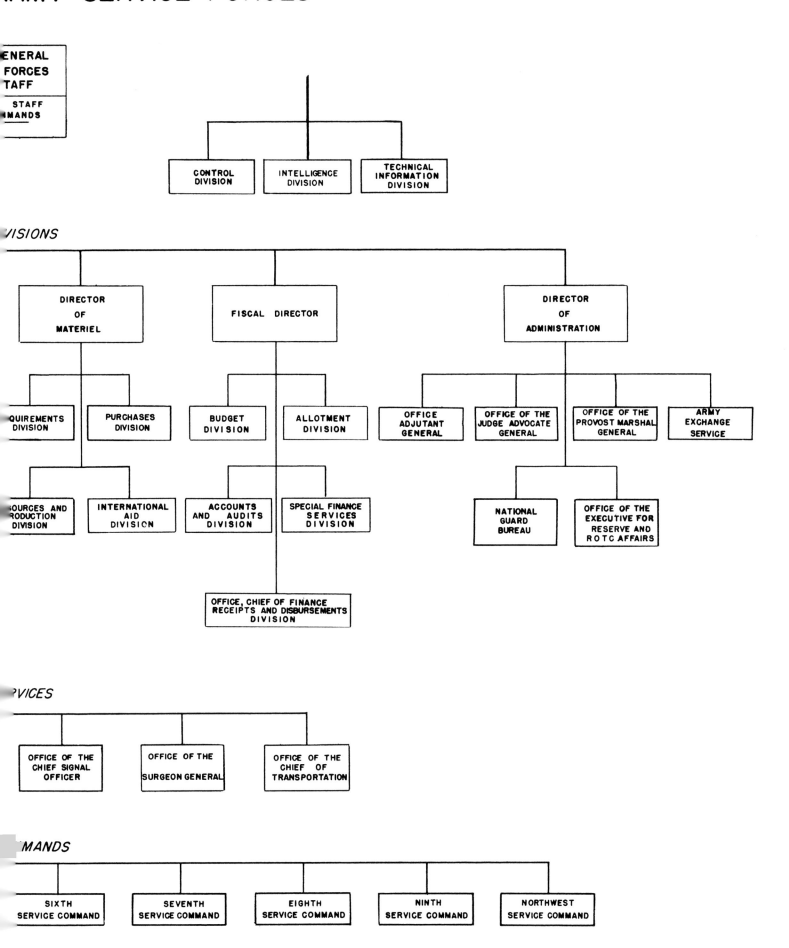

ENERAL
FORCES
TAFF

STAFF
MANDS

CONTROL DIVISION

INTELLIGENCE DIVISION

TECHNICAL INFORMATION DIVISION

VISIONS

DIRECTOR OF MATERIEL

FISCAL DIRECTOR

DIRECTOR OF ADMINISTRATION

QUIREMENTS DIVISION

PURCHASES DIVISION

BUDGET DIVISION

ALLOTMENT DIVISION

OFFICE ADJUTANT GENERAL

OFFICE OF THE JUDGE ADVOCATE GENERAL

OFFICE OF THE PROVOST MARSHAL GENERAL

ARMY EXCHANGE SERVICE

SOURCES AND RODUCTION DIVISION

INTERNATIONAL AID DIVISION

ACCOUNTS AND AUDITS DIVISION

SPECIAL FINANCE SERVICES DIVISION

NATIONAL GUARD BUREAU

OFFICE OF THE EXECUTIVE FOR RESERVE AND ROTC AFFAIRS

OFFICE, CHIEF OF FINANCE RECEIPTS AND DISBURSEMENTS DIVISION

RVICES

OFFICE OF THE CHIEF SIGNAL OFFICER

OFFICE OF THE SURGEON GENERAL

OFFICE OF THE CHIEF OF TRANSPORTATION

MANDS

SIXTH SERVICE COMMAND

SEVENTH SERVICE COMMAND

EIGHTH SERVICE COMMAND

NINTH SERVICE COMMAND

NORTHWEST SERVICE COMMAND

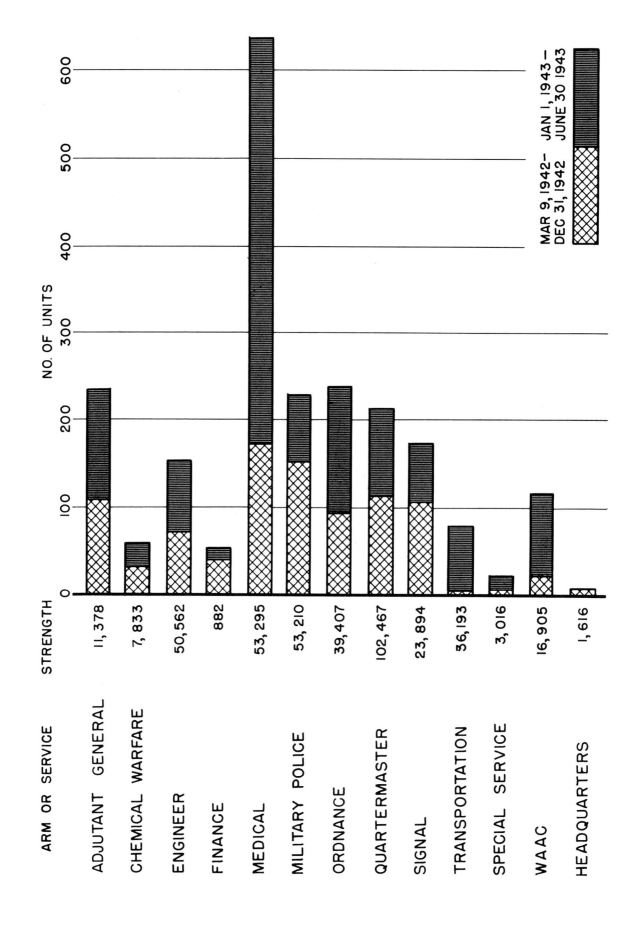

ACTIVATION OF ARMY SERVICE FORCE UNITS

NO. OF UNITS

ARM OR SERVICE	STRENGTH
ADJUTANT GENERAL	11,378
CHEMICAL WARFARE	7,833
ENGINEER	50,562
FINANCE	882
MEDICAL	53,295
MILITARY POLICE	53,210
ORDNANCE	39,407
QUARTERMASTER	102,467
SIGNAL	23,894
TRANSPORTATION	36,193
SPECIAL SERVICE	3,016
WAAC	16,905
HEADQUARTERS	1,616

MAR 9, 1942 – DEC 31, 1942

JAN I, 1943 – JUNE 30 1943

delivery. We are equipping the Chinese troops and French troops, we have been providing equipment for the British, the Australians, the New Zealanders, and the Canadians, we have furnished supplies to Latin American republics—we have been truly an arsenal of democracy. All this demands the maintenance of an elaborate system for allocation, distribution, and transportation, to be coordinated with our daily normal problem of meeting the demands of our own forces.

The requirements of logistics are seldom understood. The burdens they impose on the responsible military authorities are rarely appreciated. The conflicting demands of our theater commanders, of Allied sovereign powers, and of the home front, pose difficulties never before approximated in war. The necessity for a high degree of efficiency in management is evident and it has been found in the coordination of all the various supplies and administrative departments of the Army, under the command and leadership of Lt. Gen. Brehon B. Somervell.

Training

The vital importance of adequate training in the technical warfare of today is evident. Such training involves not only the basic elements of military science, but their coordination into teamwork involving the platoon, company, battalion, and regiment, and later, combined training of the various arms into divisions and army corps capable of a sustained and coordinated effort on the battlefield. The organization of training centers, expansion of our school system,[30] the activation of new units, the development of training doctrines, and the conduct of maneuvers, have been the primary responsibility of the Army Ground Forces (chart 20) which under the command of Lt. Gen. Lesley J. McNair, has achieved remarkable results that today are paying heavy dividends on the battlefield.[31]

While meeting this expansion, we were faced with the problem of so training our units that they would be able to compete successfully in their first battle experience with veteran organizations of the enemy. Until 1943, urgent demands of crises in various parts of the world forced us to organize special units and ship them abroad without the desired degree of preparation. Fortunately, the development of the training program, the adequacy of ammunition, and the influence of officers who have been returned to the United States after participation in combat have given us for the first time a reserve of trained units ready for dispatch to the various theaters as rapidly as shipping becomes available.

Another factor is now operating to our advantage. We are reaching the end of the expansion; already it

has been possible to reduce many training installations to a purely maintenance basis to furnish replacements for the present strength of the Army. It also has been practicable, and it is highly desirable, to lengthen the basic training period for soldiers and to extend the period of training for officer candidates; and most important of all, it is no longer necessary to drain units of their best officers and men to furnish trained cadres for new organizations or students for the officer candidate and technical schools. In other words, General McNair and his people are now free for the first time to concentrate their attention on polishing up the existing military machines and developing them to the highest degree of efficiency in preparation for the great battles to come.

Air Forces

The problems and accomplishments of the Army Air Forces (chart 21) during this emergency are so colossal in scope that the story can be properly told only by their chief, Gen. H. H. Arnold. The outstanding feature to date of America's war effort has been the manner in which our air forces have carried the war, in its most devastating form, to the enemy. Limited by appropriations prior to the emergency, they have, in a remarkably short time, been able to produce combat airplanes which have matched or surpassed those of other nations. The high degree of technical proficiency necessary to operate military airplanes in combat has been secured by a complex but remarkably efficient training program.

The Army Air Forces are now attacking the enemy on 10 different fronts throughout the world. Their victories wherever they come in contact with the enemy testify to the gallantry and skill of pilots and crews, to the mechanical efficiency of planes, and to the leadership of General Arnold and the fighting commanders of the Air Forces in the field, Kenney in New Guinea, Twining in the Solomons, Hale in Hawaii, Spaatz, Brereton, and Doolittle in Africa, Eaker in England, Butler in Alaska, Bissell in India, and Chennault with his unique contribution in China.

Planning

The orderly step-by-step development which the Army has undergone could not have been managed without the background of careful planning over a period of years. The framework for our Army today and its development through the growing pains in the early part of the emergency were laid during the period preceding Pearl Harbor. In matters of personnel, military intelligence, training, supply, and preparation of war plans sound principles and policies had been established in preparation for just such an

ORGANIZATION OF THE ARMY GROUND FORCES

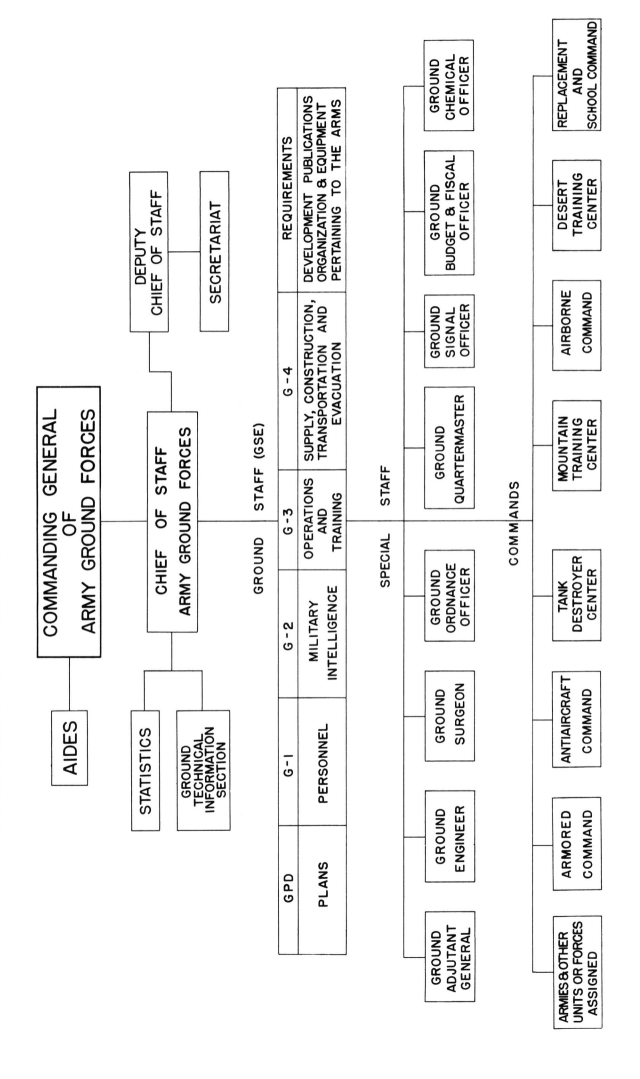

emergency as arose. When the War Department was reorganized, an increased proportion of air force officers were assigned to the General Staff and at the same time it was divorced from operating activities except in the case of the War Plans Division. The latter group became the Operations Division of the General Staff, charged with the preparation of strategic plans and the coordination of operations throughout the world. For the Army it prepares the proposals and the detailed plans for the Joint and the Combined Chiefs of Staff. Its divisions are in direct contact with every theater of war. Its members are continually traveling by air to secure first-hand knowledge of local conditions and requirements. Their participation in bombing raids, in landing operations, and in the fighting has resulted in a growing casualty list reflecting the intimate contacts they maintain with conditions in the field. The practice has been established whereby members of the Operations Division serve a period of duty in each theater, in exchange with representatives of the staff of theater commanders who serve a corresponding tour of duty in War Department Operations Division. Under the direction of Maj. Gen. T. T. Handy and his predecessors, Maj. Gen. L. T. Gerow and General Eisenhower, the Operations Division of the War Department General Staff has been a tower of strength to the undersigned in the direction and coordination of our military effort.

An outstanding feature of operations in the present war has been their amphibious character which requires close coordination with the Navy not only in the protection furnished to the transports en route to landing beaches but in actual air, antiaircraft, and gunfire support of landing parties after the troops leave the ships. In transporting more than 2,000,000 men of the Army overseas through submarine-infested waters, the Navy has lived up to its traditional record.

The development of the powerful war army of today was made possible by the determined leadership of the Constitutional Commander in Chief, and the wisdom and firm integrity of purpose of the Secretary of War. It has been dependent upon vast appropriations and the strong support of the Congress, and the cooperation of numerous Government agencies. Individuals, civilian organizations—patriotic and commercial—all have given strong support to the Army program. Outstanding has been the courageous acceptance of sacrifice by the families of those men who have already fallen in the struggle.

The end is not yet clearly in sight but victory is certain. In every emergency the courage, initiative, and spirit of our soldiers and their young leaders and of our pilots and their crews have been an inspiration at the moment, and a complete assurance of the final victory to come.

G. C. MARSHALL,
Chief of Staff.

WASHINGTON, D. C., *July 1, 1943.*

ORGANIZATION OF T

COMMA...
ARM...

CHIEF (

ASSISTANT CHIEFS OF AIR STAFF

(1) ADVISE CG/AAF
(2) ACT IN CG'S NAME
(3) SUPERVISE CARRYING OUT OF CG'S POLICY
(4) RECOMMEND NEW POLICIES AND CHANGES IN POLICIES TO CG

| DEPUTY CHIEF OF THE AIR STAFF | DEPUTY CH |

ASS'T. CHIEF OF AIR STAFF PERSONNEL	ASS'T CHIEF OF AIR STAFF INTELLIGENCE	ASS'T CHIEF OF AIR STAFF TRAINING
PLANS & LIAISON DIVISION	OPERATIONAL DIVISION	AIR CREW TRAINING DIVISION
MILITARY PERSONNEL DIVISION	COUNTER INTELLIGENCE DIVISION	UNIT TRAINING DIVISION
CIVILIAN PERSONNEL DIVISION	INFORMATIONAL DIVISION	TECHNICAL TRAINING DIVISION
SPECIAL SERVICES DIVISION	TRAINING PLANS DIVISION	TRAINING AIDS DIVISION
AIR CHAPLAIN	HISTORICAL DIVISION	PLANS, ANALYSIS & REPORTS DIVISION

| AAF PERSONNEL REDISTRIBUTION CENTER | TRAINING COMMAND | TROOP CARRIER COMMAND | SECOND AIR FORCE | THIRD AIR FORCE | FIRST AIR FORCE | FOURTH AIR FORCE |

------ Primary Interest, Supervision, and Administrative Channels of Communication.

ARMY AIR FORCES

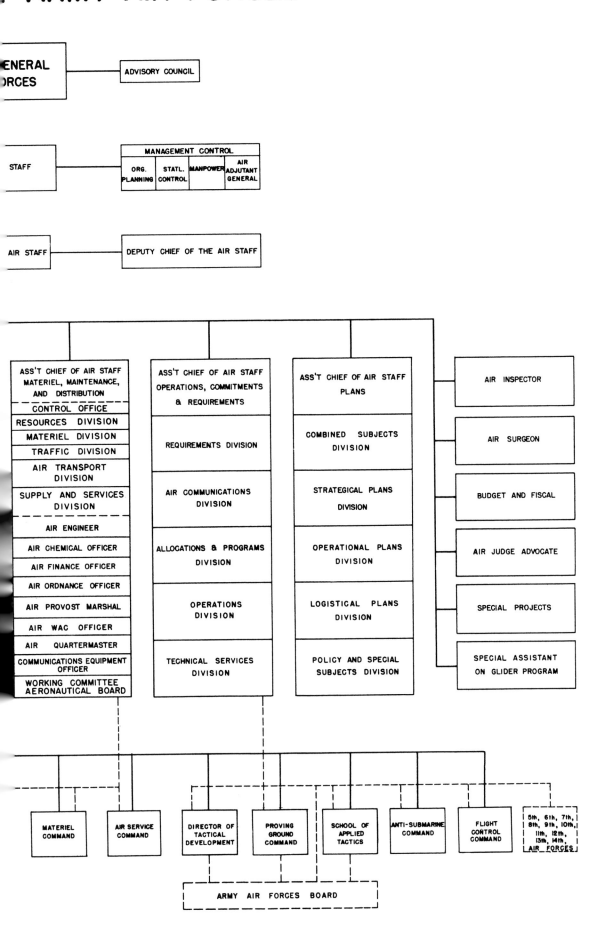

ENERAL
DRCES ——— ADVISORY COUNCIL

STAFF

MANAGEMENT CONTROL			
ORG. PLANNING	STATL. CONTROL	MANPOWER	AIR ADJUTANT GENERAL

AIR STAFF ——— DEPUTY CHIEF OF THE AIR STAFF

ASS'T CHIEF OF AIR STAFF MATERIEL, MAINTENANCE, AND DISTRIBUTION
CONTROL OFFICE
RESOURCES DIVISION
MATERIEL DIVISION
TRAFFIC DIVISION
AIR TRANSPORT DIVISION
SUPPLY AND SERVICES DIVISION
AIR ENGINEER
AIR CHEMICAL OFFICER
AIR FINANCE OFFICER
AIR ORDNANCE OFFICER
AIR PROVOST MARSHAL
AIR WAC OFFICER
AIR QUARTERMASTER
COMMUNICATIONS EQUIPMENT OFFICER
WORKING COMMITTEE AERONAUTICAL BOARD

ASS'T CHIEF OF AIR STAFF OPERATIONS, COMMITMENTS & REQUIREMENTS
REQUIREMENTS DIVISION
AIR COMMUNICATIONS DIVISION
ALLOCATIONS & PROGRAMS DIVISION
OPERATIONS DIVISION
TECHNICAL SERVICES DIVISION

ASS'T CHIEF OF AIR STAFF PLANS
COMBINED SUBJECTS DIVISION
STRATEGICAL PLANS DIVISION
OPERATIONAL PLANS DIVISION
LOGISTICAL PLANS DIVISION
POLICY AND SPECIAL SUBJECTS DIVISION

AIR INSPECTOR

AIR SURGEON

BUDGET AND FISCAL

AIR JUDGE ADVOCATE

SPECIAL PROJECTS

SPECIAL ASSISTANT ON GLIDER PROGRAM

MATERIEL COMMAND

AIR SERVICE COMMAND

DIRECTOR OF TACTICAL DEVELOPMENT

PROVING GROUND COMMAND

SCHOOL OF APPLIED TACTICS

ANTI-SUBMARINE COMMAND

FLIGHT CONTROL COMMAND

5th, 6th, 7th, 8th, 9th, 10th, 11th, 12th, 13th, 14th, AIR FORCES

ARMY AIR FORCES BOARD

NOTES

(1) *Battle maneuvers realistic.*

These maneuvers are conducted under the supervision of the Army Ground Forces, the divisions in training being organized into army corps and armies. Realism is emphasized and wherever possible they are conducted on a two-sided basis. Under Lt. Gen. Hugh A. Drum, commanding the First Army; Lt. Gen. Ben Lear, commanding the Second Army; Lt. Gen. Walter M. Krueger, later Lt. Gen. Courtney Hodges, commanding the Third Army; and Lt. Gen. John L. DeWitt, commanding the Fourth Army, extremely valuable experience has been gained in preparing our troops for battle.

(2) *Organization geared to requirements.*

A number of organizational changes have been made in tactical units to meet the requirements of the war as it developed. The World War type square Infantry division has been replaced by the hard-hitting triangular division. Rapid moving tank destroyer units have been developed, equipped with towed and self-propelled weapons capable of knocking out enemy tanks. Armored divisions have been reorganized to provide two combat teams, to improve mobility of supporting artillery, and to combine service functions. Motorized divisions have been eliminated, the transportation formerly a part of these divisions to be held in pools to meet a special situation. Horse and Mechanized Cavalry regiments have been eliminated by substituting mechanized separate squadrons. Air-borne divisions of glider and parachute troops have been established. Also there have been provided many new types of units for service functions such as port battalions to facilitate landing operations and the rapid development of new ports, petroleum distribution units, air ferrying organizations, etc. Nondivisional units except Infantry, horse Cavalry, and armored elements are being organized in battalions or smaller formations with command groups capable of directing the operations of from two to eight such units. This permits rapid assembly of exactly the type units required for any type operation and is the basis for organizing supporting troops for task forces.

(3) *American-Australian cooperation.*

The support and cooperation furnished the United States by the Australian Government and the people have been a vital factor in the conduct of the war in the Far East. All possible assistance was offered to the American commanders in that area in building up the air and supply bases and facilitating the establishment of troops units.

Previously the Australian Government had assisted us in the development of the air route from the United States to the Philippine Islands. These airdromes were of great value in the fight to stop the tidal wave of Japanese advancement. Much of Australia's resources, including aircraft factories, hospitals, warehouses, and even manpower, were assigned directly for the support of American forces in Australia.

(4) *Overseas units fully equipped.*

In general, it has been the policy to furnish 100-percent equipment, with reserves and maintenance for units scheduled to be sent overseas within 3 months. When it became apparent that units in training could not be supplied with complete allowances of numerous critical items of equipment, the War Department established a policy of providing half of the allowances. Even this goal could not be reached as the expansion of the Army rapidly exceeded increases in arms production. Munitions were assigned to various theaters of war according to a priority based upon stategic plans.

(5) *Reverse lend-lease.*

A feature of lend-lease is the so-called "reverse lend-lease," the term applied to the furnishing by other nations of supplies, equipment, services, facilities and patent rights to the armed forces of the United States without cost. The most important single contribution of reverse lend-lease in the war effort has been its saving in shipping requirements. Reverse lend-lease also reduced demands on United States raw materials, productive facilities, and manpower. It further contributed to the more efficient utilization of all the productive resources of the United Nations. Overseas commanders of American forces have been directed to utilize all available sources of local supply on a reverse lend-lease basis. Procurement organizations have been established in the principal theaters of operations to obtain supplies locally for American forces and to assist in the development of local resources. Within the United Kingdom in the fiscal year 1943, 1,500,000 ship-tons of matériel were provided the United States forces stationed there in addition to a large quantity of construction materials. Had all these supplies been shipped overseas in American vessels it would have required more than 500 fully loaded ships. In Australia and New Zealand, American forces have obtained almost all of their food requirements locally. In the Middle Eastern theater the British have provided for United States forces in the area all maintenance requirements, including food supply, clothing, and equipment.

(6) *Volume of shipping required.*

The tremendous amount of shipping required for a modern army is not generally understood. For instance, in computing initial shipping requirements an average of 6 measurement tons of cargo space per man is required. Maintenance requirements average one measurement ton per month. Also involved is the creating of a balance between shipping available for personnel and that for cargo. At the beginning of the war an acute shortage in troop-carrying capacity was met by conversions of all existing passenger ships and certain selected cargo ships. Also, additional capacity was obtained by arranging for the use of several of the larger British liners and troop ships. Late in 1942 it was found that despite the foregoing steps, cargo-carrying capabilities were again in excess of troop-carrying capacity and an extensive program of conversion of fast cargo ships was undertaken in order to maintain the proper balance.

(7) *Close cooperation by Brazil.*

Oral permission was obtained from Brazil in March 1942 for the establishment of air facilities in Belem, Natal, and Recife, permitting the unlimited transit of military aircraft and the stationing of United States Air Forces technicians in Brazil. The agreement was later formalized with permission to construct additional facilities and station United States personnel in northeast Brazil. The close cooperation of Brazil in this matter has been of inestimable value in building up our air forces in Europe and North Africa.

(8) *Alaska Military Highway.*

A project which will result in a permanent improvement in the transportation system of North America has been the construction of the Alaska Military Highway through the vaguely mapped virgin wilderness of Western Canada. The project, authorized by a joint agreement between Canada and the United States, was carried out under the direction of the Chief of Engineers. The highway was built to function as an important military supply route connecting the railway and highway system of the United States and Southern Canada with routes in Alaska, in addition to serving as a feeder road to several military airfields in Canada which previously had depended upon air transport for supplies.

On February 14, 1942, the Office of the Chief of Engineers was instructed to prepare plans for the building of the highway. Early in March 1942, Quartermaster and Engineer troops had arrived at the end of the railroad at Dawson Creek in Canada. Engineer units working on the highway from each end and in both directions from the half-way point had completed 9 miles of the road by April; by the end of October the last gap was closed on the 1,480-mile pioneer road, which had engaged approximately 10,000 Engineer troops in its construction.

Improvements currently under way provide for a 26-foot roadbed width, with surfacing placed to a width of from 20 to 22 feet. Local materials, including gravel and crushed stone, will be utilized in this surfacing. It is estimated that the cost of constructing the pioneer road, together with improving it to present proposed standards, will be $115,000,000, which figure includes the replacement of a considerable number of temporary structures destroyed during the recent spring thaw. Current improvements are scheduled for completion December 31, 1943, and are going ahead largely by contract labor forces under the immediate supervision of the Public Roads Administration and the general jurisdiction of our Northwest Service Command and division engineer of the Northwest Division.

(9) *Unity of command.*

Under the direction of the President, the Joint Chiefs of Staff, composed of the Chief of Staff to the Commander in Chief of the United States Army and Navy, the Chief of Staff of the United States Army, the Commander in Chief of United States Fleet and Chief of Naval Operations, and the Commanding General, Army Air Forces, are responsible for coordination between the Army and Navy, and in operations for which the United States has sole or primary responsibility, they are charged with the strategic conduct of the war. The Combined Chiefs of Staff, composed of the above United States members and four representatives of the British Chiefs of Staff insure complete coordination of the war effort of Great Britain and the United States. A development of the Joint Chiefs of Staff and Combined Chiefs of Staff organizations is the unity of command principle which places the responsibility and authority for a contemplated operation under one commander directly responsible to the Joint Chiefs of Staff or the Combined Chiefs of Staff. When a joint or combined force commander has been designated and the units composing his force are assigned, his command responsibilities are the same as if the forces involved were all of one service or one nation. He exercises his command through the commanders of forces which have been assigned him, and normally in operations this will consist of the assignment of their respective missions. In carrying out its mission the tactics and technique of the force concerned are the responsibility of the commander of the subordinate force.

Allied to the principles of unified command is the mechanism of operational planning on a joint and combined level. The command function of the President as Commander in Chief of the United States forces is exercised through the United States Chiefs of Staff. The British Chiefs of Staff function in a similar manner under the Prime Minister and his War Cabinet. The United States Chiefs of Staff have organized planning and supporting agencies consisting of representatives from the Army and Navy and, where applicable, from other interested governmental agencies. These United States supporting agencies assist and advise the Joint Chiefs of Staff in matters of strategy, operational and administrative planning, psychological warfare, intelligence, transportation, the assignment of materials of war, communications, meteorology, weapons, petroleum, civil affairs, and other matters. Most of the supporting agencies of the Joint Chiefs of Staff organization have a British counterpart with which they work, thus forming combined agencies to advise and assist the Combined Chiefs of Staff. An outstanding example of the success of this system is the complete harmony of action of the American and British forces in the Mediterranean area under the command of General Eisenhower.

(10) *Japanese miscalculations.*

The major miscalculation of the Japanese was the apparent expectation that the Russian Army would collapse under the German grand assault then under way against Moscow which ended in the first winter fiasco. Also unanticipated was the prolonged defense of the Philippine Islands which upset their timetable for other offensive operations in the southwest Pacific, including Australia.

(11) *Nuclei of Pacific air force.*

The air forces in the Pacific were built up piecemeal on the skeleton of the Eleventh Bombardment Group (Heavy) in Hawaii and the Nineteenth Bombardment Group (Heavy), which moved into Australia from the Philippines.

(12) *Airborne movement of troops.*

The most noteworthy feature of this project was the fact that only hastily prepared landing strips of the most primitive character could be made available. An unusual amount of skill and daring made possible its achievement.

(13) *Moves against Japan planned.*

Initially our operations in New Guinea and the Solomons were handicapped by limited resources. To determine the best use of our growing strength in resources, certain commanders and staff officers of the Central, South, and Southwest Pacific areas were assembled in Washington in March of 1943. Here the latest combat intelligence was integrated and supplemented with strategic and logistical intelligence available in War and Navy Department agencies to develop a clear picture of the enemy situation and capabilities in the areas concerned. At the same time the plans proposed by the theater commanders were coordinated with those developed in the War and Navy Departments and brought into consonance with the over-all strategical concept for the prosecution of the war. Based on these considerations a plan which set forth the objectives, allotted the available means, and prescribed command arrangements was developed and subsequently approved by the Joint Chiefs of Staff. This planning included the clearing of the Japanese from Rendova Island and New Georgia.

(14) *Bomber attacks effective.*

Large-scale daylight raids require unlimited ceilings for precise aiming from high altitudes. Days of unlimited ceilings are rare in Europe, particularly in the winter, and, in order to avoid a waste of good days, the development of accurate weather forecasting became a matter of extreme importance. It has been desirable to build up bombing missions of 300 planes or more because of the strength of the German fighter force and the antiaircraft defenses on the western front. By July 1, 1943, over 1,000 heavy bombers were based in the United Kingdom. During the last week of July, 6 American missions, averaging almost 300 heavy bombers each, were flown, all but 1 against Germany. Perhaps the greatest tribute to the heavy bomber effort was the enemy's recognition of its importance. These attacks caused him to increase his production of fighter aircraft at the expense of bombers, to allocate new production largely to the western front, to withdraw experienced single-engine fighter pilots from the Russian and Mediterranean fronts for the defense of Germany and later to withdraw fighter aircraft from Russia. The net result was that the Germans were unable to conduct any sustained offensives this summer in Russia or build up sufficient strength in the central Mediterranean to oppose the Allied offensive.

(15) *American-British conferences.*

In April 1942 I visited London for a series of conferences with the Prime Minister, the War Cabinet, and the British Chiefs of Staff regarding future operations. Plans agreed to at that time were later modifed as a result of another visit to London in July, in company with Admiral King, to permit the launching of the campaign in North Africa the following November.

Between these two visits there was interpolated a conference in Washington of the President, the Prime Minister, and Gen. Sir Alan F. Brooke, Chief of the Imperial General Staff, and the United States Chiefs of Staff. It was during this conference that the British forces in the Middle East were forced to retire to the El Alamein line. The attention of the conference thereafter was largely devoted to measures to meet the desperate situation which had developed in Egypt, supplemented by a German threat through the Caucasus toward the Abadan oil refineries in the Persian Gulf region. In this emergency 307 medium tanks and 90 self-propelled 105 mm. guns were rushed to the Middle East from New York. One transport loaded with 51 tanks and 28 105's was torpedoed and in order to replace this loss a corresponding number was taken without explanation from the American armored divisions then engaged in maneuvers. The arrival of these tanks and guns proved to be an important factor in the decisive victory of the British Eighth Army on the El Alamein line in October.

(16) *Government of occupied areas.*

Throughout military operations in foreign territory orderly civil administration must be maintained. In anticipation of this function the War Department established in May 1942 a School of Military Government at Charlottesville, Va., designed to train Army officers for these important functions. Also, in order to establish policies and plan for the coordination of civilian activities in occupied territories a War Department Civil Affairs Division was established on March 1, 1943. This Division, acting in collaboration with other Government agencies involved, coordinates civil affairs in areas occupied by the United Nations in combined operations. In general, established policies contemplate the preservation of lines of communication and channels of supply, the prevention and control of epidemics, the restoration of war production and whatever steps are possible to transform liberated peoples into effective fighting allies.

Plans for military operations also anticipate the furnishing of relief and supplies for the populations of the areas occupied. For example, Army stock piles were accumulated in North Africa in anticipation of the occupation of Sicily. These supplies included flour, sugar, milk, olive oil, meat, medicine, and soap. Plans were made for public health experts, sanitary engineers, supply and agricultural experts to accompany the invasion forces into Sicily. During the initial period of military occupation civilian supplies were distributed under the direction of the Civilian Relief Division.

The Combined Chiefs of Staff have established a Combined Civil Affairs Committee composed of the Army, Navy, and civilian representatives of the United States and the United Kingdom. This committee is charged with the responsibility of determining policies for the planning, coordination, and administration of civil affairs in areas occupied as a result of combined military operations. The Assistant Secretary of War is the chairman of this committee.

(17) *Arms supplied to French.*

At the Casablanca conference held in January 1943 it was agreed that the United States would equip the French divisions which could be formed from units then in North Africa. Arrangements were made to expedite the shipment of this equipment. The primary difficulty has been lack of transportation due to the urgency of requirements for American troops fighting in the theater. Excellent progress has been made in this matter and the French divisions are becoming an effective reinforcement as rapidly as they are equipped and trained in the technique of the new weapons. French air and naval units are included in the program.

(18) *Casablanca conference.*

In January 1943 a 10-day conference was arranged between the President, the Prime Minister, and the Combined Chiefs of Staff, together with a number of subordinate officials. While the decisions arrived at at that time cannot now be disclosed, it is permissible to state that an agreement for the operation against Sicily was reached and the logistical arrangements were immediately started. The plans for air and other operations in northwestern Europe were reviewed and confirmed. An understanding was reached regarding increased supplies for China and a series of operations in the Pacific commencing with the capture of Attu Island at the westernmost tip of the Aleutians (successfully completed on May 31) to be followed by simultaneous operations in the South and Southwest Pacific (now under way). The conference covered strategic plans throughout the world, a careful break-down of ship tonnage allotments, convoy movements, naval dispositions, etc.

(19) *Washington conference.*

A conference of the President, the Prime Minister, and the Combined Chiefs of Staff and supporting agencies took place in Washington from May 12 to May 25, 1943. The decisions reached at this conference cannot be disclosed at this time. The events of the preceding 4 months since the Casablanca conference were reviewed in the light of the victories in Tunisia and the Aleutians, the increase in shipping resulting from the success of the antisubmarine campaign, the developments or lack of developments on the Russian front, conditions in China, and the situation in the South and Southwest Pacific. At the close of this conference, I accompanied Mr. Churchill to Algiers and Tunisia for a closer survey of the situation in the Mediterranean. Incidentally, at this time decisions were taken regarding the bombing of rail communications through Rome and the destruction of the Rumanian oil refineries at Ploesti.

(20) *Civilians aid fighting units.*

In addition to lend-lease activities, a number of civilian experts have been furnished by private industrial organizations as observers to accompany field forces overseas. These experts, most of them engineers of high standing, went to such places as Cairo, Australia, Hawaii, England, the Southwest Pacific, North Africa, and elsewhere. They were given a status similar to officers and accompanied the troops in actual combat to assist in operation of equipment and to observe its performance. Reports received from them have been of great value to troops in the field and to the Army Service Forces.

In addition, several thousand civilian technicians have been employed within the United States in an advisory or supervisory capacity for the repair and reclamation of Army equipment. These technicians are also used for the instruction of mechanics of all types and as advisers to Army officers on maintenance activities. Through their assistance standards of preventative maintenance were raised, training of maintenance troops expedited, and damaged equipment speedily repaired and returned to the troops. The employment of qualified automotive and maintenance men from American industry has permitted the knowledge gained by years of experience in automotive maintenance to be passed on to the Army.

(21) *Middle East construction curtailed.*

Construction of large ordnance and aircraft depots was undertaken in the Nile Delta area, in Eritrea, and in the Levant States at a time when the enemy's success in Libya and Egypt indicated a long campaign of recovery on the part of the United Nations in the Middle East with a possible withdrawal to bases in Eritrea or the Levant. In the fall of 1942 after it appeared that the Libyan campaign coupled with the North African landings would eliminate the enemy from Africa, American support of the above depots was almost completely withdrawn, with the result that United States troops involved were then employed primarily in support of our Army (mostly air force) operations in the area and further construction was canceled. Most of the above depot activities were taken over and operated by the British.

(22) *Pacific operations planned.*

Lieutenant General Stilwell and Major General Chennault were ordered to Washington in April 1943 to present first-hand information on the situation in China to the President, the Prime Minister, and the Combined Chiefs of Staff. Similarly, Field Marshal Wavell described the situation in Burma and India, and the military and economic problems of China were described by Dr. T. V. Soong. Plans prepared by these theater commanders were supplemented by and coordinated with those of the Combined Staff Planners resulting in the development of a logistical program and plans for effective military operations which were approved by the Combined Chiefs of Staff.

(23) *Aid to Russia.*

The following assistance has been rendered to Russia by the United States in the form of military equipment: Over 3,000 airplanes, 2,400 tanks, 109,000 submachine guns, 16,000 Jeeps, 80,000 trucks, 7,000 motorcycles, 130,000 field telephones, and 75,000 tons of explosives, which have actually arrived in Russia, with a great many other items of munitions as well as foodstuffs and raw materials.

(24) *Women's Army Auxiliary Corps.*

On May 14, 1942, the President signed the bill establishing the Women's Army Auxiliary Corps. The basic purpose of this organization was to utilize the services of women wherever possible and thus release a corresponding number of soldiers for combat duty. Although the immediate authorized strength was established by the President as 25,000, by November the WAAC had justified its purpose to such an extent that the strength of 150,000 was authorized and an intensive recruiting campaign was undertaken.

The first WAAC training center was opened at Fort Des Moines, Iowa, on July 20, 1942, and within 4 weeks a basic training course for auxiliaries and a 6 weeks' course for officer candidates established. Since that time training centers have been established at Daytona Beach, Fla.; Fort Oglethorpe, Ga.; and Fort Devens, Mass. (chart 22).

The training which the women receive in these camps prepares them to take their place in Army life. The 4 weeks' basic training course is designed to inculcate the principles of Army discipline, customs, and courtesies, as well as to teach the members methods of caring for Government property. Following the basic course, WAAC's may immediately go into the field, or where special talents are indicated they may be sent to specialist schools to receive additional training. For example, women assigned to the administrative specialist schools are trained in Army administrative procedure, a matter which can be handled as efficiently by a woman as by a man. The schools for bakers and cooks teach WAAC's the fundamentals of Army cooking and efficient methods of preparation of foods for large groups as well as the principles of dietetics and balanced menus. Those assigned to motor-transport duties are not only taught the basic principles of operating Army vehicles but also elementary repair and maintenance work. Women whose tests indicate they have aptitudes may be assigned to schools for radio operators and repairmen, or given instruction in photographic techniques and developing and printing pictures and camera use and repair. Those who manifest qualities of leadership are selected for officer candidate

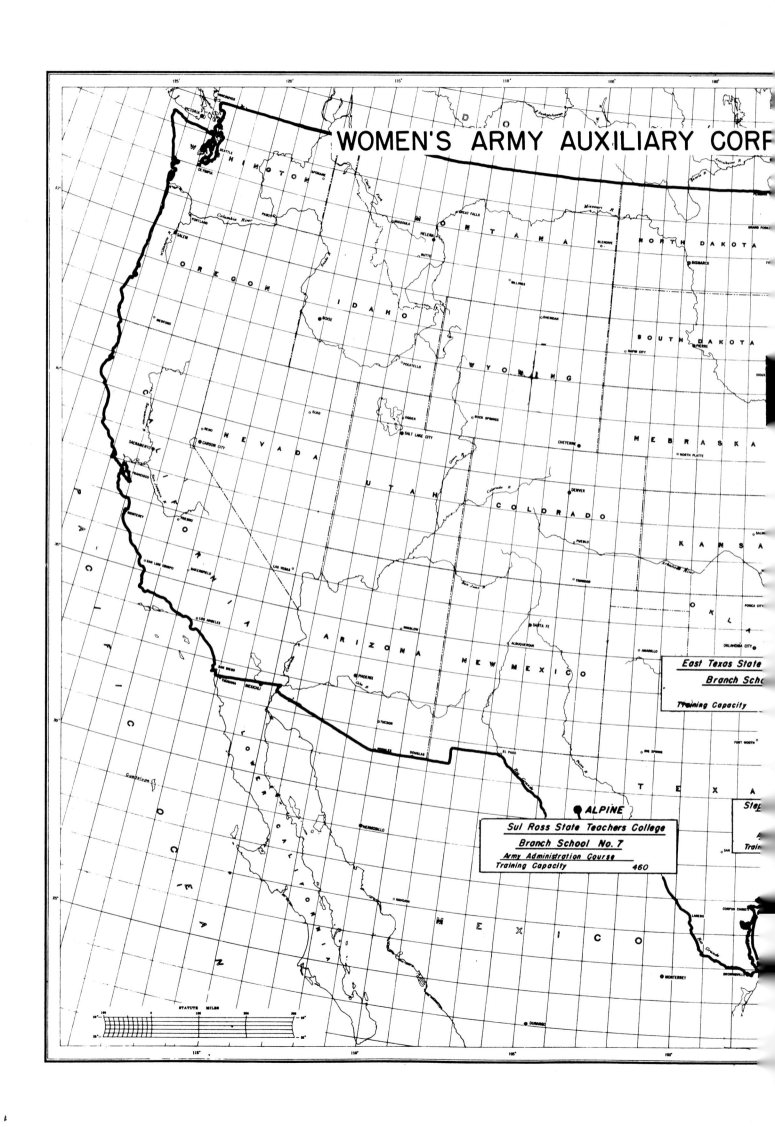

WOMEN'S ARMY AUXILIARY CORP

East Texas State

Branch Sch

Training Capacity

● ALPINE

Sul Ross State Teachers College

Branch School No. 7

Army Administration Course

Training Capacity   460

Ste

Train

TRAINING CENTERS AND SCHOOLS

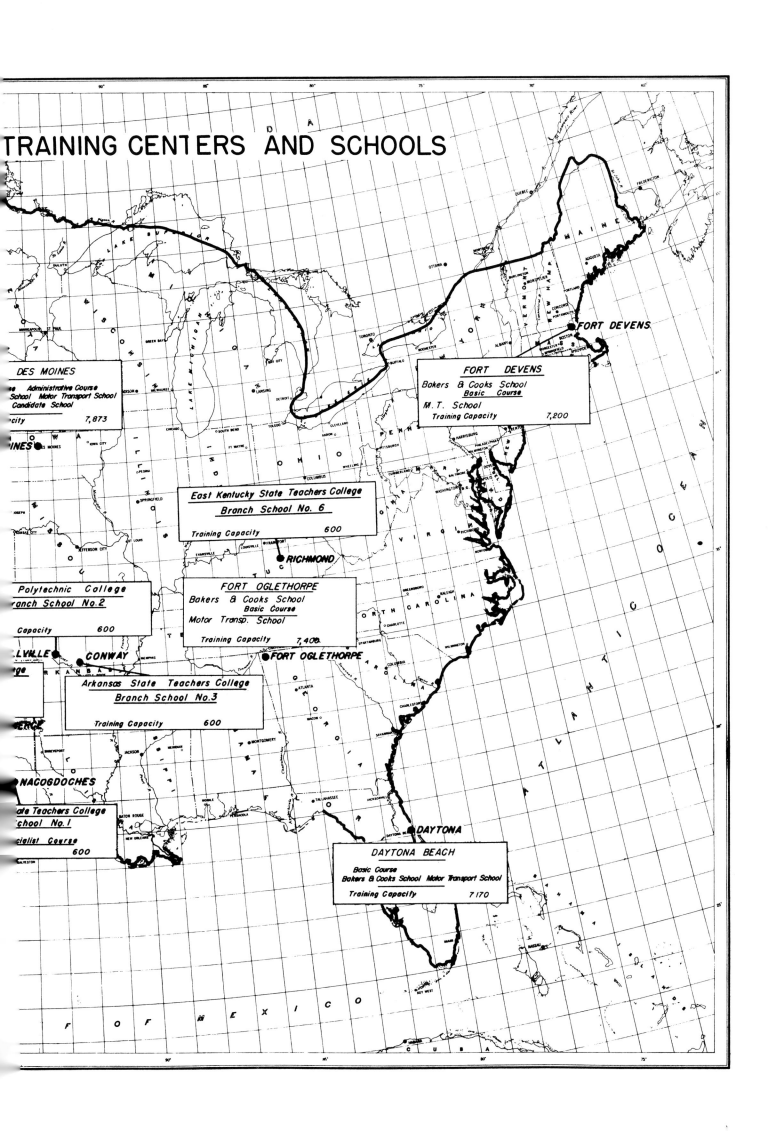

DES MOINES

Administrative Course
School Motor Transport School
Candidate School

city   7,873

FORT DEVENS

Bakers & Cooks School
Basic Course

M.T. School
Training Capacity   7,200

East Kentucky State Teachers College

Branch School No. 6

Training Capacity   600

Polytechnic College

ranch School No. 2

Capacity   600

FORT OGLETHORPE

Bakers & Cooks School
Basic Course
Motor Transp. School

Training Capacity   7,400

Arkansas State Teachers College

Branch School No. 3

Training Capacity   600

NACOGDOCHES

ate Teachers College
chool No. 1
cialist Course
                         600

DAYTONA BEACH

Basic Course
Bakers & Cooks School Motor Transport School

Training Capacity   7 170

school and there they receive more intensive training in military procedure and discipline and receive further instruction in Army administration and command responsibilities.

There is a growing demand for WAAC's services throughout the Army. Enlistees represent the highest type of American womanhood and as a whole the women have maintained the highest standards in every respect. They have fulfilled their duties in an efficient and businesslike manner and have been a definite asset to the Army. Each woman enrolled in the WAAC has postponed the induction of a man, since they are counted as a man in computing the ultimate manpower requirements of the Army.

A little over a year after the corps was established, more than 65,000 women were members and are serving in more than 240 posts, camps, and stations in the United States and abroad. In the 155 specialists jobs they have taken over they have fulfilled their primary purpose of releasing able-bodied men for active duty on the fighting front. In addition, a number have been shipped to overseas stations and are performing valuable functions in activities as chauffeurs, and in administrative capacities at the various headquarters. Plans for the increase of the Army during the calendar year of 1943 provide for approximately 150,000 WAAC's, an equivalent in size to almost 10 divisions of soldiers released for combat duty.

On July 1, 1943, the President signed a bill changing the status of the corps from an auxiliary serving with the Army to a component of the Army and giving the members the right to Army ratings, grades, privileges, responsibilities, and benefits.

(25) *Officer program.*

A factor of vital importance in the development of the Army has been the insistence that high standards of leadership be maintained throughout all echelons. The basis of the structure was a nucleus of 14,000 Regular Army officers augmented by 21,000 National Guard and 110,000 Reserve officers, the great proportion of whom were not on active duty. At the outset it was apparent that the limited number of Regular Army officers would be spread extremely thin and the orderly development during the early stages of the emergency could not have proceeded without utilizing the reservoir of Reserve officers who were brought to active duty in increasing numbers as the expansion proceeded. National Guard officers came in with their own units, and as a rule were not available for the new units organized incidental to the passage of the Selective Service Act.

In anticipation of the even greater expansion to come there was established during the summer of 1941 a number of officer candidate schools designed to give special training to enlisted men who had displayed outstanding qualities of leadership (chart 23).

Selections for attendance at officer candidate schools were based on the democratic theory that the schools were available to any man who demonstrated outstanding capabilities of leadership, who possessed the intellect as distinguished from education which would permit him to perform the functions of an officer, and who indicated that he was morally and physically qualified to train troops and lead them in combat. By June 30, 1943, officer candidate schools had given the Army more than 206,000 officers, serving in grades from second lieutenant to lieutenant colonel.

In order to meet a demand for officers who were specialists in various technical professions and who would not be involved in direct command of troops, approximately 47,000 officers were appointed from civil life, thus releasing experienced military personnel for other duties. This figure is in addition to chaplains, doctors, and former officers. These commissions were granted chiefly for duty in highly specialized positions in the Judge Advocate General's Department, Corps of Engineers, Ordnance Department, Signal Corps, and Army Air Forces. Early in 1943 when the officer shortage in the Army had been overcome, procurement from civil life was restricted to professional and technical specialists not otherwise obtainable, and a gradual reduction in the capacity and output of the officer candidate schools was initiated to keep step with the decline in the expansion rate of the Army.

General officers.—Success or failure of military campaigns and the welfare of innumerable lives are dependent upon decisions made by general officers. Our generals, therefore, are selected from men who have measured up to the highest standards of military skill, who have demonstrated a comprehensive understanding of modern methods of warfare, and who possess the physical stamina, moral courage, strength of character, and the flexibility of mind necessary to carry the burdens which modern combat conditions impose.

We had on June 30, 1943, 1,065 general officers to command and staff the Army. This represented a net increase of 722 during the past 2 years, as shown in the following table:

Rank	July 1, 1941	June 30, 1943	Net increase
General	1	5	4
Lieutenant general. . . .	8	25	17
Major general.	89	271	182
Brigadier general	245	764	519
Total.	343	1,065	722

This increase, however, did not keep pace with the expansion of the Army, for on July 1, 1941, there was

1 general officer for every group of 4,241 officers and enlisted men, while on June 30, 1943, there was 1 to 6,460.

Of these 1,065 generals, 18 were officers of the Reserve Corps, 80 from the National Guard, and 9 were promoted to brigadier general after being commissioned in lower grades directly from civil life. Of those holding commissions in the Regular Army, 47 were retired officers on active duty.

General officers—June 30, 1943

	Generals	Lieuten-ant generals	Major generals	Brigadier generals	Total
Regular Army:					
Active	3	22	238	647	910
Retired	2	2	19	24	47
Subtotal	5	24	257	671	957
Reserve			2	16	18
National Guard			12	68	80
Army of the United States		1		9	10
Total	5	25	271	764	1,065

Of the 910 active list Regular Army generals, 865 were temporary appointments only in general-officer grades, while 45 held permanent rank in those grades. Although only about 3.7 percent of the Army's commissioned strength was made up of National Guardsmen, somewhat over 7 percent of the Army's general officers had come from the National Guard.

(26) *Construction program.*

The war construction program, begun under the Quartermaster Corps and transferred to the Corps of Engineers on December 16, 1941, presented a prodigious engineering problem (chart 24). By March 31, 1943, the total cost of the entire program amounted to $9,226,464,000, of which $2,588,000,000 was for Ground and Service Forces facilities, $2,823,510,000 went for industrial facilities, and $2,503,096,000 was devoted to construction for the Air Forces. The balance represented such items as the Civil Aeronautics Administration program, storage and shipping facilities, and passive protection.

In the accomplishment of this program, 18,139,098 acres of land were acquired at a cost of $249,039,132. At the peak of employment, in July 1942, more than 1,000,000 persons were involved in some phase of the program, which figure, by March 1943, had fallen to somewhat over 350,000. At that time about 75.8 percent of the authorized projects had been completed, an additional 6.4 percent were ready for use and 17.5 percent were under construction and only 0.3 percent of the total authorized had not been started.

Housing for 4,919,617 men was provided— 3,507,552 for the ground units, 1,412,065 for the Air Forces and for civilian workers. A total of 222,154,054 square feet of depot storage space was made available; 230,235 hospital beds were provided, representing 76.2 percent of the authorized number.

The cost of Air Forces projects to March 31, 1943, amounted to $2,500,000,000. Plants for the manufacture and storage of munitions and warfare chemicals obligated approximately $3,000,000,000. Repair and upkeep of installations by the Chief of Engineers are provided for by an authorization of about $400,000,000 for the current fiscal year ending June 30, 1943. A program for camouflage and other passive protective measures to vital war factories and installations is being provided at a cost of about $40,000,000. All of this work is under the supervision of 51 Engineer Districts within the continental limits of the United States and nine extra-continental district engineer offices.

Various types of military training facilities and camps and cantonments have been built—ranging from parachute training towers to rifle ranges.

Since the health of the soldier is a vital responsibility of the Army, many health facilities, in addition to hospitals and housing, have been built. These include proper provision for food storage and cooking, incinerator plants providing for the prompt disposal of garbage and refuse, ample laundry facilities and proper heating.

Recreation centers operated by the U. S. O. have also been constructed by the Army. Attractive, modern buildings, containing club rooms and lounges, a social hall with a stage and dressing rooms, study and reading rooms, as well as a refreshment lounge and soda bar, were included in the program.

To further the high purpose of religious worship plans called for the construction of 478 chapels. In appearance, the chapels resemble the typical small church of the average American community—the slant-roofed frame building with steeple at the front. Each chapel has an electric organ and a seating capacity for about 400 soldiers and is so designed and equipped that services of any denomination can be conducted.

In January 1941 work was started on the Atlantic bases leased from Great Britain—a huge program, involving construction of permanent housing, temporary housing, airfields, fortifications, and miscellaneous technical facilities. With the approach of war, this program was accelerated and expanded to include additional bases in the Caribbean area, while in July 1941 work was started on the construction of facilities in Greenland.

Late in 1941 efforts were directed toward construction of supply routes to our own overseas pos-

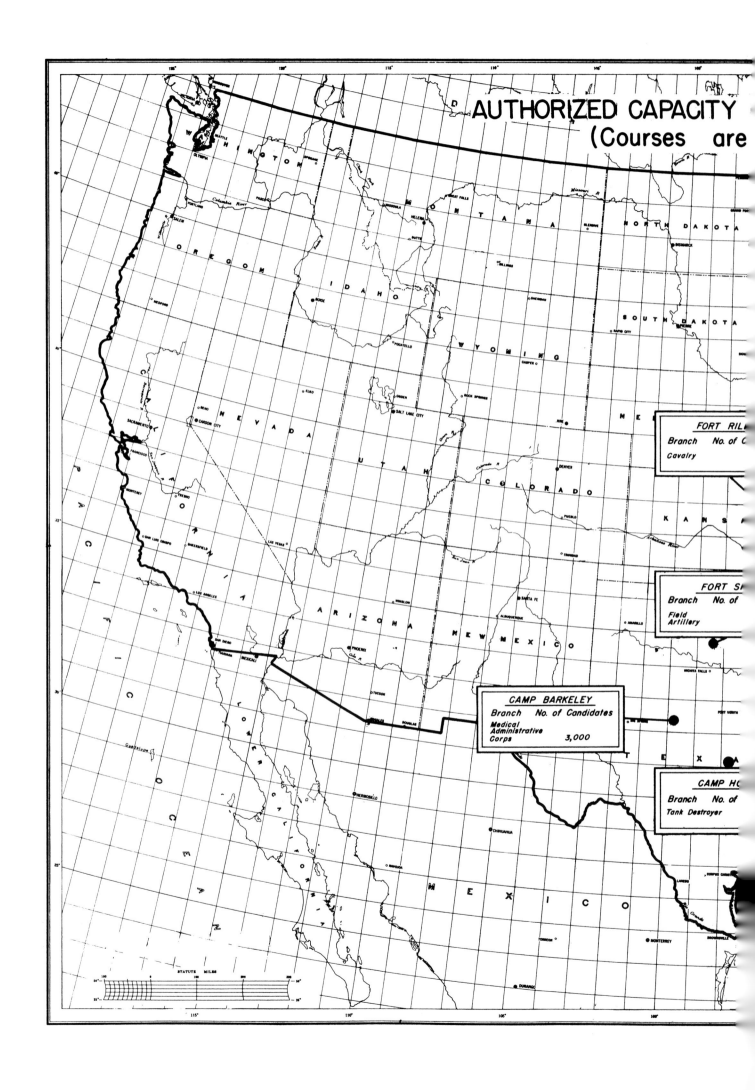

AUTHORIZED CAPACITY
(Courses are

FORT RIL
Branch   No. of C
Cavalry

FORT S
Branch   No. of
Field
Artillery

CAMP BARKELEY
Branch	No. of Candidates
Medical Administrative Corps	3,000

CAMP H(
Branch   No. of
Tank Destroyer

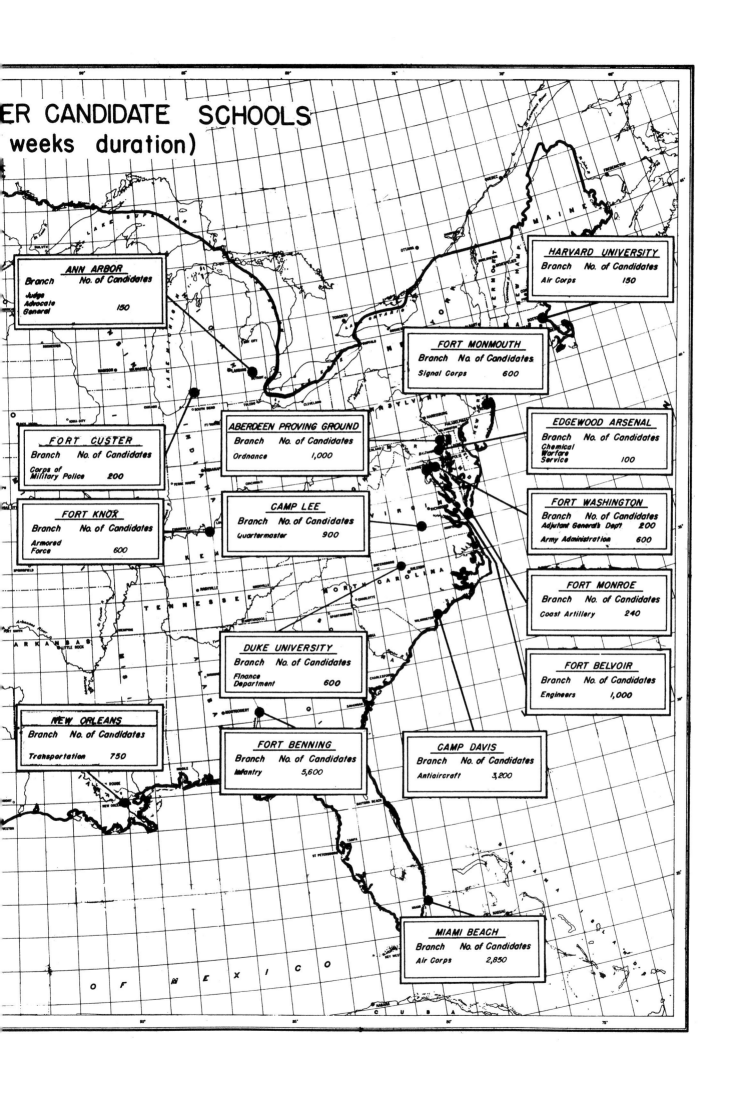

ER CANDIDATE SCHOOLS
weeks duration)

ANN ARBOR

Branch	No. of Candidates
Judge Advocate General	150

HARVARD UNIVERSITY

Branch	No. of Candidates
Air Corps	150

FORT MONMOUTH

Branch	No. of Candidates
Signal Corps	600

FORT CUSTER

Branch	No. of Candidates
Corps of Military Police	200

ABERDEEN PROVING GROUND

Branch	No. of Candidates
Ordnance	1,000

EDGEWOOD ARSENAL

Branch	No. of Candidates
Chemical Warfare Service	100

FORT KNOX

Branch	No. of Candidates
Armored Force	600

CAMP LEE

Branch	No. of Candidates
Quartermaster	900

FORT WASHINGTON

Branch	No. of Candidates
Adjutant General's Dept	200
Army Administration	600

FORT MONROE

Branch	No. of Candidates
Coast Artillery	240

DUKE UNIVERSITY

Branch	No. of Candidates
Finance Department	600

FORT BELVOIR

Branch	No. of Candidates
Engineers	1,000

NEW ORLEANS

Branch	No. of Candidates
Transportation	750

FORT BENNING

Branch	No. of Candidates
Infantry	5,600

CAMP DAVIS

Branch	No. of Candidates
Antiaircraft	3,200

MIAMI BEACH

Branch	No. of Candidates
Air Corps	2,850

MAJOR WAR CONSTRUCTION-CORPS OF ENGINEERS

VALUE OF WORK IN PLACE

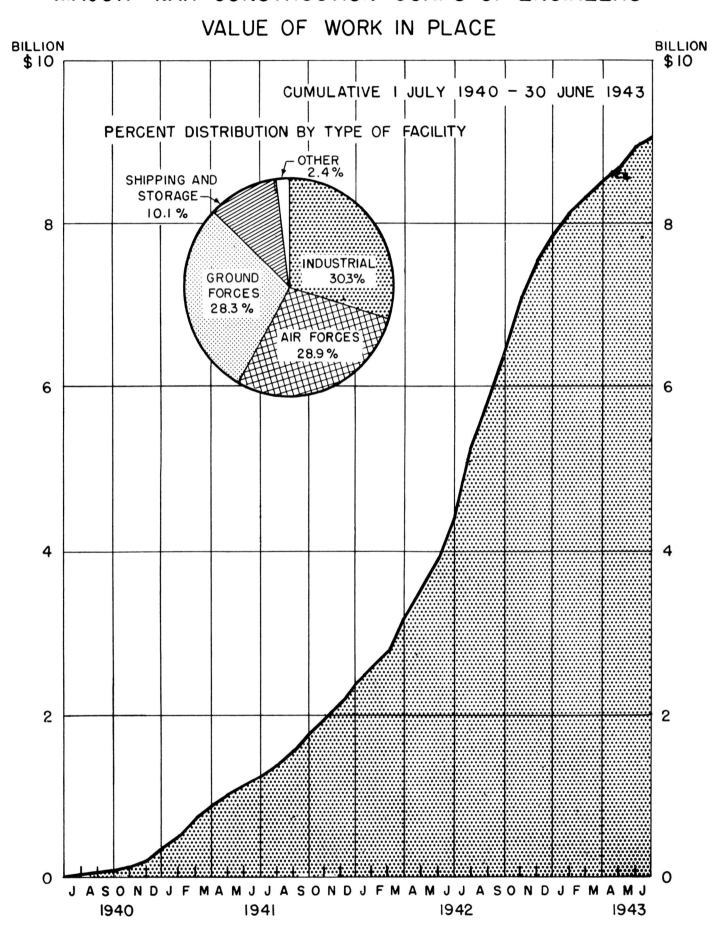

CUMULATIVE I JULY 1940 – 30 JUNE 1943

PERCENT DISTRIBUTION BY TYPE OF FACILITY

OTHER 2.4%

SHIPPING AND STORAGE 10.1%

GROUND FORCES 28.3%

INDUSTRIAL 30.3%

AIR FORCES 28.9%

sessions and to those of the Allied Nations. The first of these provided a chain of airfields for delivery of airplanes to some of our Pacific Island outposts, Australia, and the South Pacific area. Attention was also given to air routes over the North and South Atlantic; air facilities in the northeast portion of South America were expanded and work was started in the Red Sea area, Iran and Iraq to develop ports and rail and highway transportation facilities.

Construction problems of almost every variety have been encountered; some ferry-route airfields have merely been graded and permitted to freeze; others were paved with steel mats, while still others have been overlaid with concrete. Housing has varied from simple wooden structures used in theaters of operations to brick and tile buildings in South America. Housing in areas adjacent to the Arctic Circle is of special design, with plenty of insulation, vestibules, and storm windows.

(27) *Public relations.*

The War Department Bureau of Public Relations was established on February 11, 1941. During the war the guiding principle of the conduct of Army public relations has been to release all information consistent with safeguarding military security. Also by the establishment of a code of wartime practices for the press and radio, a genuine cooperation has been attained by these great news-disseminating agencies.

The global character of the war and the early dispatch of American troops to widely separated areas necessitate a world-wide organization for the prompt dissemination of news. Public relations offices in the headquarters of each theater of operations provide continuous access to important announcements by commanding generals overseas. Commanders of units in the field are instructed to assist the correspondents accredited to their organizations, and to provide them with quarters, subsistence, transportation within the area, and with the means of communication which assure that their dispatches and pictures will be carried promptly from battle zone to the home front.

As a method of providing news free from hint of propaganda, the principle has been accepted that civilian correspondents rather than public relations officers should prepare the news for the public. Within the Bureau an accrediting service considers and processes applications for the dispatch of civilian representatives both to posts in this country and to overseas theaters. Some 500 writers, photographers, and radio commentators, representing press feature services, individual newspapers, picture syndicates, and radio networks have thus far been accredited by the Bureau to theaters of operations.

The difficulties of making a full pictorial record under conditions of active warfare have been the object of special arrangement. A photographers' pool, both for still and motion pictures, operates in every theater. Under its regulations, still pictures and newsreel footage taken by one representative are made available to all. Early in 1943 facilities were set up for the dispatch by radio of still pictures from North Africa. By this means, photographs appear in the American press within a matter of hours from the time they are taken.

The News Division, subdivided in terms of the media it serves, has separate branches for press, magazine and book publishers, radio and pictorial services, assisting them to obtain such news of the Army as they desire. Through the Press Branch all news emanating from the War Department is distributed to the public. The Pictorial Branch provides pictorial news through still pictures, newsreels, and other films and maintains liaison with the film industry through the War Activities Committee, Motion Picture Industry. The Radio Branch, in addition to serving as War Department contact with the broadcasting industry, produces each week an hour's program, The Army Hour, presenting reports from the war zones, a summary of news, and developments of our training establishments. Through its Continental Liaison Branch, the News Division maintains close liaison with all public relations officers within the continental limits of the United States.

The War Intelligence Division prepares such communiques as are issued by the War Department, maintains Bureau contact with theaters of operations and its principal officers are available at all times to provide guidance on war news. This division is charged with the accrediting of all war correspondents and photographers. Lists of casualties and prisoners of war are announced to the public by this division, which also safeguards military security through the review of manuscripts intended for release to the public. The Industrial Services Division is charged with a continuous study of morale in manufacturing plants engaged in the production of war matériel.

The Bureau maintains direct contact with the arms and services through Offices of Technical Information established in all branches of the Army. In addition to news of special activities, these offices provide answers to many of the inquiries addressed to the War Department from publicity media, other organizations, and individuals.

The expansion of activity in combat zones has developed an increasing demand for the interpretation of events and for news from the battle areas. First-hand accounts of life on the battle fronts reach the public constantly from officers returned from the combat zones.

(28) *Health in the Army.*

The expansion of the Army was accompanied by a rapid development in the knowledge and application of medical science as it pertained to the Army. Of outstanding importance were the measures taken to prevent such diseases as could be prevented by inoculation and vaccination. Our soldiers have been vaccinated with an improved variety of typhoid and paratyphoid, and all have been immunized against tetanus. Also, where necessary, troops have been vaccinated against typhus, bubonic plague, cholera and yellow fever.

The necessity for giving prompt and effective care to battlefield casualties has resulted in the development of special types of equipment, including mobile X-ray units and mobile field operating units which can give immediate treatment to serious battlefield casualties. Of all developments in the present war, however, perhaps the most outstanding are the application of sulpha drugs to wounds and the use of dry human blood plasma for transfusions.

Despite the continuous expansion since 1940 the health record of the Army as a whole has made a constant improvement. For instance, the record for the fiscal year 1943 was better than that for 1942 and both represented peak attainments. The number of cases requiring medical treatment was lower during 1942 and 1943 (825 per thousand) than in the preceding two years (1,071 per thousand). Although the percentage of illness in the Army during the past 2 years was greater than during peacetime, the death rate for all causes in the United States was lower than any during the history of our Army. Equally interesting figures are available with respect to casualty rates within the Army Air Forces during this period of tremendous expansion. Despite the phenomenal rise in the total hours of flying time during the last 2 years, the rate of increase in fatalities has shown but slight rise and was actually decreasing during the first quarter of the fiscal year 1943.

Another interesting development of the present war has been the evacuation of sick and wounded by air. During the campaign in Guadalcanal and the recent campaign in New Guinea evacuation was conducted entirely by air. In cases where transportation by mule pack train through mosquito-infested jungles would have meant 14 to 21 days of difficult travel, it was accomplished in less than an hour by airplane. In New Guinea the largest number of air evacuations in a single day was 592. In April of this year during the Tunisian campaign evacuation by air was continuous, 400 men being the top figure for 1 day; the distance of transport was from 280 to 350 miles. This rapid and safe method of transporting casualties has resulted in greatly decreased mortality rates (chart 25).

(29) *Organized leisure time activities.*

Prior to the beginning of the war a Morale Branch was established in the War Department primarily for the purpose of providing entertainment and organizing the soldiers' leisure time with a view to preventing homesickness and providing wholesome recreation while off duty. Later the Morale Branch was replaced by the Special Service Division with a greatly extended scope of activities.

The Special Service Division has coordinated the contributions of the entertainment industry in cooperation with the United Service Organizations, camp shows, and the Army. Within the Zone of the Interior more than 100 entertainment units have circulated throughout 950 Army stations in the past 6 months. In addition, a large number of screen, concert, and radio stars; band and radio shows; and a total of 65 entertainment troupes have toured all theaters of operations overseas.

Of benefit to enlisted men are the service clubs, guest houses where visiting relatives may stay overnight, motion-picture theaters, and recreation halls which have been provided at various Army stations. These facilities are operated by the service commands under policies developed by the Special Service Division.

In the past year the number of theaters of the Army Motion Picture Service operating under the Special Service Division has been doubled over the previous year. The average daily attendance in 1943, was 573,756, as compared with 260,000 in 1942. Each week at least 3 Hollywood feature pictures, the gift of the American motion picture industry, are distributed among overseas stations, these pictures being released simultaneously with the release of similar programs in the United States. To keep the soldier overseas informed of what is going on in the United States 16 short-wave stations broadcast from the United States to every overseas area.

For reading material the Army Library Service has sent overseas approximately 94,000 unit sets of all current magazines together with nearly 3,000,000 books. The Army weekly newspaper Yank, published by the Special Service Division, has attained a worldwide circulation of over 400,000 and local Army newspapers, which now total over 900 are assisted by regular provision of special copy and pictorial features. A weekly news map giving a brief but clear picture of the war situation throughout the world circulates over 66,000 copies to camps, posts, and stations, while an additional 15,000 is sent to the Navy, Coast Guard, and Marine Corps; the Canadian Army; and war plants in the United States. A smaller "overseas edition" is distributed to theaters of operations and to hospitals in this country.

Four of seven feature films in the series, Why We Fight, have been completed. These motion pictures give a graphical and historical portrayal of the causes and of a depiction of the war itself and are shown to all military personnel. In addition a daily news summary is distributed daily by radio to points in all theaters.

U.S. ARMY BATTLE CASUALTIES

7 DECEMBER 1941 THROUGH 30 JUNE 1943

TOTAL CASUALTIES, OFFICERS AND ENLISTED MEN

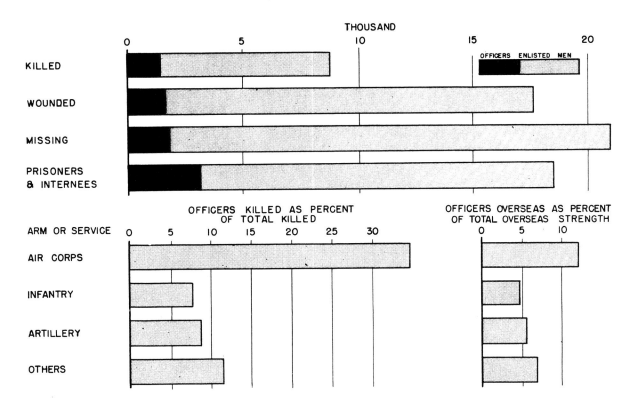

TOTAL CASUALTIES, BY ARM OR SERVICE

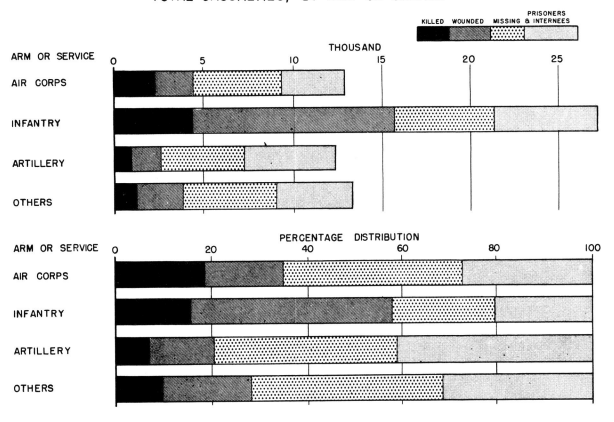

To assist soldiers moving overseas in adjusting themselves to new environments a series of Pocket Guides to foreign areas has been produced. These small volumes acquaint the soldier with the area in which he will serve. More than 2,000,000 copies have been distributed. In addition, phonograph records and instruction manuals have been produced to give instruction in 30 languages. Phrase books and dictionaries are now being produced in 20 languages.

To provide correspondence courses for off-duty use of troops, the Special Service Division, in cooperation with 81 colleges and universities, has established a series of correspondence courses whereby the soldier, at a limited financial cost, can continue his education while in the Service. On April 1, 1943, Army enrollment exceeded 20,000 persons, 50 percent of whom were soldiers overseas.

The War Department has given considerable attention to delivery of soldiers' mail as a means of maintaining morale, particularly in the active theaters. During the past year so-called V-mail service has been instituted by which letters are microfilmed and transmitted by air and reproduced at their destinations. Since the operation of V-mail service commenced 14 months ago, 110,000,000 pieces of V-mail have been processed and delivered. When in microfilm form the saving in weight is 99 percent.

(30) *Educational system expanded.*

In order to increase the output of the United States Military Academy and to provide its graduates with actual combat experience, the course of instruction there was reduced to 3 years. Of special significance was the addition of air instruction and the commissioning of many graduates directly into the Air Corps.

The Command and General Staff School at Fort Leavenworth, Kans., was tremendously expanded during the past biennium in keeping with the need for qualified general and special staff officers. Also a course was added for the training of officers in operations of the Army Service Forces.

In April 1943 an Army-Navy Staff College was established as an agency of the Joint Chiefs of Staff organization to provide for training of senior officers of the Army, Navy, and Marine Corps with special training in all phases of joint or coordinated operations of air, land, and sea forces.

(31) *Training.*

Ground Forces training.—The technical warfare of today requires that all troops be highly trained in a variety of complicated subjects. This training involves not only physical conditioning to permit men to effectively operate in climates ranging from the sub-Arctic to the Tropics, but it also requires that troops be prepared to conduct difficult amphibious operations, be qualified in jungle, mountain, and desert warfare, and also be capable of fighting as a coordinated unit in large-scale mobile operations.

Before they can undertake advanced training, all soldiers must be indoctrinated with certain basic principles, such as discipline, personal sanitation, first aid, guard duty, the use and care of weapons, etc. Accordingly, branch replacement training centers were established throughout the United States to which selectees were assigned upon their induction for a period of 13 weeks, following which they were assigned to tactical units for their advanced training (chart 26). At the beginning of the war, training centers were expanded to a capacity of 316,000 but still could not accommodate the large numbers being inducted at that time. It was consequently necessary for certain divisions which were being activated to organize their own basic training centers and give this primary training to the soldier upon his assignment to the division.

Between July 1, 1941, and July 1, 1943, 50 divisions were activated within the Army. This expansion imposed a difficult problem. To organize a division, a nucleus of trained personnel had to be available around which the division could be built. This requirement resulted in the establishment of a cadre system whereby the cadre, or nucleus, of a new division was drawn from divisions then in existence. The situation was not entirely satisfactory because divisions were being activated at such a rapid rate that a parent division, for instance, might be called upon to furnish two or more cadres while itself in the primary stages of training and development. Also, the requirement that the cadre consist of high-type personnel imposed unfortunate and practically a continuous drain on the keymen of the parent division.

Activating and transforming an infantry division into a competent fighting team of 15,000 men is a long and complicated job (chart 27). A unit of this size demands not only many of the skills and special services necessary for a civilian community of comparable size, but it must also be prepared to move with all its equipment and sustain itself in the field under combat conditions. For instance, within a typical infantry division the transportation of men, equipment, and supplies requires more than 1,500 men. The preparation of food requires more than 650 men. The administrative duties in connection with food and supplies require more than 700 men; medical, 600; communications, 1,500; repair and maintenance of equipment, 450 soldiers; while a variety of other specialized services accounts for 1,600 additional men. All of these soldiers receive not only intensive training in their specialties but also combat training to support effectively the 8,000 men in the division whose principal job is at the fighting front. (All figures are approximate.)

To meet the urgency the War Department evolved a system to insure that when the approximately 15,000 selectees arrived at their division training area there would be a minimum of lost motion and waste of time in immediately instituting the training program. For instance, the key officer personnel of a division were designated and assigned approximately 3 months before a division was to be activated. These officers were then given a course of instruction at a school pertinent to their activities, following which they arrived at the division activation area approximately 43 days before the activation date. The remainder of the officers and enlisted cadre, which was to furnish the noncommissioned officers and certain specialists, such as cooks and technicians, arrived at the division activation area approximately 38 days before the activation date with the result that when the selectees themselves arrived on D-day the division program could be launched without further delay. Normally the enlisted personnel are not assigned to a division until they have undergone a period of 13 weeks' basic training in a replacement training center and are versed in the fundamentals of being a soldier.

Following assignment to a division 13 additional weeks are spent in learning the tactics and techniques of his particular arm moving progressively through the platoon, company, battalion, and regimental training. At the end of the 26 weeks the various components of the division—the infantry regiment, field artillery battalion, and service regiment—are trained and are capable of working as a team within themselves. The following 13 weeks are devoted to divisional training. The division itself learns to operate as a team of the combined arms and services. During this period the Infantry, Field Artillery, division reconnaissance troops, Engineer battalions, Quartermaster company, Ordnance company, Medical battalion and Signal company all have been integrated to one smooth running machine— the division. The final 13 weeks are devoted to maneuvers and field exercises during which the division polishes its field training and learns to work as part of a higher unit.

To meet the need for specialized training of certain units selected for specific operations the Desert Training Center was established in March 1942, the Amphibious Training Center in May 1942, and the Mountain Training Center at Camp Hale, Calif., in September of 1942. The 30,000 square miles of the Desert Training Center terrain have been a major asset to the training facilities of the ground forces. In addition to providing experience in desert operations, the absence of restrictions on the use of land permits complete freedom of action in large-scale maneuvers. The area is organized as a theater of operations to provide training under realistic conditions and maneuvers are conducted with the accompanying problems of supply, maintenance, field bivouacs, etc., prevalent in actual combat and under the nearest permissible approach to actual combat conditions. In addition, large maneuver areas have been established

in Tennessee, Oregon, and Louisiana, where units of all the arms and services, comprising forces approximately the size of army corps, are sent at the conclusion of the division training phases for 8 weeks of intensive practical field training.

A practical aspect of the training given to ground units has been the establishment of "battle indoctrination" courses which are intended to simulate, as far as is practical, actual conditions existent on the field of battle. Exercises requiring the breaching of barbed-wire entanglements, crossing other obstacles which may be encountered in combat, such as streams, woods, towns, mined and fortified areas, all while under a screen of live ammunition fire, has been an important factor in producing units competent to enter combat against experienced and seasoned enemies.

Air Forces training.—In a general way the training schedule of an air force combat group is characteristic of any other military team (chart 28). The group, however, generally does not assemble until the completion of a period of technical training of various key individuals. This training is given in technical schools where the pilots, navigators, bombardiers, radio operators, aerial gunners, and others become expert as individuals in their specialties. This individually trained group is then assembled and undergoes a period of progressive team training in operational training units similar, with obvious modifications pertinent to the Air Forces, to Ground Forces units.

The expansion of the Army necessitated a carefully planned program to insure that the standards which had been established during peacetime were not lowered. The extent of the expansion is indicated by the fact that in the 19 years prior to 1941, the total number of pilots trained was less than 7,000. Today the rate of pilot production is about 75,000 per year not including glider, liaison, observation, and women pilots. In addition there has been incorporated a substantial training program for British, Dutch, Canadian, and Chinese pilots. The program for the training of the Chinese has had an important bearing on operations against the Japanese and is continuously expanding.

In addition to the combat flying crews who, although individual specialists, must attain a high degree of cooperative effort, the air forces have been faced with a problem of training competent ground crews—soldiers who, regardless of the weather or the hour, service planes, do rush repair jobs, keep vitally important instruments in precise order, and carry out other maintenance activities. The size of the ground crews necessarily varies with the situation but in general comprises a substantially larger number than the flying crews themselves. The expansion in the number of ground technicians trained is indicated by the fact that in the 20-year period prior to July 1, 1941, there were less than 15,000 graduates

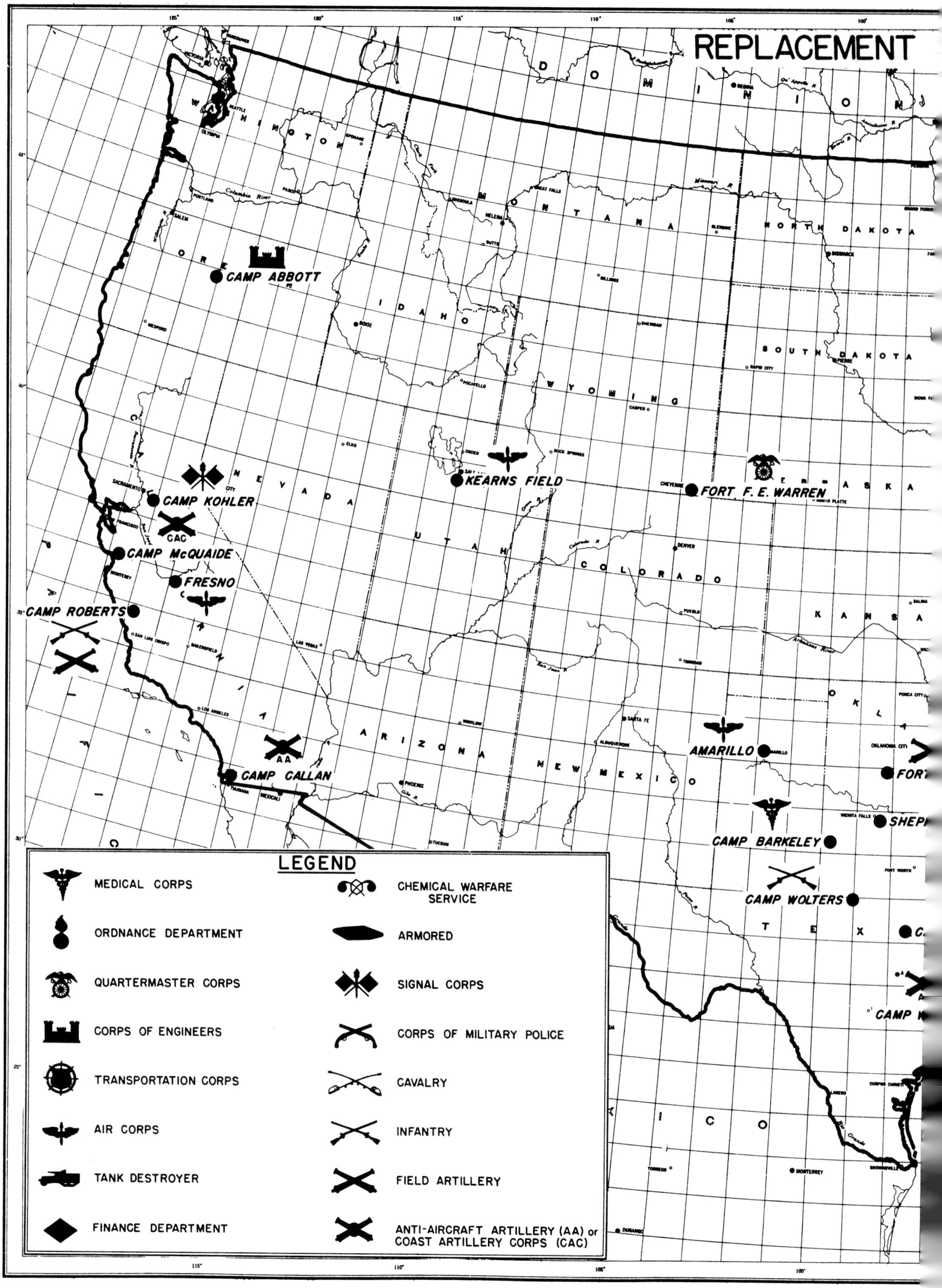
REPLACEMENT
CAMP ABBOTT
CAMP KOHLER
CAC
CAMP McQUAIDE
FRESNO
CAMP ROBERTS
KEARNS FIELD
FORT F. E. WARREN
AMARILLO
AA
CAMP CALLAN
CAMP BARKELEY
CAMP WOLTERS
WASHINGTON
OREGON
IDAHO
MONTANA
WYOMING
NEVADA
UTAH
COLORADO
ARIZONA
NEW MEXICO
NORTH DAKOTA
SOUTH DAKOTA
KANSAS
TEXAS
DOMINION
MEXICO
SEATTLE
OLYMPIA
SPOKANE
PORTLAND
SALEM
Columbia River
MEDFORD
BOISE
POCATELLO
HELENA
BUTTE
MISSOULA
GREAT FALLS
BILLINGS
SHERIDAN
CASPER
ROCK SPRINGS
OGDEN
CHEYENNE
DENVER
PUEBLO
TRINIDAD
ELKO
SACRAMENTO
SAN FRANCISCO
MONTEREY
SAN LUIS OBISPO
BAKERSFIELD
LOS ANGELES
LAS VEGAS
TIJUANA
MEXICALI
PHOENIX
TUCSON
WINSLOW
SANTA FE
ALBUQUERQUE
BISMARCK
PIERRE
RAPID CITY
NORTH PLATTE
OKLAHOMA CITY
WICHITA FALLS
FORT WORTH
LAREDO
MONTERREY
TORREON
DURANGO
BROWNSVILLE
CORPUS CHRISTI
Rio Grande
LEGEND
MEDICAL CORPS
ORDNANCE DEPARTMENT
QUARTERMASTER CORPS
CORPS OF ENGINEERS
TRANSPORTATION CORPS
AIR CORPS
TANK DESTROYER
FINANCE DEPARTMENT
CHEMICAL WARFARE SERVICE
ARMORED
SIGNAL CORPS
CORPS OF MILITARY POLICE
CAVALRY
INFANTRY
FIELD ARTILLERY
ANTI-AIRCRAFT ARTILLERY (AA) or COAST ARTILLERY CORPS (CAC)

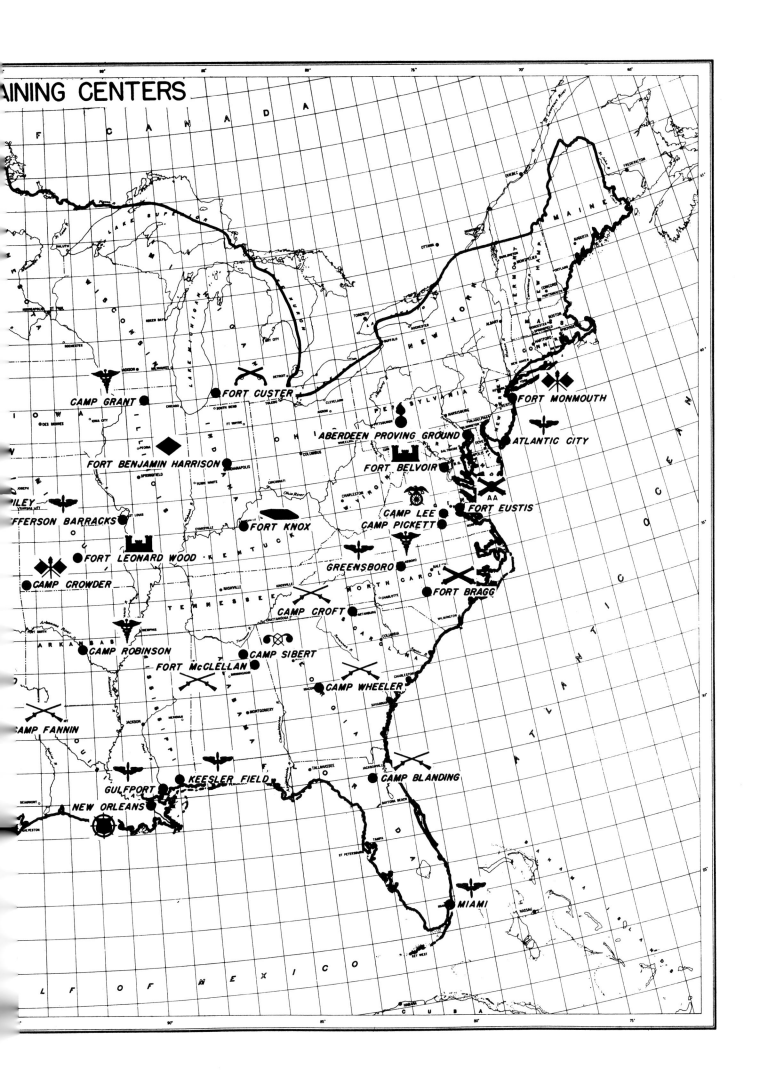

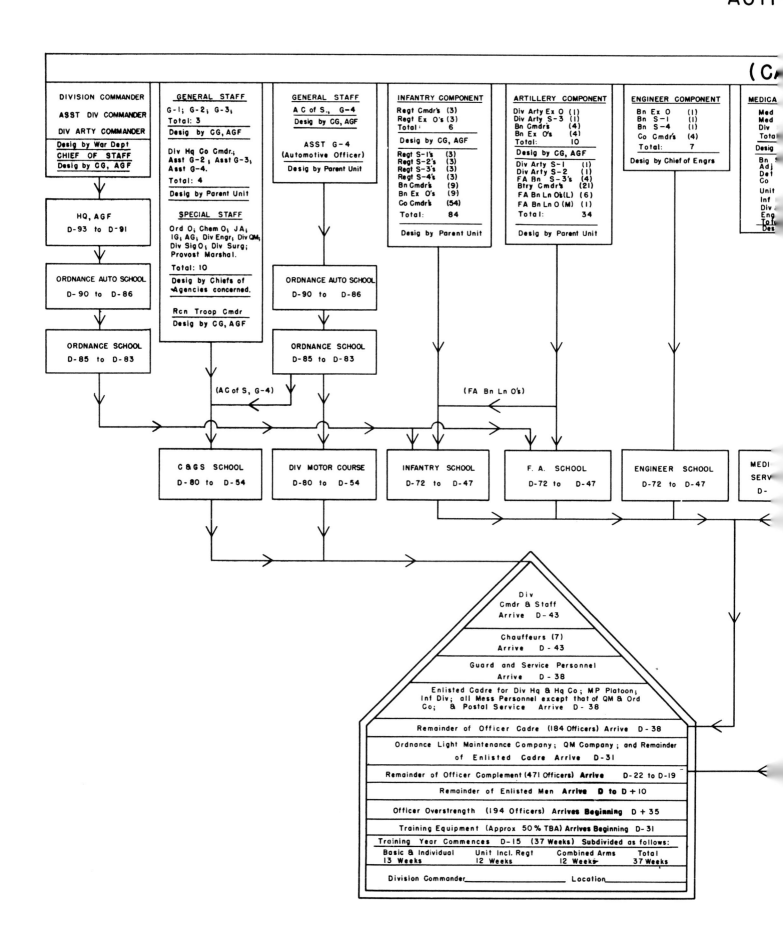

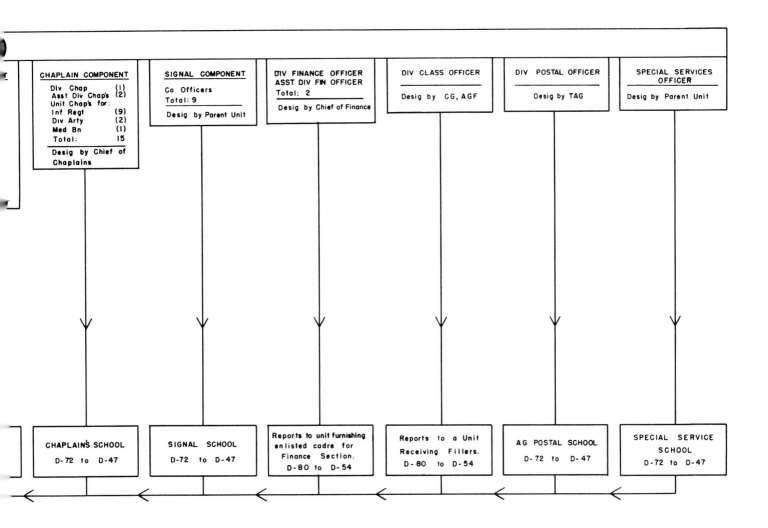

CHAPLAIN COMPONENT

Div Chap	(1)
Asst Div Chap's	(2)
Unit Chap's for:	
Inf Regt	(9)
Div Arty	(2)
Med Bn	(1)
Total:	15

Desig by Chief of Chaplains

SIGNAL COMPONENT

Co Officers
Total: 9

Desig by Parent Unit

DIV FINANCE OFFICER
ASST DIV FIN OFFICER
Total: 2

Desig by Chief of Finance

DIV CLASS OFFICER

Desig by CG, AGF

DIV POSTAL OFFICER

Desig by TAG

SPECIAL SERVICES OFFICER

Desig by Parent Unit

CHAPLAINS SCHOOL
D-72 to D-47

SIGNAL SCHOOL
D-72 to D-47

Reports to unit furnishing enlisted cadre for Finance Section.
D-80 to D-54

Reports to a Unit Receiving Fillers.
D-80 to D-54

AG POSTAL SCHOOL
D-72 to D-47

SPECIAL SERVICE SCHOOL
D-72 to D-47

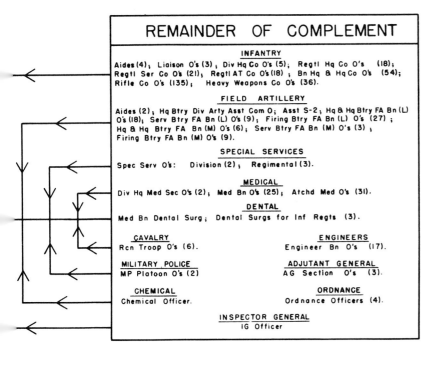

REMAINDER OF COMPLEMENT

INFANTRY

Aides (4); Liaison O's (3); Div Hq Co O's (5); Regtl Hq Co O's (18); Regtl Ser Co O's (21); Regtl AT Co O's (18); Bn Hq & Hq Co O's (54); Rifle Co O's (135); Heavy Weapons Co O's (36).

FIELD ARTILLERY

Aides (2); Hq Btry Div Arty Asst Com O; Asst S-2; Hq & Hq Btry FA Bn (L) O's (18); Serv Btry FA Bn (L) O's (9); Firing Btry FA Bn (L) O's (27); Hq & Hq Btry FA Bn (M) O's (6); Serv Btry FA Bn (M) O's (3); Firing Btry FA Bn (M) O's (9).

SPECIAL SERVICES

Spec Serv O's: Division (2); Regimental (3).

MEDICAL

Div Hq Med Sec O's (2); Med Bn O's (25); Atchd Med O's (31).

DENTAL

Med Bn Dental Surg; Dental Surgs for Inf Regts (3).

CAVALRY
Rcn Troop O's (6).

ENGINEERS
Engineer Bn O's (17).

MILITARY POLICE
MP Platoon O's (2)

ADJUTANT GENERAL
AG Section O's (3).

CHEMICAL
Chemical Officer.

ORDNANCE
Ordnance Officers (4).

INSPECTOR GENERAL
IG Officer

TRAINING A COMBAT GROUP
(HEAVY BOMBARDMENT)

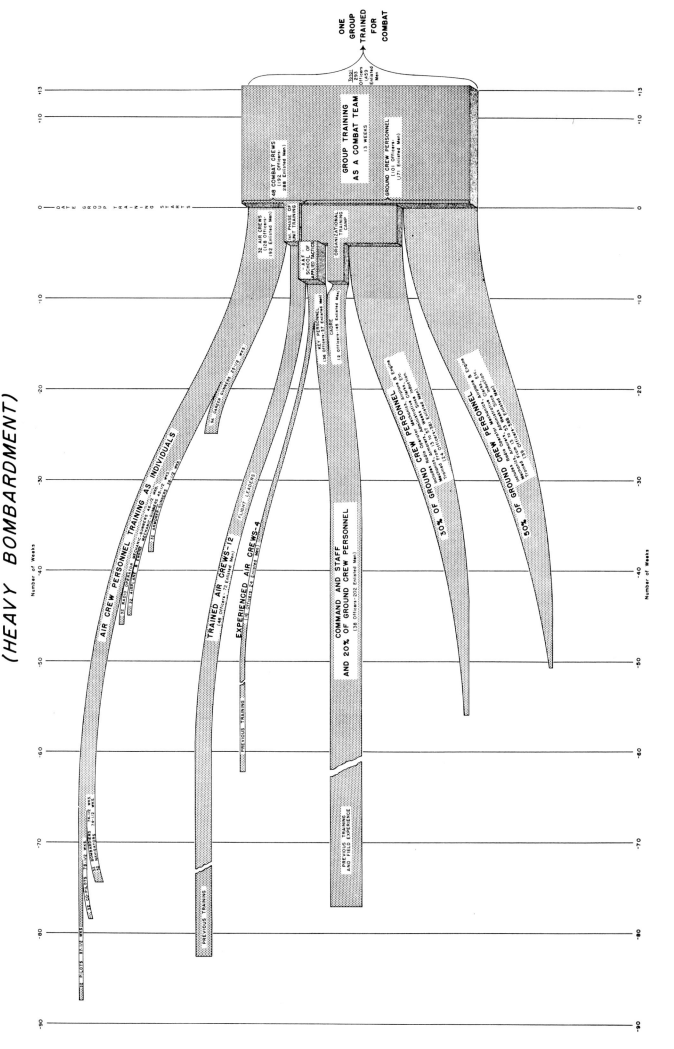

ONE GROUP TRAINED FOR COMBAT

Total 293 Officers 1,459 Enlisted Men

48 COMBAT CREWS (192 Officers 288 Enlisted Men)

GROUP TRAINING AS A COMBAT TEAM
13 WEEKS

GROUND CREW PERSONNEL (101 Officers 1,171 Enlisted Men)

Number of Weeks

AIR CREW PERSONNEL TRAINING AS INDIVIDUALS

TRAINED AIR CREWS—12

EXPERIENCED AIR CREWS—4

COMMAND AND STAFF AND 20% OF GROUND CREW PERSONNEL (38 Officers 202 Enlisted Men)

30% OF GROUND CREW PERSONNEL

50% OF GROUND CREW PERSONNEL

PREVIOUS TRAINING

PREVIOUS TRAINING AND FIELD EXPERIENCE

from the Air Corps technical training schools. During the succeeding 21 months over 503,000 men completed prescribed courses which, incidentally, had increased from 30 to 90 specialties. The total number of graduates for the period covered by this report approximates 625,000.

The welding together of the ground and air components into a coordinated team is accomplished in the operational training units which function under the four Air Forces located in the United States. During this period a bomber group, for instance, is developed into a coordinated team and then moves as a unit to combat theaters. In addition, the four Air Forces furnish operational training to replacement crews, both ground and air, which are then sent to combat theaters to replace the attrition inevitable in the aerial warfare of today.

In addition, the Army Air Forces have established a sort of postgraduate system of training in the School of Applied Tactics at Orlando, Fla. At this school officers and enlisted men participate in specialized training in all branches of air defense, bombardment, air support, and air service. In addition, the school conducts operational research, develops and tests tactical aircraft and equipment in field operations, and actually engages in every phase of aerial warfare under conditions simulating reality. Selected members of tactical groups undergo a period of training here before their unit training. As part of its component the School of Applied Tactics possesses a model task force complete with fighter, bomber, air support, and air service commands with all their respective elements, equipment, and problems.

Following completion of operational training in the United States, units are then dispatched overseas—multiengine types, flying as units wherever practicable. In the theater a further period of operational training is required to prepare the units for the particular type of targets and operating conditions which will be encountered in that parlicular theater. For instance, the problems of a fighter group in the Solomons are entirely different from those operating out of the United Kingdom. Similarly a different situation exists in the units operating in Burma, India, and China.

Biennial Report

OF THE

CHIEF OF STAFF

OF THE

UNITED STATES ARMY

July 1, 1943, to June 30, 1945

TO THE

SECRETARY OF WAR

Dear Mr. Secretary:

For the first time since assuming this office six years ago, it is possible for me to report that the security of the United States of America is entirely in our own hands. Since my last formal report to you on the state of the Army, our forces in Europe; air and ground, have contributed mightily to the complete destruction of the Axis enemy. In the Pacific, Japan has been compelled to sue for an end to the war which she treacherously started. For two years the victorious advance of the United States sea, air and land forces, together with those of our allies was virtually unchecked. They controlled the skies and the seas and no army could successfully oppose them. Behind these forces was the output of American farms and factories, exceeding any similar effort of man, so that the peoples everywhere with whom we were joined in the fight for decency and justice were able to reinforce their efforts through the aid of American ships, munitions and supplies.

Never was the strength of the American democracy so evident nor has it ever been so clearly within our power to give definite guidance for our course into the future of the human race. And never, it seems to me, has it been so imperative that we give thorough and practical consideration to the development of a means to provide a reasonable guarantee for future generations against the horrors and colossal waste of war as well as security for that freedom we recently left to the hazard of mere hope or chance.

The Nation is just emerging from one of its gravest crises. This generation of Americans can still remember the black days of 1942 when the Japanese conquered all of Malaysia, occupied Burma, and threatened India while the German armies approached the Volga and the Suez. In those hours Germany and Japan came so close to complete domination of the world that we do not yet realize how thin the thread of Allied survival had been stretched.

In good conscience this Nation can take little credit for its part in staving off disaster in those critical days. It is certain that the refusal of the British and Russian peoples to accept what appeared to be inevitable defeat was the great factor in the salvage of our civilization. Of almost equal importance was the failure of the enemy to make the most of the situation. In order to establish for the historical record where and how Germany and Japan failed I asked General Eisenhower to have his intelligence officers promptly interrogate the ranking members of the German High Command who are now our prisoners of war. The results of these interviews are of remarkable interest. They give a picture of dissension among the enemy nations and lack of long-range planning that may well have been decisive factors of this world struggle at its most critical moments.

As evaluated by the War Department General Staff, the interrogations of the captured German commanders disclose the following:

The available evidence shows that Hitler's original intent was to create, by absorption of Germanic peoples in the areas contiguous to Germany and by the strengthening of her new frontiers, a greater Reich which would dominate Europe. To this end Hitler pursued a policy of opportunism which achieved the occupation of the Rhineland, Austria, and Czechoslovakia without military opposition.

No evidence has yet been found that the German High Command had any over-all strategic plan. Although the High Command approved Hitler's policies in principle, his impetuous strategy outran German military capabilities and ultimately led to Germany's defeat. The history of the German High Command from 1938 on is one of constant conflict of personalities in which military judgment was increasingly subordinated to Hitler's personal dictates. The first clash occurred in 1938 and resulted in the removal of von Blomberg, von Fritsch, and Beck and of the last effective conservative influence on German foreign policy.

The campaigns in Poland, Norway, France, and the Low Countries developed serious diversions between Hitler and the General Staff as to the details of execution of strategic plans. In each case the General Staff favored the orthodox offensive, Hitler an unorthodox attack with objectives deep in enemy territory. In each case Hitler's views prevailed and the astounding success of each succeeding campaign raised Hitler's military prestige to the point where his opinions were no longer challenged. His military self-confidence became unassailable after the victory in France, and he began to disparage substantially the ideas of his generals even in the presence of junior officers. Thus no General Staff objection was expressed when Hitler made the fatal decision to invade Soviet Russia.

When Italy entered the war Mussolini's strategic aims contemplated the expansion of his empire under the cloak of German military success. Field Marshal Keitel reveals that Italy's declaration of war was contrary to her agreement with Germany. Both Keitel and Jodl agree that it was undesired. From the very beginning Italy was a burden on the German war potential. Dependent upon Germany and German-occupied territories for oil and coal, Italy was a constant source of economic attrition. Mussolini's unilateral action in attacking Greece and Egypt forced the Germans into the Balkan and African campaigns, resulting in over-extension of the German armies which subsequently became one of the principal factors in Germany's defeat.

Nor is there evidence of close strategic coordination between Germany and Japan. The German General Staff recognized that Japan was bound by the neutrality pact with Russia but hoped that the Japanese would tie down strong British and American land, sea, and air forces in the Far East.

In the absence of any evidence so far to the contrary, it is believed that Japan also acted unilaterally and not in accordance with a unified strategic plan.

Here were three criminal nations eager for loot and seeking greedily to advance their own self-interest by war, yet unable to agree on a strategic over-all plan for acccomplishing a common objective.

The steps in the German defeat, as described by captured members of the High Command, were:

1. *Failure to invade England.* Hitler's first military set-back occurred when, after the collapse of France, England did not capitulate. According to Colonel General Jodl, Chief of the Operations Staff of the German High Command, the campaign in France had been undertaken because it was estimated that with the fall of France, England would not continue to fight. The unexpectedly swift victory over France and Great Britain's continuation of the war found the General Staff unprepared for an invasion of England. Although the armistice with France was concluded on 22 June 1940, no orders to prepare for the invasion of Britain were issued prior to 2 July. Field Marshal Kesselring stated that he urged the invasion since it generally was believed in Germany that England was in a critical condition. Field Marshal Keitel, Chief of Staff of German Armed Forces, however, stated that the risk was thought to be the existence of the British fleet. He said the army was ready but the air force was limited by weather, the navy very dubious. Meanwhile, in the air blitz over England the German Air Force had suffered irreparable losses from which its bombardment arm never recovered.

2. *The Campaign of 1941 in the Soviet Union.* In the Autumn of 1941 after the battle of Vysma, the Germans stood exhausted but apparently victorious before Moscow. According to Jodl, the General Staff of the armed forces considered that one last energetic push would be sufficient to finish the Soviets. The German High Command had neither envisioned nor planned for a winter campaign. A sudden change in the weather brought disaster. The Red Army defense, a terrific snow storm, and extremely unseasonable cold in the Christmas week of 1941 precipitated the strategic defeat of the German armed forces. Impatient of all restraint, Hitler publicly announced that he had more faith in his own intuition than in the judgment of his military advisors. He relieved the commander in chief of the army, General von Brauschitsch. It was the turning point of the war.

3. *Stalingrad.* Even after the reverse before Moscow in 1941, Germany might have avoided defeat had it not been for the campaign in 1942 which culminated in the disaster at Stalingrad. Disregarding the military lessons of history, Hitler, instead of attacking the Soviet armies massed in the north, personally planned and directed a campaign of which the immediate objectives were to deprive the Soviet Union of her vital industries and raw materials by cutting the Volga at Stalingrad and seizing the Caucasian oil fields. Beyond these concrete objectives was evidently the Napoleonic dream of a conquest of the Middle East and India by a gigantic double envelopment with one pincer descending from the Caucasus through Tiflis and the other from North Africa across Egypt, Palestine, and the Arabian desert. The campaign collapsed before Stalingrad with the magnificent Russian defense of that city and in the northern foothills of the Caucasus, where a break-down of German transport to the front left the German armor stalled for 3 weeks for lack of fuel in the critical summer months of 1942. Field Marshal Keitel in reviewing this campaign remarks that Germany failed completely to estimate properly the reserve of Russian industrial and productive power east of the Urals. The statement of both Keitel and Jodl is that neither was in favor of the Stalingrad campaign, but that the recommendations of the High Command were overruled by Adolf Hitler.

4. *Invasion of North Africa.* Allied landings in North Africa came as a surprise to the German High Command. Field Marshal Kesselring, who, at the time, was commanding all German forces in the Mediterranean except Rommel's desert task force, states that his headquarters did expect a landing and had requested reinforcement by a division. However, Kesselring's fears were not heeded by Hitler and Goering. Allied security and deception measures for the landing operations were found to have been highly effective. Only when the Allied fleets and convoys were streaming through the Straits of Gibraltar did the Germans realize that something very special was under way, and even then false conclusions were drawn: either that the Allies intended to land in rear of Rommel in the Middle East, or that these were British reinforcements en route to the Far East, or supplies for starving Malta. Since no advance preparations had been made by the Germans to repel such an Allied invasion of North Africa, all subsequent efforts to counter the Allies suffered from hasty improvisation. Defense continued, however, because, as Field Marshal Keitel now states, since evacuation was impossible, the Germans had only the choice of resisting or surrendering.

5. *The Invasion of France.* All German headquarters expected the Allied invasion of France. According to Colonel General Jodl, both the general direction and the strength of the initial assault in Normandy were correctly estimated; but Field Marshal Keitel states that the Germans were not sure exactly where the Allies would strike and considered Brittany as more probable because of the three major U-boat bases located in that region. Both agree that the belief of the German High Command that a second assault would be launched, probably by an Army under General Patton, held large German forces in the Pas de Calais area. Both Keitel and Jodl believed that the invasion could be repulsed or at worst contained, and

both named the Allied air arm as the decisive factor in the German failure.

Prior to the invasion, important divergencies of opinion developed between Field Marshal von Rundstedt, Commander in Chief West, and Rommel, commander of the threatened Army Group. Rundstedt desired to hold his armored forces in a group around Paris and in Eastern France; Rommel to push them forward to positions in readiness close to the coast. The Rommel view prevailed. Von Rundstedt was subsequently relieved by Colonel General Von Kluge.

Soon after the Allied capture of Cherbourg, dissension again broke out in the High Command. Von Kluge and Rommel wished to evacuate all Southwestern France, blocking or destroying its usable ports. They believed that a continuation of the fight in Normandy could only end with the destruction of their Western Armies and that they should withdraw before disintegration began. Von Kluge recommended defense on the general line: lower Seine–Paris–Fontainebleau–Massif Central. Hitler refused to accept this recommendation, relieved Kluge from command, and reappointed von Rundstedt as Commander in Chief West. Under direct instructions, Rundstedt continued the battle of Normandy to its final denouement. Hitler himself ordered the Avranches-Mortain counterattack and was much surprised when it completely failed. Keitel expresses further surprise at the audacious exploitation of the American break-through at Avranches during this counterattack, and particularly of the thrust towards Brest.

6. *The Ardennes Counterattack.* The German offensive in December 1944 was Hitler's personal conception. According to Jodl, the objective of the attack was Antwerp. It was hoped that overcast weather would neutralize Allied air superiority, and that an exceptionally rapid initial break-through could be achieved. Other German officers believe that this operation was reckless in the extreme, in that it irreparably damaged the comparatively fresh armored divisions of the Sixth Panzer Army, the principal element of Germany's strategic reserve, at a moment when every available reserve was needed to repulse the expected Soviet attack in the East.

7. *The Crossing of the Rhine.* Even after the failure of the German counteroffensive in the Ardennes, the Germans believed that the Rhine line could be held. The loss of the Remagen bridge, however, exploded this hope. The entire Rhine defensive line had to be weakened in the attempt to contain the bridgehead, and the disorderly German retreat in the Saar and Palatinate rendered easy the subsequent drive eastward of the Allied Armies towards Hamburg, Leipzig, and Munich.

Not only were the European partners of the Axis unable to coordinate their plans and resources and agree within their own nations how best to proceed, but the eastern partner, Japan, was working in even greater discord. The Axis, as a matter of fact, existed on paper only. Eager to capitalize on the preoccupation of the western powers in Europe, Japan was so greedy for her own immediate conquests that she laid her strategy, not to help Germany defeat Russia and Great Britain, but to accumulate her own profit. Had the way been open Germany and Japan would have undoubtedly joined their armies in Central Asia, but to Japan this objective was secondary to looting the Far East while there was no real force to stop her. The War Department General Staff's analysis of Japanese objectives follows:

The Japanese, for many years, bolstered by a fanatical belief in divine guidance and their own spiritual and military supremacy, had planned the domination of the Far East and eventually the world. Japan in her inland empire was not self-sufficient. She required broader land areas and access to oil, rubber, and other raw materials if she were to become a major industrial world power. This principle of expansion was outlined in the "Tanaka Memorial" purportedly a secret memorandum prepared for Hirohito by the Jap Premier in 1927. Authentic or not, it provided the pattern which Japan has followed, culminating in the great Pacific conflict.

Strategically, Japan was well poised in 1941 to carry out her aims in Asia. All the major world powers who normally maintained the status quo in Asia were absorbed in the war in Europe. France had been overrun and eliminated. England was threatened by German invasion. The U. S. S. R. was attempting to repel a German invasion on her Western front reaching to the gates of the capital. The United States had become the Arsenal of Democracy, with major efforts directed toward the support and preservation of our European Allies.

The Tripartite Pact had been signed, giving Japan a free hand in Asia. She had a large and relatively well-equipped army and a moderately good air force well trained by actual combat in China. She had obtained by forced agreement a staging area in French Indo-China. She had a fairly large navy especially strong in the transport craft available. She had accumulated by great national economy a good stockpile of strategic matériels at home for the initial effort and with each successive conquest she obtained new and important areas from which other supplies of materials could be drawn, such as oil, rubber, and metal. The Japanese mistakenly believed in the hearty cooperation of "liberated" peoples of the so-called Greater East Asia Co-Prosperity Sphere with their huge labor pools. Japan considered herself ready to strike.

Japan's objective was the conquest, consolidation, and eventual domination of the whole Far East. She intended to make her conquest in a rapid surprise drive which would overpower all resistance, to form an iron ring of outer defenses against which the spiritually inferior, pacifistic combination of opponents could beat themselves into weariness, while she consolidated her gains at leisure.

The best estimate of Japan's plan for the accomplishment of her objectives appears to be the following:

1. Neutralize or destroy the U. S. Pacific Fleet by an attack on Pearl Harbor.

2. Drive rapidly south overcoming the Philippines and the Southwest and South Pacific Islands in order to cut sea routes of supply or attack from the East and gain the vast natural resources of the East Indies.

3. Cut China's supply line from the west by an invasion of Burma.

4. Form a flank by the seizure of the naval base of Singapore and the islands of Sumatra and Java.

5. Isolate or possibly invade Australia.

6. Invade the Hawaiian Islands via Midway.

7. Invade the Aleutian Islands to form a northern flank, dependent on initial successes and retained momentum.

8. Bring the American Northwest under aerial bombardment, raid our West Coast aviation industries, and then seize critical areas.

9. Stimulate unrest to eventual revolution in India.

The Japanese strategic plan initially failed when she missed the opportunity of landing troops on Hawaii, capturing Oahu and the important bases there, and denying us a necessary focal point from which to launch operations in the Western Pacific.

There can be no doubt that the greed and the mistakes of the war-making nations as well as the heroic stands of the British and Soviet peoples saved the United States a war on her own soil. The crisis had come and passed at Stalingrad and El Alamein before this Nation was able to gather sufficient resources to participate in the fight in a determining manner. Had the U. S. S. R. and the British Army of the Nile been defeated in 1942, as they well might if the Germans, Japanese, and Italians had better coordinated their plans and resources and successive operations, we should have stood today in the western hemisphere confronted by enemies who controlled a greater part of the world.

Our close approach to that terrifying situation should have a sobering influence on Americans for generations to come. Yet, this is only a prelude of what can be expected so long as there are nations on earth capable of waging total war.

On 6 August the entire world learned from President Truman's announcement that man had entered into a new era—that atomic power had been harnessed.

This discovery of American scientists can be man's greatest benefit. And it can destroy him. It is against the latter terrible possibility that this nation must prepare or perish. Atomic power will affect the peaceful life of every individual on earth. And it will at the same time affect every instrument and technique of destruction. But the atomic bomb is not alone among the scientific advances that make the possibilities of the future so terrifying. The development of aircraft and rockets and electronics has become equally incredible. In order to prevent any possible misconception of the terrible potentialities of the future, I asked the Commanding General of the Army Air Forces to prepare an estimate of the capabilities of other modern weapons. His report is confined to the certainties but, as is obvious from the atomic bomb, the developments of the war have been so incredible that wildest imagination will not project us far from the target in estimating the future. Much of the infor-

mation has until now properly been classified highly secret in our development research laboratories, at our testing establishments, or in the combat units. However, it is now so important that the people of the United States realize the possibilities of the future, that I here quote from General Arnold's report:

At the start of this war we had bombers capable of 200 miles per hour with a combat radius of 900 miles, effective operational ceilings of 24,000 feet, and bomb load capacity of 6,000 pounds. Today our development of this type aircraft has given us bombers capable of carrying 20,000 pounds of bombs to targets 1,600 miles away at speeds of 350 miles an hour and altitudes of over 35,000 feet. Radar has improved our bombing technique so that we can now attack a target effectively even though it be obscured by weather or darkness. We will produce within the next few years jet-propelled bombers capable of flying 500 to 600 miles an hour to targets 1,500 miles away at altitudes of over 40,000 feet. Development of even greater bombers capable of operating at stratospheric altitudes and speeds faster than sound and carrying bomb loads of more than 100,000 pounds already is a certainty. These aircraft will have sufficient range to attack any spot on the earth and return to a friendly base.

In 1941 our propeller-driven fighters were limited to speeds of 3oo miles an hour, a range 200 to 300 miles, and effective ceilings of 20,000 feet. Today our conventional fighters have speeds of 5oo miles an hour, combat ranges of 1,300 miles, and effective ceilings of 35,000 feet. Improvement of our jet fighters may well produce within the next five years an aircraft capable of the speed of sound and of reaching targets 2,000 miles away at altitudes of above 50,000 feet. When the barrier of compressability has been hurdled, as it surely will be, there is no practicable limit to the speed of piloted aircraft.

At the onset of this war demolition bombs ranged in size from 20 to 2,000 pounds with a few light case 4,000 pound blast bombs. The explosive filling of these bombs was standard TNT. During the war, new bombs have been developed the entire range from small 4-pound antipersonnel missiles to 22,000 pound deep penetration city smashers. At this very moment we are making a single bomb weighing 45,000 pounds to keep pace with the bomber, already under construction, which will carry such a load. Air ordnance engineers have blueprinted a bomb weighing 100,000 pounds.

When World War II began we had no rockets. So far the most spectacular rocket of the war has been the V–2. This weapon has extended artillery range to 200 miles with little sacrifice in accuracy. Defense against such weapons requires piloted and pilotless aircraft capable of fantastic speeds, or powered missiles capable of finding, intercepting, and destroying the attacker in the air and at his launching sites or by methods and devices as yet undeveloped. We can direct rockets to targets by electronic devices and new instruments which guide them accurately to sources of heat, light, and magnetism. Drawn by their own fuses such new rockets will streak unerringly to the heart of big factories, attracted by the heat of the furnaces. They are so sensitive that in the space of a large room they aim themselves toward a man who enters, in reaction to the heat of his body.

All of these weapons and their possible combinations make the air approaches of a country the points of extreme danger. Many Americans do not yet understand the full implication of the formless rubble of Berlin and of the cities of Japan. With the continued development of weapons and techniques now known to us, the cities of New York, Pittsburgh, Detroit, Chicago, or San Francisco may be subject to annihilation from other continents in a matter of hours.

The Navy, now the strongest in the world, will protect our shores against attack from any amphibious enemy who might challenge through the sea approaches, but we must also now be prepared to oppose stratospheric envelopment with the techniques and weapons discussed above. It is clear that the only defense against this kind of warfare is the ability to attack. We must secure our Nation by ourselves developing and maintaining these weapons, troops, and techniques required to warn aggressors and deter them from launching a modern devastating war against us.

With the realization of these facts will also come a highly dangerous and attractive doctrine. It will be said that to protect itself this nation need only rely on its machine power, that it will not need manpower.

This doctrine will be closely akin to the doctrine of negative defense which destroyed France. The folly of the Maginot line was proved early in the war but too late to save France. The folly of the new doctrine which has already begun to take shape in the thinking of many Americans would also be proved early—but probably too late to save America.

The only effective defense a nation can now maintain is the power of attack. And that power cannot be in machinery alone. There must be men to man the machines. And there must be men to come to close grips with the enemy and tear his operating bases and his productive establishment away from him before the war can end.

The classic proof of this came in the battle of Britain. Even with the magnificent fighter defense of the Royal Air Force, even with the incredible efficiency of the fire of thousands of antiaircraft guns, controlled and aimed by unerring electronic instruments, the British Islands remained under the fire of the German enemy until the final stages of the war.

Not until the American and British armies crossed the channel and seized control of the enemy's territory was the hail of rockets lifted from England. Not until we had physical possession of the launching sites and the factories that produced the V weapons did these attacks cease.

Such is the pattern of war in the 20th Century. If this nation is ever again at war, suffering, as Britain did in this war, the disastrous attacks of rocket-propelled weapons with explosive power like our own atomic bomb, it will bleed and suffer perhaps to the point of annihilation, unless we can move armies of men into the enemy's bases of operations and seize the sites from which he launches his attacks.

There is no easy way to win wars when two opponents are even remotely well matched. There is no easy way to safeguard the nation or preserve the peace. In the immediate years ahead the United Nations will unquestionably devote their sincere energies to the effort to establish a lasting peace. To my mind there is now greater chance of success in this

effort than ever before in history. Certainly the implications of atomic explosion will spur men of judgment as they have never before been pressed to seek a method whereby the peoples of earth can live in peace and justice.

However, these hopes are by no means certainties. If man does find the solution for world peace it will be the most revolutionary reversal of his record we have ever known. Our own responsibilities to these efforts are great. Our diplomacy must be wise and it must be strong. Nature tends to abhor weakness. The principle of the survival of the fit is generally recognized. If our diplomacy is not backed by a sound security policy, it is, in my opinion, forecast to failure. We have tried since the birth of our nation to promote our love of peace by a display of weakness. This course has failed us utterly, cost us millions of lives and billions of treasure. The reasons are quite understandable. The world does not seriously regard the desires of the weak. Weakness presents too great a temptation to the strong, particularly to the bully who schemes for wealth and power.

We must, if we are to realize the hopes we may now dare have for lasting peace, enforce our will for peace with strength. We must make it clear to the potential gangsters of the world that if they dare break our peace they will do so at their great peril.

This Nation's destiny clearly lies in a sound permanent security policy. In the War Department's proposals there are two essentials: (1) Intense scientific research and development; (2) a permanent peacetime citizen army. I will discuss these essentials in detail later in this report. The importance of scientific research is the most obvious to the civilian, but the importance of a peacetime citizen army based on universal military training is of greater importance, in my opinion.

Nothing will contribute more to an understanding of the needs of future security than a clear understanding of what has occurred in this war, the strategic decisions, the reasons for them, and the operations by which they were executed. The press and radio have given the American people a thorough day-by-day account of the progress of the war within the limitations of necessary security; never before have the details of military campaigns been so quickly, so accurately, and so completely reported. Yet because of the very bulk of the information plus the blank spots of essential secrecy it has been difficult for the public to place the developments in their proper perspective. It now becomes possible to examine them in retrospect with an emphasis more nearly approaching that which history is likely to give them.

VICTORY IN EUROPE

The Strategic Concept

The period covered by my first two Biennial Reports was a time of great danger for the United States. The element on which the security of this nation most depended was time—time to organize our tremendous resources and time to deploy them overseas in a worldwide war. We were given this time through the heroic refusal of the Soviet and British peoples to collapse under the smashing blows of the Axis forces. They bought this time for us with the currency of blood and courage. Two years ago our margin of safety was still precarious but the moment was rapidly approaching when we would be prepared to deal with our enemies on the only terms they understood—overwhelming power.

In no other period of American history have the colors of the United States been carried victoriously on so many battlefields. It is with profound satisfaction and great pride in the troops and their leaders that this report is submitted on the campaigns which crushed Italy, Germany and Japan.

It is necessary to an understanding of the Army's participation in these campaigns that reference be made to the decisions which launched them. The forces of the United States and Great Britain were deployed under a single strategic control exercised by the group known as the Combined Chiefs of Staff. As described in a previous report, this structure of Allied control was conceived at the conference of December 1941, when Prime Minister Churchill, accompanied by the chiefs of the British Navy, Army, and Air Forces, came to Washington and met with the President and the American Chiefs of Staff. It was the most complete unification of military effort ever achieved by two Allied nations. Strategic direction of all the forces of both nations, the allocation of manpower and munitions, the coordination of communications, the control of military intelligence, and the administration of captured areas all were accepted as joint responsibilities.

The President and the Prime Minister, with the advice of the Combined Chiefs of Staff, made the decision at this first conference that our resources would be concentrated first to defeat Germany, the greater and closer enemy, and then Japan.

In April 1942, President Roosevelt directed me to proceed to London, accompanied by Mr. Harry Hopkins, for a conference with the Prime Minister, the War Cabinet, and the British Chiefs of Staff, regarding the tentative plan for the invasion of the continent in a cross-Channel operation. There a general agreement was reached that the final blow must be delivered across the English Channel and eastward through the plains of western Europe. At that time the Red Army was slowly falling back under the full fury of the German assault, and it was accepted at the London Conference that everything practicable must be done to reduce the pressure on the Soviet lest she collapse and the door be opened wide for a complete conquest of Europe and a probable juncture with the Japanese in the Indian Ocean.

In the discussions at this conference, a tentative target date for the cross-Channel operations, designated by the code name ROUNDUP, was set for the summer of 1943. However, the immediate necessity for an emergency plan was recognized. It was given the code name SLEDGEHAMMER and was to provide for a diversionary assault on the French coast at a much earlier date if such a desperate measure became necessary to lend a hand toward saving the situation on the Soviet front.

Here the Western Allies faced a shortage which was to plague us to the final day of the war in Europe—the shortage of assault craft, LST's, LCI's, and smaller vessels. At least six divisions would be required for a diversionary action in order to be of any assistance to the Red Army, and all the resources of England and the United States were searched for vessels or barges that could be employed in the Channel. Outboard motors and marine engines in pleasure craft in the United States were appropriated for this purpose. An extensive building program for landing craft was agreed upon, which necessitated a heavy cut-back or delay in the construction then underway of certain major combat ships for the Pacific Fleet. Also there were added to the production program in the United States a great many items which would be required for build-up—engineering and railroad equipment and rolling stock, pipelines, hospital set-ups, communication matériel, and a multitude of items to be required for airfields, camps, docks, and depots in the British Isles for the actual Channel crossing and for the support of our troops once they were in France.

In June, the Prime Minister and General Sir Alan F. Brooke, Chief of the Imperial General Staff, returned to Washington for a further discussion of SLEDGEHAMMER and ROUNDUP, and a possible operation in the Mediterranean. During these discussions, the Allied situation in North Africa took a more serious turn, culminating in the loss of Tobruk. The discussions thereafter were devoted almost exclusively to the measures to be taken to meet the threat facing Cairo, Rommel's forces having been checked with difficulty on the El Alamein line. Further advances by his Afrika Korps, with its Italian reinforcements, and German successes along the southeastern portion of the Soviet front threatened a complete collapse in the Middle East, the loss of the Suez Canal and the vital oil supply in the vicinity of Abadan. It was a very black hour.

In July, Admiral King and I went to London for further meetings with the British Chiefs of Staff, to determine if there were not something that could be done immediately to lessen the pressure on the Soviet, whose armies were facing a crisis. Poverty of equipment, especially in landing craft, and the short period remaining when the weather would permit cross-Channel movement of small craft, ruled out the diversionary operation SLEDGEHAMMER for 1942.

After prolonged discussions, it became evident that the only operation that could be undertaken with a fair prospect of success that year was TORCH, the assault on North Africa. Landings there would be a long way from Germany, but should serve to divert at least some German pressure from the Red Army, and would materially improve the critical situation in the Middle East. It was therefore decided, with the approval of the President and the Prime Minister, to mount the North African assault at the earliest possible moment, accepting the fact that this would mean not only the abandonment of the possibility for any operation in Western Europe that year, but that the necessary build-up for the cross-Channel assault could not be completed in 1943. TORCH would bleed most of our resources in the Atlantic, and would confine us in the Pacific to the holding of the Hawaii-Midway line and the preservation of communications to Australia.

General Eisenhower, who was then established with his headquarters in London, directing the planning and assembling of American resources, was, with the generous acceptance of the British Government, appointed Commander in Chief of the British and American Forces which were to carry out the landings in North Africa. On 13 August he received the formal directive to proceed with the operation. The target date was fixed for early November.

We have since learned that the German plan at that time was to attempt the defeat of Britain by aerial bombardment and by destruction of her army and resources in the Middle East. Colonel General Jodl, Chief of the German Armed Forces Operations Staff, has disclosed that it was Hitler's plan to break through Stalingrad and Egypt, and join these two salients in the Middle East.

The heroic defense of Stalingrad and General Montgomery's crushing defeat of Rommel at El Alamein dislocated these gigantic pincers. The further development of the operations in North Africa from the east and the west, and the Soviet offensive from the Volga proved to be the turning points at which the Axis was forced on the strategic defensive.

In January 1943, the President and the Prime Minister, with the Combined Chiefs of Staff, met at Casablanca. It was then apparent that our North African operation was to be successful, even beyond original calculations. Tunisia was a lure into which the German command continued to pour great quantities of men and matériel, commitments that were certain to be disastrous for the enemy once the winter rains ceased and the low clouds over the Sicilian Strait cleared, in the face of overwhelming Allied superiority on the sea and in the air. At the conclusion of the North African campaign, enemy killed and captured numbered 349,206 Italian and German troops, and there had been captured or destroyed on land alone nearly 200,000 tons of enemy matériel.

The problem before the Chiefs of Staff at Casablanca was the next movement to be made following the completion of the Tunisian campaign. It still would have been preferable to close immediately with the German enemy in Western Europe or even in Southern France had that been possible of achievement with the resources then available to General Eisenhower. It was not.

Axis control of the Mediterranean islands and the entire reach of the southern coast of Europe from Franco's Spain to Turkey denied our communications also across the Mediterranean and forced our shipping into a 12,000-mile detour around the Cape of Good Hope. The United States was still involved in the process of a vast mobilization. The Chiefs of Staff therefore considered whether we had the strength to move directly to Italy or what might be the best intermediary steps. It was decided to assault Sicily (operation HUSKY) and, with the approval of the Heads of State, General Eisenhower was advised on 23 January:

> The Combined Chiefs of Staff have resolved that an attack against Sicily will be launched in 1943 with the target date as the period of the favorable July moon.

Even though a full-scale Mediterranean campaign now was imminent, it was resolved at Casablanca to resume amassing in the United Kingdom as quickly as possible the forces necessary to invade Western Europe. This build-up was to be one of the most tremendous logistical undertakings in military history.

It required provision for the transportation, shelter, hospitalization, supply, training, and general welfare of 1,200,000 men who had to be embarked in the United States and transported across the submarine infested Atlantic to the United Kingdom. The hospital plan alone, for example, called for 94,000 beds in existing installations, conversions, and new construction. The program was later increased by tent accommodations for 30,000 more beds. Living quarters had to be furnished for the assault forces and their supply troops. There had to be provision for 20,000,000 square feet of covering, storage, and shop space, and 44,000,000 square feet of open storage and hard standings. Parks for 50,000 military vehicles were planned; 270 miles of railroad had to be constructed. More than 20,000 railroad cars and 1,000 locomotives were to be shipped to the United Kingdom. The Air Forces required 163 fields, seven centers for combat crews and replacements, accommodations for 450,000 men, and 8,500,000 square feet of storage and shop space.

Two-thirds of the vast program of air installation required new construction by British and United States engineers. At the same time the invasion operations required detailed planning for the installations we would have to build once ashore in France—hospitals, depots, shops, railroads, pipelines, and bridging materials. There was stored in the United Kingdom, for example, all the construction materials necessary to rehabilitate completely the port of Cherbourg, the destruction of which was inevitable.

By July 1943 the flow of matériel from the United States to Britain had reached 753,000 tons a month which later was to increase to 1,900,000 tons in the month preceding the attack. It was necessary to construct and to allocate from existing resources a total of 3,780 assault craft of various types and 142 cargo ships. A great many of the assault craft were ocean-going vessels.

Not unmindful that an invasion across the English Channel against an entrenched German Army was an operation unequaled in possibility for a major disaster, the Allied commanders decided to undertake the great strategic bombardment that was to weaken Germany militarily, industrially, and economically. It was clear from the start that this program would require the tremendous resources of both American and British manpower and that critical shipping required for the build-up of the ground forces in England would have to be diverted from this purpose. The strategic bombardment of Germany was to be the mightiest air assault ever conceived. It is now certain that the decision was a sound one.

Accordingly, at Casablanca the American and British air force commanders were directed to launch and increase steadily the intensity of an assault that would continue day by day, around the clock, to reduce the enemy's capacity to resist when our armies would come to grips with the German Army on the continent. In order of priority, targets for the long-range heavy bombers were submarine construction yards, the aircraft industries, transportation, oil plants, and other critical enemy war industries.

Before the assault of Sicily was actually undertaken, the President, the Prime Minister, and the Combined Chiefs of Staff met again in Washington in May. This meeting, designated the TRIDENT Conference, may prove to be one of the most historic military conclaves of this war, for here the specific strategy to which the movements of the land, sea, and air forces of the American and British Allies conformed was translated into firm commitments. There were changes in detail and technique after the TRIDENT Conference, but the Pacific strategy was sustained, and the first great objective, the defeat of the European Axis, Germany and Italy, and their satellites, was accomplished.

It was at this Conference that the combined Chiefs of Staff decided to extend Allied influence in the Mediterranean to the point where Italy would be forced to withdraw from the war. They also approved the plan of the United States Army Air Forces to strike Germany a serious blow by reducing her great oil resources at Ploesti. The first effective attack was carried out on 1 August 1943 by a force of 178 B–24 heavy bombers. Our losses were heavy, 54 bombers, but the cost to Germany's ability to wage mechanized warfare was immense. The Axis had been obtaining 3,000,000 tons of oil a year from Rumania. The continuing Ploesti attacks materially dried up this source.

At the TRIDENT Conference plans for a direct assault from the United Kingdom into Europe's classic battlegrounds were reaffirmed. Even though we were now firmly entrenched in North Africa, to have attempted to force Germany from the south across the Alpine barrier was on the face of it impracticable. In Europe's innumerable wars no vigorously opposed crossing of the Alps had ever been successfully executed. Operation OVERLORD, the new code name for the assault of France, which replaced ROUNDUP, was formally accepted and, for the purposes of planning, the spring of 1944 was designated as the target date. General Eisenhower was directed to send to the United Kingdom beginning 1 November seven seasoned divisions which were fighting in North Africa, and which would fight in Sicily, even though this meant that at the very moment he would be committing his forces in a full-scale campaign in Italy, he would be obliged to release two Army Corps of seasoned troops.

Nor was Japan neglected at the TRIDENT Conference. It was decided to maintain an unremitting offensive pressure on the Japanese even while our forces closed in to deliver the knock-out blow to Italy and we were gathering the tremendous resources in the United Kingdom that would be necessary to force the continent. Japan would be approached both from the west and from the east. On the Asiatic mainland it was determined to build up the flow of matériel to China via the air route over the "hump" and to initiate aggressive land and air operations to reestablish surface communications with beleaguered China. In the Pacific, General MacArthur and

BALTIC SEA

Oder

Elbe · Berlin

Hamburg

Weser

G E R M A N Y

Rhine

Munie

NORTH SEA

Antwerp

SWITZERLAND

G R E A T   B R I T A I N

London

Paris

F R A N C E

Rhone

IRELAND

Brest

A T L A N T I C

P O R T U G A L

S P A I N

O C E A N

Gibraltar

M O R O C C O

N

Richard Edes Harrison

FORTRESS OF EUROPE

Victorious in North Africa, the Allied armies now had to meet and defeat the German armies of the West. It was also hoped to drive Italy out of the war, but both objectives could not be accomplished in the same operation. Behind the Alpine barrier, Nazi Germany could well feel secure from our attack. Where General Eisenhower stood in the summer of 1943, he had only two possible routes to Germany —through Southern France where his maneuver would be sharply restricted in the Rhone Valley or through Salonika in Eastern Greece where the Wehrmacht would have had the advantage of meeting both the Western Allies and the Red Army on the same front. It was imperative that the main United States and British forces be concentrated in the British Isles in preparation for a landing in France and an advance across the plains of Western Europe.

Admiral Nimitz were directed to move against the Japanese outer defenses, ejecting the enemy from the Aleutians and seizing the Marshalls, some of the Carolines, the remainder of the Solomons, the Bismarck Archipelago, and the remainder of New Guinea.

From the TRIDENT Conference, the Prime Minister, Field Marshal Sir Alan Brooke and I proceeded to General Eisenhower's headquarters at Algiers for a series of conferences lasting from 29 May to 3 June. At TRIDENT final conclusions had not been reached as to the extent to which the Mediterranean advance should continue so that General Eisenhower might be left in a position to exploit every favorable opportunity. In his villa at Algiers we discussed the future in detail, and he was authorized to proceed from operation HUSKY in Sicily as he saw fit with the intent of eliminating Italy from the war. But it was our purpose to avoid the creation in Italy of a vacuum into which the resources of the cross-Channel operation would be dissipated as the Germans had bled themselves in the North African campaign.

The Fall of Italy

Formal reports from the theater commanders on all of the operations of the last two years have not yet been received in the War Department and this general account of the operations of the United States Army during that period is based on official messages, informal reports, and other pertinent documents which are now available. They are believed to be suffficiently complete for the purposes of this report. Throughout the war, the Army was one part of a team composed of the sea, air, and ground forces of the United States and Great Britain and other members of the United Nations. It is therefore necessary to a description of the participation of the United States Army units in the fighting that the operations of the entire team be outlined.

The amphibious assault of the island of Sicily was launched on 10 July 1943. For weeks airfields, rail lines, and enemy fortifications on the island and in Sardinia and on the Italian mainland had been reduced by aerial bombardment. Pantelleria had surrendered on 11 June after an intense air and naval attack. The small islands of Lampedusa and Linosa had fallen a few days later.

The attacking force—the Fifteenth Army Group—was under General Eisenhower's deputy commander for allied ground forces, Gen. Sir Harold R. L. G. Alexander. It consisted of the American Seventh Army, under Lt. Gen. George S. Patton, Jr., on the left and the British Eighth Army, under Lt. Gen. Sir Bernard L. Montgomery, on the right. The Seventh Army assault force was made up of the II Corps, commanded by Lt. Gen. Omar N. Bradley and a separate task force under Major General Lucian K. Truscott. The II Corps consisted principally of the 1st and 45th Divisions, and a paratroop force. The task force was made up of the 3d Division with a combat team of the 2d Armored Division. In the British Eighth Army were two corps,

including four infantry divisions, two brigades, and an airborne division. These troops were embarked from Algeria, Tunisia, the Middle East, the United Kingdom, and the United States. The Naval Commander in Chief under General Eisenhower was Admiral of the Fleet Sir Andrew Cunningham. Vice Admiral Henry K. Hewitt was the senior U. S. Naval officer.

A wind which had sprung up the night preceding D-day attained near gale proportions as our convoys approached their rendezvous. The wind subsided somewhat before H-hour, but conditions continued quite unfavorable for landing. In compensation, the storm had put the beach defenders off their guard.

General Eisenhower wrote me 17 July:

. . . All the initial invasion moves were carried out smoothly, and an astonishing lack of resistance was encountered on the shoreline. Captured Italian generals say we secured complete surprise. The airborne operations, which were executed about three hours ahead of the landing, were apparently the first real notice the defenders had of what was coming. Our parachutists and the British glider troops got fairly well into their positions in spite of very high winds and bad navigating conditions. The landings on the east coast were not greatly troubled by the weather, but the 45th and 1st Divisions had an extremely bad surf. Admiral Cunningham told me that he considered the United States Navy landing operations, under Admiral Kirk (with the 45th Division), to be one of the finest examples of seamanship he had ever witnessed . . .

The wind also disrupted our airborne landings which were scheduled to be made inland from Gela a few hours before H-hour. Although scattered over a wide area and suffering heavy casualties from our own fire directed at transport formations which were off the prescribed course, the paratroops had a decisive effect on the successful landing.

General Eisenhower described these tragic difficulties as follows:

. . . The most difficult thing we have to solve is to work out methods whereby friendly aircraft can work over our troops and vessels with safety. Take for example one operation: We were quite anxious to assemble all the fighting elements of the 82d Division in the rear of Patton's line as a general reserve, since all the evidence showed that he might receive some rather serious counterattacks. Two nights after the original landing, we laid on a very carefully coordinated plan for bringing in the remainder of the 82d Division. Sea lanes were established with the Navy and all troops were carefully warned as to what to expect. In spite of this, the troop-carrying planes encountered some fire before they got over the shore and from then on we had a very unfortunate experience. Some German night bombers came in at the same moment that our troop-carrying planes did and the dropping of bombs and flares made all the ground troops open up a maximum fire. In addition to this, a local counterattack, which took place at too late an hour to warn the airborne troops, apparently allowed the enemy to establish a fire zone near the selected landing ground. The combination of all these things resulted in quite serious losses. My present reports are that we lost 23 planes, while personnel losses as yet are unestimated.

A later operation on the British front brought out the lesson that when we land airborne troops in hostile territory, we should *not do so in successive waves,* but should do it all at once. In the first wave, where we had surprise, losses were negligible, but in the two succeeding waves they were very large.

Even in the daytime we have great trouble in preventing our own naval and land forces from firing on friendly planes. This seems particularly odd in this operation, where we have such great air superiority that the presumption is that any plane flying in a straight and level course is friendly. Spaatz has written Arnold at considerable length on this subject, and he is convinced, as I am, that we are going to have to do some very earnest basic training in both ground and naval forces. Otherwise, we will finally get our air forces to the point where they will simply refuse to come over when we want them. Generally speaking, we are on the strategic offensive, which means we *must* have air superiority. Therefore, we should teach our people *not* to fire at a plane unless it definitely shows hostile intent . . .

By sunrise, three hours after the assault, beachheads had been established along 100 miles of coast, from just south of Syracuse to west of Licata. Our troops were moving inland, northeast of Gela, on D+1, when the Germans directed a heavy armored counterattack against the 1st Division. It was beaten off largely through expert use of artillery and naval gun fire. This action provided the most critical moment of the invasion.

The problems of supply over the beaches were especially acute during the first two days. The needs of the combat troops were urgent but adverse weather and occasional enemy air attacks made unloading of ships difficult and hazardous. The beach-supply operation first proved the excellence of our 2½-ton amphibious truck, the "DUKW," an official designation which quickly became popularized as "DUCK."

General Eisenhower advised me:

. . . Last Monday morning I made a quick tour along the American beaches, in order to get a visual picture of unloading operations and also to have a personal visit with Hewitt and Patton. I must say that the sight of hundreds of vessels, with landing craft everywhere, operating along the shoreline from Licata on the eastward, was unforgettable. Everybody I saw was in good heart and anxious to get ahead . . .

In the first two days of the invasion more than 80,000 men, 7,000 vehicles, and 300 tanks had been landed; several small ports had been placed in operation; at least six airfields had been captured and were being prepared for use.

Allied aircraft gave close support to ground operations, flying up to 1,200 sorties each day. Heavy bombers knocked out the few airdromes remaining serviceable to the enemy, and the ground troops were advancing rapidly. All air operations were under the Mediterranean Allied Air Forces headed by Air Chief Marshal Sir Arthur Tedder with Lt. Gen. Carl Spaatz as Commander of the Northwest African Air Forces. All heavy bombers were organized into the Strategic Air Force under Maj. Gen. James H. Doolittle.

By 16 July the battle line ran from a point just south of Catania on the east to Porto Empedocle on the west; about one-quarter of the island was in our hands. On

22 July, General Patton's forces in a rapid thrust across the western end of the island occupied the key port of Palermo. Further east the troops forged steadily ahead through rugged mountains stubbornly defended by the enemy. By the end of July only the northeastern corner of the island remained to the enemy.

Catania, the east coast bastion which had held up the advance of the British Eighth Army, fell early in August. The Germans and Italians were already withdrawing across the Strait of Messina under heavy air bombardment and continued pressure by our ground forces. On 16 August patrols of our 3d Division entered Messina from the west simultaneously with British units from the southeast and the next day organized resistance ceased. In 39 days the Sicilian campaign had ended. Through use of a heavy concentration of antiaircraft guns the Germans managed to extricate thousands of their first-line panzer and airborne troops as well as a considerable amount of light equipment over the Strait of Messina to the mainland. Nevertheless, for the Axis the loss of Sicily was a major military disaster. Their casualties totaled 167,000 of which 37,000 were Germans. Our casualties totaled 31,158 killed, wounded, and missing.

General Eisenhower reported:

. . . Nine months after the first landings in North Africa, the Allied Force had not merely cleared its shore of enemy forces, but had wrested from him the Sicilian bridge to use as our own in an advance onto the Italian mainland . . .

On to the Boot

Operation HUSKY, as we had hoped, precipitated a political disaster for the Axis. On 25 July, King Victor Emmanuel proclaimed the resignation of Mussolini. In August the President and the Prime Minister with the Combined Chiefs of Staff met at the Citadel at Quebec, the meeting being designated the QUADRANT Conference. By now the Italian Government was ready to quit. Marshal Badoglio had established contact with General Eisenhower in an effort to negotiate a surrender without the knowledge of the Germans. General Eisenhower was instructed to accept the unconditional surrender of Italy and to obtain the greatest possible military advantage from this development. He was to seize Sardinia and Corsica and attempt the establishment of air bases in the Rome area and northward, if feasible, maintaining unrelenting pressure on German forces in Northern Italy. At the same time, he was directed to coordinate his plans with the requirements of operation OVERLORD.

The Combined Chiefs of Staff at the QUADRANT Conference also conceived the operation against Southern France designated operation ANVIL and arrived at these conclusions:

Offensive operations against Southern France (to include the use of trained and equipped French forces) should be undertaken to establish a lodgment in the Toulon-Marseille area and to exploit

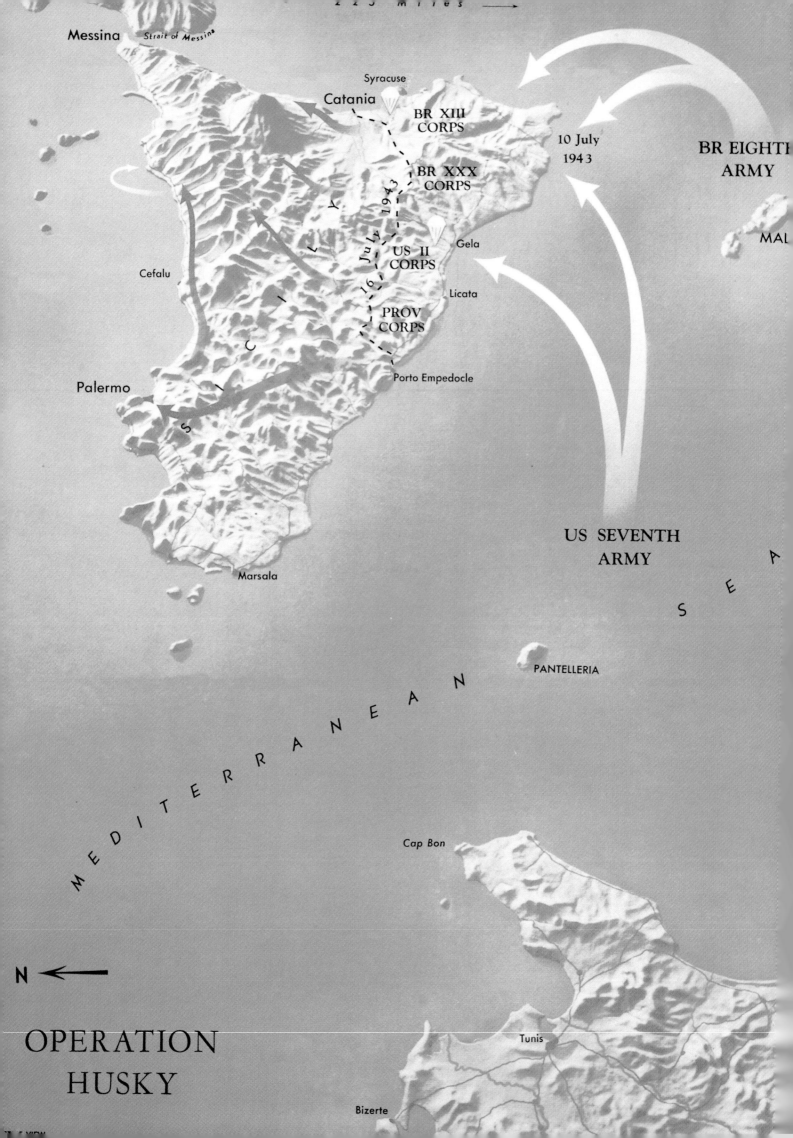

Messina · Strait of Messina

Syracuse

Catania

**BR XIII
CORPS**

10 July
1943

**BR EIGHTH
ARMY**

**BR XXX
CORPS**

MAL

S I C I L Y · 16 July 1943

Gela

**US II
CORPS**

Licata

Cefalu

Palermo

**PROV
CORPS**

Porto Empedocle

**US SEVENTH
ARMY**

S I C I L Y

S E A

Marsala

PANTELLERIA

M E D I T E R R A N E A N

Cap Bon

N ←

Tunis

OPERATION
HUSKY

Bizerte

northward in order to create a diversion in connection with OVERLORD. Air nourished operations in the southern Alps will, if possible, be initiated...

On 8 September, the day before American troops landed on the Italian mainland, the unconditional surrender of Italy was announced. On 9 September and the succeeding days the principal elements of the Italian fleet surrendered.

Compelling reasons had developed for the invasion of the Italian mainland. The operation (AVALANCHE) would enable us to capitalize on the collapse of Italian resistance; it offered a field for engaging German divisions which otherwise might operate against the Red Army and later against the forces in France; it would provide airfields from which the German homeland and the Balkans could be bombed from substantially shorter range; it would complete Allied control of the Mediterranean.

Canadian and British divisions of General Montgomery's Eighth Army crossed the Strait of Messina under cover of heavy artillery and air bombardment and landed on beaches near Reggio Calabria and Villa San Giovanni on 3 September. The beachheads were quickly secured, and the Eighth Army advanced northward through Calabria.

Six days later the U.S. Fifth Army under command of Lt. Gen. Mark W. Clark disembarked on beaches along the Gulf of Salerno. It landed with the VI Corps commanded by Maj. Gen. E. J. Dawley on the right and the British X Corps on the left. The VI Corps was composed principally of the 36th and 45th Divisions. American Rangers and British Commando units landed on the Sorrento Peninsula, north of the port of Salerno.

The enemy had suspected that we might undertake an amphibious operation against the Naples area, and as a result enemy reaction to the Salerno landings was swift and vigorous. It was evident that the German High Command had decided that its only hope of salvaging the situation arising from the surrender of the Italian Government lay in holding the Allied forces south of Naples until fresh dispositions could be made. On D-day the Germans made several local tank attacks. By 13 September the German XIV Panzer Corps was in action, and both the American and the British Corps were under heavy attack. The situation was critical.

General Eisenhower and his ground force commander, General Alexander, fully anticipated that they were in for a heavy fight at the foot of the Italian boot. They had estimated that eight German divisions were available to oppose the landings. Two were in and north of Rome. The Hermann Goering Panzer Division and the 15th Motorized Division were in the Naples area, and four more first-class divisions (the 16th and 26th Panzer, 29th Motorized, and 1st Parachute) were south of Naples. The enemy forces in

the south were heavy in armor. General Alexander, on the other hand, had to lodge assault infantry on the mainland first. The shortage of shipping made it impossible for him to bring his own heavy armor into the fight until the British 7th Armored Division started to unload on D+5. A further handicap was the necessity of making large forces available for the OVERLORD build-up at this time. The U. S. 1st and 9th Divisions and 2d Armored Division which had fought in Sicily were already staging for their movement to the United Kingdom. Later the 82d Airborne Division was withdrawn from the fighting at Salerno and sent to Britain.

The narrow margin on which we were compelled to allocate our resources so that Germany might be defeated at the earliest possible moment required superhuman effort by troops and commanders. Every available combat aircraft of both the Tactical and the Strategic Air Forces was thrown into the action. Bombers flew two missions a day, isolating the battle area and pounding German strongpoints. During the four critical days our Air Forces flew 3,000 sorties and dropped 2,150 tons of bombs in close support of the ground action. Naval gunfire supported the ground troops, and the Navy kept the stream of reinforcements coming in. On 13 September, and again the next day, reinforcing troops of the 82d Airborne Division went ashore. By the morning of 15 September the assault was firmly established, the high ground commanding the beaches had been taken, and the crisis had passed. While the fighting was in progress during these critical days General Eisenhower found time to inform me:

... We are very much in the "touch and go" stage of this operation. We got the Italian Fleet into Malta and, because of the Italian surrender, were able to rush into Taranto and Brindisi where no Germans were present. Our hold on both places is precarious but we are striving mightily to reinforce.

Our worse problem is AVALANCHE itself. We have been unable to advance and the enemy is preparing a major counterattack. The 45th Division is largely in the area now and I am using everything we have bigger than a row boat to get the 3d Division in to Clark quickly. In the present situation our great hope is the Air Force. They are working flat out and assuming, which I do, that our hold on southern Italy will finally be solidified, we are going to prove once again that the greatest value of any of the three services is ordinarily realized only when it is utilized in close coordination with the other two...

On 16 September, patrols of the Fifth and Eighth Armies met 40 miles southeast of Salerno uniting the fronts of General Alexander's Fifteenth Army Group. The critical phase of the Italian campaign had ended.

Shortage of assault shipping and landing craft continued to haunt our operations. A single division, for example, required for its landing at Salerno 30 LST's, 24 LCT's, 39 LCI's, 9 large transports, 4 freighters, and numerous miscellaneous small landing craft. Nevertheless, during the first 18 days Navy crews and

OPERATION AVALANCHE

Cassino

Termoli

Volterra

Naples

1 October 1943

Foggia

Sorrento

Salerno

BR X CORPS

US VI CORPS

Bari

US
FTH
RMY
Sept
1943

17 September 1943

Taranto

Brind

C A L A B R I A

Br 1 AB Div

Messina

Villa San Giovanni

BR EIGHTH ARMY
3 September 1943

Reggio
Calabria

I O N I A N   S E

TICAL VIEW

240 Miles

Army service troops landed over the Salerno beaches a total of 108,000 tons of supplies, 30,000 motor vehicles, and 189,000 troops.

Allied Air Established in Europe

The advance on Naples followed the successful completion of the fighting at Salerno. The Fifth and Eighth Armies under General Alexander were now deployed abreast. The Fifth occupied Naples and its harbor on 1 October and the Eighth Army reached Foggia, seizing its extensive system of airfields. Field Marshal Kesselring, commanding the German Forces in Italy, withdrew northward to delaying positions along the Volturno River. Sardinia had been evacuated by the Nazis on 20 September and on 4 October the evacuation of Corsica followed.

The capture of Foggia airfields confirmed our hold on the mainland. Fighters based in Sicily could carry enough gasoline to operate only about 15 minutes over the Salerno beachhead. Now they could be based in large numbers close to the battle area. From Foggia our heavy bombers could easily strike at the passes crossing the Alps, attack Germany air installations in Austria and factories in southern Germany, and raid industrial and transportation centers in the Balkans, aiding the Red Army. In addition the B–17's and B–24's of the Strategic Air Forces could reinforce the efforts of the Tactical Air Forces in isolating the Italian battle area.

Movement of the heavy bombers and fighter forces into Foggia was a tremendous undertaking because of the equipment necessary to establish new runways, pumping plants, pipe lines, repair shops, and warehouses. For some weeks a considerable portion of the shipping was devoted to the movement of the Air Forces onto the Italian mainland. By the end of the year 35,000 combat airmen with their supporting forces were established in Italy. There were two heavy bombardment groups, two medium groups, and two fighter groups operating from 10 airfields. The fall weather made it necessary to overlay the runways with steel mat. Pipe lines and pumping stations, largely recovered from North Africa, had to be installed to permit the necessary flow of aviation fuel to the airdromes. This buildup of air power consumed approximately 300,000 tons of shipping during the most critical months of the Italian campaign. So heavy were the shipping requirements of the Fifteenth Strategic Air Force, activated 1 November 1943 under General Doolittle, that the build-up of our ground forces in Italy was considerably delayed. This decision was a difficult one for General Eisenhower since the delay would give the enemy a heavy superiority in ground troops for a considerable period.

There were now 11 Allied divisions in the Italian line, but the Germans had at least 24 on the Italian mainland. Although 14 of these were in Northern Italy outside the combat zone, the enemy was in a position to build up a considerably greater defensive force than General Eisenhower had available for his attack. The additional Allied air power and the threat of a landing further north by General Patton's Seventh Army were counted on to deter the enemy from moving his divisions south from the Po Valley. This threat was exploited by skillful use of General Patton and his headquarters. Following the Sicilian campaign, the Seventh Army headquarters, which no longer had any divisions assigned to it, was moved to Corsica. General Patton's mysterious movements throughout the Mediterranean area kept the Germans guessing where the Seventh Army, which they had learned to fear so much in Sicily, might strike next.

Early in November the II Corps, then commanded by Maj. Gen. Geoffrey Keyes, moved to the mainland of Italy from Sicily. German plans to hold the line of the Volturno were frustrated when on the night of 12–13 October the II Corps and the VI Corps, now commanded by Maj. Gen. J. P. Lucas, of the Fifth Army forced crossings of that river. Destroying every bridge and culvert en route, the Germans withdrew to the "winter line" which they had been preparing feverishly since the Allied landings on the mainland. This defensive position stretched across the peninsula, following generally the lines of the Carigliano and Sangro Rivers, about 75 miles south of Rome.

The Slugging Battle for Rome

Winter had arrived. Heavy rains were falling and streams were in constant flood. The resources of our engineers were taxed to keep in place the temporary bridges on the vital supply routes. Vehicles and men mired deep in mud.

Despite the difficulties there was no relaxation of pressure. The purpose was to seize Rome as quickly as possible and engage the maximum number of German divisions. The offensive was a series of attacks and pauses, the immediate objectives being key terrain features. It was the hardest kind of fighting. The Germans had mined the roads, trails, natural cross-country routes of advance, and even the stream beds. To reinforce terrain barriers the enemy constructed strongpoints in which he skillfully employed mine fields, wire entanglements, log-and-earth emplacements, and automatic weapons. Machinegun and mortar emplacements, many of them dug four or five feet into solid rock, covered every approach. To deal with them the artillery was heavily reinforced by batteries of the heaviest field pieces we had produced. The 240-mm Howitzer and the 8-inch gun were rushed from the United States.

In December the Fifth Army arrived before the entrance to the Cassino corridor to Rome. The 2d Moroccan Infantry Division arrived in Italy at this time and was assigned to it. The United States had agreed

Pisa
Serchio
Leghorn
Florence
Lake Comacchio
Ravenna
Faenza
Forlì
Rimini
ELBA
1 September 1944
Lake Trasimeno
Lake Bolsena
6 June 1944
Rome
Anzio
Cisterna
Pescara
Sangro
22 January 1944
Rapido
Cassino
Gariglíano
BR EIGHTH ARMY
US FIFTH ARMY
Volturno
Naples
FROM CASSINO TO THE ARNO
US VI CORPS 22 January 1944
1 October 1943
Foggia
N
Salerno
160 Miles
PERSPEC

to equip eight French infantry and armored divisions including supporting troops. The Moroccan division was the forerunner of the *Corps Expéditionaire Français* which, under the leadership of Gen. Alphonse Juin, greatly distinguished itself in the hard fighting of the months that followed.

Allied interest in the Eastern Mediterranean shifted to the Balkans following the conclusion of the North African campaign. Maj. Gen. Lewis H. Brereton's Ninth Air Force based in Northeast Africa bombed strategic targets there, including the Ploesti airfields and, with elements of the Royal Air Force's Middle East Air Command, dropped supplies to the hard-pressed patriot forces.

The Eastern Mediterranean had constituted a separate theater under British Command until 5 December 1943 when the entire offensive in the Mediterranean was brought under one command. On that date the Combined Chiefs of Staff delegated to General Eisenhower responsibility for all operations in the Mediterranean other than strategic bombing. Three weeks later on 24 December, he was appointed Supreme Allied Commander of the invasion forces from the West, meaning from the British Isles, and was ordered to England to take over the final preparations. General Montgomery, Air Chief Marshal Tedder, and General Bradley joined him there. Gen. Sir Henry Maitland Wilson was named Supreme Commander of Allied Forces in the Mediterranean Area, to succeed General Eisenhower, and Lt. Gen. Jacob L. Devers, U. S. Army, was appointed his deputy. Lt. Gen. Sir Oliver W. H. Leese assumed command of the British Eighth Army. General Clark continued in command of the Fifth Army.

At this time Lt. Gen. Carl Spaatz was selected to command the United States Strategic Air Forces in Europe with headquarters in London, and General Doolittle was appointed commander of the Eighth Air Force, vice Lt. Gen. Ira C. Eaker, who assumed command of the Mediterranean Allied Air Forces. Maj. Gen. Nathan F. Twining was given command of the Fifteenth Strategic Air Force and Maj. Gen. J. K. Cannon continued in command of the Twelfth Tactical Air Force.

Early in January the French Corps, under General Juin, took over the right sector of the Fifth Army Front from the United States VI Corps, which was withdrawn to prepare for the Anzio landings. The Fifth Army then launched its attack against the line of the Garigliano River.

To disrupt communications in the rear of German forces in the Cassino area, the VI Corps landed on beaches near Anzio, 25 miles south of Rome, on 22 January. The landing forces included the 3d United States Division, a British infantry division, and American Ranger and parachute units. Reacting swiftly to the threat to his rear, the enemy rushed both infantry and armor to the Anzio area; the Hermann Goering Panzer Division was hastily shifted to the beachhead area and other divisions were sent down from Northern Italy. By the end of January the Allied troops in the beachhead faced a perimeter of strong German forces. With observation from the surrounding hills the Germans were able to deliver persistent accurate artillery fire throughout the flat beachhead and against ships near the shore.

Defeating the initial effort to capture Cisterna, the enemy drove in an attack to split the beachhead and annihilate our forces ashore. A masterful defense, in which the 3d and 45th Divisions suffered heavily but fought magnificently, halted the counterattacks which reached their peak of intensity on 17 February. Later in the month, the Hermann Goering and 29th Panzer Grenadier Divisions led another unsuccessful drive aimed at Anzio.

Further south the Fifth Army offensive had been halted before strong defenses of Cassino. Some of the bitterest fighting of the war raged at this point. Determined attempts to capture the town failed in the face of fanatical resistance by crack German units— notably the 1st Parachute Division, which General Alexander termed the best German division on any front. Lt. Gen. Jacob L. Devers, Deputy Allied Commander, wrote me on 22 March:

We are struggling here with time. On March 15th I thought we were going to lick it by the attack on Cassino and advance up the Liri Valley. We used air, artillery, and tanks, followed closely by infantry. I witnessed the attack from across the valley. It got off to a start with excellent weather. The bombing was excellent and severe, and the artillery barrage which followed it and lasted for two hours was even more severe and accurate, with 900 guns participating. Two groups of medium bombers, followed by 11 groups of heavies, followed by three groups of mediums, started on the minute at 8:30 a. m. and closed at 12:00 noon, the groups coming over every ten minutes up to 9:00 oclock and thereafter every 15 minutes. In spite of all this and with excellent support all afternoon with dive bombers and artillery fire, the ground forces have not yet attained their first objective. Consequently, the tanks which were to attack in mass could not get started. These results were a sobering shock to me. The infantry had been withdrawn in the early morning hours five miles to the north of Cassino. When they arrived back in the town of Cassino at approximately 1:00 o'clock close behind the barrage, the Germans were still there, were able to slow up their advance and even to reinforce themselves during the night by some unaccountable means.

The attack is still going on but it is my opinion that all we will gain will be the town of Cassino and possibly a bridgehead over the Rapido in that vicinity; General Alexander must then stop and regroup his forces, which he hopes to accomplish by the 15th of April.

After regrouping, the Fifth and Eighth Armies launched a coordinated offensive on 11 May. As the attack got underway, the U. S. VI Corps, now under Maj. Gen. L. K. Truscott, struck out from Anzio beachhead on 23 May. The attack was made by the 3d, 34th, and 45th Infantry Divisions, the 1st Armored Division, the 1st Special Service Force, the 100th Japanese

310 Miles

Brenner Pass

Bolzano

Udine

Mo

8 May 1945

Milan

Treviso

Verona

Venice

Padua

Mantua

Turin

Po

Piacenza

Via Emilia

Ferrara

ADRIATIC

Modena

Bologna

Argenta

APENNINES

Ravenna

Genoa

9 April 1945

Senio

Faenza

Savona

Forli

Rimini

La Spezia

US FIFTH
ARMY

BR
EIGHTH
ARMY

Pistoia

LIGURIAN SEA

Florence

Infantry Battalion, composed of Americans of Japanese descent, and two British divisions. The 1st Special Service Force drove east to pave the way for a junction on 25 May with other Fifth Army forces advancing northwest along the coast. These forces included the 88th and 85th Divisions which had recently arrived from the United States and entered the line in March and April. Activated after 7 December 1941 and composed almost entirely of selectees, these two new divisions fought as veteran units in their first combat assignment, overcoming extremely heavy resistance. This was the first confirmation from the battlefield of the soundness of our division activation and training program, which was described in detail in my last report.

The units from the south then moved to Anzio from which the beachhead forces were already thrusting northeastward for the final drive on Rome. On their right the French Corps under General Juin struck into the heart of the German positions covering the Liri Valley and precipitated a general withdrawal to the north of Rome. The Italian capital fell to the Fifth Army on 4 June, two days before Allied forces began the invasion of France.

We were weakened seriously in the intense fighting along the approaches to Rome by our inability to replace the casualties promptly. On 4 February General Devers had reported:

Casualties have been unusually heavy for the past 10 days, particularly in infantry. Clark reports 3d Division casualties alone total 2,400 infantry. A shortage in the 34th Division is 1,300 and in the 36th Division, 3,000. Since present operations involve simultaneous use of all divisions, it is imperative that table of organization strength be maintained.

Two weeks later he again reported:

Replacements allocated to this theater are not adequate to sustain operations in Italy on the present scale. At the present time the United States part of the Fifth Army has an effective net shortage of 13,072 officers and men.

This shortage of men needed so desperately in our battle line resulted from the inability of the Selective Service System to meet the Army's call for manpower the previous summer. In July, Selective Service had delivered 194,000 men of the Army's call of 235,000. In August and September the Army had requested 175,000 men a month and received 131,000 in August and 122,000 in September.

Pursuit to the North

Pursuit of the enemy was energetic even though we were now making heavy withdrawals in preparation for ANVIL, the attack in Southern France which was scheduled for August. Between mid-June and the last of July more than a division a week was withdrawn from the forces in Italy to train and stage for this operation. The 45th was ordered out of the line on 14 June, the 3d on 17 June, and the 36th on 27 June. The United States IV Corps under Maj. Gen. W. D. Crittenberger moved into the line in place of the VI Corps, which had been withdrawn 13 June. The French Corps of four divisions (1st Motorized Moroccan, 3d Algerian Infantry, 4th Moroccan Mountain, and 2d Moroccan Infantry) were withdrawn between 2 and 21 July, and replaced by the II Corps which had been out of the line for a rest.

To compensate partially for this heavy drain on his resources and to utilize more fully antiaircraft units which were no longer required in such large numbers as a result of our increasing air superiority, the theater commander retrained several groups as infantry to form the 473d Infantry. At this time the 442d Infantry Regiment, composed of Americans of Japanese descent, was fighting with distinction on the left flank of the Fifth Army. Thus, by the end of June, Pescara, 95 miles east of Rome, had been captured and the Allied line extended across the peninsula through Lake Trasimeno. In July the Fifth and Eighth Armies gained 50 miles. After heavy fighting lasting two weeks, Florence fell to British troops of the Fifth Army. Five days later United States troops captured Pisa. Meanwhile, the Eighth Army had passed through the Apennine Divide, and on 21 September captured Rimini in the valley of the Po.

During the withdrawal of troops for ANVIL, one American division, the 91st, had arrived to reinforce the Fifth Army. On 15 September a combat team of the Brazilian Expeditionary Force moved into the Fifth Army line in the Valley of the Serchio River. Before the end of autumn the entire Brazilian division was in the line. During this same period one of the Army's two Negro divisions, the 92d, which had reached Italy during the late summer and fall, was assigned to the IV Corps.

The advances had brought General Alexander's Allied armies up against the "Gothic Line," an elaborate transpeninsular defense system which the Germans had been preparing since early in the year. Despite the heavy diversion of troops to other theaters it was decided to launch another general offensive on 10 September for the purpose of breaking through the Apennines into the Po Valley. While the U. S. Fifth Army assaulted the Gothic Line frontally through the mountains, the British Eighth Army, now commanded by Lt. Gen. Sir R. L. McCreery attacked northwest from Rimini. This offensive involved our troops in some of the bitterest and most difficult fighting of the Italian campaign. The jagged Apennines and bad weather seemed almost insurmountable obstacles.

After three months of this costly but successful penetration of the Gothic Line, the Allied command prepared in December to drive on Bologna, but pressure against the western flank of the Fifth Army and diversion of Eighth Army units to meet the political crisis in Greece disrupted these plans. Meanwhile the Germans had time to refit and strengthen their forces and establish a new defensive position. Kesselring was under orders to hold south of Bologna. In addition to German replacements, the enemy brought up units of Mussolini's Fascist Republican Army, which had a strength of four new Italian divisions.

On 12 December 1944 Field Marshal Alexander replaced Gen. Sir Henry Maitland Wilson as Supreme Commander in the Mediterranean area. General Wilson was promoted to Field Marshal and senior representative in Washington of the British Chiefs of Staff. Lt. Gen. Mark W. Clark moved up to command the Allied armies in Italy and Lt. Gen. Lucian K. Truscott assumed command of the Fifth Army.

In January the Fifth Army was reinforced by the 10th U. S. Mountain Division which gave a fine exhibition of battle efficiency on its initial employment. During the winter, three Italian combat groups entered the line of the Eighth Army. These small gains were more than offset by a February directive from the Combined Chiefs of Staff which ordered the transfer of five British and Canadian divisions to the European Theater. The directive was later amended to send three to France, one to the eastern Mediterranean, and retain one division in Italy for possible use in the impending final battle. This movement of more than 125,000 combat troops was accomplished in complete secrecy and gave Marshal Montgomery's Northern Army Group on the Rhine additional power to the surprise of the enemy.

During the fall and winter months, the Tactical and Strategic Air Forces pounded away at communications over the Alps and in Northern Italy. With opposing ground forces so nearly equal in strength, the Air Forces represented our margin of advantage and made the maintenance of German forces in Northern Italy most difficult while our own was unmolested. In addition, Italy-based aircraft assisted the Yugoslav patriots. Closely coordinated with the attacks staged from Britain, the Strategic Air Forces struck heavy blows at oil and rail targets in Austria and southern Germany, averaging weekly bombloads of nearly 4,000 tons.

The Final Phases

Ground action on the Italian front in the late winter was limited to small but important advances in the mountains southwest of Bologna. The strategic aircraft kept up the pressure on communications and industrial targets beyond the Alps, reaching as far north as Berlin.

On 9 April, General Clark's Fifteenth Army Group launched its spring drive, known as operation GRAPESHOT. The Eighth Army led off with an attack across the Senio River west of Ravenna. In spite of unusually heavy air and artillery preparation, the offensive met stiff opposition from the German Tenth Army in approaching the Argenta Gap. Five days later,

after the enemy had presumably had time to dispose himself to meet the Eighth Army attack, the II and IV Corps of the Fifth Army threw their weight into the offensive from positions in the Apennines south and southwest of Bologna.

After a week of heavy fighting our troops broke into the Po Valley and entered Bologna from the west and south. At the same time, Polish forces of the Eighth Army entered the city from the east. The Fifth Army columns beyond the city swept up the great highway leading to Piacenza—the ancient Via Emilia—and, bypassing Modena to the east, drove toward the Po south of Mantua. Pursuing the disorganized enemy to the river, bridgeheads were quickly established across the Po on 23 April. The Eighth Army met determined resistance in Ferrara, but by the 25th had crossed the Po in force. On the same day, our forces on the Ligurian Coast captured La Spezia with its naval base. The German armies were virtually destroyed south of the Po, the bulk of their equipment being either destroyed or abandoned.

The final week of the war in Italy brought wide advances throughout northern Italy. Bridging many rivers that flow south from the Alps, the Eighth Army swept northeast along the Adriatic coastal plain, liberating Padua, Venice, and Treviso. While Fifth Army infantry and mountain troops drove into the foothills of the Alps along the Brenner route, other armored columns and motorized infantry raced up the valley of the Po and by 29 April had reached the great city of Milan.

On every side effective support was received from the Italian patriots. After seizing Genoa, our Ligurian forces drove beyond Savona to make contact with the French. Advance elements of the 442d Japanese-American regiment reached Turin. Resistance collapsed everywhere; more than 160,000 prisoners were taken by the Allied armies. By the first of May, Eighth Army troops advancing on Trieste had made contact with Yugoslav partisans at Monfalcone. On 2 May 1945 the commander of the German armies in Northern Italy found it impossible to continue the bloody struggle and capitulated.

The Italian triumph is a striking demonstration of the solidarity of the United Nations. Fighting under the Fifteenth Army Group, at some time during the Italian campaign, were Americans, British, Canadians, French, New Zealanders, South Africans, Poles, Indians, Brazilians, Italians, Greeks, Moroccans, Algerians, Arabs, Goums, Senegalese, and a brigade of Jewish soldiers.

The entire campaign was slow and bitter. The Allied troops did not have the superiority they enjoyed in Western Europe, where geography had compelled us to make the great effort. Nonetheless, the Italian campaign made a heavy contribution to the successes on the Western front, pinning down German forces which Hitler needed badly to reinforce his weakened armies, both in the east and west. The troops participating in the Italian campaign should feel as great a satisfaction in the defeat of the Axis enemy as those of the larger forces which drove into the heart of Germany from the west and made contact with the Red armies.

ORDER OF BATTLE MEDITERRANEAN THEATER OF OPERATIONS AS OF 2 MAY 1945

[The order of battle of our Allies is not shown below Army level, except to show U. S. division under their operational control.]

Unit	Commander	Location
Fifteenth Army Group	Gen. Mark W. Clark	Florence, Italy.
Fifth Army	Lt. Gen. Lucian K. Truscott	Verona, Italy.
II Corps	Lt. Gen. Geoffrey Keyes	Italy.
10th Mountain Division	Maj. Gen. George P. Hays	Italy.
85th Infantry Division	Maj. Gen. John B. Coulter	Italy.
88th Infantry Division	Maj. Gen. Paul W. Kendall	Italy.
IV Corps	Maj. Gen. Willis D. Crittenberger	Italy.
1st Armored Division	Maj. Gen. Vernon E. Prichard	Italy.
34th Infantry Division	Maj. Gen. Charles L. Bolte	Italy.
92d Infantry Division	Maj. Gen. Edward M. Almond	Italy.
British Eighth Army	Lt. Gen. Sir R. L. McCreery	Italy.
91st Infantry Division	Maj. Gen. William G. Livesay	Italy.
U. S. Army Air Forces in MTO	Lt. Gen. J. K. Cannon	Caserta, Italy.
Twelfth Air Force	Maj. Gen. B. W. Chidlaw	Florence, Italy.
XXII Tactical Air Command	Brig. Gen. T. C. Darcy	Italy.
Fifteenth Air Force	Maj. Gen. N. F. Twining	Bari, Italy.
XV Fighter Command	Brig. Gen. D. C. Strother	Italy.

OPERATION OVERLORD

This is the perspective with which the Allied Supreme Commander viewed his problem. The English Channel was the most difficult barrier to the invasion of Western Europe because of the navigational hazards and the extreme tidal variation along the French Coast. But once firmly ashore anywhere from the lowlands to the Franco-Spanish border, there would be unlimited freedom of maneuver and ample opportunity to improvise communications for the Armies driving on the German heartland.

Rome

CORSICA

SARDINIA

MEDITERRANEAN SEA

Bologna

Po

Genoa

Milan

ITALY
FRANCE

Marseille

SPAIN
FRANCE

Basle

Geneva

Belfort

Rhône

Lyon

Massif Central

Chaumont

Reims

Orléans

Loire

Bordeaux

Marne

Paris

Garonne

Seine

Angers

Nantes

Le Havre

Bay of Biscay

English

Cherbourg

Portsmouth

Channel

Southampton

N

Bristol

Brest

Plymouth

Falmouth

Richard Edes Harrison 1943

Operation OVERLORD

In November and December 1943, the Combined Chiefs of Staff had met with President Roosevelt and Prime Minister Churchill at the SEXTANT Conference in Cairo and then with the President, Prime Minister, Marshal Stalin and his Military adviser at Teheran. By that time it was clear how the defeat of Germany could be brought about—but the Allies were beset by innumerable specific problems of implementing the desired strategy.

The greatest of these by far was the critical shortage of landing craft. Those available for the top priority operation OVERLORD in Normandy still seemed insufficient and there were many other vital operations that had to be undertaken if we were to maintain the initiative on the global battlefronts. Even though an attack in the south of France was considered essential to the success of OVERLORD, the Combined Chiefs of Staff had previously directed that 68 landing ships be returned from the Mediterranean Theater to the United Kingdom beginning 15 January to meet the requirements of the cross Channel assault as then planned. Despite these additional ships, it became evident that there would not be sufficient landing craft in Great Britain by the invasion target date to provide a sufficient margin of safety for the hazardous amphibious assault. Therefore, upon their return to Cairo from Teheran, the Combined Chiefs resolved that more strenuous measures must be taken to permit a broadening of the initial landing in Normandy. The Mediterranean Theater could be bled no further. Only sufficient resources were left there for an assault force of two divisions for Southern France, and military intelligence indicated that while this force could probably overcome anticipated German resistance on the Riviera coast, the rapid development of the operation northward up the Rhone valley would not permit further reduction. The remaining possible source for additional landing ships was in the shipyards of Great Britain and the United States. Such an increase in time for OVERLORD would require a miracle of production since these shipyards were already overcrowded and working at furious speed to maintain the heavy existing schedule of landing craft production, as well as that for the construction of destroyers and destroyer escorts urgently required to combat the German submarines.

An added complication at this time was the possibility that Turkey might enter the war on the side of the United Nations, exposing herself to attack by Bulgaria. The possibility of operations to support her in the eastern Mediterranean had to be considered.

At the same time there was grave concern over the situation then obtaining in Asia. The Generalissimo, Chiang Kai-shek, met with President Roosevelt, Prime Minister Churchill, and their military advisers at Cairo, and all were convinced that a determined effort must be made to reestablish surface communications with our Chinese Allies in 1944. Agreement was reached for operation CAPITAL in which the forces of Admiral Mountbatten and General Stilwell were given the mission of investing Northern and Central Burma. It was realized that the success of these operations could be made much more certain by an amphibious landing in the Bay of Bengal, but there were not sufficient landing craft to insure the success of our European offensive and at the same time undertake a landing on the shores of Burma.

Victory in this global war depended on the successful execution of OVERLORD. That must not fail. Yet the Japanese could not be permitted meanwhile to entrench in their stolen empire, and China must not be allowed to fall victim to further Japanese assaults. Allied resources were searched through again and again, and strategy reconsidered in the light of the deficiencies. These conclusions seemed inescapable: France must be invaded in 1944, to shorten the war by facilitating the advance westward of the Soviet forces. At the same time German technological advances such as in the development of atomic explosives made it imperative that we attack before these terrible weapons could be turned against us. In addition, the pressure on the Japanese in the Pacific must not be relaxed. Communications with China must be reopened. Resources were allocated accordingly. The balance was extremely delicate but we had to go ahead.

When General Eisenhower was selected as the Supreme Allied Commander for OVERLORD after the resumption of the conference at Cairo in December, he received this directive:

> You will enter the continent of Europe and, in conjunction with the other Allied Nations, undertake operations aimed at the heart of Germany and the destruction of her armed forces.

Accompanied by his Deputy Commander, Air Chief Marshal Sir Arthur Tedder, General Eisenhower arrived in Britain in mid-January. Almost immediately he wrote:

> It is obvious that strong and positive action is needed here in several directions. The location of various headquarters, the exact pattern of command, the tactics of the assault, and the strength in units and equipment, are all questions that have not yet been definitely settled. The most important of all these questions is that of increasing the strength of the initial assault wave in OVERLORD.

The search for greater resources for OVERLORD continued until it seemed that the time and energy of the Allied commanders was almost completely absorbed by a problem that defied solution. We had gone to the shipping experts and the shipyard owners to urge them to bend greater than human efforts to step-up the output of their precious landing craft. The shipyards broke all records to meet our requirements but there still were not enough landing craft in sight.

After intensive calculations which taxed the endurance of the military and naval planners, two major decisions were made. The target date of invasion was advanced from early May to early June, even though this pushed us closer to the time when weather conditions would turn against us. The operations in Southern France, which were originally to be made simultaneously with the attack on Normandy, were delayed months so that landing craft could be used first in the Channel, then rushed to the Mediterranean to do double duty both in OVERLORD and ANVIL.

The Preparations

At the time of the QUADRANT Conference at Quebec in August 1943, there had been but a single United States division in the United Kingdom and our trans-Atlantic shipping effort was concentrated on filling the heavy requirements of the Mediterranean campaign. By late August 1943, shipping was partially released from this heavy southern commitment and troops again began to pour into the British Isles. On D-day, 6 June 1944, the strength of the United States Army in that theater was 1,533,000; in the interim an average of 150,000 men had been transported each month.

The build-up of this force, together with a corresponding accumulation of supplies of all kinds, involved a tremendous job of transportation, and special credit must be given to the Navy for its vital part in the undertaking. An enormous administrative task was also involved, since facilities for quartering and training such large forces had to be provided within the limited area of the United Kingdom. The efficiency of the preinvasion build-up is exemplified by the speed with which units landing in Britain were provided with their essential arms and equipment. Through a system of preshipping and storing, the Army Service Forces were able to have equipment distributed and waiting for each unit on its arrival. Within a maximum of 30 days after debarking, divisions were fully equipped and ready for action.

The units arriving in the United Kingdom from America were well trained, especially in fast-moving corps and army operations over large areas; those coming from the Mediterranean were battle-tested. Nonetheless, everything possible was done during their staging period in the United Kingdom to increase their combat efficiency despite the limited terrain available in a densely populated and cultivated countryside. The troops which were to make the assault landings maneuvered realistically on beaches and ground which approximated the target areas. In the early spring of 1944, joint exercises of the ground, sea, and air forces which were to make the attack were held along the southern coast of England. It was a full-dress rehearsal.

Three weeks before the invasion General Eisenhower wrote:

There is no question at all as to the readiness of the troops. They are well trained, fit, and impatient to get the job started and completed. In forecasting future possibilities, it is, of course, necessary that we seek ways and means to bring to bear those factors in which we enjoy a great superiority over the enemy. These are control of the sea, command of the air, including resources in airborne troops and armor. I am trying to visualize an operation in which we would bring in behind the initial beachhead a great strength in armor and seek an opportunity to launch a big armored attack in conjunction with a deep and very heavy penetration by airborne troops.

Victory in the Air

By 1 July 1943 the Allied strategic air assault of Air Chief Marshal A. T. Harris' Royal Air Force Bomber Command by night and General Eaker's Eighth Air Force by day on the fortress of Europe was in full swing and was producing important results. Single raids in which the air force delivered bomb loads of more than 500 tons had been carried out. Serious inroads had been made on the combat power of the German fighter force.

These results had been obtained with an American air fleet of less than 1,000 heavy bombers and 1,000 planes of other types. By D-day, the strength of the United States air forces in the United Kingdom exceeded 3,000 heavy bombers and 6,500 first-line planes of other types. The attacks on Germany continued with increasing intensity and shattering power.

The climax in air war came in February 1944, when the Luftwaffe made a powerful effort to sweep our day bombers from the skies. The battle raged for a week. It was fought over Regensburg, Merseburg, Schweinfurt, and other critical industrial centers. The German fighter force was severely crippled, and our attacks continued with unabated fury.

From the time of the Eighth Air Force's first heavy bomber attack on 17 August 1942 until V-E Day, United States airmen had dropped more than 1,550,000 tons of bombs on western European targets. During 1943, following successful attacks on the enemy's submarine yards and bases, the effort of our precision bombers was concentrated against aircraft and ballbearing manufacturing plants, airdromes, and communications. The German fighter command, already outclassed in aerial combat, was further reduced by inability to get replacements. The RAF Bomber Command concentrated upon the destruction of the Ruhr-Rhineland industries and the undermining of the morale of industrial workers.

In order to exploit more fully the flexibility of our bombardment, particularly against German industrial targets, the Eighth and Fifteenth U. S. Air Forces were combined on 1 January 1944 to form "The U. S. Strategic Air Forces in Europe." Lt. Gen. Carl Spaatz was placed in command. The component forces con-

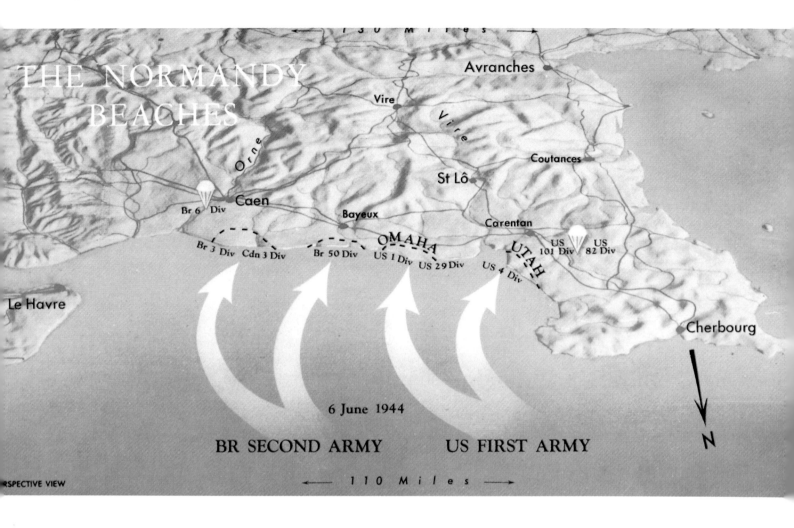

THE NORMANDY BEACHES

Avranches

Vire

Coutances

St Lô

Caen

Br 6 Div

Bayeux

Carentan

Br 3 Div   Cdn 3 Div   Br 50 Div   OMAHA   UTAH   US   US
                                        US 1 Div   US 29 Div   US 4 Div   101 Div   82 Div

Le Havre

Cherbourg

6 June 1944

BR SECOND ARMY   US FIRST ARMY

N

PERSPECTIVE VIEW

← 110 Miles →

tinued to be based in the United Kingdom and in Italy respectively.

In the late spring of 1944, synthetic fuel plants and crude oil refineries became the prime targets. Captured documents now show that the bombing campaign succeeded in reducing production between May and October 1944 to five percent of the former monthly output.

The attack on German industry was coupled with strikes on German communications. Vital rail junctions and the canals which were so important in the enemy's transportation system were repeatedly bombed. During a single month—May 1944—more than 900 locomotives and 16,000 freight cars were destroyed in Western Europe. The effects of this phase of the air assault were enormous, for transportation and communications are the life arteries of a modern industrial state engaged in total war.

Medium bombers and fighter-bombers of Lt. Gen. Lewis H. Brereton's Ninth Air Force, which moved from the Middle East during the fall of 1943, struck enemy airfields in diversionary attacks so timed as to reduce the concentration of enemy fighters which might oppose the passage of the heavy United States bomber formations. Diversionary fighter sweeps further dislocated the enemy's air opposition. As the range of fighters was increased through the installation

of additional fuel tanks, they were employed more and more to escort bombers to targets deep in Germany.

As the aerial offensive mounted the enemy was forced to withdraw fighters from the support of his armies in the East to meet the threat from the West. This was an important factor in enabling the Soviet air forces to maintain superiority on their front.

It was not merely overwhelming numbers of planes which gave our air assault its great effectiveness. There were important, almost revolutionary, improvements in techniques and in equipment. To reduce the excessive aircraft losses in long, round-trip bombing flights exposed to constant enemy interception, a system of shuttle-bombing between bases in the United Kingdom and North Africa was initiated in mid-August 1943. The shuttle-bombing run was shortened as the advance in Italy continued. A shuttle system between Italy and the U. S. S. R. was inaugurated with a heavy raid on rail communications in Central Europe on 2 June 1944. Soon thereafter, shuttle-flights were made between the United Kingdom and the new Ukrainian bases.

Radar bombing technique, first employed in the fall of 1943, improved constantly. All-weather bombing approached reality; our bombers used the cover of darkness and inclement weather to achieve surprise, yet still hit their target with precision.

In the spring of 1944, three months before D-day, the Allied air forces, while still hammering at their strategic targets, began directly to prepare the way for the invasion. Through destructive attacks on key bridges and rail centers, the "invasion coast" was effectively isolated. As a result of this preparatory bombing, the ability of the enemy to shift reserves to the critical area was severely restricted. Since the outcome of an amphibious operation hinges on the relative ability of the opposing forces to build up strength in the critical areas, this air preparation was a decisive factor in the success of OVERLORD. Even with favorable Channel weather, it would have required at least 15 weeks for the Allies to land as many divisions as the Germans had available in Belgium and Northern France.

The Assault

The beaches of Normandy were chosen for the assault after long study of the strength of German coastal defenses and the disposition of German divisions. The absence of large ports in the area was a serious obstacle, but it was offset in some measure by the relative weakness of the German defenses and elaborate construction in Britain of two artificial harbors to be emplaced off the beaches.

The selection of target dates and hours for the assault required an accurate forecast of the optimum combination of favorable weather, tide, and light conditions. Moonlight was desirable for the airborne operations. D-day was scheduled for 5 June; this date was changed to 6 June because of unfavorable but clearing weather. Hundreds of craft, en route from distant ports on the west coast of England, were already approaching the invasion area; they had to backtrack or seek shelter in the overcrowded harbors on the south coast. The final forecast for the attack day predicted high winds; the sea was still rough, but rather than accept a delay of several weeks until tide and moon provided another favorable moment, General Eisenhower made the fateful decision to go ahead.

At 0200 hours on 6 June 1944, the American 82d and 101st Airborne Divisions, as well as British airborne troops, were dropped in vital areas in the rear of German coastal defenses guarding the Normandy beaches from Cherbourg to Caen.

The seaborne assault under the over-all command of Field Marshal Montgomery was made on a broad front; British and Canadian forces commanded by Lt. Gen. Sir Miles C. Dempsey and American forces commanded by Lt. Gen. Omar N. Bradley deployed against 50 miles of coast line. Aerial bombardment of beach defenses along the coast began at 0314, preliminary naval bombardment at 0550, shortly after sunrise. At 0630 the first waves of assault infantry and tanks landed on the invasion beaches.

German defenses on all beaches were formidable; they consisted first of bands of underwater obstacles designed to break up formations of landing craft; mines were freely used to make these obstacles more lethal. The beaches themselves were heavily mined and strung with wire. Concrete pillboxes and gun emplacements were sited to deliver withering crossfire along the beaches. All exits leading inland from the beaches were blocked by antitank walls and ditches, mine fields, and barbed wire. Further inland, mortars and artillery were sited to deliver indirect fire on the beaches. Open fields were blocked against glider landings by patterns of heavy stakes, but complete intelligence gathered up to the moment of assault provided detailed knowledge of enemy dispositions and enabled the troops to breach the defenses.

In the American sector, the beach areas totaled 10,000 yards in length. Every 75 yards a landing craft loaded with assault infantry touched down at H-hour. Assault veterans charged down the ramps, picked their way through the bands of obstacles, and immediately provided cover for the work of naval and engineer demolition crews which followed close behind. Each crew had a specific task to perform in clearing lanes for subsequent waves of craft carrying infantry, artillery, vehicles, and supplies. Naval gunfire and air bombardment hammered at artillery and mortar positions, pillboxes, and gun emplacements.

Resistance by German ground elements was stubborn, and bitter fighting developed in many sectors. Our long campaign against the Luftwaffe had greatly weakened its capacity for combat and, as a result, there was no effective air opposition to our highly vulnerable initial landings. Reinforcements continued to pour ashore, and by nightfall on D-day, five American divisions, the 1st, 4th, 29th, and 82d and 101st Airborne, with tanks, artillery and other reinforcements, were firmly established. Also ashore were advance detachments of the headquarters of Maj. Gen. Leonard T. Gerow's V Corps and Maj. Gen. J. Lawton Collins' VII Corps. The British build-up in their sector was on a corresponding scale. Additional divisions still afloat were being landed in a steady stream, constantly augmenting the superiority which our assault troops had already established over the German defenders.

By the second morning it was clear that the beachhead was secure and that the greatest and longest step toward the destruction of the German armies of the west had been taken. The "crust" of the German coastal defense system had been broken. The German boast that an invading force could not remain ashore for nine hours had been flung back on the now desperate defenders.

Shortly after D-day the Combined Chiefs of Staff met in London in order to be immediately available should an emergency arise requiring a prompt decision on

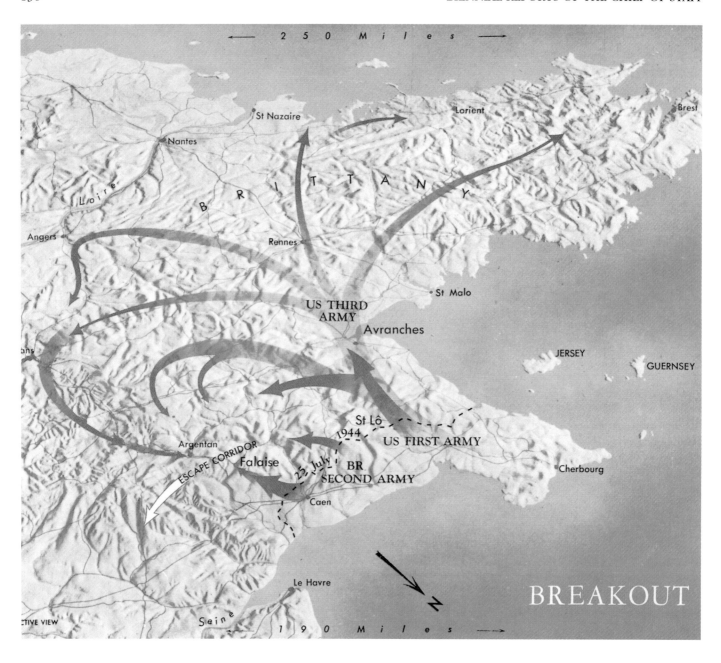

some matter beyond General Eisenhower's jurisdiction as Supreme Commander. The assault went so well that it was possible on 12 June for the Combined Chiefs to visit the beaches of Normandy and observe at first hand the magnitude of the undertaking and the gallant and skilfull manner in which the Allied forces were overcoming the resistance of the veteran German soldiers.

Our Army feels great pride in the Normandy assault. So must the Navy and our British Allies. The Navy's mission was to transport the troops across the Channel, to land them properly on the beaches, and to support the landings with gun and rocket fire. If the Allied navies had not performed this task brilliantly, the invasion would have failed before it was well begun. The combined planning of British and American staffs, working together as a single team with excellent knowledge of enemy dispositions, resulted in precise execution of an operation so complicated that it almost defies description; its success must be attributed in great measure to wholehearted

Allied cooperation, as well as to the stout hearts and fearless courage of the men. The destruction of rail and road communications by the air forces and their constant strafing of the highways continued to prevent the enemy from concentrating a superior force against the beachhead.

The Breakout

The second phase of the invasion had two objectives: first, the capture of the port of Cherbourg; and, second, the build-up of sufficient forces and matériel to enable the forces to break out from the beachhead and strike toward Germany. Now the fighting grew fiercer. After a bitter and costly struggle, Cherbourg fell on 27 June to the 4th, 9th, and 79th Divisions of General Collins' VII Corps. Damage in the harbor was so extensive and difficult of repairs that until the late fall thousands of tons of matériel were still pouring over the beaches. Other Allied forces had, by 1 July, deepened the beachhead by advances up to 20 miles in the area between Caen and St. Lo against increasingly stubborn resistance in the aggressively defended hedgerows of the Cotentin Peninsula.

General Eisenhower wrote on 5 July:

> The going is extremely tough, with three main causes responsible. The first of these, as always, is the fighting quality of the German soldier. The second is the nature of the country. Our whole attack has to fight its way out of very narrow bottlenecks flanked by marshes and against an enemy who has a double hedgerow and an intervening ditch almost every 50 yards as ready-made strong points. The third cause is the weather. Our air has been unable to operate at maximum efficiency and on top of this the rain and mud were so bad during my visit that I was reminded of Tunisian wintertime. It was almost impossible to locate artillery targets although we have plenty of guns available. Even with clear weather it is extraordinarily difficult to point out a target that is an appropriate one for either air or artillery.

In spite of the lack of a major port, the build-up in the beachhead was completed late in July. On 1 August the 12th U. S. Army Group, later designated the Central Group of Armies, became operational under the command of General Bradley. Its two armies—the First, under Lt. Gen. Courtney H. Hodges, and the Third, under Lt. Gen. George S. Patton, Jr., totaling 13 infantry and 5 armored divisions,[1] had been assembled in the beachhead area. The Canadian First Army under General Crerar and the British Second Army under General Dempsey composed the 21st Army Group, later designated the Northern Group of Armies, commanded by Field Marshal Montgomery. These armies were still dependent on beachhead supply for their sustenance. Even with unseasonable bad weather which severely damaged and almost destroyed one of the two artificial port installations and halted unloading operations many times, an average of some 30,000 tons of supplies and 30,000 troops were handled every day. These achievements, without precedent in history, were not anticipated by the German defenders and, consequently, their plans for the defense of the French coast had not taken them into account.

General Bradley was able, on 25 July, to mount the offensive which broke out of the beachhead at St. Lo and Avranches and carried the lines swiftly forward to the Meuse River. Preceding the ground attack 1,500 heavy bombers and hundreds of other combat aircraft dropped more than 3,390 tons of bombs on enemy positions on a narrow front. The crushing power of the air attack and its paralyzing effect on the enemy's movement blasted the way for rapid penetration of German lines. While observing preparations for the attack, one of the Army's outstanding soldiers, Lt. Gen. Lesley J. McNair, was killed by misdirected bombs of our own air force. Though his loss was a tremendous shock to our divisions, which he had organized and trained, he undoubtedly died in the way he preferred—in battle. General McNair was utterly fearless.

The break-out gave General Eisenhower an opportunity to deliver mighty blows at the shaken enemy. At the height of this action he wrote:

> My entire preoccupation these days is to secure the destruction of a substantial portion of the enemy forces facing us. Patton's Third Army, on the marching wing of our forces, is closing in as rapidly as possible. His deployment through the bottleneck near Avranches was exceedingly difficult but we have now got the strength on that wing to proceed definitely about our business. We have detached only one corps for the conquest of the Brittany Peninsula so as to have the maximum forces for the main battle. Within a week there should be real developments on the present front.

He seized his opportunity, directing a vigorous pursuit of the shattered German forces. There followed a campaign which for speed and boldness has few parallels. Following the First Army's breakthrough, the Third Army, under General Patton, utilizing a heavy preponderance of armor, thrust forward from the Avranches breach on 2 August and cut off the Brittany Peninsula by 6 August, isolating the bulk of the 2d Parachute and 265th, 266th and 343d German Infantry Divisions. The next move was to establish a southern flank along the Loire to protect our main effort heading eastward against attack from the south. These were preparatory moves. While they were in progress, General Hodges' First Army and the British Second Army were repulsing and crushing heavy attacks which the enemy launched in the desperate hope of driving a wedge to the sea through Avranches to cut off General Patton's forces.

On 13 August the Third Army swept north from Le Mans around the southern flank of the German Normandy position in the direction of Argentan. Simultaneously, Canadian forces of the British Second Army drove south from Caen toward Falaise. This pincers movement created the "Falaise pocket," in which 100,000 enemy troops were captured, thousands more were killed or wounded, and thousands more thrown into disorder as they escaped toward the Seine through the "Falaise-Argentan corridor" held open by desperate German resistance. The Germans realized that the battle for Normandy was lost and they began withdrawing beyond the Seine under heavy pressure from both the ground and the air. The Seine crossings were raked by fighter patrols. Turning eastward from Le Mans and Argentan, the Third Army raced for the river with such speed that supply by air was often necessary to maintain its momentum. By the capture of Mantes on 18 August the German escape route was confined to crossings of the lower Seine northwest of Elbeuf.

Continental Envelopment

Meanwhile, on 15 August, operation ANVIL was executed by the U. S. Seventh Army under Lt. Gen. Alexander M. Patch in landings on the southern coast

---

[1] U. S. Divisions in France, 27 July 1945, Infantry: 1st, 2d, 4th, 5th, 8th, 9th, 28th, 29th, 30th, 35th, 79th, 83d, 90th; Armored: 2d, 3d, 4th, 5th, and 6th.

215 Miles

Dijon

Dole

Geneva

Lyon

27 August 1944

Grenoble

MARITIME ALPS

Valence

Rhône

Gap

Avignon

FRENCH
ARMY

US SEVENTH
ARMY

Nimes

Argens

Cannes

St Raphaël

Marseille

Toulon

Commandos

1st Sp Serv

N

OPERATION ANVIL

US
COR
15 Au
194

JULY 1, 1943, TO JUNE 30, 1945

of France, which further weakened the fast-deteriorating position of the German Army in France. Preparations for this operation under the general supervision of the Supreme Allied Commander, Mediterranean Theater of Operations, had been under way, while the campaigns in Italy and Northern France were in progress. The very threat of such a landing had held substantial German forces of the First and Nineteenth armies immobilized in the south of France, preventing their deployment against our forces in Normandy. A naval force, comparable in size to the one which participated in the American landings in Normandy, had been assembled. An air offensive, conducted chiefly by the Allied Strategic Air Forces, prepared the way for the invasion by sustained attacks on vital enemy communications and installations in Southern France.

The Seventh Army landed southwest of Cannes in ideal weather. The area had been selected as the most favorable approach to the Rhone Valley. The landing force consisted of elements of General Truscott's VI Corps, our 1st Special Service Force, and French commandos. A British-American Airborne Task Force jumped astride the Argens River west of St. Raphael the night preceding the seaborne assault and seized the pass through which our forces would debouch. By 28 August the beachheads were firmly established and the advance up the Rhone Valley was well under way.

The operations had been substantially aided by the efforts of the French underground. The landing of our VI Corps had been followed up immediately by the landing of divisions of the French I and II Corps of General de Tassigny's First French Army, which quickly captured Marseille and Toulon; by 1 September Nice had fallen. While the main force swept west to the Rhone, before moving northward, a task force from the American 36th Division under Brig. Gen. Frederic B. Butler headed directly north from the landing beaches through Gap, seized Grenoble and then turned northwest toward the Rhone to cut off the German columns retreating up the Rhone Valley. This drive into the rear of the German Nineteenth Army greatly facilitated the rapid advance of the main body of the VI Corps up the Rhone Valley. Lyon fell on 3 September and the advance northward continued unabated.

On 15 September other United States and French forces were combined into the 6th Army Group (later designated the Southern Group of Armies) commanded by Lt. Gen. Jacob L. Devers. He was succeeded as Deputy Theater Commander in the Mediterranean by Lt. Gen. Joseph T. McNarney, former Deputy Chief of Staff of the U. S. Army.

The Liberation of France

On 25 August the 2d French Armored Division of the First U. S. Army entered Paris, as the battered remnants of the German army which had defended the Normandy coast fell back north of the Seine. The Germans had suffered at least 400,000 casualties, of which more than 200,000 were prisoners of war. The units which had escaped destruction were forced to abandon the major portion of their equipment.

As the enemy withdrew he had left behind substantial garrisons to defend the critical seaports: Brest, St. Nazaire, Lorient, Dieppe, and LeHavre. In order to prevent the Allies from developing harbor facilities to sustain the advance of the gathering millions, the Germans freely expended thousands of men to make the supply problem difficult if not impossible of accomplishment.

Despite these obstructions, by 5 September (D+90) 2,086,000 Allied troops and 3,446,000 tons of stores had been put ashore in France. This was an outstanding logistical achievement, but nevertheless we were still in urgent need of additional ports if we were to support adequately the fast-moving offensive across France that was operating on a dangerously thin supply basis. Many divisions had a very limited supply on hand.

On 5 September the Ninth U. S. Army under the command of Lt. Gen. William H. Simpson began operations under the 12th Army Group for the reduction of Brest and other French ports, where four German divisions were bottled up. Dieppe fell on 31 August; LeHavre on 11 September; Brest on 19 September. The most strenuous efforts were made to put these ports into operating condition. Tonnage began moving through Dieppe on 7 September and through Le Havre on 9 October. Brest was too heavily damaged and too distant from future fields of operations to justify immediate reconstruction.

The defeated German armies now were streaming across France, heading for the shelter of the Siegfried Line. They were under constant air attack. On the ground General Bradley's First and Third Armies, driving northeast from Melun and Troyes reached the Aisne and the Marne, sweeping aside the German rear guards. Field Marshal Montgomery's forces crossed the lower Seine, invested LeHavre, and pushed on to the Somme. On crossing the Aisne, the 7th Corps of the First Army turned northward and raced on to Mons in a brilliant stroke that cut off five of the retreating German divisions. The pocket thus formed yielded over 22,000 prisoners with heavy additional losses of killed and wounded.

Overrunning Reims and Chalons, our Third Army pushed eastward, nourished often by air supply, and by 7 September had reached the line of the Moselle from Nancy to the vicinity of Metz. On 11 September elements of the Third Army contacted Seventh Army columns northwest of Dijon. Four days later the 6th Army Group passed to operational control of Supreme Headquarters, Allied Expeditionary Forces, severing its fighting connection with the Mediterranean theater, though its supply was continued for some time from Italy. On 16 September approximately 20,000 occupational troops of the German Army from the Biscayne Bay area, moving northeastward toward Germany, surrendered to the commander of the U. S. 83d Division southwest of Orleans.

To the north, our First Army had crossed the Belgian frontier on 2 September, captured Liege on the 8th, crossed Luxembourg, and entered Germany on the 11th. The enemy had been kept completely off balance. As the Allies approached the German border, supply lines were stretched to the limit and the marching columns of the armies were maintained only by the full use of air transportation, fast double-lane, one-way track routes, such as the famous Red Ball Express from the Normandy beaches to Paris, and other emergency measures. Logistical difficulties now began to slow down the advance. Time was needed for the opening of additional ports and for the relaying and repair of hundreds of miles of French railroads.

The following extract from a report by General Eisenhower indicates the severity of the campaign in France and illustrates the tremendous needs of our armies during this campaign, in addition to the routine consumption of huge quantities of gasoline and rations:

Losses of ordnance equipment have been extremely high. For instance, we must have as replacement items each month 36,000 small arms, 700 mortars, 500 tanks, 2,400 vehicles, 100 field pieces. Consumption of artillery and mortar ammunition in northwestern Europe averages 8,000,000 rounds a month. Our combat troops use up an average of 66,400 miles of one type of field wire each month. (The AEF during the entire First World War expended less than 10,000,000 rounds of artillery and mortar ammunition.)

The British 21st Army Group liberated Brussels on 3 September and Antwerp the next day. They crossed the Dutch frontier on 12 September and by the 15th the Channel coast was cleared as far north as Zeebrugge with the exception of the isolated enemy forces holding out in key ports.

On 9 September 1944 General Eisenhower reported:

The hostile occupation in force of the Dutch Islands at the mouth of the Schelde is certain to delay the utilization of Antwerp as a port and thus will vitally influence the full development of our strategy.

Again on 21 September he wrote:

Right now our prospects are tied up closely with our success in capturing the approaches to Antwerp. All along the line maintenance is in a bad state—reminiscent of the early days in Tunisia—but if we can only get to using Antwerp it will have the effect of a blood transfusion.

The efforts of the British forces on the north flank were to be devoted for several weeks to clearing the enemy from these islands. After bitter fighting involving heavy losses, featured by river crossings and amphibious landings, the last of the positions was cleared on 9 November. By 27 November the port of Antwerp was in operation but under heavy fire of the vicious German V-weapons which fell at one time at the rate of one every 12½ minutes and caused thousands of Allied civilian and military casualties and cast grave doubt for a time as to the advisability of continuing the operation of the port.

The ports of southern France were vital to the U. S. Seventh Army and the French First Army in the Southern Group of Armies. Toulon and Marseille were in operation late in September. Since then 14 divisions were moved through Southern French ports, in addition to an average daily unloading of over 18,000 tons of supplies. Two railways were placed in early operation, including the double-track main line through Lyon and Dijon, and thousands of tons of supplies moved daily over these lines and by truck to forward railheads. Port capacities and transportation facilities were sufficient to meet the requirements of the entire Southern Group of Armies and also to assist in the supply of the Central Group of Armies until the stubborn defense of the water entrance to Antwerp was reduced.

After the port of Antwerp became operational, it handled on an average of over 25,000 tons of stores daily, despite the V bombs. This tremendous increase in our over-all port capacity made it unnecessary to devote more precious time and manpower to reopen the shattered ports in Brittany, which, although now in our hands, were much more distant from the front lines than Antwerp.

Having overcome the acute shortage of port facilities, the primary bottleneck in the supply line then became transportation from the port supply dumps to the front lines. To improve this situation our Engineers, Transportation Corps, and other supply troops in Lt. Gen. J. C. H. Lee's communications zone performed miracles in repairing and building railways, operating large high-speed truck convoys, and extending fuel pipelines from the ports and terminals of 16 cross-Channel pipelines to the forward areas. At one time 70 miles of pipe were being laid in a single day.

The Westwall

As the Siegfried Line was approached, and the port and enlarged transportation facilities became adequate, General Eisenhower advised the War Department that tactical plans for the final assault of this fortification required greater ammunition resources than those provided, and requested a maximum production effort in the United States. He forecast the expenditure of some 6,000,000 artillery and 2,000,000 mortar shells monthly in order to reduce the Siegfried Line. In this country an urgent demand

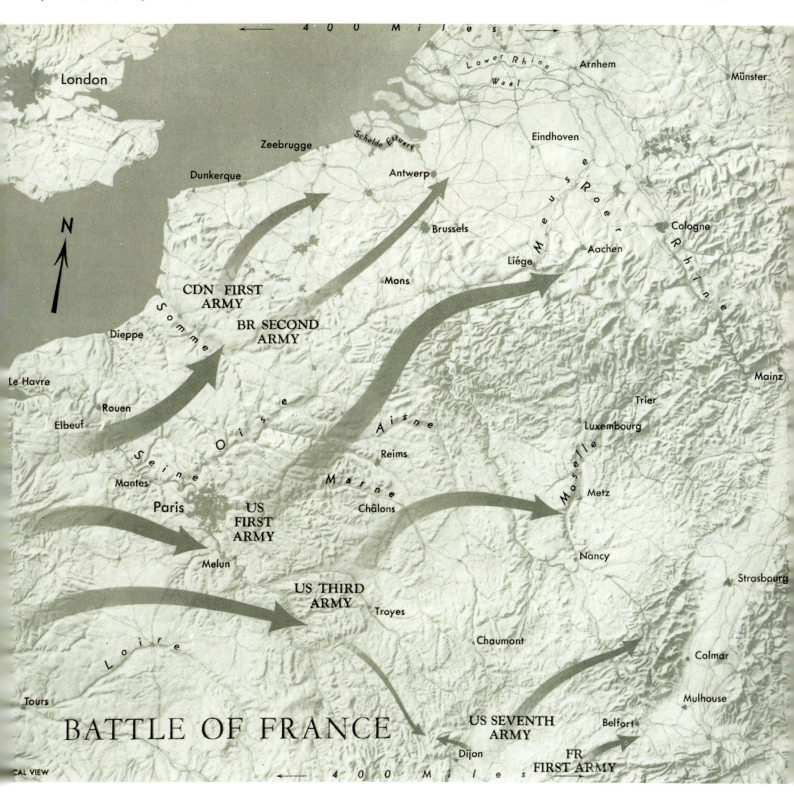

was made for maximum production; fast rail and water transportation was utilized to make shipments direct from the production lines to the gun positions, and rationing to less active theaters, as well as stabilized fronts in the European theater itself, became rigid. Only by these measures was it possible to serve the thousands of guns behind the major assault efforts and secure an adequate supply of ammunition for the final battles against Germany.

Field Marshal Montgomery struck through the air at the northern flank of the Seigfried Line on 17 and 18

September. The U. S. 82d and 101st and one British airborne division, all elements of Lt. Gen. Lewis H. Brereton's newly formed First Allied Airborne Army, landed in Holland astride the Meuse, Waal, and Lower Rhine rivers in the Eindhoven-Arnhem area. This was the largest airborne operation ever attempted, requiring the employment on the first two days of 2,800 planes and over 1,600 gliders. Several airborne operations had been planned for the period following the break-through in Normandy, but so rapid was the Allied advance that events overtook the plans in each

PATH OF THE RED ARMY

Along this highroad to Berlin was destroyed two-thirds of the German
Wehrmacht. As Soviet forces drove westward and General Eisenhower's
armies drove eastward through France, Adolph Hitler had only rivers and
man-made defensive lines to prolong his end. The mountain barriers of
Southern Europe gave him small safety.

Gibraltar

Marsei

MEDITERRANEAN SEA

AFRICA

Rome

Messina

ITALY

ADRIATIC SEA

YUGOSLAVIA

Vier

Budapest

GREECE

Krakc

Athens

AEGEAN SEA

POL

BULGARIA

Bucharest

Danube

ROMANIA

Istanbul

Dniester

TURKEY

Odessa

BLACK SEA

Dnieper

Dniepropetrovsk

ATLANTIC OCEAN

PORTUGAL

Bay of Biscay

Brest

Loire

FRANCE

Paris

GREAT BRITAIN

London

IRELAND

Rhine

Rotterdam

GERMANY

NORTH SEA

Prague

Bremen

Elbe

Berlin

DENMARK

Oder

Copenhagen

NORWAY

Oslo

Vistula

arsaw

Danzig

BALTIC SEA

SWEDEN

D

Stockholm

LITHUANIA

Kaunas

Riga

LATVIA

FINLAND

Tallinn

ESTONIA

Helsinki

Smolensk

Leningrad

Richard Edes Harrison

instance. The operation in Holland achieved only partial success. The American 82d and 101st Airborne Divisions, landing near Eindhoven, seized crossings of the Meuse and Waal Rivers. The British Second Army was able to establish contact with these divisions after the second day. The important bridgeheads were held in the face of desperate German counterattacks. The British airborne division, landing in the more remote and exposed Arnhem area north of the Lower Rhine, was subjected to concentrated attacks by superior enemy forces. It was finally forced to withdraw south of the river.

Meanwhile, to the south, our First Army was forcing its way into Germany. Aachen was strongly defended, and a bitter battle ensued before it fell on 21 October. On 3 October the Ninth Army had been brought up from the western coast of France and entered the line between the First and Third Armies. Then on 23 October the Ninth Army was moved to the northern flank of the First Army above Aachen. By the end of November the Third Army, driving toward the Saar, had reduced the formidable Metz area and the defenses along the Moselle and Seille Rivers. A Southern Army Group offensive into Alsace-Lorraine brought the 2d French Armored Division of the U. S. Seventh Army to Strasbourg on the Rhine in late November and the First French Army to the river between Mulhouse and the Swiss border. Between the two armies remained a sizable portion of the Alsace known as the Colmar pocket.

During the third week in September the Combined Chiefs of Staff were again in conference at Quebec with President Roosevelt and Prime Minister Churchill. The whole of Northern France and substantial parts of Belgium and Luxembourg were in Allied hands. But General Eisenhower reported that enemy resistance was stiffening as he approached the German frontier. He reported that it was his intention to prepare with all speed to destroy the German armies in the west and occupy the German homeland. He considered that his best opportunity to defeat the defenders in the west was to strike at the Ruhr and Saar, confident the enemy would be compelled to concentrate most of his available resources in defense of these essential areas. He preferred the northern approach into Germany through the Cologne plain for reasons which the map makes obvious.

Early in October I made a hurried 9-day inspection trip to the Western Front, visiting American corps and divisions from the Vosges Mountains north to Holland. At that time many of the infantrymen had been in almost constant combat since D-day in June. After many computations and exchanges of radio messages with the War Department to determine the effect on our hard-pressed and delicately balanced shipping situation, it was decided to rush the movement from the United States of the infantry regiments of 9 of the 11 remaining divisions ahead of the scheduled departures of the entire divisions. This was for the purpose of relieving those regiments which had been in combat for an excessively long period and to give immediate increased strength and striking power to our armies facing a most difficult winter campaign.

With the promise of a large increase of supplies through the port of Antwerp in late November, and with more than 3,000,000 troops on the Continent, General Eisenhower in mid-November launched a charging offensive to penetrate the Siegfried Line and place himself in position to cross the Rhine.

Not in years had European weather been so unfavorable for grand-scale military operations. Resistance was bitter. The Siegfried defenses were formidable as anticipated, and our divisions paid heavily for each inch of ground they tore from the fanatical Nazi defenders. Nevertheless, by 4 December the Second British Army had cleared the west bank of the Meuse and the Ninth Army had reached the Roer. East of Aachen troops of the First Army fought splendidly through bloody Hurtgen Forest, taking heavy casualties and inflicting heavy losses on the stubborn enemy. The dams of the Roer were seriously inhibiting General Eisenhower's progress. He wrote:

> He (the enemy) is assisted in that area, however, by the flooded condition of the Roer River and the capability he has of producing a sudden rush of water by blowing the dams near Schmidt. Bradley has about come to the conclusion that we must take that area by a very difficult attack from the west and southwest.
>
> There can be no question of the value of our present operations. The German is throwing into the line some divisions with only six weeks training, a fact that contributes materially to his high casualty rate. As explained in my most recent appreciation to the Combined Chiefs of Staff, our problem is to continue our attacks as long as the results achieved are so much in our favor, while at the same time preparing for a full-out heavy offensive when weather conditions become favorable, assuming the enemy holds out. Unless some trouble develops from within Germany, a possibility of which there is now no real evidence, he should be able to maintain a strong defensive front for some time, assisted by weather, floods, and muddy ground.

The Wehrmacht's Last Blow

General Eisenhower was determined to give Germany no chance to recoup from the blows already delivered. Despite shortages in troops and supplies, his attitude was offensive, and, consequently, he was compelled to hold some sectors of the front with comparatively weak forces in order to gather strength at his points of attack. To the 75 miles between Monschau and Trier he could assign only four divisions of the First Army, or sacrifice his effort to bring about a decision elsewhere. It was here that the German armies of the west, commanded by Field

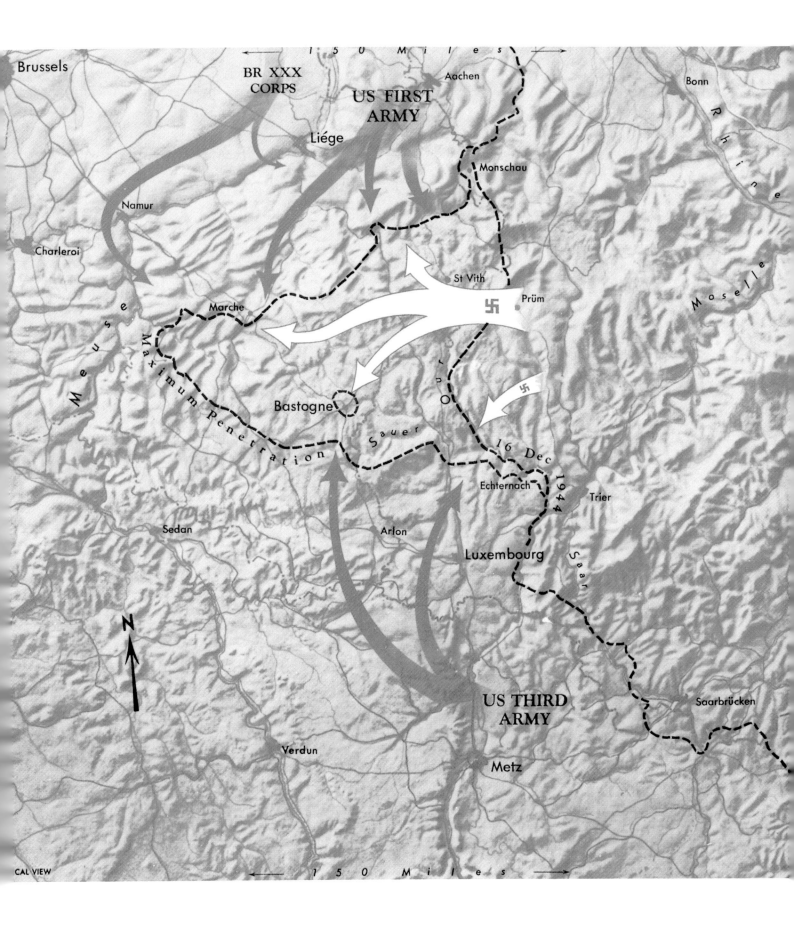

Brussels

BR XXX
CORPS

US FIRST
ARMY

Aachen

Bonn

Liége

Monschau

Namur

Charleroi

St Vith

Prüm

Marche

Maximum Penetration

Bastogne

Sauer

Echternach

Sedan

Arlon

Luxembourg

Trier

US THIRD
ARMY

Verdun

Metz

Saarbrücken

Meuse

Our

Saar

Moselle

Rhine

16 Dec 1944

N

150 Miles

150 Miles

CAL VIEW

Marshal von Rundstedt and acting on the direct orders of Hitler, made their last desperate effort to stave off the disaster.

On 16 December von Rundstedt attacked with a force of 24 divisions. He had been able, because of heavy fog which continued for days, to assemble his forces in secrecy in the heavily forested foreground. When the blow came, eight panzer divisions broke through our VIII Corps line on a 40-mile front. Diversionary attacks in other sectors and considerable air and artillery support assisted the main offensive in Luxembourg.

General Eisenhower reacted promptly and decisively and subsequent results have proved the eminent soundness of his plan. All available reserves in the Central Army Group were used to strengthen the northern and southern flanks of the penetration and the XXX British Corps of the Northern Army Group was deployed to hold the line of the Meuse and the vital Liege area. With communications seriously disrupted, Field Marshal Montgomery was charged with the operation of forces north of the penetration, involving temporary operational control over most of the U. S. First and Ninth Armies while General Bradley coordinated the effort from the south. The 82d and 101st Airborne Divisions were brought up from theater reserve to retard the momentum of the enemy thrust, with the 101st, reinforced by armor and artillery, holding the important road center at Bastogne. The shoulders of the penetration at Monschau and Echternach were stubbornly held by infantry divisions moved in from the north and from the south, outstanding among which were the 1st, 2d, 4th, and 99th Divisions.

The Ardennes battle deserves a prominent place in the history of the U. S. Army. The splendid stand of the 7th Armored Division at St. Vith, the tenacity of the 101st Airborne and elements of the 10th Armored Division at Bastogne, and the numerous examples of superb fighting qualities shown by the troops of other units were in the finest American tradition.

The tide of battle began to turn when the U. S. Third Army brought its full weight to bear on the southern flank of the salient, where General Patton stopped the advance of the German columns with available reserves and was attacking on a two-corps front by 22 December with the III and XII Corps. This shift from an offensive across the Saar to a general attack in southern Luxembourg was a brilliant military accomplishment, including corps and army staff work of the highest order. Elements of the 5th Division which were fighting in the Saar bridgehead on the morning of 20 December moved 69 miles, and were in contact with the enemy north of the Sauer River by nightfall.

General Devers' 6th Army Group was required to assume responsibility for the entire front from Saarbrucken south, adding over 25 miles to its already extended front. In order to defend this front adequately, full use was made in the Seventh Army of the infantry regiments of three divisions which were just arriving in the theater from the United States in advance of their division headquarters and supporting troops.

The weather ceased to favor the enemy between 23 and 26 December, permitting our overwhelming tactical air forces to strike terrific blows at the German armor and supply columns. On 26 December the 4th Armored Division relieved encircled Bastogne. The crisis had passed, for by this time the German salient was being assaulted from the north, west, and south. At the points of extreme penetration, the enemy had driven more than 50 miles into the American lines, but he was unable to shake loose our valiant units fighting desperately to hold the critical shoulders of the bulge. The depth of his advance was accordingly limited and it was possible to interdict by artillery fire all the important supply roads for the leading troops at the tip of the salient.

The reduction of the Ardennes salient involved our First and Third Armies in heavy fighting under severe winter conditions, but progress was steady and by the end of January the bulge was eliminated at a cost which later proved fatal to the enemy. In the single day of 22 January, the air force destroyed or damaged more than 4,192 pieces of heavy equipment, including locomotives, rail cars, tanks, and motor and horse-drawn vehicles.

The Germans gained an initial tactical success and imposed a delay of about six weeks on the main Allied offensive in the north, but failed to seize their primary objectives of Liege and Namur. They lost 220,000 men, including 110,000 prisoners, and more than 1,400 tanks and assault guns. The operation was carried out by the Fifth and Sixth Panzer Armies, supported by the Seventh Army, thus stripping the Reich of all strategic reserves and seriously depleting the resources required to meet the powerful Soviet offensive in January.

"Possibly more serious," reported General Eisenhower, "was the widespread disillusionment ensuing from the failure to seize any really important objective and the realization that this offensive for which every effort had been brought to bear and on which such great hopes were pinned, had in no sense achieved anything decisive."

In mid-January the Second British Army launched an attack in the Sittard area and within a fortnight reached the Roer Valley, 10 miles inside the Reich. Regrouping of the Allied armies for further offensive action proceeded during January.

In an effort to divert the punishing blows from his forces withdrawing from the Ardennes, the enemy attacked in the Bavarian Palatinate. Here there was ground to give, and the U. S. Seventh Army withdrew to the Maginot defenses west of the Rhine, permitting the detachment of divisions for the heavy fighting in the Bulge.

Closing The Rhine

On 20 January the First French Army launched an attack in the southern Alsace to destroy the enemy's forces in the Colmar pocket and clear the west bank of the Rhine. The operation involved a drive through Colmar by the American XXI Corps, commanded by Maj. Gen. F. W. Milburn, and simultaneous attacks by forces of the First French Army under General de Tassigny from the Mulhouse area. The climax of the battle was a night assault on the bridgehead town of Neuf-Brisach by infantry of the U. S. 3d Division using assault boats and scaling ladders on the moats and walls of the fortified town, very much after the fashion of medieval battles. After this aggressive action, the German position in the Alsace rapidly deteriorated and by 9 February the Allies held a loosely defended line along the west bank of the Rhine from Strasbourg to the Swiss border, freeing troops for use in other sectors. The offensive in the Alsace cost the Germans more than 25,000 men.

The reduction of the Colmar pocket and the seizure of the Roer River dams to the north in the vicinity of Schmidt were both necessary preludes to clearing the enemy from the west bank of the Rhine and a full-scale drive into the heart of Germany. The U. S. First Army now attacked toward Schmidt while the Third Army threw its weight against tbe Siegfried Line in the Prüm-Trier area. By 10 February the First Army had obtained control of the Erft and the Schwammenauel dams, and the following day had cleared the entire west bank of the Roer. Although failing to prevent the flooding of the Roer Valley, this action forced the Germans to release the waters at a time when our operations would not be endangered, thus removing the most serious threat to General Eisenhower's plan for the invasion of northern Germany.

The Combined Chiefs of Staff met at Malta in early February preliminary to a meeting with President Roosevelt, Prime Minister Churchill, and Marshal Stalin in the ARGONAUT Conference at Yalta a few days later. En route to the Conference, I met General Eisenhower briefly at a secret rendezvous near Marseilles where we discussed his future plans that were later approved at Malta, providing for the closing of the Rhine, the destruction of enemy forces west of the river, the seizure of bridgeheads across the river in the north and south and coordinated drives into the heart of Germany. At Yalta the general plan for the final destruction of Nazi Germany was established.

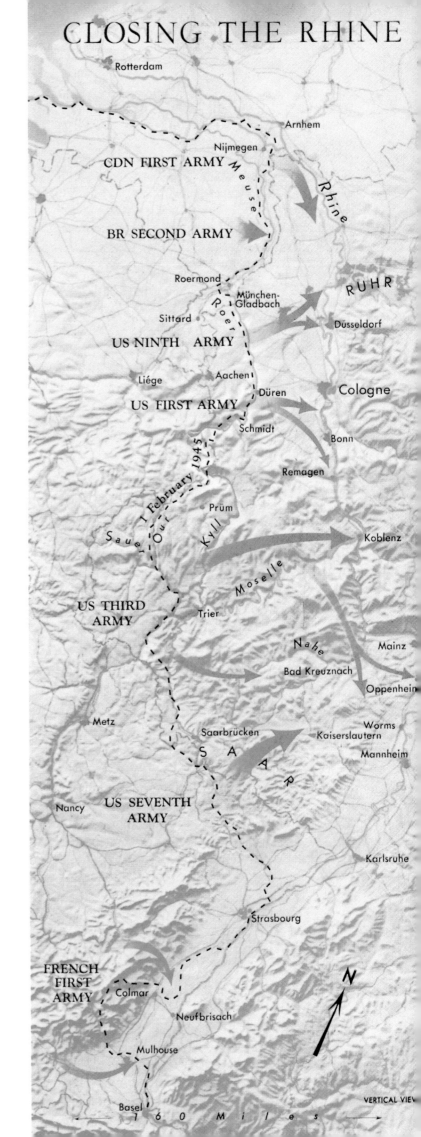

CLOSING THE RHINE

VERTICAL VIEW

0   60   Miles

In executing General Eisenhower's plan, a coordinated drive by the First Canadian Army from the Nijmegen bridgehead along the watershed between the Meuse and the Rhine s necessary and an attack by the U. S. Ninth Army across the Roer toward Dusseldorf was to follow shortly afterward. On 8 February the First Canadian Army began its attack following a heavy air and artillery preparation. Initially, the Canadian advance was rapid, but flooded terrain delayed the start of the Ninth Army attack, permitting the enemy to concentrate against the Canadians.

In preparation for the Ninth Army offensive, the Tactical and Strategic Air Forces flew almost 10,000 sorties on 22 February, covering rail and transportation targets throughout the length and breadth of Germany. These blows from British, French, and Italian bases were designed to paralyze the German rail system and isolate the Western Front. The next day the Ninth Army attack was launched and, although there was some delay in establishing bridgeheads over the flooded Roer, the general progress was quite rapid. By 1 March Roermond and Munchen-Gladbach were captured and the following day the armored columns reached the Rhine north and south of Dusseldorf. Meanwhile, in the Prüm-Trier area, the Third Army drove across the Our and Sauer Rivers, capturing Prüm on 13 February. Successive bridgeheads were established across the Saar and the Kyll Rivers and on 2 March Trier fell to our troops. From the launching of the operations on 8 February to 1 March more than 66,000 German prisoners were captured by the Northern and Central Army Groups.

The Watch That Failed

Advancing on the right of the Ninth Army, the First Army captured the ruins of Cologne on 7 March against stout resistance. On the same day elements of its 9th Armored Division, probing to the Rhine further south, found the Ludendorff Bridge at Remagen intact and immediately crossed to the east bank, developing a small bridgehead. Such a windfall had been hoped for but not expected. The prompt seizure and exploitation of the crossing demonstrated American initative and adaptability at its best, from the daring action of the platoon leader to the Army commander who quickly redirected all his moving columns in a demonstration of brilliant staff management. He established powerful elements across the river immediately in accordance with direct orders from General Eisenhower. The bridgehead provided a serious threat to the heart of Germany, a diversion of incalculable value both to the main effort in the Ruhr and to the reduction of the Saar-Palatinate. It became a springboard for the final offensive to come.

In the meantime, the Third Army was forcing its way through the rugged Eifel hills. By 7 March, constant pressure had crushed the German front north of the Moselle. General Patton's armor broke out and dashed forward to the Rhine near Koblenz on the 9th. Contact was established with General Hodges' First Army units southeast of Remagen, and by 11 March the Allies controlled the west bank of the Rhine from Nijmegen in Holland to its junction with the Moselle at Koblenz.

Once the Eifel sector had been mopped up, General Patton was ready to assist the Seventh Army in reducing the Saar pocket. General Eisenhower wrote me:

> Tomorrow morning the XX Corps of Patton's Army begins a local attack in the Trier area as a preliminary to the general attack by Seventh Army on the 15th. So far as we can determine there is not a single reserve division in this whole area. If we can get a quick break-through, the advance should go very rapidly and success in the region will multiply the advantage we have secured in the bridgehead at Remagen. It will probably be a nasty business breaking through the fortified lines, but once this is accomplished losses should not be great and we should capture another big bag of prisoners. I have given Seventh Army 14 divisions for their part of the job, and XX Corps (Third Army) jumps off with four. Patton will throw in another subsidiary effort from north to south across the Moselle with about four to five divisions.

On 14 March General Patton established a bridgehead across the Moselle, southwest of Koblenz. The following day his troops lunged southward from the Moselle bridgehead, other Third Army forces drove east from Trier, and the Seventh Army attacked northward between Saarbrucken and the Rhine. Despite dense mine fields and the formidable Siegfried Line fortifications, the Seventh gained steadily, pinning down strong enemy formations and leaving the Third Army tanks free to cut to pieces the rear of the German position. On 16 March a spearhead of the 4th Armored Division broke through for a gain of 32 miles and seized two bridges across the Nahe River south of Bad Kreuznach. From this point on, resistance south of the Moselle crumbled. Armored divisions of the Third and Seventh Armies enveloped the Saar, and the Rhine cities of Worms and Mainz fell to our swift columns.

While pocketed German forces in the Saar were still in process of being mopped up, Third Army infantry of the Corps under Maj. Gen. Manton S. Eddy, achieved a brilliant surprise by crossing the Rhine at Oppenheim south of Mainz late on 22 March with decidedly sketchy and improvised means. In two days this bridgehead was expanded to a width of 15 miles, and on the third day the 4th Armored Division broke through the enemy lines to a depth of 27 miles, seizing an undamaged bridge over the Main River. The daring armored thrusts in the Saar had criss-crossed and intermingled elements of the two armies. Under the skillful direction of General Bradley and General Devers, the Army commanders regrouped their mingled corps and divisions without loss to the momentum of the offensive.

The Knockout

In six weeks the combined efforts of the Allied armies had achieved a major objective. The German soil west of the Rhine had been cleared of all hostile forces. The river itself had been forced in two fortuitous crossings, and the freedom of action of the German defense on the east bank was seriously curtailed. General Eisenhower was now ready to launch his offensive beyond the Rhine.

Several considerations governed the selection of the area north of the Ruhr for the main effort. A drive in this sector was the quickest means of denying what vestiges remained of the once rich Ruhr industries to the enemy. That stretch of the Rhine between Emmerich and Wesel was one of the two best sites for a forced crossing, and the Germans had brought up only relatively inferior forces to oppose such an operation. Once across that river the gently rolling terrain north of the Ruhr was most suitable for mobile and tank operations, the type of warfare it was desired to force upon the enemy because of his shortages in tanks, vehicles, and motor fuel.

After a heavy aerial and artillery preparation, the Second British Army began an assault crossing of the Rhine during the evening of 23 March. Next morning, the U. S. 17th and the 6th British Airborne Divisions were dropped north and northeast of Wesel. British troops crossing the river soon established contact with the airborne forces. The U. S. Ninth Army crossed between Wesel and Duisburg early on the 24th, meeting light to moderate resistance. Within two days seven bridges had been built across the river and the British-American bridgehead stretched 25 miles along the Rhine to a maximum depth of 6 miles.

General Eisenhower was with the Ninth when it jumped off. He described the attack in a letter:

I have just finished a rapid tour of the battle front. Yesterday and the day before I was with the Ninth Army to witness its jump-off and the early stages of the Rhine crossing. Simpson performed in his usual outstanding style. Our losses in killed, during the crossing, were 15 in one assault division and 16 in the other. I stayed up most of one night to witness the preliminary bombardment by 1,250 guns. It was an especially interesting sight because of the fact that all the guns were spread out on a plain so that the flashes from one end of the line to the other were all plainly visible. It was real drumfire.

I have noted so many unusual and outstanding incidents in the forward areas that it would almost weary you to tell you of the fine performances of American and other troops. For example, the Engineers of VII Corps laid a Treadway bridge across the Rhine in 10 hours and 11 minutes. While not actually under fire, this job was done under battlefield conditions with all the necessary precautions taken to prevent unusual damage by a sudden concentration of enemy artillery fire. It was a brilliant performance.

During the critical week ending 22 March, United States aircraft alone made 14,430 heavy bomber attacks, 7,262 medium bomber attacks, and 29,981 fighter sorties against targets in Europe.

By 25 March hard fighting in the Remagen area had extended the bridgehead to a depth of 10 miles and a length of over 30. The German High Command, expecting an immediate drive on the Ruhr from this direction, had concentrated strong forces of Army Group "B" north of the Sieg River. To their great surprise, General Hodges broke out of the bridgehead to the southeast on 26 March, when his armor drove to Limburg, seized a bridge over the Lahn River, and raced along the superhighway toward Frankfurt. Other armored columns of the First Army, speeding eastward as fast as 40 miles a day, reached Marburg and Giessen by 28 March, and then swung northward through the hill country west of Kassel. Troops of the Third Army crossed the river at Mainz to reduce the German pocket bypassed between Mainz and Frankfurt while, to the east, other Third Army forces drove on toward Kassel and the line of the Fulda River. With solid contact between their advancing corps, the First and Third Armies were now executing a massive thrust to the northeast into the heart of Germany. The complete rout of the German military establishment was now under way.

In the sector of Field Marshal Montgomery's Northern Army Group, the U. S. Ninth Army pressed into the northwest section of the Ruhr. Still further to the north, resistance on the right flank of the British Second Army slackened considerably toward the end of March, and armored troops broke through to Dulmen. Meanwhile, on the left flank of the Second Army, the enemy withdrew, and British units crossed the Dutch border on a 30-mile front.

During the last week of March both of General Devers' armies in the south crossed the Rhine. The Seventh sent the XV Corps, commanded by Maj. Gen. W. H. Haislip, across on a 15-mile front between Gernsheim and Mannheim. Our troops took Mannheim and advanced 25 miles east of the Rhine. The II Corps of the First French Army crossed the Rhine near Germersheim and established contact with the Seventh Army south of Heidelberg. By 1 April, French troops had advanced 18 miles.

The magnitude of the offensive smothered resistance all along the Western Front. The shattered condition of the German transport system and the sustained speed of the Allied advance prevented the enemy from coordinating a defensive line in any sector. He did offer bitter resistance at isolated points but these were bypassed by the armored columns, leaving pockets to be mopped up later. During the month of March nearly 350,000 prisoners were taken on the Western Front.

The entrance of the Fifteenth Army, under command of Lt. Gen. L. T. Gerow, into the line of the 12th Army Group on 30 March gave more freedom of action to the First and Ninth Armies, enabling them to

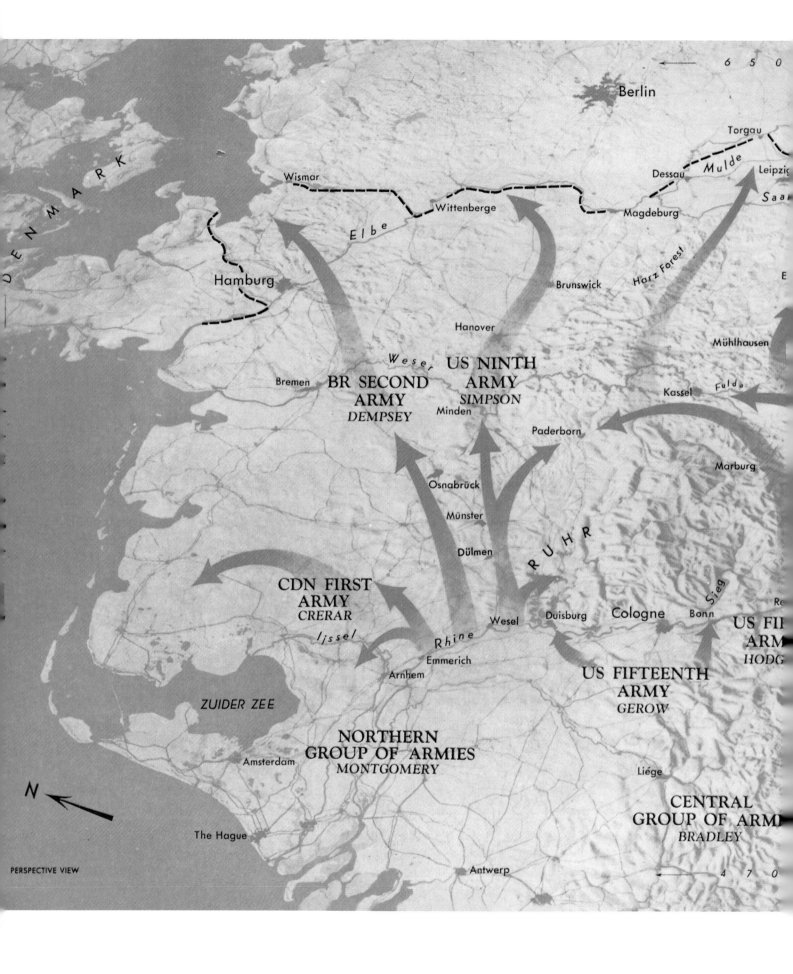

Berlin

Torgau

DENMARK

Dessau *Mulde* Leipzig

Wismar

Wittenberge Magdeburg *Saa*

Elbe

Hamburg

Brunswick *Harz Forest*

Hanover

Mühlhausen

Weser US NINTH

Bremen BR SECOND ARMY Kassel *Fulda*

ARMY SIMPSON

DEMPSEY Minden Paderborn

Osnabrück Marburg

Münster

Dülmen *R U H R*

CDN FIRST *Sieg*

ARMY Wesel Duisburg Cologne Bonn Re

CRERAR US FI

Ijssel ARM

Rhine HODG

Emmerich

Arnhem US FIFTEENTH

ARMY

ZUIDER ZEE GEROW

NORTHERN

GROUP OF ARMIES

Amsterdam MONTGOMERY Liége

N

CENTRAL

GROUP OF ARM

The Hague BRADLEY

Antwerp

Prague

Dresden

Chemnitz

Approximate Extent of Advance

Pilsen

Linz

Asch

Salzburg

Berchtesgaden

Danube

Regensburg

Inn

Munich

Nürnberg

Innsbruck

Brenn
Pass
Vipite

Main

Stuttgart

Frankfurt

Lake Constance

Mainz

Heidelberg

Gernsheim

FRENCH FIRST ARMY
DE TASSIGNY

Oppenheim

Mannheim

**US THIRD
ARMY**
PATTON

Germersheim

Karlsruhe

Black Forest

**US SEVENTH
ARMY**
PATCH

Strasbourg

Saarbrücken

Basel

SOUTHERN GROUP OF ARMIES
DEVERS

Luxembourg

Belfort

Metz

Nancy

M i l e s

increase the weight of the offensive into Germany. Ninth Army tanks immediately broke out of the area north of the Ruhr and swept eastward in a powerful thrust toward Münster. On 1 April the enveloping columns of these armies made contact west of Paderborn, cutting off the Ruhr and a large area to the south, in the largest pocket of envelopment in the history of warfare.

Elements of 18 German divisions from the First Parachute, Fifth Panzer, and Fifteenth Armies were encircled in this skillful maneuver. Leaving strong forces to contain and reduce this giant encirclement, the First and Ninth Armies continued eastward toward the line of the Weser. Spearheading the Allied offensive, they headed for Leipzig and a prearranged junction with the Soviet forces. There was no loss of momentum, no respite for the enemy forces, and by the end of the first week of April both armies had crossed the Weser in the area north of Kassel.

On 6 April, General Eisenhower wrote me:

> As you can see from the reports, our plans have been developing almost in exact accordance with original conceptions. You must expect, now, a period in which the lines on your map will not advance as rapidly as they did during the past several weeks because we must pause to digest the big mouthful that we have swallowed in the Ruhr area. It should not take too long and, of course, in the meantime, maintenance will be pushed to the limit to support our next main thrust. My G–2 [Major General Strong of the British Army] figures that there may be 150,000 German soldiers left in the Ruhr but a number of these will change into civilian clothes before we liquidate the whole thing. He is confident, however, that we will capture at least 100,000. [Actually 300,000 were captured.] The enemy has been making efforts to break out of the area but our persistent policy of knocking out his communications to the eastward, and his lack of mobility within the pocket, both make it very difficult for him to launch a really concerted attack. I am confident that he can do nothing about it.

The Ninth Army advance from the Weser to the Elbe was featured by armored gains of 20 to 30 miles a day against little or no resistance. By mid-April our troops were along the Elbe near Wittenberge and Magdeburg and had established bridgeheads across the river. In rear of the armored columns, the cities of Hanover and Brunswick fell to Ninth Army infantry. Bypassing Leipzig and strong resistance in the Harz Forest, the First Army drove eastward to the Mulde Valley south of Dessau.

While these extensive operations continued, the battle progressed against the trapped Germans in the Ruhr. With the Fifteenth Army holding the west face of the pocket along the Rhine, and armor and infantry of the Ninth and First Armies driving in from the north, east, and south, the formidable enemy forces were crushed in just 18 days. More than 300,000 prisoners were taken in this unique victory, won far behind our forward positions and squarely astride our lines of communication.

Soon Leipzig and the Harz Mountains were in American hands, and the Ninth and First Armies closed on the line of the Elbe-Mulde, the forward limit, which had been arranged with the Soviets. To establish contact with our Allies from the Eastern Front, First Army patrols pushed east of the Mulde to Torgau, where the long-awaited juncture with the Red Army occurred on 25 April.

In the north, the British Second Army advancing on the Osnabrück-Bremen axis had crossed the Weser on a broad front near Minden early in April and was at the outskirts of Bremen by the middle of the month. From their Weser crossings the British struck northward toward Hamburg, reaching the Elbe southeast of the city. The Canadians forced the Ijssel River and pressed on through the Dutch towns, liberating the remaining sections of eastern and northern Holland.

Far to the south, the Third Army, after capturing Mühlhausen, Gotha, and Erfurt, crossed the Saale River and turned southeast toward the mountains of Czechoslovakia and the Danube Valley. This advance was designed to establish firm contact with the Soviet forces in Austria and to prevent any effective reorganization of the enemy remnants in mountainous regions to the south. On the right, the Seventh Army encountered bitter resistance in Nürnberg, but quickly captured the city and then swung south into the Bavarian plain. On the first of May the Third Army was advancing into Czechoslovakia on a hundred-mile front southeast of Asch; along the Danube other elements had driven 20 miles into Austria. The Seventh Army had taken Munich, birthplace of the Nazi party, and was sweeping southward toward the Inn River. Along the upper Rhine, the First French Army captured Karlsruhe and Stuttgart in turn and proceeded with the reduction of enemy forces caught in the Black Forest. By the first of May the French had cleared the Swiss border west of Lake Constance and were driving into western Austria alongside the Seventh Army.

In northern Germany, the British Second Army, reinforced by the XVIII American Corps under Maj. Gen. Matthew B. Ridgway, broke out from the Elbe River late in April and reached the Baltic on 2 May. This action established contact with Soviet forces at Wismar and cut off the Danish Peninsula. Further resistance on this front was hopeless. On 5 May, the German commander surrendered all forces in northwest Germany, Holland, and Denmark.

Along the Danube, the Third Army continued the advance into Austria and entered Linz on 5 May. Next day Pilsen fell to our forces in Czechoslovakia. General Patch's Seventh Army swept across the Inn on a wide front and drove 40 miles to capture Salzburg and Hitler's stronghold at Berchtesgaden. Other Seventh Army troops who had taken Innsbruck drove through the Brenner Pass to establish contact with the Fifth Army at Vipiteno. Since its landing on the Riviera, the Seventh Army had advanced an average of more than 3 miles a day against what had been the most formidable army in the world. At noon on 6 May, Army Group "G," comprising all German forces in Austria, surrendered unconditionally to our Sixth Army Group, just 11 months after the landing in Normandy.

The powerful Wehrmacht had disintegrated under the combined Allied blows, and the swift advances into the mountains of Austria and Bohemia had prevented the establishment of an inner fortress. Surrounded on all fronts by chaos and overwhelming defeat, the emissaries of the German government surrendered to the Allies at Reims on 7 May 1945, all land, sea, and air forces of the Reich.

ORDER OF BATTLE EUROPEAN THEATER OF OPERATIONS (AS OF 7 MAY 1945)

[The order of battle of our Allies is not shown below Army level, except where American forces are under their operational control.]

Unit	Commander	Location
Supreme Headquarters Allied Expeditionary Forces	General of the Army, Dwight D. Eisenhower	Main Headquarters, Versailles, France.
		Advance Headquarters, Rheims, France
Northern Group of Armies (21st Army Group)	F/M Sir Bernard L. Montgomery	Suchteln, Germany.
First Canadian Army	Gen. H. D. G. Crerar.	Holland.
Second British Army	Lt. Gen. Sir Miles C. Dempsey	Germany.
XVIII Corps (Airborne)	Maj. Gen. M. B. Ridgway	Germany.
5th Armored Division	Maj. Gen. L. E. Oliver	Germany.
7th Armored Division	Maj. Gen. R. W. Hasbrouck	Germany.
82d Airborne Division	Maj. Gen. J. M. Gavin	Germany.
8th Infantry Division	Maj. Gen. B. E. Moore.	Germany.
Central Group of Armies (12th Army Group)	Gen. Omar N. Bradley	Wiesbaden, Germany.
Ninth Army	Lt. Gen. William H. Simpson	Braunschwieg, Germany.
XIII Corps	Maj. Gen. A. C. Gillem, Jr.	Germany.
35th Infantry Division	Maj. Gen. Paul W. Baade	Germany.
84th Infantry Division	Maj. Gen. A. R. Bolling	Germany.
102d Infantry Division	Maj. Gen. F. A. Keating	Germany.
XVI Corps	Maj. Gen. J. B. Anderson	Germany.
29th Infantry Division	Maj. Gen. C. H. Gerhardt.	Germany.
75th Infantry Division	Maj. Gen. R. E. Porter.	Germany.
79th Infantry Division	Maj. Gen. I. T. Wyche.	Germany.
95th Infantry Division	Maj. Gen. H. L. Twaddle	Germany.
XIX Corps	Maj. Gen. R. S. McLain	Germany.
2d Armored Division	Maj. Gen. I. D. White	Germany.
8th Armored Division	Maj. Gen. J. M. Devine	Germany.
30th Infantry Division	Maj. Gen. L. S. Hobbs.	Germany.
83d Infantry Division	Maj. Gen. R. C. Macon	Germany.
First Army	Gen. Courtney H. Hodges	Weimar, Germany.
78th Infantry Division	Maj. Gen. E. P. Parker, Jr.	Germany.
VII Corps	Lt. Gen. J. L. Collins	Germany.
3d Armored Division	Brig. Gen. Doyle O. Hickey	Germany.
9th Infantry Division	Maj. Gen. L. A. Craig	Germany.
69th Infantry Division	Maj. Gen. Emil F. Reinhardt	Germany.
104th Infantry Division	Maj. Gen. Terry Allen	Germany.
VIII Corps	Maj. Gen. Troy H. Middleton	Germany.
6th Armored Division	Brig. Gen. George W. Read, Jr.	Germany.
76th Infantry Division	Maj. Gen. William R. Schmidt	Germany.
87th Infantry Division	Maj. Gen. Frank L. Culin, Jr.	Germany.
89th Infantry Division	Maj. Gen. Thomas D. Finley	Germany.
Third Army	Gen. George S. Patton, Jr.	Erlangen, Germany.
4th Infantry Division	Maj. Gen. Harold W. Blakeley	Germany.
70th Infantry Division	Maj. Gen. A. J. Barnett	Germany.
III Corps	Maj. Gen. James A. Van Fleet	Germany.
14th Armored Division	Maj. Gen. Albert C. Smith	Germany.
28th Infantry Division	Maj. Gen. Walter E. Lauer	Germany.
V Corps	Maj. Gen. Clarence R. Huebner.	Germany.
9th Armored Division	Maj. Gen. John W. Leonard	Germany.
16th Armored Division	Brig. Gen. John L. Pierce	Czechoslovakia.
1st Infantry Division	Maj. Gen. Clift Andrus	Czechoslovakia.
2d Infantry Division	Maj. Gen. Walter M. Robertson	Czechoslovakia.
97th Infantry Division	Brig. Gen. Milton B. Halsey	Czechoslovakia.

XII Corps	Maj. Gen. Stafford Leroy Irwin	Germany.
4th Armored Division	Maj. Gen. William M. Hoge	Czechoslovakia.
11th Armored Division	Maj. Gen. Holmes E. Dager	Austria.
5th Infantry Division	Maj. Gen. Albert E. Brown	Germany.
26th Infantry Division	Maj. Gen. Willard S. Paul	Austria.
90th Infantry Division	Maj. Gen. Herbert L. Earnest	Czechoslovakia.
XX Corps	Lt. Gen. Walton H. Walker	Germany.
13th Armored Division	Maj. Gen. John Milliken	Germany.
65th Infantry Division	Maj. Gen. Stanley E. Reinhart	Austria.
71st Infantry Division	Maj. Gen. Willard G. Wyman	Austria.
80th Infantry Division	Maj. Gen. Horace L. McBride	Austria.
Fifeenth Army	Lt. Gen. Leonard T. Gerow	Bad Neunahr, Germany.
66th Infantry Division	Maj. Gen. Herman F. Kramer	France.
106th Infantry Division	Maj. Gen. Donald A. Stroh	France.
XXII Corps	Maj. Gen. Ernest N. Harmon	Germany.
17th Airborne Division	Maj. Gen. William M. Miley	Germany.
94th Infantry Division	Maj. Gen. Harry J. Malony	Germany.
XXIII Corps	Maj. Gen. Hugh J. Gaffey	Germany.
28th Infantry Division	Maj. Gen. Norman D. Cota	Germany.
Southern Group of Armies (6th Army Group)	Gen. Jacob L. Devers	Heidelberg, Germany.
Seventh Army	Lt. Gen. Alexander M. Patch	Schwabischgmund, Germany.
12th Armored Division	Maj. Gen. Roderick R. Allen	Germany.
63d Infantry Division	Maj. Gen. Louis Hibbs	Germany.
45th Infantry Division	Maj. Gen. Robert T. Frederick	Germany.
100th Infantry Division	Maj. Gen. W. A. Burress	Germany.
XXI Corps	Maj. Gen. Frank W. Milburn	Germany.
101st Airborne Division	Maj. Gen. Maxwell D. Taylor	Germany.
36th Infantry Division	Maj. Gen. John E. Dahlquist	Austria.
XV Corps	Lt. Gen. Wade H. Haislip	Germany.
20th Armored Division	Maj. Gen. Orlando Ward	Germany.
3d Infantry Division	Maj. Gen. John W. O'Daniel	Germany.
42d Infantry Division	Maj. Gen. Harry J. Collins	Germany.
86th Infantry Division	Maj. Gen. Harris M. Melasky	Austria.
VI Corps	Maj. Gen. Edward H. Brooks	Germany.
10th Armored Division	Maj. Gen. William H. H. Morris, Jr.	Austria.
44th Infantry Division	Maj. Gen. William F. Dean	Austria.
103d Infantry Division	Maj. Gen. Anthony C. McAuliffe	Austria.
First French Army	Gen. Jean J. de Lattre de Tassigny	Lindau, Germany.
SHAEF Reserve		
First Allied Airborne Army	Lt. Gen. Louis H. Brereton	Maison LaFitte, France.
13th Airborne Division	Maj. Gen. Elbridge G. Chapman, Jr.	France.
US Strategic Air Forces in Europe*	Gen. Carl A. Spaatz	Rheims, France.
Eighth Air Force	Lt. Gen. James H. Doolittle	High Wycombe, Bucks, England.
1st Air Division	Maj. Gen. Howard McC. Turner	England.
2d Air Division	Maj. Gen. Wm. E. Kepner	England.
3d Air Division	Maj. Gen. Earle E. Partridge	England.
Ninth Air Force	Lt. Gen. Hoyt S. Vandenberg	Weisbaden, Germany.
IX Bomb Division	Maj. Gen. Samuel E. Anderson	Belgium.
IX Tactical Air Command	Maj. Gen. Elwood R. Quesada	Germany.
XIX Tactical Air Command	Maj. Gen. Otto P. Weyland	Germany.
XXIX Tactical Air Command	Brig. Gen. Richard E. Nugent	Germany.
First Tactical Air Force (Prov.)	Maj. Gen. Robt. M. Webster	Heidelberg, Germany.
XII Tactical Air Command	Brig. Gen. Glenn O. Barcus	Darmstadt, Germany.
1st French Air Command	Gen. de Brig. Paul Gerardot	Issenheim, France.
IX Troop Carrier Command	Maj. Gen. Paul L. Williams	Louvecienne, France.

*Exercised operational control over Fifteenth Air Force shown under Mediterranean Theater of Operations.

VICTORY OVER JAPAN

The Road to China

Of all the battle fronts of the global war, the situation in East Asia two years ago was the bleakest for the United Nations. In seeking to capitalize on the preoccupation of the Western Powers in Europe and the sneak attack on the American fleet at Pearl Harbor, the Japanese had established an immense perimeter of conquest in the Far East. By July 1942 it extended more than halfway across the Pacific, southward almost to Australia, and westward to the mountain barriers of the India-Burma front. The advance eastward of the Japanese had been halted in the critical battles of Midway and the Coral Sea. But Japan still held tremendous areas replete with the natural resources essential to the conduct of modern warfare.

So far, our advance back over these areas taken by the Japanese in their initial stride had been slow and painful. It seemed to many Americans that if we had to repeat again and again the bloody struggles for Guadalcanal and the Papuan Coast of New Guinea by what was popularly termed "island hopping," the decision in the war with Japan was distant many years. Army and Navy commanders were well aware of the difficulties and paucity of means. Nevertheless, we had undertaken offensive operations in the Pacific and Far East with only the small forces then available because it was imperative that the Japanese be halted and placed on the defensive.

Japan's rush into Burma had isolated China except for the thin line of air supply over the 500 miles of the Himalayan Hump between Assam, India, and the Yunnan plateau. The Japanese had attacked China at the most propitious time for carrying out their dreams of conquest of Asia and Oceania. In the face of almost a complete lack of war matériel, China had refused to submit. But her condition by the early summer of 1943 had grown truly desperate.

China's most critical needs were in trucks and rolling stock, artillery, tanks, and other heavy equipment. It was impossible to fly this matériel over the Himalayas in the essential quantities. In fact, except as it supplied the American Fourteenth Air Force commanded by General Chennault with gasoline, bombs, and ammunition, the Hump air route at that time gave China little material assistance. If the armies and government of Generalissimo Chiang Kai-shek had been finally defeated, Japan would have been left free to exploit the tremendous resources of China without harassment. It might have made it possible when the United States and Britain had finished the job in Europe, and assaulted the Japanese home islands, for the government to flee to China, and continue the war on a great and rich land mass.

The Combined Chiefs of Staff recognized that Germany had to be defeated first and that the quickest approach to Japan was across the Pacific, spearheaded by our Navy. Nevertheless, they believed that China must be given sufficient support to keep her in the war.

Accordingly, when this critical phase of the global war was discussed at Casablanca in January 1943, the Combined Chiefs directed that preparations be made to reestablish surface communications to China and to step up the flow of supply over the Hump even though at that time Allied resources were being heavily taxed to bring the North African campaign to a successful conclusion and to extend control over the Mediterranean. We knew they would be much more heavily taxed as we gathered our strength for the invasion of France.

At the TRIDENT Conference in Washington four months later the position of the Allies in Asia was reconsidered, and it was agreed that top priority must be given the Air Transport Command to increase the capacity of the aerial route over the Hump to 10,000 tons a month. It was also resolved that vigorous action must be taken to begin a Burma campaign in the fall at the end of the 1943 monsoon.

Three months later in the QUADRANT Conference plans were laid in greater detail to realize the maximum effect that could be obtained in Asia with the resources then available. The penetration into Burma from India was a task of unusual difficulty. Communications between the Port of Calcutta and Assam were limited to one railroad which changes from broad to meter gauge and which must cross the sweeping Brahmaputra River in ferries because the monsoon floods make bridging impossible. Nowhere along the India-Burma frontier is there an easy west-to-east passage. The jungles that cover the barrier of the Himalayan foothills are malaria-ridden, infested with acute dysenteries and endemic typhus.

The United States and Great Britain had insufficient landing vessels even to give assurance of the success to the operations planned for the Mediterranean and Western Europe. It was impossible at that time to mount an amphibious attack on Burma from the south.

Operation CAPITAL

At the QUADRANT Conference the Southeast Asia Command was created under Admiral, the Lord Louis Mountbatten. Lt. Gen. Stilwell, who commanded the China-Burma-India U. S. Theater, was made his deputy. All the resources the United States could make available to him were allocated for the task of reestablishing land communications to China. It was urgently desired to furnish greater Allied resources in the East than were allotted. They simply were not available.

In the new command structure the Combined Chiefs of Staff continued to exercise general jurisdiction over operations in Southeast Asia and over the allocation of American and British resources. Operations in the Chinese theater of war were under the command of the Generalissimo, with Stilwell as his Chief of Staff. All Royal Air Force and Army Air Forces combat strength on the Burma front, including the U. S. Tenth Air Force, was formed into the Eastern Air Command under Maj. Gen. George E. Stratemeyer.

It was decided that an offensive in North Burma should be undertaken in the winter of 1943 and 1944, and that the Ledo Road from Assam, then under construction by American engineers, should be extended to the old Burma Road at Mongyu as rapidly as the offensive operations progressed. It was also decided to build a pipe line from Calcutta to Assam and another one paralleling the Ledo Road. These lines would greatly increase the flow of motor fuels to China.

At the same conference it was decided to enlarge the capacity of the Hump route to 20,000 tons a month. The plan for the bombing of the Japanese Islands by B–29's operating out of China was reviewed and accepted at the QUADRANT Conference. The air plan for the reduction of Japan, adopted at the conference, foresaw the establishment of superfortress bases in the Pacific to subject Japan to the same devastating air attack that was to prepare Germany for assault by our ground forces. The target of the air route and new overland supply route to China established at this first Quebec conference, was 85,000 tons per month of general stores and 54,000 tons of petroleum products, which would move via the pipe line.

These decisions regarding the Ledo Road, the increase of Hump tonnage, the construction of pipe lines, and the campaign in North Burma generally presented a most difficult and trying problem to the Combined Chiefs of Staff. Ocean tonnage, transport planes for possible airborne operations to break the stalemate in Italy, an increase in the inflow of troops into the United Kingdom for OVERLORD, assistance for General MacArthur's campaign in the Southwest Pacific, and other urgent requirements all had to be taken into consideration in the light of our limitations in resources. Sacrifices would be required somewhere but if made at the wrong place they would cost the lives of Allied soldiers and delay final victory.

Since the operations in Burma could not begin until the monsoon had ended in Assam and the floods had receded, the Allied staff chiefs with the President and Prime Minister had the opportunity to meet with Chiang Kai-shek in Cairo in November 1943 before our projected offensive began. At the Cairo Conference the Combined Chiefs of Staff made further efforts to find the resources to increase the scope of the Burma campaign by adding amphibious operations in the Bay of Bengal. These resources were available nowhere in this world unless we abandoned the great basic decision to close with the German enemy in Western Europe in 1944. The alternative would have permitted the Japanese to exploit their prizes of conquest in the Pacific islands. It was determined, however, that by means of the projected Allied attacks across the India-Burma frontier, it would be possible to drive the Japanese from Northern Burma and achieve the objective of reopening surface communications to China.

The preliminaries to these operations began late in October just prior to the conference at Cairo and Teheran. The Chinese 22d and 38th Divisions moved from their forward positions in front of the advancing Ledo Road into the Hukawng Valley. These troops had been trained in the center established at Ramgarh, India, through the energy and wisdom of General Stilwell and with the approval of the Generalissimo.

In February the Chinese advances down the Hukawng Valley were joined by a specially trained American infantry combat team known as the GALAHAD Force commanded by Brig. Gen. Frank D. Merrill. These troops had been gathered in a call for volunteers that went to all United States jungle trained and veteran infantry units in the Pacific and in the Western Hemisphere. Marching over the most difficult terrain under intolerable weather conditions, the Chinese and American forces virtually destroyed the Japanese 18th Division, which had captured Singapore in the Japanese advance. In May 1944 they fought their way into the airfield at Myitkyina, the key to Northern Burma.

During most of this campaign the Japanese were effectively blocked from reinforcing Northern Burma through the Irrawaddy Valley by columns of seasoned British and Indian jungle troops, commanded by the late Maj. Gen. Orde C. Wingate. These columns were known as long-range penetration groups. Some of them marched from India to establish their strangleholds on Japanese communications; others were taken in by glider in an airborne operation directed by U. S. Col. Philip G. Cochran, who commanded a specially organized composite air group known as Air Commandos. While General Stilwell's forces were advancing on Myitkyina troops of the Generalissimo commanded by Marshal Wei Li Haung crossed the Salween River from the east.

Patrols of the two forces finally met at Tengchung in the summer of 1944, establishing the first thin hold on Northern Burma.

During the fall of 1943 the Japanese, anticipating the attack in Burma, had been building their strength for a counteroffensive to prevent the reestablishment of surface communications with China. Japanese forces attacked eastward across the Salween in the Lungling area and were met and stopped by the Chinese in time to permit completion of the road from Ledo. Another strong Japanese force struck toward India while the Allied operations were in progress in an effort to seize the large British base at Imphal and sever the Bengal-Assam Railroad below the bases on which Hump air transportation and General Stilwell's operations were dependent. By April 1944 Imphal was cut off and the Japanese threatened Dimapur on the railroad. British and Indian troops flown to the sector met the attack, turned it back, and reestablished contact with the Indian divisions in the Imphal plain. After heavy and prolonged fighting, the hostile divisions were dispersed and cut up with heavy losses. At the same time, British and Japanese troops in the Arakan to the south were engaging in see-saw fighting along the coast of the Bay of Bengal.

The reentry into Burma was the most ambitious campaign yet waged on the end of an airborne supply line. From the first advance by the Chinese into the Hukawng Valley in October until after the fall of Myitkyina town the next August there were at all times between 25,000 and 100,000 troops involved in fighting and dependent largely or entirely on food, equipment, and ammunition that could be air-supplied, either by parachute, free drop, or air-landed.

The air supply was maintained by troop carrier squadrons, British and American, commanded by Brig. Gen. William D. Old, under the direction of General Stratemeyer's Eastern Air Command. Night and day troop carrier C-46's and 47's shuttled from numerous bases and air strips in the Brahmaputra Valley to points of rendezvous with the Allied ground columns in the Burma jungles. Each trip had to be flown over one or more of the steep spines which the Himalayas shove southward along the India-Burma frontier to establish one of the most formidable barriers to military operations in the world. The troop carrier squadrons at the height of the campaign averaged 230 hours of flying time for each serviceable plane a month for three months. The normal average monthly flying time is 120 hours.

At two critical stages of the campaign the troop carrier squadrons assisted by Air Transport Command planes made major troop movements in a matter of hours and days that would have required weeks and months by surface transport.

The first was the movement of British and Indian troops to meet the threat on the Bengal-Assam Railroad at Dimapur. The second was the movement of two Chinese divisions, the 14th and 50th, from Yunnan, China, across the Hump to the troop carrier base at Sookerating, in Assam, India. This operation was accomplished in just eight days. The Chinese troops were picked up by Air Transport Command planes in China and landed at the troop carrier field where they were entirely refitted, armed, and flown to a staging area in the Hukawng from where they entered the battle for Myitkyina.

Only by air supply was the Burma campaign at all possible. The jungle covered ridges between India and Burma have effectively resisted the advance of civilizations. They are inhabited by mountain tribes of Kachins, Chins, and the headhunting Nagas. Before United States Engineers accomplished the Herculean job of driving the Ledo Road, now known as the Stilwell Road, across the mountains and through the jungles, a road from the Brahmaputra to the Irrawaddy Valley was considered an impossibility.

Fall of Burma

The mission that the Joint Chiefs of Staff had given General Stilwell in Asia was one of the most difficult of the war. He was out at the end of the thinnest supply line of all; the demands of the war in Europe and the Pacific campaign, which were clearly the most vital to final victory, exceeded our resources in many items of matériel and equipment and all but absorbed everything else we had. General Stilwell could have only what was left and that was extremely thin. He had a most difficult physical problem of great distances, almost impassable terrain, widespread disease and unfavorable climate; he faced an extremely difficult political problem and his purely military problem of opposing large numbers of enemy with few resources was unmatched in any theater.

Nevertheless General Stilwell sought with amazing vigor to carry out his mission exactly as it had been stated. His great efforts brought a natural conflict of personalities. He stood, as it were, the middle-man between two great governments other than his own, with slender resources and problems somewhat overwhelming in their complexity. As a consequence it was deemed necessary in the fall of 1944 to relieve General Stilwell of the burden of his heavy responsibilities in Asia and give him a respite from attempting the impossible.

At the same time it became obvious the mission of reestablishing communications with China would be accomplished, and as the future objectives of the forces in Southeast Asia and China were to grow continually more divergent, it appeared advisable to make a clear division of the two theaters. Accordingly, the American administrative area of China-Burma-India was separated into the India-Burma and the China theaters. Lt. Gen. Daniel I. Sultan, who had been General Stilwell's deputy, was given command of the India-Burma theater. Maj. Gen. Albert C. Wedemeyer, formerly Chief of the War Department Strategical Planners and later a member of Admiral Mountbatten's staff, was appointed commander of our forces in China, succeeding General Stilwell as the Generalissimo's Chief of Staff.

No American officer had demonstrated more clearly his knowledge of the strength and weakness of the Japanese forces than General·Stilwell and the steps necessary to defeat them in Asia. He was brought back to the United States to reorient the training of the Army Ground Forces for the war against Japan. Then after the death of General Buckner on Okinawa he was returned to the field to command the U.S. Tenth Army.

The Burma campaign continued with intensity during the monsoon season of 1944. Chinese, American, and British troops were then disposed along the Chindwin River north of Kalewa and from the upper Irrawaddy to Lungling. It was planned to drive southward through Central Burma to Mandalay, and Admiral Mountbatten prepared for operation DRACULA to seize Rangoon amphibiously from the south. At the close of the monsoon, Chinese, American, and British troops under the immediate command of General Sultan advanced southward astride the Irrawaddy, captured Shwegu in early November, and

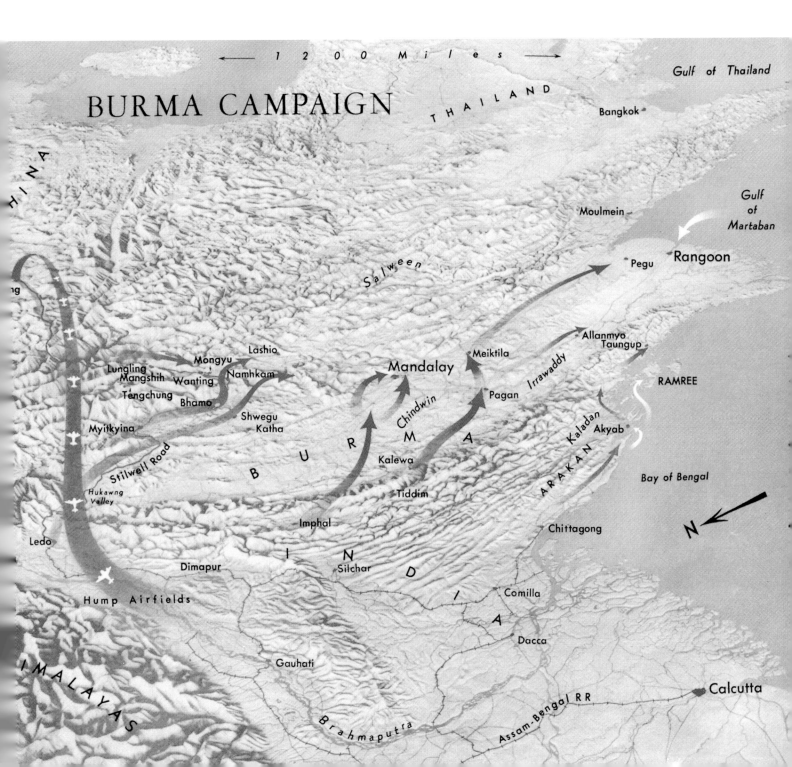

by December had cleared the projected trace of the supply road to Bhamo.

The Japanese in Burma had never recovered from General Stilwell's thrusts and from the losses inflicted by British and Indian forces on their 15th, 31st, and 33d Divisions in their abortive effort to sever the Bengal-Assam Railroad. As fast as the combat forces moved ahead, United States Engineers, commanded by Brig. Gen. Lewis A. Pick, shoved the road forward behind them, operating their bulldozers so far forward that they were frequently under fire. On 28 January 1945 a convoy of American trucks and matériel from India crossed the Burma-China frontier. The Stilwell Road was open.

In Western Burma the British broke south through Tiddim across the Chindwin against Japanese delaying actions. Southward in the Arakan, British operations cleared the Kaladan River delta on the Arakan Coast and provided air strips at Akyab and on Ramree Island.

The Japanese retreat in Burma was in full swing by the end of January 1945. General MacArthur's successive landings in the Philippines and United States fleet operations in the China Sea had cut the Japanese supply line to Burma. In mid-February, a British column crossed the Irrawaddy near Pagan and drove to Meiktila. The seizure of this road and rail center with its airfields undermined the whole Japanese position in Central Burma. In the meantime, other British-Indian forces were closing on Mandalay from the north and west. Japanese trapped in Mandalay held out against the British until 21 March. Forty days later British airborne troops descended along the western shore of the Rangoon River south of the port and assault troops came ashore the following day. The Japanese had already fled Rangoon and the British forces entered on 3 May. The port facilities were captured in good condition.

The Burma campaign had all but ended. A few Japanese units were able to withdraw eastward into Thailand and into the Moulmein area of Southern Burma, but thousands of the enemy were cut off in isolated pockets with little hope of escape. Admiral Mountbatten reported the fighting had already cost Japan 300,000 casualties of which 97,000 were counted dead.

The Asiatic operations had been maintained at the end of the most precarious supply lines in history. The efforts of the United States service forces to strengthen them were prodigious. United States port battalions at Calcutta worked in intolerable heat and humidity with native labor weakened by disease, heat, and famine. Despite these handicaps, they established records exceeding those of every other military port in the world for quick unloading and turn-around of our ships. At the same time, the capacity of the tiny Bengal-Assam Railroad was more than doubled by

American railway battalions which refused to let the disease and heat of the steaming Brahmaputra Valley dissipate their energies as they have weakened white men and brown for centuries. During 1943 and 1944 the flow of United States arms and matériel through Calcutta and up the valley had become great enough to support not only the Herculean job of building the Ledo Road and destroying the Japanese forces in its path, but to increase steadily the capacity of the Himalayan air route and the flow of arms to the undernourished armies of China.

Reverse in China

In the latter stages of the Burma campaign, American troops of the MARS force, a brigade of two regiments which succeeded the GALAHAD force, were flown to China together with two of the Chinese divisions that had been fighting in Burma.

By January 1945, Hump cargo had been increased to the amazing rate of 46,000 tons a month. This vital and hazardous traffic stands as one of the great logistical accomplishments of the war against Japan. It alone made possible the indispensable support which General Chennault's Fourteenth Air Force was able to give the Chinese armies and the attacks by China-based superfortresses on Japan's home islands. In June of this year when the Marianas bases had been sufficiently developed, the China-based B-29's were sent to the Pacific where they could be more easily supplied.

In May 1944, however, the Japanese had launched a strong drive southward from Tung Ting Lake in Hunan Province. In the late summer they began a complementary drive west from Canton. These salients joined near the American air base at Kweilin severing unoccupied China, and overran seven of the principal bases from which the Fourteenth Air Force had been throwing its weight against shipping in the China Sea. In April 1945, the Japanese drove out of Paoching against our important air base at Chihkiang. Supported by the Fourteenth Air Force, Chinese troops slowed, stopped, then threw back this Japanese column with heavy losses. The offensives in China were the most serious the Japanese were able to mount in 1944 and 1945.

By the spring of this year the impact of the smashing attack across the Pacific islands had been felt deep in Asia. Fearing for the safety of their homeland, the Japanese had begun to withdraw large forces from South and Central China. Behind them Chinese troops were applying every pressure their present strength would permit. Under General Wedemeyer, American officers in increasing numbers were helping speed the retraining and reequipping of Chinese soldiers who had been fighting the Japanese for eight long years. The War Department made available to him two

Chinhsien

Peiping

Tientsin

Port Arthur

Lanchow

Tsingtao

YELLOW SEA

Kaifeng

Yellow

Changan

Laohokow

Nanking

Shanghai

Chengtu

Yangtze

Chungking

Tung Ting Lake

Wenchow

Chihkiang

Paoching

Suichwan

Foochow

Kweilin

Liuchow

Amoy

FORMOSA

Nanning

Swatow

Canton

Hong Kong

Hanoi

Haiphong

Gulf of Tonkin

JAPANESE OPERATIONS
AGAINST U. S. AIRFIELDS

Japanese Holdings in July 1944

HAINAN

LUZON

1 2 7 5 Miles

of the Army commanders who had helped defeat the German Wehrmacht, General Truscott of the Fifth Army in Italy and General Simpson of the Ninth Army. At the same time the Air Forces in China were reorganized, the 10th Air Force from India was moved into China and both the 10th and 14th were placed under the general direction of General Stratemeyer. While this reorganization was in progress, General Chennault, who had commanded the original American Volunteer Group of "Flying Tigers" and then became the first commander of the 14th Air Force, asked to be relieved.

The War Department granted his request and named Maj. Gen. Charles B. Stone to succeed him.

General Stillwell had been able to provide some training and equipment for 35 Chinese divisions in his training centers in Yunnan. Under the direction of the Generalissimo, General Wedemeyer was continuing this mission with full vigor and greatly increased resources now moving over the road from India. We were determined that when the final battle of Japan was fought the armies of the Emperor would find no comfort anywhere on earth.

ORDER OF BATTLE U. S. FORCES IN CHINA THEATER (AS OF 14 AUGUST 1945)

Unit	Commander	Location
Headquarters, U. S. Forces, China Theater	Lt. Gen. A. C. Wedemeyer	Chungking, China.
U. S. Army Air Forces, China Theater	Lt. Gen. G. E. Stratemeyer	Chungking, China.
Tenth Air Force	Maj. Gen. H. C. Davidson	Liuchow, China.
Fourteenth Air Force	Maj. Gen. C. B. Stone, 3d	Kunming, China.

Unremitting Pressure

It had always been the concept of the United States Chiefs of Staff that Japan could best be defeated by a series of amphibious attacks across the far reaches of the Pacific. Oceans are formidable barriers, but for the nation enjoying naval superiority they become highroads of invasion.

Japan's attack on our fleet at Pearl Harbor gave her a tremendous but, nevertheless, temporary advantage. The Japanese had reckoned without the shipyards of America and the fighting tradition of the United States Navy. Even before parity with the Japanese fleet had been regained, the Navy successfully maintained communications with Australia and had undertaken limited offensives in the Solomons to halt the enemy advance. A desperate courage stopped the Japanese before Australia in the now historic battle of the Coral Sea and then shortly afterward utterly smashed the Japanese advance toward the United States itself in the decisive action at Midway.

The broad strategic allocation of resources among the theaters was controlled by the Combined Chiefs of Staff, but the actual control of operations in the Pacific had been retained by the U. S. Chiefs of Staff. At the Casablanca Conference, the Combined Chiefs agreed that Japan must be prohibited from further expansion and from consolidating and exploiting her current holdings. This resolution was agreed upon even though we were at the very moment having great difficulty in concentrating sufficient resources to defeat the European Axis.

It has been declared axiomatic that a nation cannot successfully wage war on two fronts. With a full appreciation of the difficulties and hazards involved, we felt compelled to wage a war not only on two fronts, but on many fronts. Thus we arrived at the concept of global war in which the vast power of American democracy was to be deployed all over the earth.

At the TRIDENT Conference of May 1943 in Washington when the specific strategy of the global war was conceived, it was determined to step up the pace of the advance on Japan. Then a few months later, in August 1943, at the QUADRANT Conference in Quebec, the specific routes of the advance on Japan were laid out. Gen. Douglas MacArthur was directed to continue his operations up the New Guinea coast to reach the Philippines by the fall of 1944. Operations in the Gilberts, the Marshalls, and the Marianas were agreed to, and it was forecast that by the spring of 1945 we would be able to secure a lodgment in the Ryukyus on the threshold of the Japanese homeland.

Admiral King was confident that somewhere during these advances, probably during the Marianas or the Philippine campaigns, the United States fleets would meet and decisively defeat the Japanese Navy. No long-range military forecast could have been more accurate.

At the QUADRANT Conference General Arnold proposed an air plan for the softening of Japan. It was later approved and carried into execution. It called for the establishment of bases in China, in the Marianas, and other Pacific Islands from which would operate the huge B-29 superfortresses then only just going into production.

Pacific Pincers

At the turn of the year 1943 Army forces in the South Pacific area were added to General MacArthur's strategic command. It was the intention of the Joint Chiefs of Staff to maintain the initiative, advancing by amphibious flanking actions on the Philippines and the Japanese Islands from the south and from the east. The advance across the tremendous reaches of the Central Pacific was placed under command of Admiral Chester W. Nimitz. There were two axes of the operations on the southern flank—one in New Guinea commanded by Lt. Gen. Walter Krueger, the other in the Solomons under Admiral William F. Halsey.

It was General MacArthur's intention to proceed by a series of envelopments up the coast of New Guinea and into the Philippines. We now enjoyed superiority both on the sea and in the air. He was therefore able to land his troops where the Japanese were weakest and confine their stronger forces in pockets from which, because of incredibly difficult terrain and our air and sea superiority, they could never break out. As a result there were at the time of surrender hundreds of thousands of Japanese troops isolated in the jungles of the Pacific islands, dying on the vine and of no further use to their Emperor. As General MacArthur reported toward the end of 1944:

> The enemy garrisons which have been bypassed in the Solomons and New Guinea represent no menace to current or future operations. Their capacity for organized offensive effort has passed. The various processes of attrition will eventually account for their final disposition. The actual time of their destruction is of little or no importance and their influence as a contributing factor to the war is already negligible. The actual process of their immediate destruction by assault methods would unquestionably involve heavy loss of life without adequate compensating strategic advantages.

Even with the intense preoccupation in the campaigns in Europe during the past two years, this great nation had been able steadily to increase the resources available in the Pacific until at the moment of German collapse General MacArthur and Admiral Nimitz were established on the threshold of the Japanese homeland and the industries and cities of Japan were crumbling under our aerial bombardment. The U. S. Navy dominated the Pacific. The Commonwealth Government, under President Osmeña, had been reestablished in power and in residence in the Philippines.

On 1 July 1943, General MacArthur had four American divisions and six Australian divisions under his control. His air force had less than 150 heavy bombers. Admiral Nimitz had nine Army and Marine divisions. Yet in the spring of 1945 these two commanders were ejecting the Japanese from the Philippines and the Ryukyus—already on the home stretch to Japan.

Following the completion of the extremely difficult Buna campaign late in June 1943, difficult because of the paucity of facilities and the character of the terrain, two regimental combat teams landed on Woodlark and Kiriwina Islands off the eastern tip of New Guinea. The operation was small but it was typical of the general method of the offensive in the Southwest Pacific. Deceived by feints, the Japanese were taken by surprise. Airfields were quickly established on these two islands, from which effective support could be provided for the operations which were to follow, and which permitted the rapid transit of fighter aircraft, if necessary, between the Solomons and New Guinea.

The capture of New Georgia Island with its important Munda airfield was accomplished by Maj. Gen. Oscar W. Griswold's XIV Corps. The first landing in force was made 30 June on nearby Rendova Island. Japanese ground reaction was slight, but in the air the enemy tried hard to disrupt the landing. The next day Marine 155-mm guns on Rendova were shelling Munda airdrome six miles across the water. Elements of 37th and 43d Divisions then landed on New Georgia enveloping the western end of the island. After our forces were reinforced by troops of the 25th Division, Munda was captured on 5 August. Bypassing the strongly held island of Kolombangara, the XIV Corps had captured Vella Lavella by 9 October.

General MacArthur reduced Salamaua with an Australian force which advanced overland from the west and an American regimental combat team which made an amphibious landing south of the town. On 4 September, while the Japanese were still resisting at Salamaua, an Australian force landed a few miles east of Lae. The next day, supported by air and screened by smoke, a U. S. parachute regiment dropped to seize the airdrome at Nadzab, 19 miles northwest of the town. This daring move permitted the airborne movement to Nadzab of an Australian division, which then participated with their forces to the east in a concentric attack on Lae. After difficult fighting the town was occupied on 16 September.

Salamaua had fallen five days previously. General MacArthur then moved quickly toward Finschhafen. Employing mostly Australian forces, he occupied the town on 2 October. By February 1944 the Huon Peninsula was completely in our hands. During these operations and those which followed, extensive air attacks were maintained against the enemy's supply lines, barges, and airfields, contributing materially to the success of the ground operations.

Meantime New Zealand troops occupied two islands in the Treasury Group of the northern Solomons late in October. Preceded by diversionary landings in northwest Choiseul, the 3d Marine Division of Lt. Gen. A. A. Vandegrift's I Marine Amphibious Corps landed on 1 November at

THE GREAT OCEAN

Here are the broadest water distances of Earth. The short route to Japan across the top of the world was blocked by weather. So the Army and Navy were compelled to step their way over the Equator to the down-under lands of Australia and New Guinea and back up to the Philippines and the Ryukyus. Vast as the Pacific Ocean is, it became the broad highway for American invasion forces when the Navy drove the remnants of the defeated Japanese fleet back to their harbors after the battle of the Philippines.

TIBET

MANCHURIA

C H I N A

SOUTH CHINA SEA

FORMOSA

LUZON

RYUKYUS

OKINAWA

JAPAN

Tokyo

BORNEO

LEYTE

CELEBES

MOROTAI

IWO JIMA

GUAM

SAIPAN

AUSTRALIA

NEW GUINEA

Hollandia

ENIWETOK

P R O C E

GUADALCANAL

KWAJALEIN

MARSHALL IS

Brisbane

GILBERT IS

47   Hrs   By   Air

EUROPE

SIBERIA

RILE

ATTU

KISKA

Dutch Harbor

ALASKA

CANADA

UNITED STATES

San Francisco

PACIFIC

Nautical   Miles

HAWAIIAN

6193

Pearl Harbor

ISLAND

Empress Augusta Bay in western Bougainville. This permitted the establishment of a naval base and three airfields within fighter range of the enemy concentrations at Rabaul, 235 miles distant. From these airfields the remaining Japanese installations in the Solomons could more extensively be neutralized by Maj. Gen. Nathan F. Twining's Thirteenth Air Force, thus obviating the immediate necessity of conducting a campaign to annihilate the enemy or to complete the capture of the islands. On 11 November elements of the 37th Division entered the line, and on 15 December command of the beachhead passed to our XIV Corps, which had been reinforced by the Americal Division. Meanwhile a naval task force under Admiral Halsey had smothered Japanese air and naval power at Rabaul.

In the Central Pacific Area the primary mission of the Army command under Lt. Gen. Robert C. Richardson, Jr., was the training of units en route to the combat zones further south and west. Amphibious and jungle training centers were established under battle-tested instructors in the Hawaiian Islands. The effectiveness of this training was demonstrated in every area of the Pacific Ocean.

In the fall of 1943 a series of operations was initiated which, less than a year later, had given us mastery of the Pacific. Attacks directed against the enemy along several axes forced him to deploy his relatively inferior air strength over a wide area, without sufficient strength at critical points. The vast sea area favored the employment of superior American naval strength. The small islands were not suitable for the employment of large Japanese ground forces.

The first step was the seizure of the Gilbert Islands, designated operation GALVANIC. Preluded by attacks by carrier task forces on Marcus and key islands in the Marshalls, Baker, Nukufetu, and Nanumea Islands were occupied by United States forces at the beginning of September. Early in October, Wake was heavily bombarded. After a preparatory naval and air bombardment by both Marine and Navy planes and Maj. Gen. Willis H. Hale's Seventh Air Force, the invasion of the Gilberts began on 21 November. The 2d Marine Division landed on Tarawa. A combat team of the 27th Division landed on Makin. The Jap fought stubbornly on both islands. The larger enemy force on Tarawa made the operation difficult and costly for our troops. Abemama to the south was seized without opposition.

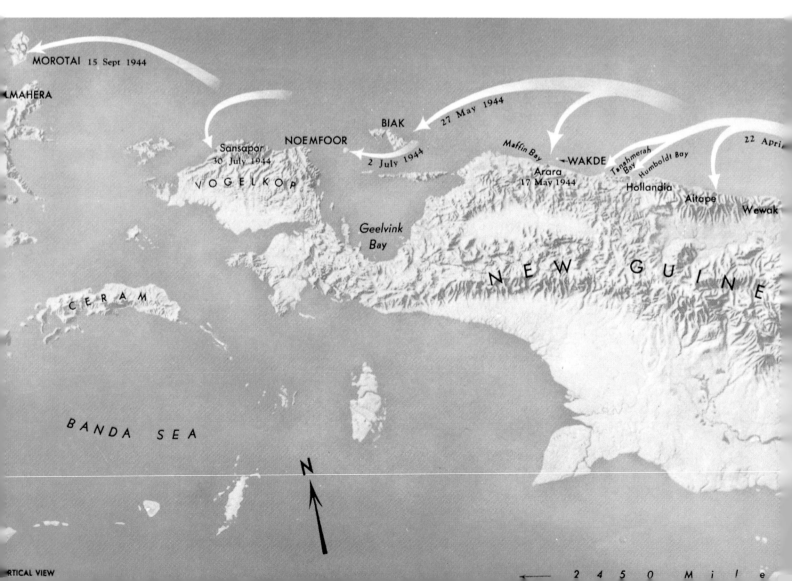

These operations opened a phase of warfare new to most of our troops. The enemy was concentrated within restricted areas, heavily fortified in pillboxes, and protected by mines and beach obstacles. Landing forces faced intense cross-fires. The enemy could be dislodged only by shattering bombardment and powerful hand-to-hand infantry assault. Amphibious tractors proved to be one of the effective assault weapons. They could be floated beyond the range of shore batteries, deployed in normal landing boat formations, and driven over the fringing reefs on to and up the beaches.

From the Gilberts, Admiral Nimitz turned to operation FLINTLOCK—the seizure of several atolls in the Marshall Islands. On 31 January 1944, after two days of intense air and naval bombardment, the 7th Division, veteran of Attu, landed on the southern islands of Kwajalein Atoll, while the 4th Marine Division attacked the northern tip at Namur and Roi. These divisions were part of the V Marine Amphibious Corps, commanded by Maj. Gen. Holland M. Smith. By 8 February all resistance had ceased. General Richardson wrote me after a flight to the Marshalls:

As a result of the air, naval, and artillery bombardment, the scene at Kwajalein was one of great devastation. The destruction was complete. Upon approaching it from the lagoon side, it gave the appearance of no-man's land in World War I and was even greater, I think, than that of Betio on Tarawa. With the exception of rubble left by concrete structures, there were no buildings standing. All those which had been made of any other material except concrete had been completely burned or destroyed. The result was that there were practically no stores left except a few packages of rice and a little clothing and ammunition scattered here and there.

Majuro, with its excellent naval anchorage, was also occupied. Then after heavy attacks by carrier planes, a combat team of the 27th Division and a Marine combat team landed on Eniwetok Atoll on 19 February and completed its capture on 22 February. Control of the Marshalls enabled the interdiction by air of the enemy naval base at Truk until the advance into the Carolines could definitely isolate it. Truk also came under attack by Thirteenth Air Force B–24's based in the Admiralties.

Concurrent with these moves were operations in the Southwest against the western end of New Britain, to establish control of Vitiaz and Dampier Straits. On 15 December 1943 a reinforced cavalry regiment landed on three beaches in the Arawe area. The airdrome on Cape Gloucester was a desirable link in the chain of bases necessary to permit the air forces to pave the

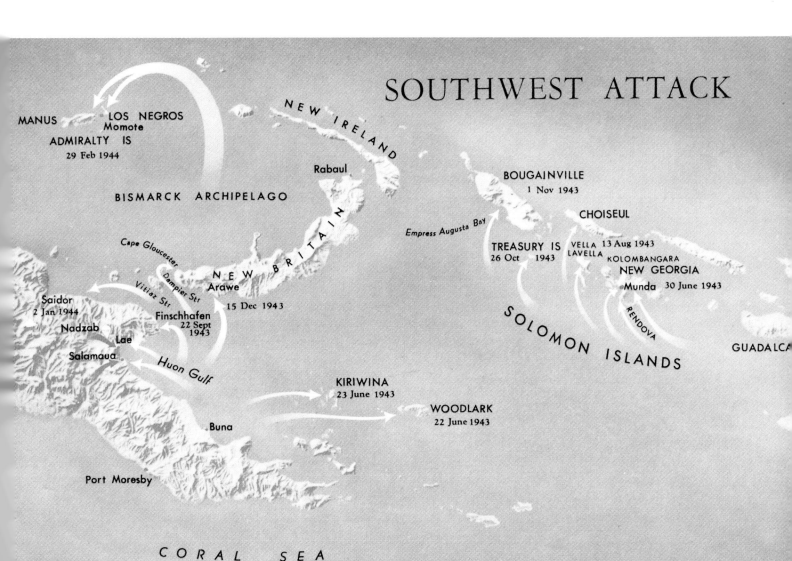

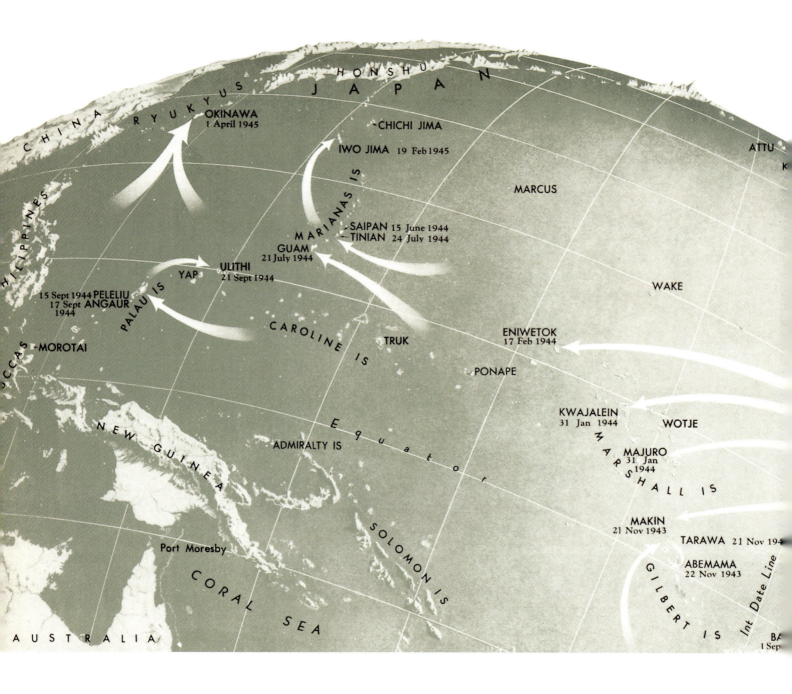

way for further advances. During a period of weeks the area was subjected to intensive aerial bombardment and on 26 December the 1st Marine Division landed and 4 days later captured the airdrome. By mid-March joint operations of the Marines and the Army's Arawe Force had secured western New Britain. While this fighting was in progress General MacArthur's advance westward continued. On 2 January 1944 a regimental combat team of the 32d Division made a jump of 110 miles to land near Saidor, on the north coast of New Guinea, and by 7 January an airstrip was in use.

The Admiralty Islands, lying west of the Bismarck Archipelago, were strategically important because of their airfields and harbor. An operation was originally scheduled for April 1944, but on 29 February General MacArthur accompanied advance elements of the 1st Cavalry Division, transported on Vice Admiral Thomas

C. Kinkaid's Seventh Fleet destroyers and high-speed transports to reconnoiter Los Negros Island. He was prepared to follow in force if the situation warranted. Little opposition was found, and the remainder of the division was committed. Momote airdrome was captured, and the beachhead secured after a series of fanatical counterattacks. During the remainder of March and the early part of April, the occupation of Manus and the adjacent islands was completed.

The next move to Hollandia and Aitape on 22 April involved a leapfrog advance westward of more than 400 miles. Since the landings were beyond the effective range of Army fighters, air support was provided by naval carriers. At Hollandia were located three excellent Jap airfields, and Humboldt Bay was suitable as an advanced naval and supply base. The airfields were found to be hard to reach overland, so General MacArthur occupied Aitape and based fighters on the airstrip there. Three main landings were made by troops of the 24th, 32d, and 41st Divisions of Lt. Gen. Robert L. Eichelberger's I Corps, one just east of Aitape, one in Humboldt Bay, and one in Tanahmerah Bay. The Jap was taken by surprise; fewer than 5,000 of his troops were in the entire Hollandia area. By 30 April airfields there were in our hands. General Krueger's Sixth Army Headquarters moved into Hollandia 6 July 1944; General MacArthur brought his headquarters up from Brisbane on 8 September 1944. On this same date General Eichelberger was assigned to command the newly activated Eighth Army with headquarters also at Hollandia.

The Hollandia-Aitape operation cut off more than 50,000 Japanese troops to the eastward. The advance westward was continued in mid-May when elements of the 41st Division made an unopposed landing near Arara. A few days later a regiment of the same division captured the offshore island of Wakde with its airstrip and extended the beachhead on the mainland to include Maffin Bay.

Later in the month our 41st Division landed 330 miles farther west on Biak Island, strategically located off Geelvink Bay. The 8,000 well-equipped Japanese troops on the island put up fierce resistance, and it was 22 June before Biak's three airfields were in use. In another surprise attack, this time supported by paratroops, a regimental combat team occupied Noemfoor Island in early July. The possession of the airfield at this point gave much needed breadth and depth to the air deployment, permitting the further penetration and dislocation of enemy supply lines in the Southwest Pacific. By this time Japanese air had almost disappeared from the New Guinea area except for an occasional raid on landing craft or over established beachheads.

A landing at Sansapor on 30 July by elements of our 6th Division secured air and naval bases still further west, on the Vogelkop Peninsula. Although 18,000 Japanese garrisoned the Vogelkop Peninsula, General MacArthur again caught the enemy off balance and resistance was slight.

In a little over 12 months American forces in the Southwest Pacific, with the assistance of Australian units, had pushed 1,300 miles closer to the heart of the Japanese Empire, cutting off more than 135,000 enemy troops beyond hope of rescue. The operations had been conducted under adverse weather conditions and over formidable terrain, which lacked roads in almost every area occupied, and made troop movements and supply extraordinarily difficult. Malaria was a serious hazard, but with suppressive treatment and rigid mosquito control, it no longer was a serious limitation to tactical operations.

In the Pacific, men who had engaged in combat for long months had to be withdrawn to rear positions to recuperate. Consequently, the theater commanders endeavored to maintain replacement pools sufficiently large to provide a margin for the lost time of recuperation and transportation to and from the battle area. For every unit engaged in combat operations, more than its equivalent had to be present in the theater to assure this margin.

The prompt "roll up" of the bases, personnel, and matériel in Australia and the islands of the South Pacific permitted the same equipment to be utilized again and again, so that despite the lower priority given Pacific operations they could be continued. Only skeleton organizations remained in Australia, to procure supplies and maintain air transport.

Similar to the preparation of Western Europe for invasion, each advance northward toward Japan was preluded by air attack. Under Lt. Gen. George C. Kenney, the Fifth Air Force and later the Far East Air Forces, which included both the Fifth commanded by Maj. Gen. Ennis C. Whitehead and the Thirteenth commanded by Maj. Gen. St. Clair Streett, effectively stopped the flow of supplies to bypassed Japanese units. The Japanese aerial threat to our own operations was swept from the skies, and direct support was provided for the successive amphibious advances. At the same time, General Kenney's forces forayed far to the westward, striking powerful blows at strategic targets in Timor, the Celebes, Java, and Borneo. These attacks seriously impaired the ability of the Japanese to maintain their widely scattered forces and reminded the captive peoples of those islands that Allied strength was rapidly growing and the enemy's hold was becoming more and more insecure.

Operation FORAGER to capture the Marianas was next on Admiral Nimitz's schedule. On 15 June Lt. Gen. Holland M. Smith's V Marine Amphibious Corps, consisting of the 2d and 4th Marine Divisions, followed by the 27th Infantry Division, landed on Saipan. On 9 July, after 25 days of extremely heavy fighting, the island was in their possession, though mopping-up operations continued for months.

On 21 July the 77th Infantry Division, the 3d Marine Division, and a Marine brigade of the III Marine Amphibious Corps under Maj. Gen. R. S. Geiger landed on Guam. The assault made steady progress. Resistance ceased on 10 August. Shortly after the Saipan operation had ended our XXIV Corps artillery, which had supported that action, began the neutralization of Tinian, assisted by fighter aircraft of the Seventh Air Force. On 24 July elements of the 2d and 4th Marine Divisions assaulted that island and secured it in 9 days of heavy fighting.

Bombers of the Seventh Air Force, now operating from Saipan under Maj. Gen. Robert W. Douglass, soon were striking Iwo Jima and Chichi Jima in the Bonins. Even before the capture of the Marianas was complete, airfields were under construction on Saipan and Guam, from which Superfortresses could begin the strategic bombardment of the main Japanese Island of Honshu. The first major strike was delivered 24 November 1944.

With the rapid increase in the size of the Pacific Ocean Command, it became necessary to consolidate the Central and South Pacific Army forces. On 1 August 1944, Headquarters, U. S. Army Forces, Pacific Ocean Areas, was established under General Richardson's command. Concurrently, two subordinate administrative commands, the Central Pacific Base Command and the South Pacific Base Command, were organized. All Army Air Forces in the area were placed under Headquarters, U. S. Army Air Forces in the Pacific Ocean Area, commanded by the late Lt. Gen. Millard F. Harmon, who came from the South Pacific Area. In addition, General Harmon was designated Deputy Commander of the Twentieth Air Force to represent General Arnold in the theater. General Harmon after a long record of splendid service was lost in a transPacific flight, on 28 February 1945. He was succeeded by Lt. Gen. Barney McK. Giles who at the time of his appointment was Deputy Commander and Chief of Staff of the Army Air Forces.

Reconquest of the Philippines

Toward the end of August Admiral Halsey's Third Fleet began a probing operation in the western Carolines and the Philippines. His carrier planes struck at Yap and the Palau Islands on 7 and 8 September, and the next two days bombed Mindanao. On the morning of the 12th, Admiral Halsey struck the central Philippines and arrived at a conclusion which stepped up the schedule by months.

The OCTAGON Conference was then in progress at Quebec. The Joint Chiefs of Staff received a copy of a communication from Admiral Halsey to Admiral Nimitz on 13 September. He recommended that three projected intermediate operations against Yap, Mindanao, and Talaud and Sangihe Islands to the southward be canceled, and that our forces attack Leyte in the central Philippines as soon as possible. The same day Admiral Nimitz offered to place Vice Admiral Theodore S. Wilkinson and the 3d Amphibious Force which included the XXIV Army Corps, then loading in Hawaii for the Yap operation, at General MacArthur's disposal for an attack on Leyte. General MacArthur's views were requested and 2 days later he advised us that he was already prepared to shift his plans to land on Leyte 20 October, instead of 20 December as previously intended. It was a remarkable administrative achievement.

The message from MacArthur arrived at Quebec at night, and Admiral Leahy, Admiral King, General Arnold, and I were being entertained at a formal dinner by Canadian officers. It was read by the appropriate staff officers who suggested an immediate affirmative answer. The message, with their recommendations, was rushed to us and we left the table for a conference. Having the utmost confidence in General MacArthur, Admiral Nimitz, and Admiral Halsey, it was not a difficult decision to make. Within 90 minutes after the signal had been received in Quebec, General MacArthur and Admiral Nimitz had received their instructions to execute the Leyte operation on the target date 20 October, abandoning the three previously approved intermediary landings. General MacArthur's acknowledgment of his new instructions reached me while en route from the dinner to my quarters in Quebec.

That day the 1st Marine Division of General Geiger's III Marine Amphibious Corps, with a combat team of the 81st Infantry Division in reserve, landed in Peleliu in the Palau group. Two days later the 81st Division landed on Angaur, an island south of Peleliu.

The War Department on 16 September relayed to General MacArthur a report from General Stilwell to the effect that the Japanese offensive in central China would soon result in capture of the eastern China airfields from which Maj. Gen. Claire L. Chennault's Fourteenth Air Force had planned to support operations in the northern Philippines. MacArthur replied that Admiral Halsey's carrier task force had so severely reduced hostile air capabilities in the Philippines, Formosa, and the Ryukyus that it would be possible to move directly from Leyte to Lingayen Gulf without the support of Chennault's air force. Admiral Halsey's carrier planes had destroyed almost 2,000 Japanese aircraft in the probing attacks during September.

On 22 September another combat team of the 81st Division moved to Peleliu, where heavy resistance was being met. Capture of this island was completed by 30 September except for a few isolated enemy groups which held out in caves for another two months. On 21 September, patrols of the 81st Division landed on Ulithi, meeting no opposition. The main body landed two days later.

The landing on Peleliu coincided with General MacArthur's move to seize Morotai north of Halmahera with the 31st and 32d Divisions. Despite uniformly stubborn resistance the Japanese had lost a series of islands which were important stepping stones for the return to the Philippines and the ultimate conquest of Japan.

The advance of our forces westward across the Pacific had been accompanied by the steadily expanding strategic operations of the Eleventh Army Air Force in Alaska, the Seventh Air Force in the Central Pacific, and the Fifth and Thirteenth Air Forces in the Southwest Pacific. In the operations fleet carriers had played a vital part. During the campaigns through the Southwest Pacific and the western mandated islands, General Kenney's aircraft and those of the Pacific Ocean Areas swung their powerful attacks back and forth in mutual support of the various operations. At the same time the westward advance had resulted in an ability to strike from the air at the foundations of the Japanese war potential—their shipping, petroleum, and aircraft industries.

Battle of the Visayas

On 19 October two assault forces, the 3d commanded by Admiral Wilkinson and the 7th commanded by Rear Admiral Daniel E. Barbey, approached the east coast of Leyte with the Sixth Army under General Krueger aboard. It was an armada of combat and assault vessels that stretched across the vast Pacific horizon. In the covering naval forces were the battleships *California, Mississippi, Maryland, Pennsylvania, Tennessee,* and *West Virginia* with their screen of cruisers and destroyers. The troops and matériel with which we were to seize Leyte were loaded in 53 assault transports, 54 assault cargo ships, 151 landing ships (tank),72 landing craft (infantry), 16 rocket ships, and over 400 other assorted amphibious craft. The air cover was provided by planes from 18 escort carriers.

Out to sea Admiral Halsey's mighty carrier task force, which helped prepare the way for the landings by air bombardment, now stood watch for possible Japanese naval opposition to the landings. That day a Japanese search plane discovered this great amphibious force and reported its presence to Admiral Kurita's Singapore fleet, which then constituted 60 percent of Japan's major naval units. This report precipitated one of the decisive battles of history.

The X and XXIV Corps of the Sixth Army went ashore on schedule the following day after the Navy had paved its way with drum-fire bombardment. Three days later General MacArthur directed the ground forces to secure their beach areas and await the outcome of the naval battle which was now impending. The Japanese made the decision to commit their fleet in the battle to prevent America's return to the Philippines. Admiral King has described the great naval action which followed in his recent report. Every American who reads it must be filled with tremendous pride in the achievements of our fighting Navy.

By the 26th it was apparent that the Third and Seventh Fleets had virtually eliminated Japan as a sea power. Her fleet had suffered a crippling blow.

In April 1944 the defense of the Philippines, the Japanese Empire of conquest in the south and west, the Netherlands Indies, Malaya, Thailand, Borneo, French Indo-China, the Moluccas and New Guinea, had been in charge of Field Marshal Count Hisaichi Terauchi. From his headquarters at Manila he controlled 17 Japanese armies totaling about 925,000 men. Terauchi was a typical Japanese jingoist. He had been Minister of War and commanded the armies which set out in 1937 to sack China. In the fall of 1943

he had assumed command of the southern armies with headquarters at Singapore. He moved his headquarters to Manila a half year later when the Philippines were added to his area. The 14th Area Army in the Philippines was then under command of Lt. Gen. Shigenori Kuroda. A month before the forces of General MacArthur and Admiral Nimitz were at his throat, Terauchi's staff had prepared for him the following estimate of American intentions:

A two-pronged attack on Luzon is planned. MacArthur's Army, aided by naval cooperation from Nimitz, will advance in the southern Philippine Islands. The other attack will be directed at the northern Philippines from the Pacific Ocean.

Nimitz will provide MacArthur's forces with direct cooperation support with a part of his naval forces. His main forces will be prepared to engage our navy in the northern Philippines and Taiwan area and overcome any air resistance.

The anti-axis Far East Air Army under Kenney will overcome any air resistance over the Philippines and together with the enemy air force stationed in China will operate over the North China Sea to isolate the Philippines.

In the six days of the great naval action the Japanese position in the Philippines had become extremely critical. Most of the serviceable elements of the Japanese Navy had been committed to the battle with disastrous results. The strike had miscarried, and General MacArthur's land wedge was firmly implanted in the vulnerable flank of the enemy. Terauchi no longer had an effective fleet to cover his forces in the Philippines or his communications to the empire of Malaysia so easily conquered two and one-half years before. There were 260,000 Japanese troops scattered over the Philippines but most of them might as well have been on the other side of the world so far as the enemy's ability to shift them to meet the American thrusts was concerned. If General MacArthur succeeded in establishing himself in the Visayas where he could stage, exploit, and spread under cover of overwhelming naval and air superiority, nothing could prevent him from overrunning the Philippines.

Terauchi decided that the battle must be fought in the difficult terrain of the Leyte mountains and rice paddies. He relieved Kuroda as commander of the 14th Area Army and replaced him with General Tomoyoki Yamashita, who had conquered Singapore in 1942 and then moved to the Philippines to wind up the campaign after Lt. Gen. Masaharu Homma had been unable to budge the American forces holding out on Bataan. Yamashita was one of Japan's best known generals. For his victories in Singapore and Bataan he had been given the First Area Army in Manchuria, one of the two top field commands in the Kwantung Army.

To General Makina, commander of the 16th Division, then fighting a delaying action against the U. S. Sixth Army under General Krueger, Yamashita relayed this message:

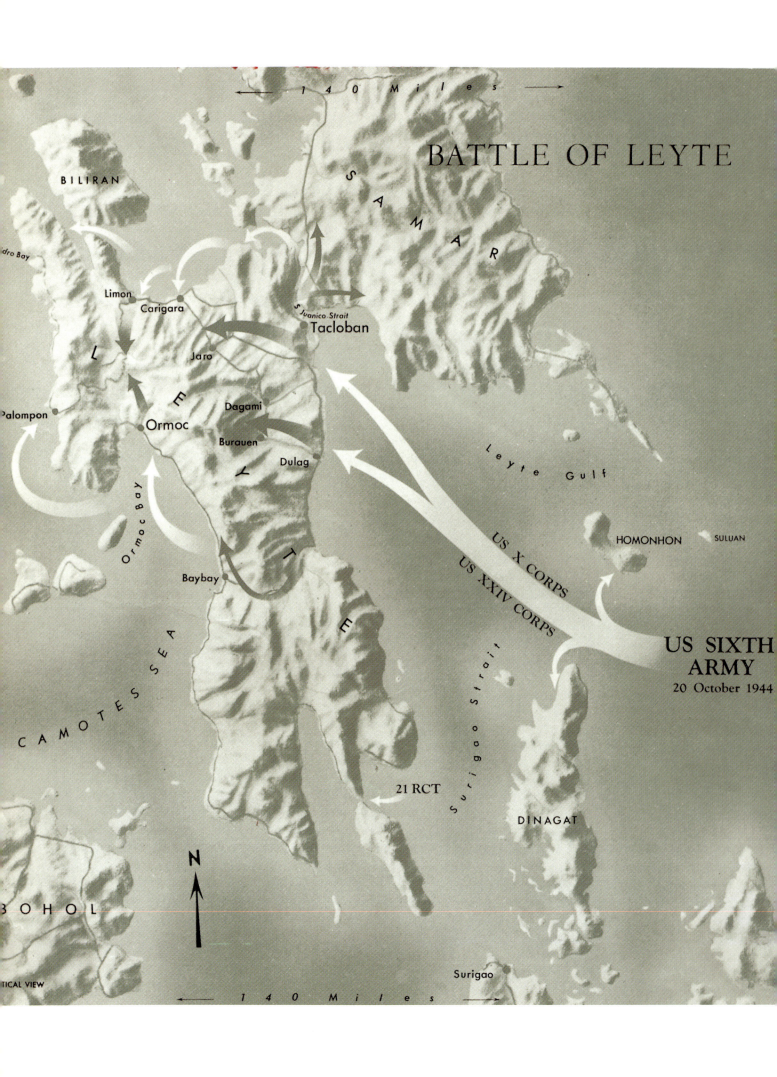

BATTLE OF LEYTE

BILIRAN

SAMAR

← 1 4 0 M i l e s →

dro Bay

Limon
Carigara
S.Juanico Strait
Tacloban

L

Jaro

E

Dagami

Palompon

Ormoc

Burauen

Y

Dulag

Leyte   Gulf

Ormoc Bay

T

HOMONHON   SULUAN

Baybay

E

US X CORPS

US XXIV CORPS

C A M O T E S   S E A

US SIXTH
ARMY
20 October 1944

Surigao Strait

21 RCT

DINAGAT

N

TICAL VIEW

BOHOL

Surigao

← 1 4 0 M i l e s →

The Army has received the following order from his Majesty, the Emperor:

"Enemy ground forces will be destroyed."

General MacArthur's advance continued. After securing the high ground overlooking Leyte Gulf, Maj. Gen. J. R. Hodge's XXIV Corps penetrated inland to secure Dagami and Burauen. The X Corps, under Maj. Gen. F. C. Sibert, swept across the San Juanico Strait to seize the south coast of Samar and landed troops in a short amphibious operation on the north coast of Leyte.

By 5 November the American forces had reached the vicinity of Limon at the northern end of the valley road leading to Ormoc, the principal Japanese installation on the island. Bitter fighting for Leyte was now in progress, rendered the more difficult by typhoons which inaugurated the rainy season.

During the naval battle and the weeks following, the Japanese were able to transport reinforcements to Leyte, but by mid-December General Kenney's land-based fighters and Admiral Halsey's carrier planes had strangled this stream of reinforcements. On 1 November United States air patrols located four large transports unloading, escorted by four destroyers and two destroyer escorts.

Army planes struck and sank one, possibly two transports. On 3 November, another three transports were seen unloading at Ormoc, but the Japanese maintained sufficient air patrol overhead and continued striking the United States fields on the east coast so that their unloading operations could not completely be interrupted. On 7 November three large transports and four small transports unloaded, covered by seven destroyers and two destroyer escorts. On 9 November ten destroyers and two heavy cruisers brought in four more large troop transports. Kenney's planes attacked and sank two transports, one destroyer, and six freighters. On 11 November another convoy started into Ormoc Bay. Carrier planes, now reinforced after the great naval battle, attacked. Two transports were sunk. Four destroyers were also sent to the bottom and the fifth was badly damaged. One destroyer escort was sunk. On 7 December an entire convoy of six transports, four destroyers, and three destroyer escorts were sunk in San Isidra Bay by United States planes. On 11 December three transports and three destroyers were sunk off Palompam, and the following day another destroyer was sunk and one destroyer escort and two transports were badly damaged. By now the Japanese were able to commit no more of their valuable ships to the battle for the central Philippines and attempted to supply their troops already on Leyte by sailboat.

The Japanese took heavy troop losses in these repeated sinkings, but they had at the same time made some formidable reinforcements. By the middle of November troops of the U. S. 24th Division, reaching into the remnants of the Japanese 16th Division west of Jaro, killed a messenger and learned that the Japanese 1st Division was now on the island. Yamashita was therefore committing his best troops. The 1st Division was one of Japan's finest from the Kwantung Army.

When United States forces from the south and across the Pacific began to gather speed, the 1st Japanese Division had been moved to China. After General MacArthur's assault force had been sighted, the 1st Division was rushed from Shanghai to Manila and then on to Leyte.

In the Ormoc valley the Japanese 1st Division fought fiercely and delayed but could not stop Krueger's advance. By the end of November American troops were closing on Limon and another column threatened Ormoc from the south. Violent rain storms and deep mud harassed the supply lines. Forward units were dependent on hand-carry. Casualties were evacuated by native bearers.

But by 1 December seven divisions were well established ashore, five airfields were in operation, and the waters of the Visayas under firm naval control.

The 77th Division landed south of Ormoc on 7 December and captured the town four days later along with great quantities of enemy supplies. Toward the end of December the 7th, 24th, 32d, 77th, and 96th Divisions, the 1st Cavalry Division, and the 11th Airborne Division closed out organized Japanese resistance on the island.

It was at Kilometer 79 on the Ormoc highway that the Japanese 1st Division command post, defended by 500 exhausted, defeated soldiers made the last stand. This little band, made up of every element General Kataoka had been able to reassemble, quit on the night of 21 December and fled south and west. Men of the 32d Division found this letter, written by an unknown Japanese soldier:

I am exhausted. We have no food. The enemy are now within 500 meters from us. Mother, my dear wife and son, I am writing this letter to you by dim candle light. Our end is near. What will be the future of Japan if this island should fall into enemy hands? Our air force has not arrived. General Yamashita has not arrived. Hundreds of pale soldiers of Japan are awaiting our glorious end and nothing else. This is a repetition of what occurred in the Solomons, New Georgia, and other islands. How well are the people of Japan prepared to fight the decisive battle with the will to win...?

Marshal Terauchi, realizing that the Philippines were slipping from his grasp fled with his headquarters to Saigon, Indo-China.

Command of the battle of Leyte passed to Eichelberger's Eighth Army on 26 December. For Krueger's Sixth Army there was other business.

While mopping-up continued on Leyte, General MacArthur had sent a landing force of two regiments into southern Mindoro. Within 24 hours American

EUROPEAN THEATER

OF OPERATIONS

London
10 JUNE 1944

Quebec
19 AUG 1943
13 SEPT 1944

Washington

Yalta
4 FEB 1945

MEDITERRANEAN

Casablanca
15 JAN 1943

Malta
30 JAN 1945

PERSIAN

Teheran
28 NOV 1943

AMERICAN

THEATER

THEATER OF

Cairo
23 NOV 1943

GULF

COMMAND

OPERATIONS

MIDDLE   EAST   SOUT

CENTRAL   AFRICA

COM

THEATER

THEATERS OF OPERATIONS

The decision to pool the resources of the United States and Great
Britain in joint effort to defeat Germany, Italy and Japan was taken
in the initial War Conference between the President, the Prime Minister
with their Chiefs of Staff held in Washington in December, 1941. To
implement this decision and establish this coordinated strategic control,
there was created the agency known as the Combined Chiefs of Staff.
It was the mission of the Combined Chiefs to propose the operations
to be undertaken, allocate the resources of the two nations accordingly,
define Theaters of Operations, and recommend the Allied Commanders
for these theaters. The map shows the operational areas established.
The Combined Chiefs met periodically, usually with their Chiefs of
State, in the International Conferences, here shown.

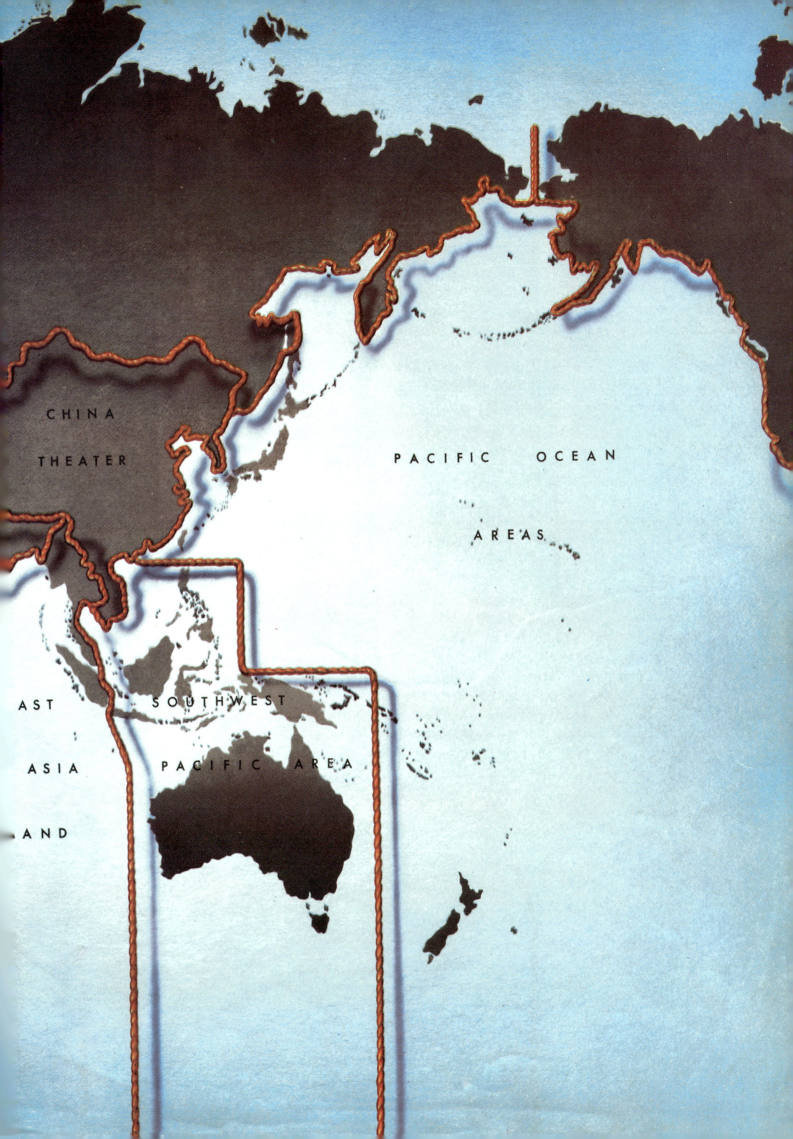

CHINA

THEATER

PACIFIC OCEAN

AREAS

AST

ASIA

AND

SOUTHWEST

PACIFIC AREA

planes and PT boats were operating off the southern coast of Luzon.

Battle of Luzon

In the first week of January a new American assault force gathered east of Leyte, slipped through the Surigao Strait over the sunken wrecks of Japanese warships that had gone down in their attempt to turn aside the invasion more than two months before, and passed into the Mindanao and Sulu Seas. This American force was treading its way through the heart of the Philippine Archipelago and through waters where the Japanese Navy and air forces had for two years maintained unchallenged supremacy, to invade Luzon by effecting a landing in Lingayen Gulf, its classic point of greatest vulnerability.

No opportunity was overlooked to conceal this bold plan from the Japanese. While the assault force was proceeding up the west coast of Luzon, Kenney's planes and the guerrillas under MacArthur's direction concentrated on the destruction of roads, bridges, and tunnels to prevent General Yamashita from shifting forces to meet the assault. The guerrillas in southern Luzon conducted noisy demonstrations to divert Japanese attention to the south. Navy mine sweepers swept the Balayan, Batangas, and Tayabas Bays on the south coast of Luzon. Landing ships and merchantmen approached the beaches until they drew fire, then slipped out under cover of night. United States transport planes flew over Batangas and Tayabas and dropped dummies to simulate an airborne invasion. The Tokyo radio reported that American troops were trying to land on Luzon but had been driven off. Japanese forces on the island, harassed by guerrillas and by air, drove north, south, east, and west in confusion, became tangled in traffic jams on the roads, and generally dissipated what chance they might have had to repel the landing force. On 9 January the U. S. Sixth Army, now composed of the I and XIV Corps, hit the beaches in Lingayen Gulf. By nightfall, 68,000 troops were ashore and in control of a 15-mile beachhead, 6,000 yards deep.

The landing had caught every major hostile combat unit in motion with the exception of the 23d Infantry Division to the southeast of the beachhead in the central Luzon plain and its supporting 58th independent mixed brigade 25 miles to the north of Lingayen Gulf. Yamashita's inability to cope with General MacArthur's swift moves, his desired reaction to the deception measures, the guerrillas, and General Kenney's aircraft combined to place the Japanese in an impossible situation. The enemy was forced into a piecemeal commitment of his troops. The Japanese 10th and 105th Divisions in the Manila area which were to secure Highway No. 5 on the eastern edge of the central Luzon plain failed to arrive in time. The brunt of defending this withdrawal road to the north fell to the 2d Japanese Armored Division which seemingly should have been defending the road to Clark Field.

General MacArthur had deployed a strong portion of his assault force on his left or eastern flank to provide protection for the beachhead against the strong Japanese forces to the north and east.

In appreciation of the enemy's predicament the Sixth Army immediately launched its advance toward Manila across the bend of the Agno which presumably should have been a strongly held Japanese defense line.

The troops met little resistance until they approached Clark Field. The I Corps, commanded by Maj. Gen. Innis P. Swift, had heavy fighting on the east flank where the Japanese were strongly entrenched in hill positions. For the time being they were to be held there to keep the supply line for the advance on Manila secure.

On 29 January troops of General Hall's XI Corps under strategic direction of the Eighth Army landed on the west coast of Luzon near Subic Bay, meeting light opposition. They drove eastward to cut off the Bataan peninsula where General MacArthur had made his stand three years before, denying the Japanese the use of Manila harbor for months.

The 11th Airborne Division on 31 January made an unopposed amphibious landing at Nasugbu in Batangas Province south of Manila. Three days later the division's parachute regiment jumped to Tagaytay ridge dominating the Cavite area. That night troops of the 1st Cavalry Division raced through Novaliches and reached Grace Park in the northeastern portion of the city of Manila. On 6 February the airborne troops reached Nichols Field. As the troops of the Sixth Army closed on Manila from the north, northwest, and south, the situation of Japanese forces in the city was rendered hopeless but they fought bitterly from house to house. Organized resistance ceased on 23 February when American infantry penetrated the old walled city.

Preceded by heavy air and naval bombardment, elements of the 38th Division landed on 15 February at Mariveles on the tip of Bataan. Resistance was light and our soldiery rapidly advanced along the perimeter road west of Manila Bay. While the battle for the city still raged, MacArthur moved to open Manila Bay and begin preparation of the Philippines as a major base for the next United States advances in the far Pacific.

Corregidor had gone under Allied bombardment on 23 January, and in less than a month Kenney's airmen dropped 3,128 tons of bombs on the two and three-fourths square-mile island that controls Manila Bay.

On the morning of 16 February, two long trains of Army C–47 transports approached the "Rock," close to the 500-foot sheer cliffs. A sudden 18-mile-an-hour wind swept the air clear of the smoke and dust of the naval and air bombardment that had ceased a few minutes earlier. Then the troop carriers began to sow the sky. 'Chutes spilled out white and troops of the veteran 503d Parachute Regiment drifted downward toward the lighthouse and golf course on the little island, against scattered small arms fire from the Japs on the ground. Simultaneously, troops of the 34th Infantry Regiment hit the shore in assault boats at San José South Dock. They ran into a heavy mine field covering the entire length of the beach, but little fire from Japs on the island.

Fighting in the tunnels built by Americans in an attempt to make Corregidor impregnable prior to World War II, the Japs continued their suicidal resistance for nearly two weeks. Toward the end there was a series of terrific explosions on the islands as the Japs destroyed the tunnel system and themselves with it. Americans sealed up remaining caves and an estimated 300 Japs. A total of 4,215 Japs were killed on the island, an unknown number blown up. Of the 3,038 Americans who took back Corregidor, 136 were killed, 8 were missing, and 531 wounded.

Manila Bay was open in early March. In less than two months General MacArthur accomplished what the Japanese had needed six to do after Pearl Harbor.

In late February, elements of the Eighth Army's 41st Division effected an unopposed landing at Puerto Princesa, Palawan Island. The force captured the town with its two airstrips and completely occupied Puerto Princesa Peninsula. The airfields gave control of a wide area of the China Sea greatly facilitating the severance of Japanese communication with Malaysia and Burma.

On 10 March other 41st Division troops landed on the western tip of Mindanao, second largest island in the Philippine group. Initial resistance was light and the city of Zamboanga fell the following day, but heavy fighting followed in the foothills and continued for weeks.

Landings were made during March on Panay, Cebu, and Negros. Reconnaissance parties went ashore on Jolo, Tawitawi, and other islands in the Sulu Archipelago, extending our holdings to within 40 miles of Borneo. In each case the landings were effected most skillfully with a minimum of resistance but stubborn and prolonged fighting usually followed in the hills.

Driving north from the central plain of Luzon, the Sixth Army Divisions met a fanatical enemy in the mountain ranges between Baguio and Balete Pass. East of Manila, infantry fought for long weeks across successive, bitterly-contested mountain ridges. Other elements cleared the area south of Laguna de Bay and advanced along the highway toward the Bicol Peninsula. On 1 April, a reinforced combat team landed at Legaspi in southeast Luzon. With the help of guerrillas, this force cleared the southeastern tip of the island and then moved northward toward our other troops advancing from central Luzon.

In mid-April, with the campaign in the Visayas drawing to a close, General Eichelberger sent the X Corps of his Eighth Army ashore on Central Mindanao north of Cotabato. By this time our troops were well established in the Zamboanga area and guerrilla forces were in possession of large areas in Northern Mindanao. Driving eastward to Davao Gulf, infantry of the 24th Division, X Corps, took Davao City on 4 May after house-to-house fighting. A column of the 31st Division drove north up the valley of the Pulangi River to Kibawe. Meanwhile, on Luzon, the important city of Baguio had fallen to the 33d and 37th Divisions.

Allied gains in the Southwest Pacific were extended on 1 May by an amphibious force of Australian and Netherland East Indies troops which landed on oil-rich Tarakan Island, off the northeast coast of Borneo. By the end of the month all important installations on the island were in Allied hands.

In mid-May another landing was made on Mindanao, this time at Agusan on the guerrilla-held north coast. In two days the assault troops had driven 12 miles south and seized the town and airfield of Del Monte.

On 13 May, after months of extremely hard fighting, Balete Pass, gateway to the Cagayan Valley, was captured. East of Manila, on the same day, the 1st Cavalry Division reached the sea at Binangonan Point, thus dividing the last enemy pocket in central Luzon and cutting to the rear of the strong enemy positions in the Marikina watershed.

The Net Closes

The superforts were now blasting the great cities of the Japanese Islands on an ever-increasing scale. Chief targets were aircraft plants. Docks and small manufacturing plants received their share of the punishment.

On 19 February the V Marine Corps supported by Admiral R. A. Spruance's Fifth Fleet landed along the south coast of Iwo Jima, 775 miles from the main Japanese Island of Honshu. The fighting was exceptionally heavy and it was a month before organized resistance terminated. The Japanese defense grew more desperate as our advance moved toward the shores of their homeland.

Iwo Jima was of vital importance to the air assault on Japan. Japanese interceptors which came up to meet the B–29 strike on Tokyo on 7 April 1945 found a strong Mustang escort with our bombers. The Iwo fields saved hundreds of battle-damaged B–29's unable to make the full return flight to their bases in the Marianas, 800 miles further to the south.

Meanwhile Philippine-based aircraft were establishing command over Formosa and the China Coast and our naval carrier planes, as well as the superforts, delivered strikes at the very heart of Japan. It was now possible to drive forward into the Ryukyus along the main Japanese archipelago bordering the East China Sea.

The offensive on the Ryukyus was launched on 26 March when the 77th Division of Lt. Gen. Simon B. Buckner's Tenth Army landed on Kerama Retto west of Okinawa. In three days the force had secured all islands in the Kerama chain and had emplaced artillery within range of the key island, Okinawa.

Under cover of an intense naval bombardment, the XXIV Army Corps and the III Marine Corps established beachheads on the west coast of long, narrow Okinawa on 1 April. Aided by a realistic feint toward the thickly populated southern tip of the island, our forces met little resistance in the landing and in consolidating positions ashore. After driving across the inland, the Marines swung northward against light to moderate opposition; the Army corps turned south toward Naha, principal city of the island, where it was confronted by the main Japanese force elaborately entrenched.

By the end of the first week, four United States divisions were ashore and Marine fighters were operating from the Yontan airfield. The III Marine Corps had driven 20 miles northward.

General Hodge, commander of the XXIV Army Corps wrote:

It is going to be really tough. There are 65,000 to 70,000 fighting Japs holed up in the south end of the island, and I see no way to get them out except blast them out yard by yard. Our attack is set to go soon, and I think we are ready.

The Japs have tremendous amounts of artillery and have used it far more intelligently than I have ever seen them use it to date. With best estimate, it shows around 500 or more individual weapons of 75-mm or better, including some 169–175 of caliber 105 or better. The most powerful weapon of long-range we have encountered to date is the 150 rifle with range of 27,000 yards which fires occasionally upon the two airfields from the vicinity of Shuri. They are using quite a few of the Spigot mortars (320-mm), 250-mm mortars, and aerial bombs up to 250 kilograms fitted as rockets. They are also using large sized rockets somewhere in the 5-, 6- to 8-inch class.

The terrain is decidedly rugged and cut up with many cliffs, natural and man-made, limestone and coral caves, and organized over long periods of time, and well-manned.

After mopping-up all of the northern part of the island, the Marines took over a sector in the south to throw their weight into the drive for Naha. Progress continued slow against the bitterest sort of opposition but by the middle of June, our troops had broken through the heavily fortified Naha and Shuri defense lines and had compressed the Japanese into two pockets on southern Okinawa.

The ferocity of the ground fighting was matched by frequent Japanese air assaults on our shipping in the Okinawa area. By the middle of June, 33 U. S. ships had been sunk and 45 damaged, principally by aerial attacks. In the Philippines campaign U. S. forces first met the full fury of the kamikaze or suicide attacks,

but at Okinawa the Japanese procedure was better organized and involved larger numbers of planes; also the Baka plane appeared, something quite new and deadly. This small, short range, rocket-accelerated aircraft, carried more than a ton of explosives in its war head. It was designed to be carried to the attack, slung beneath a medium bomber, then directed in a rocket-assisted dive to the target by its suicide pilot. It was in effect, a piloted version of the German V-1.

By mid-June, the Japanese had lost twenty percent of their total combat aircraft strength in the battle for Okinawa; in all, 3,400 Japanese planes were shot down over the Ryukyus and Kyushu and 800 more were destroyed on the ground. During the same period our losses totaled more than a thousand aircraft.

The pattern of fanatical Japanese resistance continued in the southernmost tip of the island. Each successive strong point was cleared only by heroic efforts of our soldiers and marines. By the end of June we had suffered 39,000 casualties in the Okinawa campaign, which included losses of over 10,000 among naval personnel of the supporting fleet. By the same date, 109,629 Japanese had been killed and 7,871 taken prisoner.

With victory just within his grasp, the Tenth Army Commander, General Buckner, was forward with his assault infantry, observing the progress of this final drive to clean up the island on 18 June. An enemy artillery salvo squarely bracketed his observation post, and General Buckner died a soldier's death a few minutes later. This splendid leader was replaced by General Joseph W. Stilwell, then Commander of the Army Ground Forces. The Ground Forces Command was given to General Jacob L. Devers, the veteran commander of the Southern Group of Eisenhower's Armies.

General Buckner had won his battle. Within three days of his death, all organized resistance had ceased on Okinawa, our first strategic base within the shadow of the Japanese homeland.

The 9th Australian Division on 10 June made an unopposed landing at Brunei Bay, in northwest Borneo, seizing the naval anchorage and airfields. By overland and amphibious operations the Australians quickly drove south to important oilfields at Seria and Miri. The establishment of air and naval facilities at Brunei Bay, combined with those in the Philippines, completed a chain of mutually supporting strategic bases from which Allied air and naval forces could cover the Asiatic coast from Singapore to Shanghai, interdicting the enemy's overland communications and escape routes in Indo-China and Malaya.

Meanwhile, General Krueger began the final operations against the Japanese on Luzon when the 37th Division drove northward from Balete Pass into the Cagayan Valley. North of Baguio, our forces met stiff resistance from Japanese remnants who had gathered

for a last stand among the precipitous mountains. Further north, Philippine guerrillas cleared large areas of northwest Luzon. On 21 June these forces, assisted by Rangers of the Sixth U. S. Army, captured Aparri, Luzon's northernmost port, and were astride the main road through the valley at Tuguegarao.

On 23 June a paratroop force of the 11th Airborne Division dropped just south of Aparri. This force drove 25 miles southward during the next three days to establish contact with forward elements of the 37th Division.

The seizure of the Cagayan Valley virtually terminated the campaign in Luzon, though sizable pockets of desperate Japanese remained to be eliminated. In the liberation of the Philippine Islands, General MacArthur's armies had killed by that time 317,000

and captured 7,236 Japanese against a U. S. casualty figure of approximately 60,628 killed, wounded, and missing.

On 1 July Australian forces landed at Balikpapan in southeastern Borneo. Preceded by a heavy aerial and naval bombardment, assault troops suffered only light casualties in seizing their beachheads. By the middle of July, Balikpapan Harbor was open to Allied shipping.

From California to the coast of China the vast Pacific abounded with American power. In the Philippines, the Marianas and the Ryukyus, our forces under steadily increasing reinforcements from the European continent massed for the final phase of the Pacific war. The enemy's shipping had been largely sunk or driven from the seas. The few remaining fragments of his once powerful naval

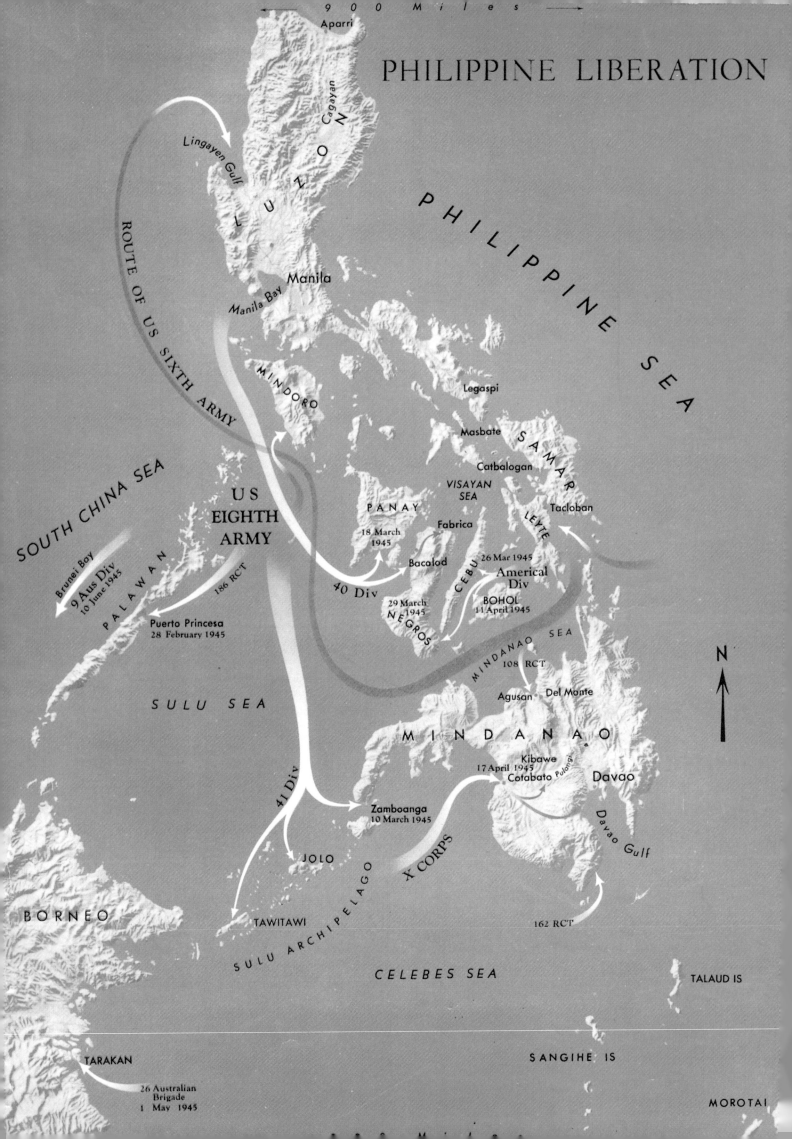

PHILIPPINE LIBERATION

9 0 0 M i l e s

Aparri

LUZON

Cagayan

Lingayen Gulf

ROUTE OF US SIXTH ARMY

Manila

Manila Bay

MINDORO

PHILIPPINE SEA

Legaspi

Masbate

SAMAR

Catbalogan

VISAYAN SEA

SOUTH CHINA SEA

US EIGHTH ARMY

PANAY

18 March 1945

Fabrica

Tacloban

LEYTE

Brunei Bay

9 Aus Div
10 June 1945

PALAWAN

186 RCT

Bacolod

40 Div

CEBU

26 Mar 1945

Americal Div

Puerto Princesa
28 February 1945

29 March
1945

NEGROS

BOHOL
11 April 1945

MINDANAO SEA

108 RCT

SULU SEA

Agusan   Del Monte

N

MINDANAO

Kibawe
17 April 1945

Cotabato   Pulangi

Davao

41 Div

Zamboanga
10 March 1945

X CORPS

Davao Gulf

JOLO

BORNEO

TAWITAWI

SULU ARCHIPELAGO

162 RCT

CELEBES SEA

TALAUD IS

TARAKAN

SANGIHE IS

26 Australian
Brigade
1 May 1945

MOROTAI

force were virtually harbor bound and the industries and communications of Japan were rapidly crumbling under the mounting tempo of our aerial bombardment. Lord Mountbatten's forces in southeastern Asia were closing in on Malaysia and the Netherlands East Indies. Chinese armies, newly equipped, trained, and determinedly led, were gradually assuming the offensive.

The day of final reckoning for a treacherous enemy was at hand.

Final Victory

By direction of the Joint Chiefs of Staff, General MacArthur assumed command of all United States Army Forces in the Pacific on April 6. Both he and Admiral Nimitz, Commander of Naval Forces in the Pacific, were directed to prepare for the final operations against Japan. By June General MacArthur had created a new command known as the United States Army Forces in the Western Pacific under Lt. Gen. W. D. Styer to replace the old Southwest Pacific Area. General Richardson was redesignated Commander of the Army Forces of the Middle Pacific.

On 10 July the Joint Chiefs of Staff ordered another revision of the Pacific Command.

The formerly China-based 20th and 21st Bomber Commands were deactivated. The 21st became the 20th Air Force and the personnel of the 20th Bomber Command was transferred to the Eighth Air Force, which had been redeployed from Europe. General Twining, who had started in the Pacific war with the 13th Air Force in the Solomons, later moved to command of the 15th Air Force in Italy, was given command of the new 20th Air Force. General Doolittle retained command of the 8th.

Both Air Forces which now controlled the mightiest fleet of superbombers ever assembled, were combined into the U. S. Strategic Air Force, the Command which controlled the American Air assault on Germany. General Spaatz retained command of USSTAF in the Pacific. General Giles became his deputy. General LeMay, who once had commanded the B–29 fleet in China, then built up the superfortress attack in the Pacific, became his Chief of Staff.

Strategic control of the superfortress fleet remained with the Joint Chiefs of Staff with General Arnold as their agent.

During July the superbombers had steadily increased the scale of their attacks on the Japanese homeland. From the Marianas bases, the B–29's averaged 1,200 sorties a week. Okinawa airfields which now occupied almost all suitable space on the island began to fill with heavy bombers, mediums and fighters which united in the aerial assault on the Japanese islands, her positions on the Asiatic mainland and what was left of her shipping. Fighters from Iwo Jima swept the air over the Japanese Islands, strafed Japanese dromes and communications and gave the superbombers freedom of operation. The Third Fleet augmented by British units hammered Japan with its planes and guns sailing boldly into Japanese coastal waters. The warships repeatedly and effectively shelled industries along the coasts.

These mighty attacks met little opposition. Terrific air losses during the fierce battles of Japan's interdefenses had made the enemy desperate. Knowing that invasion was not long off, he husbanded his now waning resources for the final battle. Defending the homeland the enemy had an army of 2,000,000, a remaining air strength of 8,000 planes of all types, training and combat.

General MacArthur was massing troops and planes in the Philippines and in Okinawa and in bases to the south of the Philippines for the showdown. He, in cooperation with Admiral Nimitz,* was preparing to execute two plans for the invasion of Japan: the first known as operation OLYMPIC, provided for a three-pronged assault on southern Kyushu in the fall of 1945 by the Sixth United States Army, consisting of the I and the XI Army Corps and the V Marine Amphibious Corps. The three groups were to land in the order named at Miyazaki, Ariaka Wan, and on the beaches west of Kagoshima to isolate the southernmost Japanese island and destroy the defending forces there. Preceding the main assault were to be preliminary operations in Koshiki Retto and a diversionary feint off Shikoku by the IX Corps.

The second phase of the Japanese invasion, operation CORONET, was to be carried out in the early spring of 1946. The Eighth and Tenth Armies, consisting of nine infantry divisions, two armored divisions and three Marine divisions were to assault the Kanto or Tokyo plain of eastern Honshu. These two veteran Pacific Armies were to be followed ashore by the First Army, which had spearheaded our victory in Europe and was now to be redeployed for the final battle of the Pacific. In this attack the First Army would have contained 10 infantry divisions. The three armies had the mission of destroying the Japanese Army on the main home island and to occupy the Tokyo-Yokohama area. On Kyushu we would have held a one-corps reserve of three infantry divisions and one airborne. From here the plan was to fan out to the north and clean up the remainder of the Japanese islands. Supporting the clean-up would ultimately have been an air garrison equivalent to 50 groups.

These were our plans for final victory in World War II should Japan fight to a last ditch national suicide. But we had other plans which we anticipated might bring a much speedier end to the war. For years the full resources of American and British science had been working on the principle of atomic fission. By

---

* Naval aspects of the plans are not discussed here.

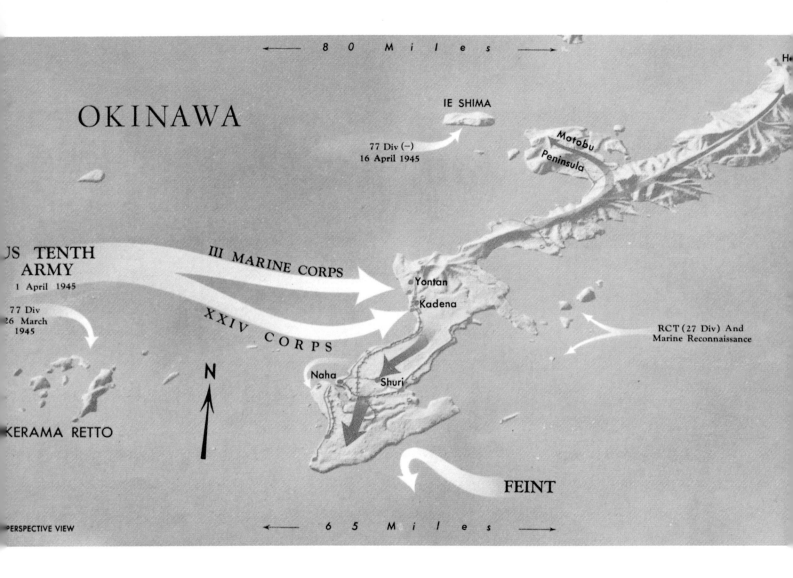

the spring of this year we knew that success was at hand. While President Truman was meeting with the British Prime Minister and Generalissimo Stalin at Potsdam, a new and terrible bomb was taken to a deserted area of New Mexico and detonated. The results were even more terrifying than was anticipated. A report was rushed to the Secretary of War and the President at Potsdam, Germany, and it was decided to use this weapon immediately in an effort to shorten the war and save thousands of American lives. From Potsdam General Spaatz received orders to drop the atomic bomb on the industrial installations of one of four selected cities from which he could make his own selection according to weather and target any time after the 3d of August. He chose the military base city of Hiroshima.

On 6 August the bomb was dropped. The results are well known.

Two days later the Soviet Union declared war on Japan and within a few hours the Red Army was again on the march, this time driving with powerful blows into the pride of Japanese military power, the Kwantung Army of Manchuria. The first Red offensives were across the Manchuria borders and southward on the island of Sakhalin. The advance by the Red divisions was swift. They struck first to isolate Manchuria and then Korea. In rapid thrusts from outer Mongolia and Trans Baikal, the Soviet forces drove deep into Manchuria and struck the Khinghan range, captured the communications center and bases at Hailar and crossed the Khinghan barrier into Harbin, key city of central Manchuria. To the south strong mobile forces crossed the desolate Gobi desert toward southern Manchuria.

Then, on 9 August, the Strategic Air Forces loosed a second atomic bomb on Nagasaki, which displayed greater destructive blast and fire than the Hiroshima bomb. The smoke of the Nagasaki detonation rose 50,000 feet into the air and was visible for more than 175 miles.

The week of 6 August had been one of swift and sudden disaster to the nation which fired the first shot in the series of conflicts that led to World War II. Japan was being made to pay in full for her treacheries at Mukden and at Shanghai, at Pearl Harbor and at Bataan. The enemy situation was hopeless. On 10 August the Japanese Government sued for peace on the general terms enunciated by the Allied powers at the Potsdam Conference.

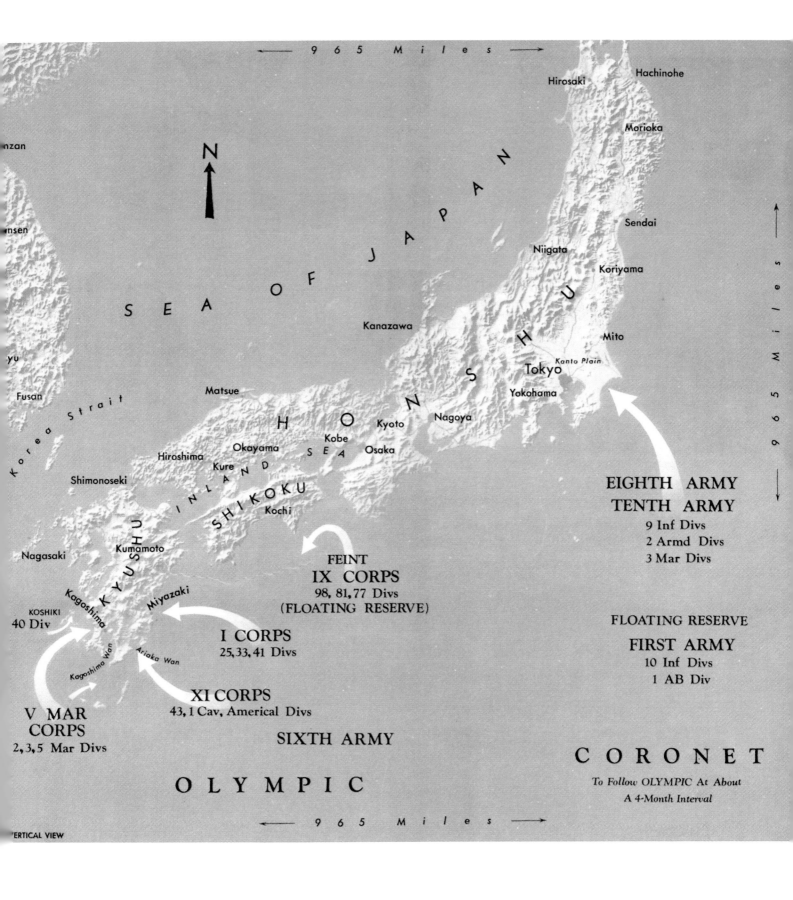

EIGHTH ARMY
TENTH ARMY
9 Inf Divs
2 Armd Divs
3 Mar Divs

FLOATING RESERVE
FIRST ARMY
10 Inf Divs
1 AB Div

CORONET
To Follow OLYMPIC At About
A 4-Month Interval

FEINT
IX CORPS
98, 81, 77 Divs
(FLOATING RESERVE)

I CORPS
25, 33, 41 Divs

XI CORPS
43, 1 Cav, Americal Divs

SIXTH ARMY

V MAR
CORPS
2, 3, 5 Mar Divs

KOSHIKI
40 Div

OLYMPIC

VERTICAL VIEW

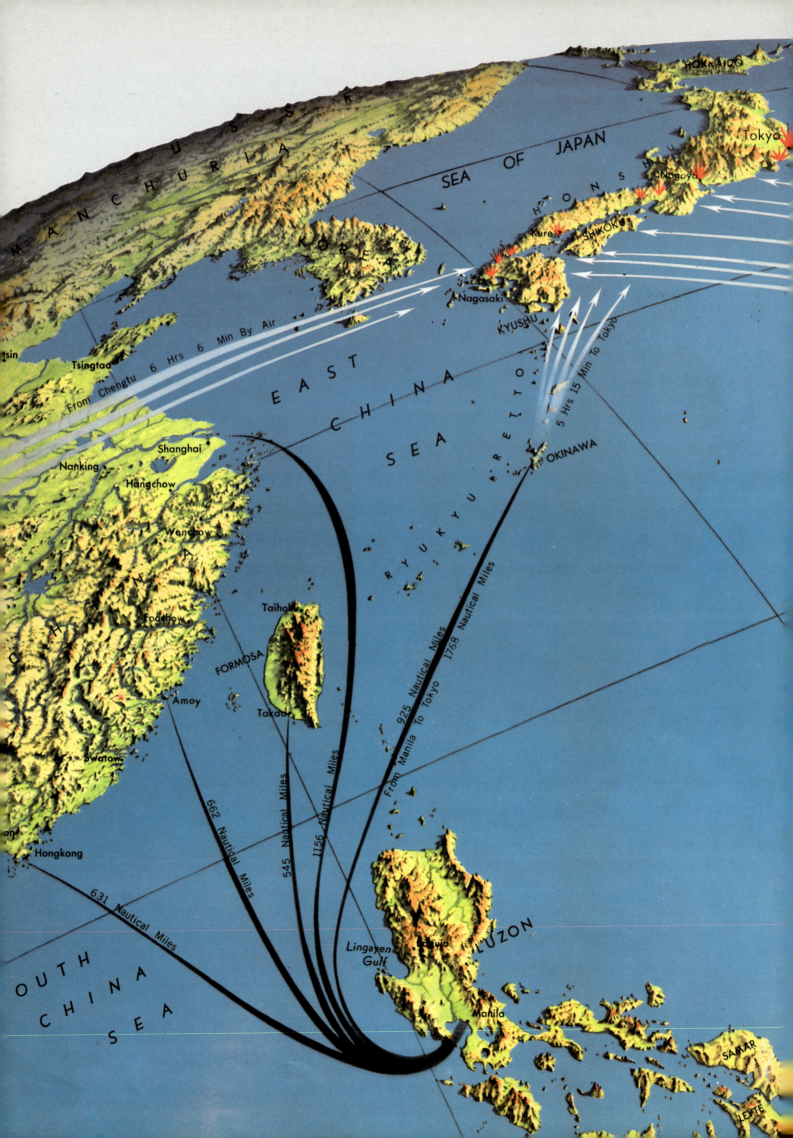

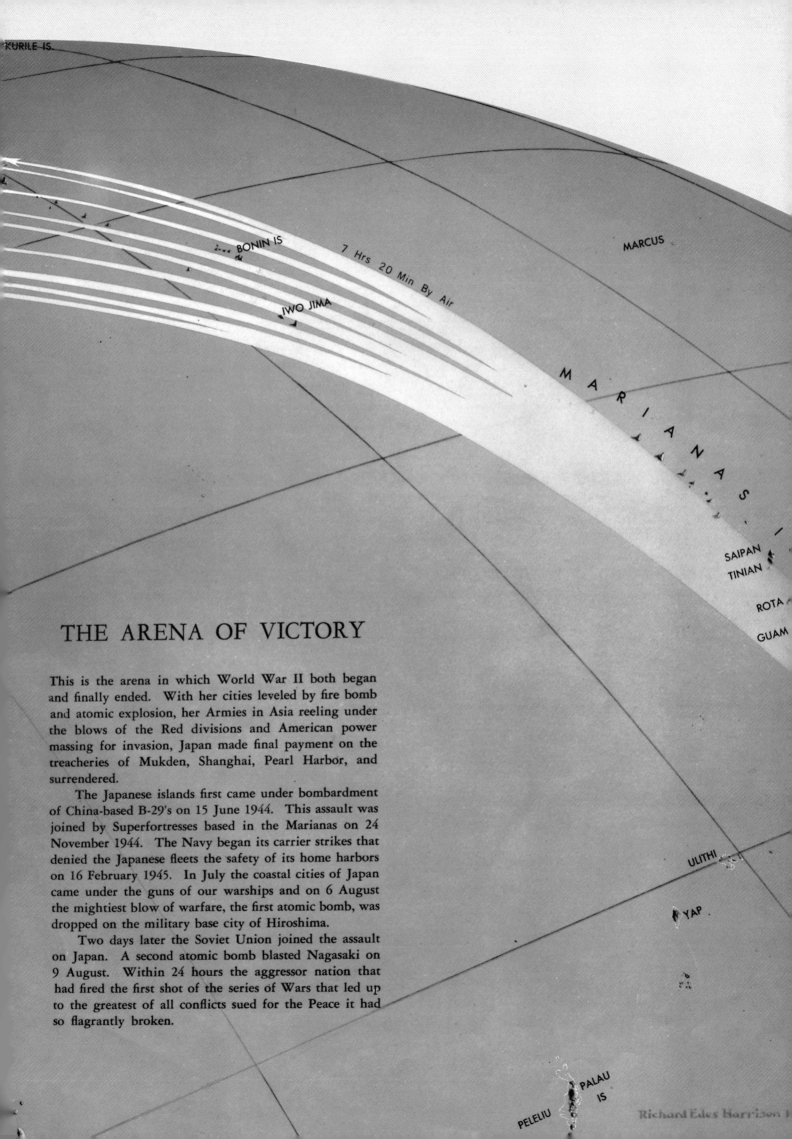

KURILE IS.

BONIN IS

IWO JIMA

7 Hrs 20 Min By Air

MARCUS

M A R I A N A S

SAIPAN
TINIAN
ROTA
GUAM

ULITHI

YAP

THE ARENA OF VICTORY

This is the arena in which World War II both began and finally ended. With her cities leveled by fire bomb and atomic explosion, her Armies in Asia reeling under the blows of the Red divisions and American power massing for invasion, Japan made final payment on the treacheries of Mukden, Shanghai, Pearl Harbor, and surrendered.

The Japanese islands first came under bombardment of China-based B-29's on 15 June 1944. This assault was joined by Superfortresses based in the Marianas on 24 November 1944. The Navy began its carrier strikes that denied the Japanese fleets the safety of its home harbors on 16 February 1945. In July the coastal cities of Japan came under the guns of our warships and on 6 August the mightiest blow of warfare, the first atomic bomb, was dropped on the military base city of Hiroshima.

Two days later the Soviet Union joined the assault on Japan. A second atomic bomb blasted Nagasaki on 9 August. Within 24 hours the aggressor nation that had fired the first shot of the series of Wars that led up to the greatest of all conflicts sued for the Peace it had so flagrantly broken.

PALAU
IS

PELELIU

Richard Edes Harrison

ORDER OF BATTLE U. S. ARMY FORCES IN THE PACIFIC (AS OF 14 AUGUST 1945)

Unit	Commander	Location
General Headquarters, U. S. Army Forces the Pacific	General of the Army Douglas MacArthur	Manila, Luzon, Philippine Islands.
Sixth Army	Gen. Walter Krueger	Luzon, Philippine Islands.
40th Infantry Division	Brig. Gen. D. J. Myers	Panay, Philippine Islands.
11th Airborne Division	Maj. Gen. J. M. Swing	Luzon, Philippine Islands.
I Corps	Maj. Gen. I. P. Swift	Luzon, Philippine Islands.
25th Infantry Division	Maj. Gen. C. L. Mullins	Luzon, Philippine Islands.
33d Infantry Division	Maj. Gen. P. W. Clarkson	Luzon, Philippine Islands.
41st Infantry Division	Maj. Gen. J. A. Doe	Mindanao, Philippine Islands.
IX Corps	Maj. Gen. C. W. Ryder	Leyte, Philippine Islands.
77th Infantry Division	Maj. Gen. A. D. Bruce	Cebu, Philippine Islands.
81st Infantry Division	Maj. Gen. P. J. Mueller	Leyte, Philippine Islands.
XI Corps	Lt. Gen. C. P. Hall	Luzon, Philippine Islands.
43d Infantry Division	Maj. Gen. L. F. Wing	Luzon, Philippine Islands.
Americal Infantry Division	Maj. Gen. W. H. Arnold	Cebu, Philippine Islands.
1st Cavalry Division	Maj. Gen. W. C. Chase	Luzon, Philippine Islands.
Eighth Army	Lt. Gen. R. L. Eichelberger	Leyte, Philippine Islands.
93d Infantry Division	Maj. Gen. H. H. Johnson	Morotai Island, New Guinea, and Philippine Islands.
96th Infantry Division	Maj. Gen. James L. Bradley	Okinawa, Ryukyus Islands, and Mindanao, Philippine Islands.
X Corps	Maj. Gen. F. C. Sibert	Mindanao, Philippine Islands.
24th Infantry Division	Maj. Gen. R. B. Woodruff	Mindanao, Philippine Islands.
31st Infantry Division	Maj. Gen. C. A. Martin	Mindanao, Philippine Islands.
XIV Corps	Lt. Gen. O. W. Griswold	Luzon, Philippine Islands.
6th Infantry Division	Maj. Gen. C. E. Hurdis	Luzon, Philippine Islands.
32d Infantry Division	Maj. Gen. W. H. Gill	Luzon, Philippine Islands.
37th Infantry Division	Maj. Gen. R. S. Beightler	Luzon, Philippine Islands.
38th Infantry Division	Maj. Gen. F. A. Irving	Luzon, Philippine Islands.
Tenth Army	Gen. J. W. Stilwell	Okinawa, Ryukyus Islands.
XXIV Corps	Lt. Gen. J. R. Hodge	Okinawa, Ryukyus Islands.
7th Infantry Division	Maj. Gen. A. V. Arnold	Okinawa, Ryukyus Islands.
27th Infantry Division	Maj. Gen. G. W. Griner, Jr.	Ie Shima and Okinawa, Ryukyus Islands.
U. S. Army Forces, Middle Pacific	Lt. Gen. R. C. Richardson, Jr.	Oahu, Hawaiian Islands.
98th Infantry Division	Maj. Gen. A. M. Harper	Oahu, Hawaiian Islands.
U. S. Army Forces, Western Pacific	Lt. Gen. W. D. Styer	Luzon, Philippine Islands.
Far East Air Forces	Gen. G. C. Kenney	Okinawa, Ryukyus Islands.
Fifth Air Force	Lt. Gen. E. C. Whitehead	Okinawa, Ryukyus Islands.
Seventh Air Force	Brig. Gen. T. D. White	Saipan, Marianas Islands.
Thirteenth Air Force	Maj. Gen. P. B. Wurtsmith	Leyte, Philippine Islands.

ORDER OF BATTLE U. S. ARMY STRATEGIC AIR FORCES (AS OF 14 AUGUST 1945)

Headquarters, U. S. Army Strategic Air Forces, Guam, Marianas Islands:

Commanding General	Gen. Carl Spaatz.
Deputy Commander	Lt. Gen. B. McK. Giles.
Chief of Staff	Maj. Gen. C. E. LeMay.

Eighth Air Force, Okinawa, Ryukyus Islands:

Commanding General	Lt. Gen. James H. Doolittle.

Twentieth Air Force, Guam, Marianas Islands:

Commanding General	Lt. Gen. Nathan F. Twining.

OCCUPATION

Orderly civil administration must be maintained in support of military operations in liberated and occupied territories. In previous wars, the United States had no prepared plan for this purpose. In this war it was necessary to mobilize the full resources of both liberated and occupied countries to aid in defeating the enemy. The security of lines of communication and channels of supply, the prevention of sabotage, the control of epidemics, the restoration of production in order to decrease import needs, the maintenance of good order in general, all were factors involved. It was important to transform the inhabitants of liberated countries into fighting allies.

The Civil Affairs Division was created on 1 March 1943 to establish War Department policies designed to handle these problems. In joint operations, the Division works closely with a similar agency in the Navy Department, as well as with related civilian agencies to determine and to implement United States policies. The Army and Navy are represented on the Joint Civil Affairs Committee under the Joint Chiefs of Staff which is charged with planning for civil affairs in both Europe and the Pacific. In combined operations, United States policies are coordinated with those of the British through the Combined Civil Affairs Committee of the Combined Chiefs of Staff.

Army officers were trained at the School of Military Government established at the University of Virginia and at Civil Affairs training schools to serve in military government and civil affairs activities in the field. The operation of these schools is a responsibility of The Provost Marshal General, under directives prepared by the Civil Affairs Division.

In French North Africa the civil administration was conducted by the French Government. The British managed civil affairs in the territory east of the Tunis-Tripoli border.

In Sicily for the first time, civil affairs officers, American and British in equal numbers, went ashore with assault troops. For the remainder of the Sicilian campaign these officers accompanied combat troops into towns and areas where their services were necessary. In the initial stages of the Sicilian campaign, military government was a responsibility of combat commanders, and civil affairs officers went with fighting troops to take the burden of dealing with the civil populace off the commander's shoulders. They organized the civil administration so as to secure the cooperation of the Sicilians, and thus relieve tactical commanders from the necessity of diverting detachments from combat troops for security. Allied Military Government of Occupied Territories was extended in Sicily as rapidly as the enemy was cleared from a community.

A similar procedure was followed in the early phases of the invasion of the Italian mainland. Civil affairs officers, attached to the 15th Army Group, were placed under the commanding generals of the Fifth and Eighth Armies. A mobile Allied Military Government headquarters moved with each army.

After Italy capitulated and became a cobelligerent against Germany, the Allied Control Commission for Italy was established by the Combined Chiefs of Staff to supervise the activities of the Italian Government and to insure that the terms of the surrender were observed. The Supreme Allied Commander in the Mediterranean Theater is president of the Commission. Originally, it was a United States–British military agency. Now the percentage of civilian personnel is progressively increasing. Early in 1945 the Allies reestablished diplomatic relations with Italy and since that time diplomatic representatives have dealt with political matters. The major portion of the Italian peninsula has been transferred from the control of AMG to that of the Italian Government.

Experience gained in Sicily and Italy and practices followed there have been utilized in all subsequent operations.

Public safety, health, supply, agricultural, and other experts in the various phases of civil affairs accompanied the invasion forces into Sicily and Italy. The security of the armies and their property, the protection of local resources for the use of the armies, and the keeping of public order were achieved by public safety officers who worked largely through the Royal Carabinieri and other Italian police. Emergency civilian relief supplies, food, medicine, soap, and coal were accumulated in North Africa before and during the Italian campaign. They were supplemented by shipments from the United Kingdom and the United States. In one year more than two million long tons of relief supplies were distributed in Italy. However, scarcity of food remained the most difficult civil affairs problem in that country. This was complicated by the Fascist-born black market, by lack of shipping space for nonmilitary goods, and by partial paralysis of inland transportation facilities which had been crippled by the enemy and by Allied bombings. Yet the bread ration rose from 125 to 200 grams, and finally to 300.

Conditions favorable to epidemics were created by undernourishment, lack of soap and water, broken sewers, dead animals, overcrowding, and refugees. The united efforts of the medical personnel of the armies and the public health experts of AMG, who directed and assisted the Italian medical profession, kept epidemics under control. Outbreaks of typhus were suppressed. The public was informed of the danger from rodents and vermin as plague carriers. Refugees were deloused. Demolished water supply and sewer systems were restored. The services of a few experts prevented malaria from levying a heavy toll on our fighting men.

Many fugitives from Nazi oppression, chiefly Yugoslavs, had escaped into Italy. They have been cared for by the Army, and thousands have been evacuated to the Near East. A camp, capable of housing a group of 40,000 displaced persons, was opened by the Army at Philippeville, Algeria, and approximately 1,000 such refugees have been established in a temporary camp at Oswego, N. Y.

Upon recommendation of the American Commission for the Protection and Salvage of Artistic and Historic Monuments in War Areas, selected officers were assigned to the Mediterranean and European Theaters to furnish technical advice on the preservation and restoration of art and archives. As a result of a concerted program of education, troops have been able to save many priceless works from destruction.

In France and other liberated countries of Northwestern Europe, the aims and activities of civil affairs personnel were the same as in Italy. However, special conditions required revised methods. In Italy there was a progressive movement from full military government toward looser forms of control, including increased participation by civilians and the Italian Government. In the European Theater of Operations, civil affairs personnel was required to shift abruptly from cooperative management of civil affairs in liberated areas to full blown military government in Germany.

The War Department coordinated negotiations on the United States military level with the French Committee of National Liberation. They drew up agreements for the administration of civil affairs and, after approval by the U. S. Joint Chiefs of Staff, these were signed by General Eisenhower for the United States and General Koenig for the French Committee. The British executed a similar agreement on a governmental level.

Under these agreements, civil affairs in Corsica and France were effected through a French Delegate acting in accordance with French law. Later General Eisenhower was represented by a SHAEF Military Mission in France. The French civil administration cooperated effectively and it was unnecessary for General Eisenhower to invoke his paramount powers of control even in forward areas. So well did this understanding work that, as early as 24 October 1944, a zone of interior was proclaimed in France, which had the effect of formally restoring practically complete control over all governmental problems to the French Provisional Government. United States and United Kingdom officials had the aid of French officers in helping the armies keep their lines of communication open and supplies flowing forward. The French Provisional Government furthered the campaign in a variety of ways. During the autumn rains, "duckbill" type tread extensions were needed to give tanks better traction on muddy terrain. The French contributed 600 tons of their sparse steel stocks to make 400,000 "duckbills." They provided storm boats for the spring campaign requiring river crossings. It has been estimated that by the end of February 1945 the French Provisional Government had made available to the Allies supplies, labor, services, installations, transportation, and other facilities valued at approximately 225 million dollars.

Prior to the invasion of Normandy, the Governments of Belgium, Luxembourg, the Netherlands, and Norway had military missions attached to the staff of the Supreme Allied Commander in London. As these governments were reestablished on the continent, General Eisenhower designated a SHAEF Military Mission to each nation.

In Albania, Greece, and Yugoslavia, the interests of the United States in the administration of civil affairs is limited to the activities concerned with relief and rehabilitation.

Since D-day in Europe, our military authorities have carried out a civilian relief import program for the liberated peoples of Europe in coordination with the British. The relief supplies have consisted mostly of limited quantities of food, medical supplies, clothing and fuel. The United States share of this program, exclusive of petroleum products, for the northwest Europe and the Mediterranean areas, is approximately 3,900,000 tons for the year ending 30 June 1945.

In addition to imports of specific supplies for the civilian populations, the military authorities have actively assisted the liberated countries in the construction or repair of railroads, highways, and bridges, the reactivation of public utility services, and the construction or repair of port facilities and inland waterways. The Army has also been of assistance to the liberated governments in its efforts to aid in the resumption of essential industries such as coal mining, fishing, and others which would provide supplies to further the military effort and reduce shipping required for relief imports.

Military responsibility for provision of civilian supplies, except coal, for France was terminated 1 May 1945. It is expected that termination of military responsibility for furnishing civilian supplies throughout liberated northwest Europe, including coal for France, will be terminated on or about 1 September 1945.

The American Armies have accumulated so great a crop of prisoners that their handling has been a problem of immense complexity. Following the termination of hostilities in Europe our forces were holding 130,000 Italian prisoners and 3,050,000 German prisoners as well as an additional 3,000,000 German troops who were disarmed after the unconditional surrender. Of these, 370,000 German and 50,000 Italian prisoners are in the United States and Hawaii, and their disposition is a matter of immediate concern. It is the policy of the War Department to return to Europe all prisoners held in the United States as soon as this movement is practicable logistically.

The total capture in combined European operations has been divided equally between the United States and the British Commonwealth Governments. In addition to those prisoners who were the direct responsibility of the United States, this Government agreed to take 175,000 of the British captures with the understanding they would be returned as soon as possible.

The country has benefited from the utilization of the labor of these prisoners of war. Our critical manpower shortage has been relieved by 62,075,800 prisoner working days; the U. S. Treasury has been enriched by $35,196,800 paid by private contractors for this labor. In addition, their use on military installations has an estimated value of $108,825,469. After the capitulation of Italy, 110,000 Italian prisoners volunteered for Italian Service Units which perform noncombatant work helpful to the Allied war effort.

In the utilization of prisoners of war in continental United States, under the direction of The Provost Marshal General, the principle has been followed that such labor will not be permitted to compete with American civilian labor or to impair American wage standards and working conditions. Before a private contractor may employ prisoner of war labor, he must obtain from either the War Manpower Commission or the War Foods Administration a certification that civilian labor is not available for the project.

The policy of the United States with respect to treatment to be accorded to prisoners of war held by this country is in accordance with Geneva Prisoners of War Convention, which was ratified by the United States on 16 January 1932, and thus has the power of law. In following the provisions of the convention, the enemy prisoners have received firm treatment. At the same time a program of reorientation has been instituted to impress upon prisoners the vitality and strength of democratic institutions in the United States.

Prior to the unconditional surrender, military government in Germany was established by General Eisenhower throughout the areas occupied by his forces. Military government detachments followed in the wake of the advancing armed forces and established rigid control over the civil population, taking the first steps necessary to reestablish German administration free from Nazi influence. Some 5,500,000 displaced civilians and liberated United Nations prisoners of war were uncovered in Germany. By the end of June nearly 3,000,000 had been repatriated to their home lands. Suspected war criminals and persons whose freedom might endanger the security of the occupying forces were taken into custody.

The remarkable efficiency of handling both prisoners and displaced persons along the routes of an advancing victorious army was the fruit of an intensive effort to establish a new conception in the organization of military police. Our experience in the old AEF indicated that a highly trained military police force could be of tremendous value to military operations. Up to that time military police were used simply to enforce discipline and the regulations to which troops were subject. A careful study of World War operations coupled with experience in the first maneuvers brought the concept of using military police for helpful control of military traffic moving to and during battle. For this purpose special training schools were established by the Provost Marshal General. Insofar as possible older men were selected for the training. The returns on this effort were especially rich in the drive across France which heavily depended on the forwarding of the troops and supplies which had been put ashore in Normandy. Later in the collapse of German resistance the military police performed miracles in regulating the dense, rather chaotic traffic on the roads, burdened with combat troops and their supplies surging forward and millions of prisoners or displaced persons straggling in the opposite direction.

With the unconditional surrender of the German armed forces on 8 May, rigid military government was established throughout the whole of General Eisenhower's area of responsibility. The redeployment of forces into the national zones of occupation agreed upon by the four powers in the European Advisory Commission began. On 5 June General Eisenhower met in Berlin with Field Marshal Montgomery, Marshal Zhukov, and General De Lattre and on behalf of the United States signed the declaration by which the four governments assumed supreme authority and power in Germany. The Control Council in Germany was set up in accordance with the four-power protocol of the European Advisory Commission. At the end of June, General Eisenhower's responsibility as a Supreme Allied Commander for military government in Germany terminated and, as Commander in Chief of

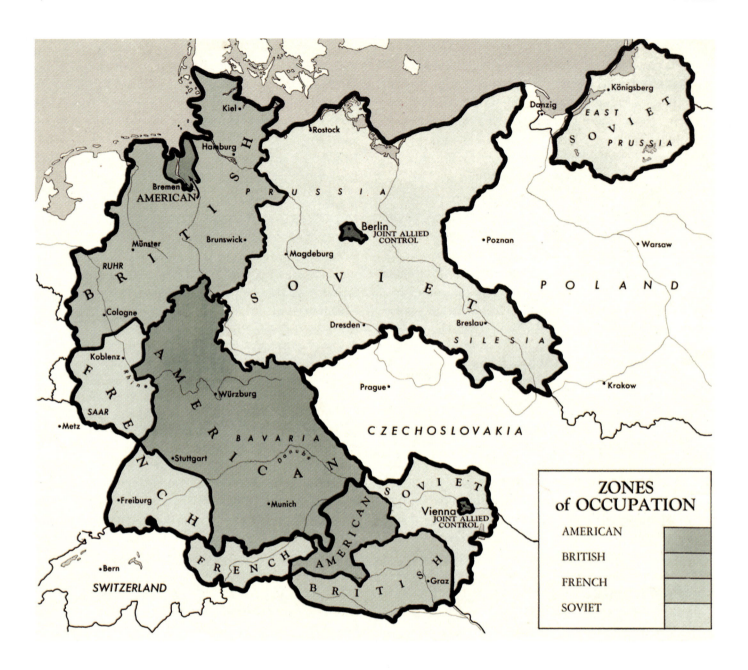

the United States Occupation Forces in Germany, he became responsible for the military government of the United States zone of occupation. The United States zone of occupation includes the whole of Bavaria, Wurtemburg, Hesse and Hesse-Nassau, and the northern portion of Baden, and, in addition, a portion of Berlin and the ports of Bremen and Bremerhaven. Lieutenant General Lucius DuB. Clay serves as Deputy Military Governor of the United States zone and as General Eisenhower's representative on the Coordinating Committee of the Control Council. He is assisted by a staff of specially chosen civilian and military experts.

In the closing days of the German campaign Allied Military Government was established in Austria. Officers and men, especially trained to deal with the problems of Austria, accompanied the tactical forces into those portions of the country occupied by United States, British, and French forces and took over control of all civil affairs. The military government in

Austria differs substantially from that in Germany. Although the program of denazification and demilitarization of Germany is being extended in Austria, the United Nations will endeavor to promote conditions which will lead to the establishment of a free and independent Austria. Allied control in Austria is conducted through quadripartite administration by Soviet, British, French, and United States commanders, each of whom has been made responsible for a zone of occupation. Combined command of United States and British forces in Austria has been terminated. Matters of concern to Austria as a whole are dealt with by the four national commanders sitting in Vienna. General Clark has been designated the Commanding General of United States forces in Austria and, as such, will be the United States representative on the Governing Body of the Allied Administration in Austria. Though Austria has become a part of the European Theater of Operations, General Clark, in his role as the United States representative in the Allied Administration in Austria, is responsible directly to the United States Joint Chiefs of Staff.

The liberation of the Philippines would have involved major problems of civil affairs had the Commonwealth Government and local officials of inflexible loyalty not shown from the very first landings immediate competence to reorganize administration and reestablish orderly government. By agreement with the Commonwealth Government it has been understood throughout the whole of the Philippine campaign that military responsibility for civil affairs was limited to the provision of necessary emergency relief to the population. Through military channels 140,000 tons of civil relief supplies were shipped to the Philippines between November 1944 and 1 July 1945.

The first major operation requiring the establishment of military government over large numbers of Japanese people was at Okinawa. In that testing ground of policies, for the main islands of Japan, valuable experience was gained by military government personnel of the Army working with naval personnel.

The capitulation of Japan has been followed by the occupation of various strategic portions of the four main Japanese Islands by Allied Forces under the supreme command of General MacArthur.

An important element of the surrender was the clear statement by the Allied Powers that from the moment of the capitulation, the Emperor and the Japanese Government would be under the absolute authority of the Supreme Commander. Initially, military government has not been established in the same manner as in Italy or Germany. The will of the Allied Powers as exemplified in the surrender instrument is being imposed upon the Japanese through the channel of the Emperor and the Japanese governmental machinery.

OUR WEAPONS

The Nation's state of unpreparedness along with that of the British Empire gave the Axis nations an overwhelming initial advantage in matériel. The Japanese campaigns in China, the Italian compaign in Ethiopia, and the participation of German and Italian troops in the Spanish Civil War afforded these enemies an opportunity to test their new weapons on the battlefield. This is a matter of very great importance, preliminary to decisions for quantity production of any weapon. Since we had some time in which to mobilize our resources, the vastly superior industrial establishment of the United States eventually overcame the initial advantage of the enemy.

During the past two years the United States Army was well armed and well equipped. The fact is we dared to mount operations all over the world with a strategic inferiority in numbers of troops. Were it not

for superiority in the air and on the sea, in mobility and in firepower we could not have achieved tactical superiority at the points chosen for attack nor have prevented the enemy from bringing greater forces to bear against us.

From the time of the landing in France to the time the Allies had reached the German frontiers, the German armies of the West exceeded numerically the attacking forces. General MacArthur invaded the Philippines with a lesser force than that with which the Japanese held the islands. In the immediate strategic area Japanese strength far outnumbered us. By no other criterion can the quality and quantity of our weapons better be judged. Yet we were in some instances outdone by both Germany and Japan in the development of specific weapons. It is truly remarkable that our superiority was as general and as decisive as it proved to be.

Overshadowing all other technological advance of the war was the Allied development of the atomic explosive. The tremendous military advantage of this terrifying weapon fell to us through a combination of good luck, good management and prodigious effort. The harnessing of atomic power should give Americans confidence in their destiny but at the same time we must be extremely careful not to fall victim to overconfidence. This tremendous discovery will not be ours exclusively indefinitely. In the years of peace between the two world wars we permitted Germany to far outpace us in the development of instruments which might have military use. As a consequence German development of long-range rockets and pilotless aircraft, stemming from years of peacetime research, was far more advanced than our own, which began in earnest only after the war had already started. The fact that we overtook Germany's head start on atomic explosive is comforting, but certainly should not lull us again into a state of complacent inertia.

In the development of aircraft and ships U. S. factories and productive "know-how" soon gave the Allies both a qualitative and quantitative advantage over Germany and Japan. By the time the great air battles of Europe and the far Pacific were joined, U. S. planes were superior in numbers and types to the enemy's. Our development of the long-range heavy bomber, now exemplified by the B-29, has been unmatched. The Germans themselves admit they did not even foresee our developments in the long-range fighter. They first introduced the jet engine in combat, but this was not because we had made no progress in this field. By the time their jet fighters were ready to take the air, the only areas in which they could give them operational tests were swept by our fighters. They had either to test them in combat or not at all. The German jet fighters were limited to a maximum endurance of a little over an hour. Ours already had the endurance to fly nonstop from San Francisco to New York.

Another noteworthy example of German superiority was in the heavy tank. From the summer of 1943 to the spring of 1945 the German Tiger and Panther tanks outmatched our Sherman tanks in direct combat. This stemmed largely from different concepts of armored warfare held by us and the Germans, and the radical difference in our approach to the battlefield. Our tanks had to be shipped thousands of miles overseas and landed on hostile shores amphibiously. They had to be able to cross innumerable rivers on temporary bridges, since when we attacked we sought to destroy the permanent bridges behind the enemy lines from the air. Those that our planes missed were destroyed by the enemy when he retreated. Therefore our tanks could not well be of the heavy type. We designed our armor as a weapon of exploitation. In other words, we desired to use our tanks in long-range thrusts deep into the enemy's rear where they could chew up his supply installations and communications. This required great endurance—low consumption of gasoline and ability to move great distances without break-down.

But while that was the most profitable use of the tank, it became unavoidable in stagnant prepared-line fighting to escape tank-to-tank battles. In this combat, our medium tank was at a disadvantage, when forced into a head-on engagement with the German heavies. Early in 1944 it was decided that a heavy American tank, on which our Ordnance experts had been continuously experimenting since before the war, must be put into mass production. As a result the M-26 (Pershing) tank began to reach the battle lines last winter. This tank was equal in direct combat to any the Germans had and still enjoyed a great advantage in lighter weight (43 tons), speed, and endurance. At the same time work was begun on two new models, the T-29 and T-30, which weighed 64 tons, one mounting a high-velocity 105-mm rifle, the other a 155-mm rifle.

Following the fierce fighting in North Africa and in the Papuan campaign in New Guinea, it became clear that our lack of preparedness and research in military instruments during peacetime would have to be overcome by extreme measures. Accordingly, in the late spring of 1943 I selected an expert ordnance officer, Col. William A. Borden, and directed him to work under me independently of normal War Department channels in the development and modification of weapons and improved techniques. His first efforts were devoted to increasing the effectiveness of our weapons against the Japanese in jungle fighting. As a result, the 105-mm and 155-mm mortars, flame throwers, ground rockets, improved launching devices, skid pans for towing heavy artillery in mud, improved bazooka ammunition, and colored smoke grenades were developed and the production and shipment to the theaters were expedited.

Later the Secretary of War decided to establish a division of the War Department Special Staff to be charged with coordinating the experience of our troops in the field with the Nation's scientific developments in order to keep us abreast in the race for newer and more deadly means for waging war. The New Developments Division was organized by Maj. Gen. Stephen G. Henry in October 1943. Officers were sent to the theaters to observe troops in combat to search for ways in which to apply our civilian scientific knowledge to the problems of the battlefield. They then returned and coordinated and expedited experimentation with new types of weapons and equipment by the appropriate Army Service Forces agency. When some item was developed it was taken to the theaters for trial and if successful put into production. Some examples: flame-throwing tanks, air rockets, improved ground rockets, self-propelled heavy artillery and electronic devices for locating enemy mortar and gun positions.

In addition, the New Developments Division studied and interpreted the intelligence available on new enemy weapons, particularly the proposed targets for air bombardment of the V-1 launching sites and supply channels to them. The air reduction for these sites so seriously interfered with the effectiveness of the V-1 that its threat to the invasion of France never materialized.

In August 1944 Brig. Gen. Borden succeeded General Henry as Chief of the New Developments Division when the latter officer was appointed Chief of the Personnel Division of the War Department General Staff. Special emphasis was then placed on the development of guided missiles, heavy tanks, recoilless artillery, rockets, radar, and night viewing devices, as well as expediting the production and shipment overseas of improved types of many of our new weapons or devices.

In most respects, our battle clothing was as good as can be supplied to any soldier of any country. The "layering" principle saves the greatest possible protection, and at the same time the greatest freedom of movement. The rubber-bottomed, leather-topped shoepac, worn with heavy ski socks and a felt innersole, overcame the heavy incidence of trench foot among our troops fighting in cold and extremely wet climates. No clothing has ever been invented that will make the exposure men must endure in combat pleasant. It has been possible only to develop sufficient protection to prevent large-scale casualties from such exposure. This we accomplished both in Europe and in the battlefields of the East. The principal difficulty in meeting this problem was control of the wasteful habits of our men in their use and misuse of the clothing and equipment issued.

The American Army was unquestionably better fed than any in history. However, feeding in combat can never be like that in garrison or cantonment, nor remotely like home cooking. Field rations must be non-perishable, compact, and easily carried by the individual soldier. The problem of providing troops with appetizing food has plagued armies down through the centuries. The development of field rations for the United States Army in this war was almost revolutionary. The combat rations "C" and "K" were given a range of variety that combat troops would not have dreamed of a few years ago. The "C" ration, the subject of much amusing criticism, was supplied with 10 different meat components: meat and beans; meat and vegetable stew; meat and spaghetti; ham, eggs, and potatoes; meat and noodles; meat and rice; frankfurters and beans; pork and beans; ham and lima beans; and chicken and vegetables. These were rations that could be made available to men actually under heavy fire. Where there was more time for the preparation of food, troops were given the "10-in-1" ration which contains canned vegetables and fruits, canned desserts, chocolates and other candies, roast beef, roast pork and similar meat components, even canned hamburgers. When troops in the field were not under fire, they were fed the "B" ration which offered a wide selection considering the circumstances. Since under conditions where the "B" ration was fed, there were usually few, if any, facilities for refrigeration and preserving foods, this ration was composed of canned vegetables, meats, fruits, and dehydrated potatoes and eggs and similar items. It certainly did not compare with the fresh eggs and meats and vegetables common to the American family table, but it was a vast improvement over past issues of campaign rations. In the rear areas where food could be shipped quickly and preserved under refrigeration, the "A" ration was fed. This is as good food as can be served large numbers of men. Compared with these American Army rations was the Japanese ration of 1½ pounds of rice and small quantities of meat or fish a day. The Japanese soldier, however, thrived on this diet because he had been accustomed to little more at home.

In major ground campaigns to destroy the enemy's forces and end his resistance, such as we fought in North Africa, Italy, France, and Germany, one of the basic factors in the final decision is the armament and equipment of the infantry divisions and the manner in which they are employed. A nation with the belligerent tradition of Germany, concentrating its resources on a powerful army and enjoying every initial advantage from years of preparation for war, should have the upper hand in many if not all of the basic infantry weapons.

In two of these basic items the German Army held an advantage almost to the end of the war. The first was the triple-threat 88-mm rifle which our troops first encountered in North Africa. Even at that time the U. S. Army had a similar weapon, the 90-mm rifle,

with greater penetrating power but the Germans had theirs on the battlefields and in quantity, with the "bugs" worked out in previous battle experience over a period of years. The United States forces did not have the 90-mm in quantity at the time and were compelled to work out its shortcomings in opposition to a proven weapon.

As a result the 88 was a powerful German weapon, ahead of ours in quantity and technique almost to the end of the war. In the Spanish Civil War the Germans were careful to conceal the role of the 88 as an anti-tank and antipersonnel weapon, revealing it only as an antiaircraft piece. When we first encountered it, it was serving all three purposes with deadly effect. A single 88 could fire several rounds of armor-piercing shells at our tanks, then suddenly begin firing air-bursting fragmentation shells at our infantry following their tanks, and a few minutes later throw up an anti-aircraft fire at planes supporting the ground operation. The 90-mm rifle had no such flexibility. It could not be depressed low enough for effective antitank fire. Our technique of handling the gun had not been sufficiently developed so that interchangeable ammunition was available to the gun when it was needed, and we did not have the numbers of the weapons the Germans had.

A second marked German advantage during most of the European war was in powder. German ammunition was charged with smokeless, flashless powder which in both night and day fighting helped the enemy tremendously in concealing his fire positions. United States riflemen, machine gunners, and gunners of all types had to expose their positions with telltale muzzle flashes or puffs of powder smoke. German preparations had given them time to develop this high-grade powder and manufacture tremendous quantities of it. They had it there and they used it. These facts should be considered along with our policy regarding the manufacture of explosives after the last war and the scientific development that should or would have followed in the plants of the great commercial manufacturers had they not been subjected to bitter attack as "Merchants of death."

Careful planning and husbandry of the Army's meager peacetime resources and the nature of this Nation's machine economy gave the American armies in Europe two good advantages over the German enemy. One of ours was the Garand semi-automatic rifle, which the Germans were never able to duplicate. It is interesting to trace the planning and decisions that gave us the Garand rifle and the tremendous small arms fire power that went with it, noting especially that the War Department program for the Garand was strenuously opposed.

The base of fire of a rifle platoon is its automatic weapons. The riflemen concentrate their fire on the impact area blocked out by the automatics. The base of fire of a United States rifle squad in this war has been its Browning automatic rifle. Prior to the war the Army had several hundred thousand of these weapons in war reserve. The developments of the war indicated it might be well to replace the automatic rifle with another type of small automatic weapon, but if we had, we would have jammed production facilities, replacing a type of weapon already in stock. Instead, it was decided to modify the automatic rifle and devote production to the Garand rifle.

The Germans, on the other hand, shifted their rifle squad automatic weapon to a new type of light machine gun developed just before the war. Their standard rifle at the end of the war was still bolt-operated. They had produced a few semi-automatic rifles but they were never effective and did not reach the battlefield in numbers. In their efforts to improve the firepower of their infantry, the Germans then beat us to quantity production of the machine pistol, which we did not have in large numbers on the battlefields until well near the end of the European war. Our superiority in infantry firepower, stemming from the use of the semi-automatic rifle, was never overcome.

The greatest advantage in equipment the United States has enjoyed on the ground in the fighting so far has been in our multiple-drive motor equipment, principally the jeep and the 2½-ton truck. These are the instruments which have moved and supplied United States troops in battle while the German Army, despite the fearful reputation of its "panzer armies" early in the war still depended heavily on animal transport for its regular infantry divisions. The United States, profiting from the mass production achievements of its automotive industry, made all its forces truck-drawn and had enough trucks left over to supply the British armies with large number of motor vehicles and send tremendous quantities to the Red Army.

The advantage of motor vehicle transport did not become strikingly clear until we had reached the beaches of Normandy. The truck had difficulty in the mountains of Tunisia and Italy, but once ashore in France our divisions had mobility that completely outclassed the enemy. The Germans discovered too late the error of the doctrine which a member of their general staff expressed to General Wedemeyer, then in Berlin, in the late thirties: "The truck has no place on the battlefield." He meant by this that an unarmored vehicle was too vulnerable to be brought within immediate fire areas.

The appearance of an unusually effective enemy weapon, or of a particularly attractive item of enemy equipment usually provoked animated public discussion in this country, especially when stimulated by criticism of the Army's supposed failures to provide the best. Such incidents posed a very difficult problem for the War Department. In the first place, the morale of the fighting man is a matter of primary importance. To destroy his confidence in his weapons or in the higher command is the constant and intense desire of the enemy. The American soldier has a very active imagination and usually, at least for the time being, covets anything new and is inclined to endow the death-dealing weapons of the enemy with extraordinary qualities since any weapon seems much more formidable to the man receiving its fire than to the man delivering it. If given slight encouragement, the reaction can be fatal to the success of our forces. Commanders must always make every effort to show their men how to make better, more effective use of what they have. The technique of handling a weapon can often be made more devastating than the power of the weapon itself. This was best illustrated by the correct, the intended, tactical employment of the United States medium tank.

Another factor involved is the advantage given to the enemy by informing him which of his weapons is hurting us most. And along with this goes the similar embarrassment of not wishing to disclose to the enemy the state of the measures you are most certainly taking to correct any demonstrated weakness in a particular weapon or in armament generally. If a machine gun is found to jam after one or two bursts or at high altitudes you don't give the enemy this important information. Nor do you wish to sacrifice surprise by advising him in advance of the improved weapon to come or actually in process of deployment.

In some of the public discussions of such matters, criticism was leveled at the Ordnance Department for not producing better weapons. This Department produced with rare efficiency what it was told to produce, and these instructions came from the General Staff of which I am the responsible head, transmitting the resolved views of the officers with the combat troops or air forces, of the commanders in the field.

In the other categories of weapons and equipment of the infantry divisions, machine guns, mortars, artillery, individual equipment, the United States and the German armies were so nearly equal that neither had any marked advantage. The German infantry rocket, the Panzerfaust, had greater hitting power than the United States bazooka which had been developed first. We believe that our use of massed heavy artillery fire was far more effective than the German techniques and clearly outclassed the Japanese. Though our heavy artillery from the 105-mm up was generally matched by the Germans, our method of employment of these weapons has been one of the decisive factors of our ground campaigns throughout the world.

In the field of aircraft armament, United States matériel was excellent. The .50-caliber aircraft machine gun was one of the most reliable weapons of the war. The latest version of this gun had a cyclic rate of 1,200 rounds a minute. The German 30-mm aircraft cannon had as an American counterpart a 37-mm aircraft cannon. The newest version of this United States weapon had a velocity of 3,000 foot-seconds. The Japanese primarily used a 37-mm gun built on obsolete design principles. The 75-mm aircraft cannon which some United States planes carry was a heavier gun than any other air force has ever mounted.

American bombs and the newest fusing and control devices which guide them to their targets had no counterpart. United States heavy military equipment such as tractors, earth-moving machinery, railroads and rolling stock, bridging equipment, and similar items stood the test of battle splendidly.

Radar equipment developed by the United States and Britain was superior to the electronics devices of either Germany or Japan. Our radar instruments, for example, which tracked aircraft in flight and directed the fire of antiaircraft guns was more accurate than any possessed by the enemy. American radar detection equipment, which picked up planes in the air and ships at sea, had greater range than the German. Japanese radar was greatly inferior.

Great emphasis was placed on airborne radar by the United States and British and the use of this device was a very important factor in the control of the submarine menace. Close personal supervision over this War Department program was exercised by the Secretary of War. Radar bombsights together with radio navigational aids permitted accurate bombing of German and Japanese targets under adverse weather conditions.

In the field of amphibious assault craft, the United States and Great Britain made great progress. This resulted from the fact that in every major campaign we waged in this war, we had to cross water and attack enemy-held positions. There was nothing anywhere which compared or even resembled our big landing ships with ramp prows and the dozens of other type craft which have put our armies ashore from North Africa to Okinawa. The initial development of these special types was stimulated by Lord Louis Mountbatten and the staff of the special British Commando forces under his direction.

Not only did the Nation's industrial establishment equip our Army, but it also contributed heavily to the hitting power of the other United Nations. The allocation of military lend-lease matériel to the Allied Powers exceeded a dollar value of 20 billions. A United States armored division can be fully equipped for 34 millions. The equipment of an infantry division represents a dollar expenditure of 10 millions. Translated into these terms, the dollar value of the arms alone turned over to our Allies would equip 588 armored divisions, or 2,000 infantry divisions.

To the British Empire went enough aircraft to equip four air forces the size of our Ninth as it went into action on D-day in Western Europe. At that time the Ninth was the largest air force in the world. American raw materials made possible a large percentage of Britain's own war production. But in addition fully fabricated equipment shipped to Britain in the last two years included 76,737 jeeps, 98,207 trucks, 12,431 tanks, and 1,031 pieces of heavy artillery.

The Soviet Union received thousands of tons of American raw materials to feed its own factories as well as fully fabricated equipment. In the two years covered by this report we shipped the Soviets 28,356 jeeps, 218,888 trucks, 4,177 tanks, and 252 pieces of heavy artillery. The mobility and supply of the great Red Army was further increased by American locomotives, rails, and rolling stock. Aircraft sufficient to equip two air forces the size of the Ninth were sent to the Soviets.

Almost all of the equipment used by the revitalized French Army, which had 12 fully equipped divisions in action at the time of Germany's surrender, came from the United States. The French tactical air force which largely covered the operations of this army was also American-equipped.

The amount of aid that could be given to China was curtailed by the limitations of the air route over the high altitudes and storms of the Himalayan Mountains. The Chinese divisions and supporting troops which played a major part in the opening of the Stilwell road were American trained and equipped. The Chinese armies which successfully stopped the Japanese advance short of Chungking and Kunming had some American equipment. Total aid to China now exceeds $500,000,000, and to this should be added the tremendous expenditures in war resources, planes, and facilities required in India and Burma in order to transport the material into China.

In return for lend-lease arms and matériel, United States forces fighting over the world received reciprocal aid known as reverse lend-lease from those Allies in a position to give it. By the end of 1944 reciprocal aid had reached a dollar value of 4 billions. It consisted largely of housing facilities, base installations, and foodstuffs. During the period of the build-up for the European invasion, United States forces in the British Isles received the equivalent of one shipload of equipment, food, and matériel for every two shipped them from the United States.

Rations of our troops in the United Kingdom were supplemented by 436,000,000 pounds of foodstuffs, principally fresh fruits and vegetables, grown in Britain, and tea and cocoa and other products imported from the Empire. For our forces in the Pacific and Asia, Australia supplied 1,835,000,000 pounds of foodstuffs; New Zealand, 800,000,000 pounds; and India, 524,000,000. A large percentage of our base construction in Australia, New Zealand, and India was done under reverse lendlease. From the British refineries at Abadan, in the Persian Gulf, our forces received 259,000,000 gallons of aviation fuel.

THE TROOPS

Manpower Balance

The process of mobilization for this war reached its peak and immediately started to decline with the surrender of Germany. In the summer of 1943 the firm decision was reached to build up the Army to an effective strength of 7,700,000 enlisted men believed necessary to meet our strategic commitments.

At the close of the European war the operating strength of the Army plus ineffectives was approximately 8,300,000. The ineffectives consisted of 500,000 men undergoing hospitalization, including 100,000 in the process of being discharged because they were no longer fit for either active or limited service, and 100,000 en route overseas as replacements, in all totaling approximately 600,000 men.

This spring, as it became evident that victory in Europe was close at hand, a new strength ceiling of 6,968,000 officers and men was set, based on the requirements of war in the Pacific only. It then became possible to proceed immediately with the demobilization of those individuals who were most entitled to discharge.

The technique for the mobilization of American manpower in this war was unique. The special nature of the war introduced many new factors. Perhaps greater than any other single advantage of the United Nations was the productive capacity of American industry. It was therefore necessary not to cut too deeply into the manpower of the Nation in the process of acquiring the men urgently needed by the Army and the Navy. We had the problems of arming both ourselves and the Allied Nations while, at the same time, we created huge armed forces necessary to the successful prosecution of the war. Furthermore, our lines of communication were to be extended entirely around the world, requiring large forces of men to work them and absorbing even larger forces in transit over the thousands of miles to and fro without profit to the military enterprise.

Fighting across the oceans, we needed a very powerful Navy and a large merchant fleet to transport and maintain our armies and to carry munitions to our Allies. At the same time, it was our purpose to exploit every possible scientific device and technique to secure victory at the smallest cost in lives of our men. These various efforts demanded large numbers of men and women, and necessitated their allocation among the various programs with exceeding care, so that the right numbers of men would be doing the most important things at the most important time. The mere statement of this requirement fails to indicate the exceeding difficulty involved in its application to the special claims of each industry and the demands of each theater commander. To resolve the conflicting requirements posed a most difficult problem for a democracy at war.

It was estimated that the absolute ceiling on the number of American men physically fit for active war service lay between 15 and 16 million. The requirements of the naval and merchant shipping program had to be given a high order of priority. The Army decided to establish its strength ceiling at 7,700,000. Before we could bring the enemy to battle we had to secure our lines of communication and build our training and service installations. Within this total strength of the Army the minimum requirements of the Service Forces were set at 1,751,000. It was decided at the outset that the first offensive blows we could deliver upon the enemy would be through the air, and anticipated that the heavier and more effective our air assault, the sooner the enemy's capacity to resist would be destroyed. So the Air Forces were authorized to bring their strength to 2,340,000 men and were given the highest priority for the best qualified both physically and by educational and technical ability of the military manpower pool.

Each theater of operations had requirements for men over and above those allocated for its armies, air forces, and service installations. The troop basis allowed 423,000 men for these troops which would be directly attached to theater headquarters and major command installations throughout the world.

This left the Ground Forces with a maximum of 3,186,000 men within the limitations of the 7,700,000 effective troop strength. Yet when we entered the war it was almost impossible to compute accurately how many ground combat troops we would need to win. The precise results to be attained by modern aerial warfare could only be an educated guess.

It was known that we would take our heaviest casualties both from gunfire and disease on the ground where men must fight on the most intimate terms with the enemy. We had to estimate accurately the strength and the quality of the ground forces with which the enemy nations could oppose us, and we also had to estimate with a reasonable degree of accuracy the forces the Allied Nations could put into the battle. From 7 December 1941, until after Stalingrad and El Alamein, it was almost impossible to forecast what would be the results of the seesawing ground battles raging in Eastern Europe and North Africa. In addition, the decisions as to the relative strength of our various combat arms were limited by the capacity of our training establishment, which was then in process of being expanded.

With all these unknown quantities, in early 1942 we established a troop basis of 3,600,000 men which would permit the organization of 71 divisions: 59 infantry (including 18 National Guard), 10 armored, and two cavalry. This force was the largest we then had the ability to train, equip, and provide a nucleus of trained officers and noncommissioned officers. In mid-1942, when the original build-up in the United Kingdom for the invasion of France and the North African operation began to take shape, we found we needed more and still more service troops. The demand was insatiable. The over-all strength of the Army by the end of the year had increased to 5,397,674 men. Throughout 1942, however, the planners were at work estimating the requirements for 1943 which we believed would carry the Army to its peak of mobilization and would give us the necessary strength to force a victorious decision. The projection was 8,248,000 officers and men. At first it was estimated this would provide the Army with 105 divisions. Later it became evident that the men for only 100 divisions could be found within this strength. By the middle of 1943 we determined that this projected mobilization might impose too great a strain on the Nation's manpower, if all of the ambitious efforts planned for the global war were to remain in balance. Fortunately for our dilemma, Stalingrad was now past history and the great Soviet armies were showing a steadily increasing offensive power. The ceiling was therefore reduced to 7,700,000 shortly after the TRIDENT Conference in Washington, the meeting at which the over-all strategy became sufficiently firm to permit more precise planning. This amounted to a reducion of 548,000 men. The projected number of divisions was reduced to 90, including three special or "light" divisions that were being trained for jungle and mountain warfare. Later the 2d Cavalry Division, then in North Africa, was inactivated to provide urgently required service troops to support the amphibious landing in southern France. At the same time the Air Forces mobilization was fixed at 273 combat groups containing five very heavy bombardment (B–29's and 32's), 96 heavy bombardment (Flying Fortresses and Liberators), 26 medium bombardment, 8 light bombardment, 87 fighter, 27 troop carrier, and 24 reconnaissance groups.

On the face of it this appeared to be a critically small ground force for a nation as large as ours. Germany with a prewar population of 80,000,000 was mobilizing 313 divisions. Japan was putting 120 in the field; Italy 70; Hungary 23; Rumania 17; Bulgaria 18. Among the major Allies, the Soviets had a program for more than 550 divisions; the British for more than 50; the Chinese more than 300, though their divisional strength was often little more than regimental according to our method of computation. We were, however, second of the Allies in the mobilization of men and

women for military service, third among all the belligerent nations. The Soviet war effort was putting 22,000,000 men and women into the fight. By the time of their defeat, the Germans had mobilized 17,000,000. Our peak mobilization for the military services was 14,000,000. The British Empire mobilized 12,000,000; China 6,000,000.

This war brought an estimated total of 93,000,000 men and women of the Axis and United Nations into the conflict. And fortunately for us the great weight of numbers was on the side of the United Nations. Total Allied mobilization exceeded 62,000,000; total enemy mobilization, 30,000,000. The figures show how heavily the United States was concentrating on aerial warfare, on the production and movement of arms for its own troops and those of its Allies, and the meaning in terms of manpower of waging war from 3,000 to 9,000 miles from our shores.

Our ground strength was, for the size of our population, proportionately much smaller than that of the other belligerents. On the other hand it was, in effect, greater than a simple comparison of figures would indicate, for we had set up a system of training individual replacements that would maintain 89 divisions of ground troops and 273 combat air groups at full effective strength, enabling these units to continue in combat for protracted periods. In past wars it had been the accepted practice to organize as many divisions as manpower resources would permit, fight those divisions until casualties had reduced them to bare skeletons, then withdraw them from the line and rebuild them in a rear area. In 1918 the AEF was forced to reduce the strength of divisions and finally to disband newly arrived divisions in France in order to maintain the already limited strength of those engaged in battle. The system we adopted for this war involved a flow of individual replacements from training centers to the divisions so they would be constantly at full strength. The Air Forces established a similar flow to replace combat casualties and provide relief crews.

This system enabled us to pursue tremendous naval and shipping programs, the air bombardment programs and unprecedented, almost unbelievable, production and supply programs, and at the same time to gather the strength necessary to deliver the knock-out blows on the ground. There were other advantages. The more divisions an Army commander has under his control, the more supporting troops he must maintain and the greater are his traffic and supply problems. If his divisions are fewer in number but maintained at full strength, the power for attack continues while the logistical problems are greatly simplified.

When we had planned the size of the Army it had been impossible to foresee all of the ways in which the circumstances of waging three-dimensional war over the world would drain our manpower. It was clear that in this, as in all wars, men would fall victim to enemy action and disease; others would become ineffective because of sheer nervous and physical weariness that comes after long months of active participation in battle. But since the nature and technique of war, if not the fundamentals, are ever-changing, it is impossible to forecast casualties in one war from the experience of past ones. Both the intensity and the nature of our casualties have varied from month to month throughout this war, depending on the terrain and climate in which our forces were fighting and the quality of enemy resistance. Once an error was discovered it required months to correct it because of the days and distances between the training camps in the United States and the battle fronts of the world. Yet the necessity of estimating approximately a year in advance the numbers of men that would be needed in the various elements of the Army and the total over-all strength required that both the casualty rates and the requirements for transportation, rest, and rehabilitation be forecast accurately.

Some of the forecasts were accurate; others were not. An exact forecast of the rate of ground force attrition had to be tied directly to the effectiveness of such factors as aerial bombardment, artillery, enemy morale, enemy fighting ability, and a myriad others that defied long-range calculation. As the war progressed we learned, by unceasing study of the experience we were gaining daily, what to expect in specific situations. But even here these calculations could never be made absolute. After the North African campaign, it seemed that we could reasonably expect heavy casualties in our armored units. So in preparation for the Sicilian operation we built up a sizable backlog of tank drivers and crewmen and at the same time geared the training program in the United States to this expectation.

But once ashore in Sicily our armor raced around the island against feeble opposition and received few casualties. Then we moved directly into the battle for Italy's jagged terrain, where armor was difficult to employ, and found ourselves with a surplus of armor personnel and a critical shortage of infantrymen for the job of clearing a clever and stubborn enemy out of positions ideal for defense.

The final manpower crisis occurred during the prolonged and very heavy fighting in the fall of 1944 and the winter of 1944–45, both in Europe and in the Philippines. However, our own tribulations of this nature were much less serious, it is believed, than those of our Allies and certainly of the German enemy, whose divisions at times were reduced below 5,000.

In the Siegfried Line fighting prior to the final advance to the Rhine, the weather was atrocious and most of the troops had been continuously engaged since the landing in Normandy in June. The lack of port facilities prior to the opening of Antwerp to Allied shipping made it impossible to maintain divisions in normal corps reserve and thus permit the rotation of units between the fighting line and comfortable billets in rear areas. Divisions for this purpose were available in England and in northwestern France, but the state of the railroads and the flow of supplies made it impossible to maintain them at the front. All this resulted in a great strain on the fighting troops, and when a shortage in replacements was added, the situation grew very serious. It was just at this moment that the Germans launched their final offensive effort in the Ardennes.

This shortage in replacements at such a vital moment was the final effect of long-accumulating circumstances. The Army's manpower balance had been disturbed in the fall of 1943 by shortages in deliveries of inductees by the Selective Service System, which amounted during one 3-month period to about 100,000 men. A second factor was the miscalculation after North Africa that resulted in too many men being trained for the armored forces, the artillery and special troops, and too few by far for the infantry. Another factor was our failure in the early phases of the war to compensate in the over-all strength ceiling for the number of men who would be required to fill the long overseas pipelines and the time involved between the completion of the training of the individual in the United States and his final arrival in the division. Still another was the heavy pressure brought to bear on the War Department to hold down or reduce its demands for manpower. It will be recalled that for more than a year a rather vigorous attack was maintained against the War Department's estimates of manpower requirements. This limited our ability to get the men we needed when we needed them.

The Air Forces became involved in their own special type of imponderables. It was found that casualties suffered in the air had a serious reaction on the fighting effectiveness unless they were replaced the same day. Vacant chairs at mess had an unexpectedly depressing effect on the survivors of heavy fighting. The strain of frequent missions produced an unanticipated degree of fatigue which required relief crews in addition to the normal complement. It was finally found necessary during the period of the Eighth Air Force's heaviest fighting and losses to provide three combat crews per operating plane and to return the men to the United States after 25 missions. In the Mediterranean where the losses at this time were much lighter, 50 missions could be flown before the strain demanded the relief of the crews.

For a considerable period in the southwest Pacific and in the Aleutian Islands, the Air Forces carried an almost intolerable burden of fighting and endurance. The climate, the isolation, the insufficiency of numbers in the face of Japanese opposition all combined to make necessary a heavy increase in replacements.

Another unknown factor was discovered in the tropical regions. It was found that the ground service crews had to work all night virtually every night in maintaining their planes, and were consequently exposed to the malarial mosquito during her most active hours. These men suffered so much from over-fatigue and the cumulative effect of heavy doses of atabrine that their replacement for recuperation became necessary long before the estimated period.

To implement the replacement system we had established the Ground and Service Force Replacement Training Centers.[1] It required more than a year to train the many elements of a new division because of the difficulties of teaching men and units the team-work so essential under the trying conditions of bat-tle. But it was possible and practicable in a much shorter time to train an individual soldier so that he was competent to join a veteran team as a replacement where the battle experienced soldier can quick-ly fit him into the divisional structure. At the replacement training centers men were made ready to join the divisions and replace casualties in a concentrated training period of 17 weeks. At these training centers they were given six weeks of basic military training and intense physical conditioning. In the remaining period they acquired competence in handling the weapons with which they would fight or the equip-ment with which they would work and in learning the tactics of squads, platoons, companies, and battalions, the tactical units which actually engaged in combat.

An infantryman, for example, became proficient in his primary weapons and familiarized with the M1 rifle, the carbine, the hand grenade, the rifle grenade, the automatic rifle, the .30 caliber medium machine gun, the 60-mm mortar, and the two-man rocket launcher. These were the weapons that every infantry rifleman might be called upon to use. Not only were men taught to handle their weapons with proficiency in the replacement training centers, but they were taught to take care of themselves personally. There was intensive instruction in personal sanitation, malaria control, processing of contaminated water, cook-ing, and keeping dry in the open and all the other lore that a good soldier must understand. But most impor-tant, our replacements were taught the tricks of sur-vival in battle. As the Army acquired battle veterans, both officers and enlisted men were returned to the United States for duty as instructors in the replace-ment training centers. These veterans, who learned how to survive in combat, passed on knowledge to new men and thereby increased both their effective-ness and their chances of survival in their first experi-ence in combat. The training of replacements was made as realistic as possible to manage in training. Problems of street fighting, jungle fighting, and close combat were staged in realistic fashion with live ammunition, and men learned to crawl under sup-porting machine gun fire, to use grenades, and advance under live artillery barrages just as they must in battle. Although this training cost us a few casual-ties in this country, it is certain that for every casualty we took in this manner, we saved the lives of many men in battle.

After the completion of their replacement training, men received a furlough at home before reporting to oversea replacement depots where their long journey to the fighting fronts began. In the theaters of opera-tions they again staged through replacement depots which were established in the rear of each army group, army, and corps. When division commanders needed new men to replace casualties, they called on corps replacement depots and the men moved for-ward to the line.

Where it was possible, the replacements were absorbed in the division in its inactive periods, or in regiments in reserve positions, and each new man was

---

[1] Army Ground Forces:

Antiaircraft Artillery	Fort Bliss, Tex.
Armored	Fort Knox, Ky.
Cavalry	Fort Riley, Kans.
Field Artillery	Fort Bragg, N. C.
Field Artillery	Fort Sill, Okla.
Infantry	Camp Blanding, Fla.
Infantry	Camp Croft, S. C.
Infantry	Camp Fannin, Tex.
Infantry	Camp Gordon, Ga.
Infantry	Camp Hood, Tex.
Infantry	Camp Livington, La.
Infantry	Camp Roberts, Calif.
Infantry	Camp Rucker, Ala.
Infantry	Camp Wheeler, Ga.
Infantry	Camp Wolters, Tex.
Infantry	Fort McClellan, Ala.
Infantry Advanced	Camp Howze, Tex.
Infantry Advanced	Camp Maxey, Tex.
Infantry Advanced	Camp Robinson, Ark.
Tank Destroyer	Camp Hood, Tex.

Army Service Forces:

Adjutant General	Camp Lee, Va.
Chemical Warfare Service	Camp Lee, Va.
Engineers	Fort Belvoir, Va.
Engineers	Camp Claiborne, La.
Engineers	Fort Lewis, Wash.
Engineers	Fort Leonard Wood, Mo.
Finance	Fort Benjamin Harrison, Ind.
Medical	Camp Crowder, Mo.
Medical	Fort Lewis, Wash.
Ordnance	Aberdeen Proving Ground, Md.
Ordnance	Flora, Miss.
Quartermaster Corps	Fort Francis E. Warren, Wyo.
Quartermaster Corps	Camp Lee, Va.
Signal	Camp Crowder, Mo.
Special Service	Camp Lee, Va.
Transportation Corps	Camp Gordon Johnston, Fla.
Transportation Corps	Indiantown Gap, Pa.
Transportation Corps	Camp Plauche, La.
Transportation Corps	Fort Francis E. Warren, Wyo.

teamed up with a veteran so that he could learn to know his squadmates before he saw action. But when the battle was moving at a fast pace, replacements at times had to join units engaged with the enemy.

By the spring of 1944, as most of the shortcomings of the replacement system had become evident, the War Department took vigorous corrective action. A directive was sent to every theater requiring the establishment of retraining centers so that every man in the Army would be put to his most efficient use.

Since the early critical days of the mobilization, the Service Forces, the Ground Force training commands, and particularly the Air Forces had acquired great numbers of the best qualified of our men. The shortage of physically qualified men for infantry and artillery became apparent about midway in the activation of the new divisions. Later we started approaching the bottom of the manpower barrel, and it grew increasingly difficult to get men physically fit for combat out of the remaining civilian manpower pools. The only way in which the battle line could be kept firm was with suitable men already in the Army. To do this we speeded up the training program and stripped the divisions training in this country of nearly 90,000 infantrymen. At this same time the overseas divisions were returning increasing numbers of sick, wounded, and injured men to the hospitals as the intensity of the fighting developed and sickness took its toll. It was our purpose to fill up the service units with these hospitalized men who still could serve their country but no longer could endure the extreme hardships of the fox holes, and to send forward fresh men to take their place, after a necessary period of retraining.

In the United States we resolved to move out all physically fit men from the service and training commands and replace them with men who had been wounded or weakened by disease and the hardships of the front, with men who had been overseas so long that they were entitled to return home under the rotation policy, and where possible with civilians.

To reduce the requirements for military personnel in the United States in order to send the maximum number of physically fit men overseas, expert personnel audit teams under the direction of the War Manpower Board headed by Major General Lorenzo D. Gasser were dispatched to every service and training command. General Gasser's teams achieved remarkable results.

Through the economies effected by the personnel audit teams and the policies established by the War Department Personnel Division, 143,000 combat-fit men in the Ground Forces training installations and units, such as antiaircraft no longer necessary because of our air superiority, were placed in retraining for use as infantry. The Air Forces gave up another 65,000; the Service Forces 25,000. From the defense commands 12,000 men were extracted and at the same time the theaters produced 100,000 from their communication zones for the retraining program.

To assist General Eisenhower in combing out able-bodied men from his Communications Zone and replacing them with battle casualties, Lt. Gen. Ben Lear, who was then commanding the Army Ground Forces, was made Deputy Commander of the European Theater. This gave Eisenhower an outstanding general officer who would devote his entire attention to this critical readjustment of personnel.

To keep the over-all effective strength of the Army within the troop basis of 7,700,000, the call on Selective Service had been reduced from 160,000 a month in early 1944 to 60,000 in the fall. But when the replacement crisis reached its peak in the winter, there was no remaining alternative but again to call on Selective Service for more men. The call was increased to 80,000 in February of this year and 100,000 a month thereafter to the end of June.

No opportunity was overlooked to replace men with personnel of the Women's Army Corps, both in the United States and overseas. The WAC, now in its fourth year, presently has a strength of approximately 100,000, including 6,000 officers. Approximately 17,000 are on duty in the theaters. The Corps also contributed greatly to the critical shortage of hospital personnel by recruiting and training 100 general hospital companies to assist Army doctors and nurses in caring for the sick and wounded. Training of WAC personnel was consolidated at Fort Des Moines in July with the closing of the center at Fort Oglethorpe, Ga.

Early in 1944 the Army imposed restrictions on the movement overseas of combat replacements under the age of 19. It was the policy to send no man under this age to the battle lines so long as others were available. A few months later the policy was stiffened to prevent the use of men under 19 in infantry and armored units under any circumstances. By fall the Army had exhausted these resources, yet the need for men in General Eisenhower's armies continued to grow more pressing. The replacement training centers were filled largely with men who had been inducted when they reached the age of 18. It was a clear question of either relinquishing our momentum in the battles of Europe or using troops of this age. Certainly there is no military reason for not doing so. Men of 18, 19, and 20 make our finest soldiers. The excellent Marine divisions are made up largely of men of these age groups. They have stamina and recuperative power far beyond that of older men and this physical superiority often determines the issue in heavy and prolonged fighting. The only reason for not using 18-year olds in combat was the expressed preference of a great many Americans who felt there were moral reasons for not exposing men so young to the great risk of battle. The Army made every effort to accede to these views, but when it became a question of risking the victory or using men who could make it possible, there was no alternative. A new policy was then adopted to supersede the use of men under 19 in combat as soon as Germany surrendered and the terrific pressure on our available manpower was relieved. Congress in extending the Selective Service Act in May 1945 imposed a formal requirement, that 18-year-olds have at least a total of six months of training before they were sent into battle.

It is remarkable how exactly the mobilization plan fitted the requirements for victory. When Admiral Doenitz surrendered the German Government, every American division was in the operational theaters. All but two had seen action; one had the mission of securing the vital installations in the Hawaiian Islands; the other was an airborne division in SHAEF Reserve. To give General Eisenhower the impetus for final destruction of the German armies of the west, two divisions, already earmarked for future operations in the Pacific, the 86th and 97th, were halted on the West Coast in February, rushed across the United States and onto fast ships for Europe. When these troops left the New York Port of Embarkation there were no combat divisions remaining in the United States. The formed military forces of the nation were completely committed overseas to bring about our victory in Europe and keep sufficient pressure on Japan so that she could not dig in and stave off final defeat.

The significance of these facts should be carefully considered. Even with two-thirds of the German Army engaged by Russia, it took every man the Nation saw fit to mobilize to do our part of the job in Europe and at the same time keep the Japanese enemy under control in the Pacific. What would have been the result had the Red Army been defeated and the British Islands invaded, we can only guess. The possibility is rather terrifying.

Price of Victory

Even with our overwhelming concentration of air power and fire power, this war has been the most costly of any in which the Nation has been engaged. The victory in Europe alone cost us 772,626 battle casualties of which 160,045 are dead. The price of victory in the Pacific was 170,596 including 41,322 dead. Army battle deaths since 7 December 1941 were greater than the combined losses, Union and Confederate, of the Civil War. I present the following comparisons of the battle deaths we have suffered in all our wars so that there can be no misunderstanding of the enormous cost of this conflict, for which we were so completely unprepared:

	Number of months duration	Total battle deaths	Average battle deaths per month
American Revolution	80	4,044	50
War of 1812	30	1,877	62
Mexican War	20	1,721	86
Civil War (Union Losses)	48	110,070	2,293
Civil War (Confederate Losses)	48	74,524	1,552
Spanish-American	4	345	86
World War I	19	50,510	2,658
World War II	44	201,367	4,576

Army casualties in all theaters from 7 December 1941 until the end of the period of this report total 943,222, including 201,367 killed, 570,783 wounded, 114,205 prisoners, 56,867 missing; of the total wounded, prisoners, or missing more than 633,200 have returned to duty, or have been evacuated to the United States.

The great strategic bombardment strikes on Germany and the inauguration of the Mediterranean campaign pushed our total casualty rate above 5,000 a month in 1943. In the first five months of 1944 the increasing tempo of the air attack and the fighting in Italy drove our losses, killed, wounded, missing, and prisoners, to 13,700 men a month. Once ashore in Western Europe, the casualty rate leaped to 48,000 a month and increased to 81,000 by December. The average for the last seven months of the year was 59,000.

Out in the Pacific the advance on Japan cost 3,200 men a month throughout 1944. In the first seven months of this year the rate increased to 12,750 as we closed on the Japanese Islands.

The heaviest losses have been on the ground where the fighting never ceases night or day. Disregarding their heavy losses to disease and exposure, the combat divisions have taken more than 81 percent of all our casualties. However, though the percentage of the total is small, the casualties among the combat air crews have been very severe. By the end of July the Army Air Forces had taken nearly 120,000 casualties. Of this total 36,698 had died. The air raids over enemy territory gave Air Force casualties the heaviest weighting of permanency. The wounded of the Ground Forces drove their total casualties high, but with the exceptional medical care the Army has had in this war, the wounded had good chances to recover.

The following break-down for the European Theater of Operations (which does not include Italy) demonstrates where our casualties were taken:

Assignment	Number of casualties	Percentage of casualties
Theater troops	1,094	.18
Army group, army and corps troops	60,998	10.35
Infantry divisions	392,990	66.69
Armored divisions	62,417	10.60
Airborne divisions	22,008	3.73
Total combat divisions	477,415	81.02
Total field forces	539,507	91.55

Assignment	Number of casualties	Percentage of casualties
Troops under air commanders	1,699	.29
Strategic air forces	37,500	6.36
Tactical air forces	6,346	1.08
Total air forces.	45,545	7.73
Communications zone troops.	4,217	.72
Grand total	589,269	100.00

In the Army at large, the infantry comprises only 20.5 percent of total strength overseas, yet it has taken 70 percent of the total casualties. Enemy fire is no respecter of rank in this war; 10.2 percent of the casualties have been officers, a rate slightly higher than that for enlisted men.

The improvement of battle surgery and medical care, on the other hand, reduced the rate of death from wounds to less than one-half the rate in World War I, and permitted more than 58.8 percent of men wounded in this war to return to duty in the theaters of operations.

As staggering as our casualties have been, the enemy forces opposing us suffered many times more heavily; 1,592,600 Germans, Italians, and Japanese troops were killed for the 201,367 American soldiers who died. It is estimated that permanently disabled enemy total 303,700. We captured and disarmed 8,150,447 enemy troops.

The break-down of German and Italian losses against American, British, and French forces in the war in Europe follows:

	Battle dead	Permanently disabled	Captured	Total
Tunisia.	19,600	19,000	130,000	168,600
Sicily	5,000	2,000	7,100	14,100
Italy	86,000	15,000	357,089	458,089
Western Front . .	263,000	49,000	7,614,794[1]	7,926,794
Total	373,600	85,000	8,108,983[1]	8,567,583

[1] Includes 3,404,949 disarmed enemy forces.

The break-down of Japanese losses in the Eastern battlefronts, including China, since Pearl Harbor is as follows:

	Battle dead	Permanently disabled	Captured	Total
Southern Pacific .	684,000	69,000	19,806	772,806
Central Pacific . .	273,000	6,000	17,472	296,472
India-Burma	128,000	38,000	3,097	169,097
China	1,26,000	126,000	1,059	253,059
Aleutians	8,000	1,000	30	9,030
Total.	1,219,000	240,000	41,464	1,500,464

Constant efforts were made to ameliorate conditions under which American prisoners of war were held in Germany. The number of Americans taken prisoner by Germany and her satellites in the European war reached a final total of approximately 98,000. Until the final stages of administrative disintegration brought about by the success of our arms, it was possible to make our protests known and to secure some measure of relief for United States personnel in enemy hands. Nevertheless, Germany consistently failed to respect its obligations to provide a proper scale of food and clothing for Allied prisoners. When our forces overran prisoner camps, it was discovered that outrageous brutalities and atrocities had been inflicted upon Allied personnel. Every case is being investigated. The perpetrators will be punished.

Every effort was made to better the situation of American prisoners of war in Japanese hands but they produced only limited results. Though the United States did secure from the Japanese Government an agreement to accept the Geneva Prisoners of War Convention, to which Japan is not a party, in treatment of American prisoners and civilian internees, that Government failed to observe its obligations. With the cooperation of the Soviet Government there was inaugurated in 1944 a service for transmission of mail and some supplies to prisoners of war and civilian internees in the Far East. Funds were made available, to the maximum extent permitted by the Japanese Government, for prisoners of war and civilian internees in Japan proper, China, Manchuria, and the Netherlands East Indies. The Japanese did not agree to exchange sick and wounded prisoners of war, and our prisoners taken by the Japanese enemy were recovered only as a result of successful military operations. Nearly 16,000 Americans were taken prisoner in the fighting with Japan.

American troops who have been prisoners of the enemy are returned to the United States, with the highest priority next to that of sick and wounded, and high-point personnel of the forward combat units who are being returned for discharge. Rehabilitation treatment has been given them both overseas and in the United States. Sixty days temporary duty at home is granted each prisoner to permit him to rest and recuperate. Exprisoners from the Philippines have been promoted one grade since their release. Opportunity also is being given to all prisoners recovered in Europe to achieve the rank or grade which they presumably would have acquired but for the fact of capture. Many of these former prisoners of war are being discharged on the point system and other separation procedures.

The remarkable reduction in the percentage of deaths from battle wounds is one of the most direct and startling evidences of the great work of the Army medical service. In the last two years Army hospitals treated 9,000,000 patients; another 2,000,000 were treated in quarters and more than 80,000,000 cases passed through the dispensaries and received outpatient treatment. This tremendous task was accomplished by 45,000 Army doctors assisted by a like number of nurses and by more than one-half million enlisted men, including battalion-aid men, whose courage and devotion to duty under fire has been as great as that of the fighting men they assisted.

One of the great achievements of the Medical Department was the development of penicillin therapy which has already saved the lives of thousands. Two years ago pencillin, because of an extraordinarily complicated manufacturing process, was so scarce the small amounts available were priceless. Since then mass production techniques have been developed and the Army is now using 2,000,000 ampoules a month.

Despite the fact that United States troops lived and fought in some of the most disease-infested areas of the world, the death rate from nonbattle causes in the Army in the last two years was approximately that of the corresponding age group in civil life—about 3 per 1,000 per year. The greater exposure of troops was counterbalanced by the general immunization from such diseases as typhoid, typhus, cholera, tetanus, smallpox, and yellow fever, and, obviously, by the fact that men in the Army were selected for their physical fitness.

The comparison of the nonbattle death rate in this and other wars is impressive. During the Mexican War, 10 percent of officers and enlisted men died each year of disease; the rate was reduced to 7.2 percent of Union troops in the Civil War; to 1.6 percent in the Spanish War and the Philippine Insurrection; to 1.3 percent in World War I; and to 0.6 percent of the troops in this war.

Insect-borne diseases had a great influence on the course of operations throughout military history. Our campaigns on the remote Pacific Islands would have been far more difficult than they were except for the most rigid sanitary discipline and the development of highly effective insecticides and repellents. The most powerful weapon against disease-bearing lice, mosquitoes, flies, fleas, and other insects was a new chemical compound commonly known as DDT. In December 1943 and early 1944, a serious typhus epidemic developed in Naples. The incidence had reached 50 cases a day. DDT dusting stations were set up and by March more than a million and a quarter persons had been processed through them. These measures and an extensive vaccination program brought the epidemic under control within a month. Shortly after the invasion of Saipan an epidemic of dengue fever developed among the troops. After extensive aerial spraying of DDT in mosquito-breeding areas, the number of new cases a day fell more than 80 percent in two weeks. The danger of scrub typhus in the Pacific Islands and in Burma and China was reduced measurably by the impregnation of clothing with dimethyl phthalate.

The treatment of battle neurosis progressed steadily so that between 40 and 60 percent of men who broke down in battle returned to combat and another 20 to 30 percent returned to limited duties. In the early stages of the War less than 10 percent of these men were reclaimed for any duty.

The development of methods of handling whole blood on the battlefield was a great contribution to battle surgery. Though very useful, plasma is not nearly as effective in combating shock and preparing wounded for surgery as whole blood. Blood banks were established in every theater and additional quantities were shipped by air from the United States, as a result of the contribution of thousands of patriotic Americans. An expendable refrigerator was developed to preserve blood in the advanced surgical stations for a period of usefulness of 21 days.

So that no casualty is discharged from the Army until he has received full benefit of the finest hospital care this Nation can provide, the Medical Service has established a reconditioning program. Its purpose is to restore to fullest possible physical and mental health any soldier who has been wounded or fallen ill in the service of his country.

To insure that men are properly prepared for return to civilian life the Army established 25 special convalescent centers. At these centers men receive not only highly specialized medical treatment, but have full opportunity to select any vocational training or recreational activity, or both, they may desire. Men, for example, who have been disabled by loss of arms or legs are fitted with artificial limbs and taught to use them skillfully in their former civilian occupation or any new one they may select. Extreme care is taken to insure that men suffering from mental and nervous disorders resulting from combat are not returned to civil life until they have been given every possible treatment and regained their psychological balance.

Beyond the Call Of Duty

It is impossible for the Nation to compensate for the services of a fighting man. There is no pay scale that is high enough to buy the services of a single soldier during even a few minutes of the agony of combat, the physical miseries of the campaign, or of the extreme personal inconvenience of leaving his home to go out to the most unpleasant and dangerous spots on earth to serve his Nation. But so that our troops might know that the Nation realizes this simple truth, the Army made it a determined policy to decorate men promptly for arduous service and for acts of gallantry while they were fighting.

Exclusive of the Purple Heart, which a man receives when he is wounded, often right at the forward dressing station, the Army awarded 1,400,409 decorations for gallantry and meritorious service since we entered the war. The Nation's highest award, the Congressional Medal of Honor, was made to 239 men, more than 40 percent of whom died in their heroic service; 3,178 Distinguished Service Crosses have been awarded; 630 Distinguished Service Medals; 7,192 awards of the Legion of Merit; 52,831 Silver Stars; 103,762 Distinguished Flying Crosses; 8,592 Soldiers Medals; 189,309 Bronze Stars; and 1,034,676 Air Medals. Exclusive of the Air Medal and the Purple Heart, the Infantry received 34.5 percent of all decorations, the Air Corps 34.1 percent, the Field Artillery 10.7 percent, Medical Personnel 6.0 percent, and all other arms and services 14.7 percent.

The War Department has designated 34 specific campaigns during the course of this war. For participation in each of these campaigns a small star of bronze metal is authorized to be worn on the theater service ribbon, a star of silver metal to be worn in lieu of five bronze stars. A small bronze arrowhead is awarded for those who make combat parachute jumps or glider landings or who are in the assault wave of amphibious landings. For example, the men who fought with the 1st, 3d, and 9th Infantry Divisions from the invasion of North Africa to the defeat of Germany are entitled to wear the bronze assault arrowhead and eight bronze battle stars. In addition to the specific campaigns approved by the War Department, a theater commander may authorize additional bronze stars for antisubmarine, air, and ground combat participation not included within these campaigns.

Since my last report, two infantry badges and a medical badge have been authorized. The expert infantry badge was awarded to those who demonstrated proficiency in their specific duties after completion of training. The combat infantry badge was given to those who have shown outstanding skill as infantrymen in combat and the medical badge was presented to recognize the medical personnel who went into combat with infantry troops unarmed to serve the injured.

Battle participation stars had been awarded for the following campaigns up to the time of the Japanese surrender:

European-African-Middle Eastern Theater

Egypt-Libya	11 June 1942 to 12 February 1943
Air Offensive, Europe	4 July 1942 to 5 June 1944
Algeria-French Morocco	8 to 11 November 1942
Tunisia:	
Air	8 November 1942 to 13 May 1943
Ground	17 November 1942 to 13 May 1943
Sicily:	
Air	14 May to 17 August 1943
Ground	9 July to 17 August 1943
Naples-Foggia:	
Air	18 August 1943 to 21 January 1944
Ground	9 September 1943 to 21 January 1944
Rome-Arno	22 January to 9 September 1944
Normandy	6 June to 24 July 1944
Northern France	25 July to 14 September 1944
Southern France	15 August to 14 September 1944
North Apennines	10 September 1944 to 4 April 1945
Rhineland	15 September 1944 to 21 March 1945
Ardennes	16 December 1944 to 25 January 1945
Central Europe	22 March to 11 May 1945
Po Valley	5 April to 8 May 1945

Asiatic-Pacific Theater

Central Pacific	7 December 1941 to 6 December 1943
Burma	7 December 1941 to 26 May 1942
Philippine Islands	7 December 1941 to 10 May 1942
East Indies	1 January to 22 July 1942
India-Burma	2 April 1942 to 28 January 1945
Air Offensive, Japan	17 April 1942 (campaign not yet completed)
Aleutian Islands	3 June 1942 to 24 August 1943
China	4 July 1942 (campaign not yet completed)
Papua	23 July 1942 to 23 January 1943
Guadalcanal	7 August 1942 to 21 February 1943
New Guinea	24 January 1943 to 31 December 1944*
Northern Solomons	22 February 1943 to 21 November 1944*
Eastern Mandates:	
Air	7 December 1943 to 16 April 1944*
Ground	31 January to 14 June 1944*
Bismarck Archipelago	15 December 1943 to 27 November 1944*
Western Pacific:	
Air	17 April 1944 to (campaign not yet completed)
Ground	15 June 1944 to (campaign not yet completed)
Southern Philippines	17 October 1944 to 4 July 1945*
Luzon	9 January 1945 to 4 July 1945*
Central Burma	29 January 1945 to 15 July 1945
Ryukyus	26 March 1945 to 2 July 1945*

* Battle participation credit for the campaigns noted by asterisks may be awarded by the appropriate theater commander to units or individuals who actually engaged the enemy in the combat zone after the closing date.

Information and Recreation

In this war a very special effort was made to care for the minds of men in service as well as their bodies. This is continuing during the occupation and demobilization period. Millions of Americans have now been overseas in many parts of the world for several years. The conditions under which they lived during the war, the exposure to extreme danger, the monotony, the starvation for the comforts of living to which citizens of our Nation are accustomed placed heavy strains on their mental and nervous processes. From the beginning, the Army recognized that this strain must be counteracted by healthy informational and recreational activities.

At first, responsibility for both information and recreation was given to the Special Services Division of the Army Service Forces. Later, to permit greater specialization, this section was relieved of its informational duties and the Information and Education Division was created.

The Special Services Division continues to establish policy and assist the theaters in establishing and operating recreational and entertainment programs. Each month it has shipped to the theaters, for example, more than 4,000,000 copies of books selected by the Council on Books in Wartime, and 10,000,000 magazines to keep troops supplied with reading material. In each theater a Special Service officer directs the distribution of motion pictures, athletic and other recreational equipment, the routing of entertainment groups selected by the United Service Organizations, and the activities of the Red Cross Military Welfare Services Program. In each unit other Special Service officers are asigned to make the fullest use of all facilities offered by the theater command and improvise, wherever possible, additional recreational and entertainment programs.

During the feast two years the theaters of operations have done outstanding jobs in organizing shows and athletic programs of their own with soldier talent to supplement that shipped from the United States.

The Information and Education program is designed to keep our troops abreast of developments in their own areas and throughout the world. This division publishes the magazine "Yank," and assists the overseas theaters in publishing their own daily and weekly newspapers. At the present time there are eight editions of the daily newspaper "Stars and Stripes" published in England, France, Germany, Italy, Africa, and Hawaii. In the Asiatic theater there is a weekly newspaper known as the "CBI Roundup," published at New Delhi.

For men still in hospitals who are separated from their units by reason of injury or illness, Information and Education Division also publishes the weekly journal "Outfit" devoted solely to bringing news of combat and service units to their absent members, who otherwise lost all touch with their organizations and suffered a feeling of abandonment or ingratitude. Fifty-five thousand copies of this magazine are distributed each week in 154 hospitals all over the world.

The information and Education Division also conducts periodic surveys of how our troops are thinking—studies which the War Department utilizes in determining policies which affect troops individually. The point system of discharge was based directly on these expert surveys of soldier opinions.

It operates the Army News Service, an objective digest of United States press association and newspaper reports radioed over the world each day to supply news for Army newspapers and mimeographed or typewritten daily news sheets which are made available to troops by unit Information and Education officers. Information and Education also prepares and distributes radio programs for broadcast to troops throughout the world. During the great Campaign these programs were made available even in the most forward areas by mobile radio transmitters. This is the well-known Armed Forces Radio Service radio which carries a flavor of home to Americans from Germany to the islands of the far Pacific.

Through the Armed Forces Institute, which has established 10 oversea branches, troops have an opportunity to improve their educational or technical background. Prior to the end of the war more than a million members of the Armed Forces had taken advantage of these correspondence courses, self-teaching materials, and off-duty classes.

The information program also includes the small pocket-sized soldier guides to the customs and languages of the countries where our men serve, the weekly news map series published world-wide, and educational posters covering a wide field of subjects from promotion of bond sales among the troops to malaria control. The division also distributes information films such as Colonel Frank Capra's "Why We Fight" series, a series known as "GI Movies" and the Army-Navy Screen Magazine. "GI Movies" is a compilation of existing commercial short subjects and those produced by the Army Pictorial Service, such as comedies, travelogues, and similar educational subjects. The Army-Navy Screen Magazine is a periodic compilation of newsreel and new short subjects of special interest to troops. It includes the "By Request" films. A group of men in New Guinea wanted to see pictures of a snowstorm. Soldiers all over the world asked for pictures of the Statute of Liberty. One enlisted man wanted to hear a quartet sing "Down By the Old Mill Stream." These and similar requests are met in the Army-Navy Screen Magazine.

The big job ahead for both Information and Education and Special Services is the provision of constructive activity for troops in Europe awaiting return to the United States, and serving in our occupation forces.

At the present time, there is in full swing in the European theater a tremendous program of education and recreation to make sure that American soldiers have healthy and profitable activities for their spare time in the months they must wait for shipping space to become available to return them to the United States for discharge.

Three extensive programs offering educational opportunities to all who would take advantage of them have been established. The broadest is the school program for men in the smaller units now operating in both the European and Mediterranean theaters. These schools are conducted on the battalion or regimental level. Prior to V-E Day theaters had been shipped sufficient text books by the Armed Forces Institute to get these schools promptly under way. The courses have been selected from the entire range of secondary and vocational schooling, including subjects at the junior college level—algebra, elementary chemistry, history, languages, etc. Literacy training is also being provided. Individual soldiers may select any course of study they wish and pursue it in their own units while awaiting shipment home.

Opportunity for advanced study and technical refresher courses have also been provided. A centralized technical school has been established at Tidworth, England, with a capacity of 4,000 students for each two-month period. It opened in mid-August to troops and WAC personnel who wish to refresh their vocational skills prior to returning to their civilian jobs. Entrance qualifications require that applicants have three or more years of apprentice training in their craft. A university center has been established at Shrivenham, England, and another in France. These centers conduct a series of five 2-month courses at college level. Each has a capacity of 4,000 students per period. The qualifications for entrance in these courses are at least a high school education. Instruction is by Army personnel chosen for their civilian experience in education and these will be supplemented by eminent United States educators. Men who do not want to enroll in any of the conducted courses will still have the opportunity to take correspondence courses.

Troops on occupational duty now have little leisure, but as Europe stabilizes they will find more and more opportunity for profitable work. It is anticipated that 1,250,000 men and women in the European theater will take advantage of this opportunity to improve their education.

At the same time the recreational programs will be carried on at full pace. An extra allocation of equipment was on hand in Europe the day of German surrender. Baseball, football, golf, swimming, tennis, and other equipment that Americans use in sport is available to the troops. Motion pictures are on hand everywhere since fighting ceased. Numerous post exchanges have been established throughout the occupation zone. The exchanges offer food and refreshment as they do in the United States and sales counters where soldiers can buy Swiss watches, French perfumes, and other authentic European goods at noninflationary prices.

In the Pacific both the educational and recreational programs will be stepped up to meet the need of troops in occupation there.

Army Management

During the past two years the contributions to the war effort of three major commands and the War Department General Staff have been on a vast scale.

The Air Forces have developed in a remarkable manner. Young commanders and staff officers, catapulted into high rank by reason of the vast expansion, and then seasoned by wide experience, now give the Air arm the most effective form of military leadership—the vigorous direction of young men with the knowledge and judgment of veterans. Theoretical conceptions have been successfully demonstrated in action and modified or elaborated accordingly; new conceptions are welcomed and quickly tested; the young pilots and combat crews daily carry out the dangerous and difficult missions with a minimum of losses and a maximum of destruction for the enemy. In personnel, in planes, technique, and leadership, the Army Air Forces of more than two million men have made an immense contribution to our victories. Through aggressive tactics and the concept of strategical precision bombing they have made these victories possible with a minimum of casualties.

The Army Ground Force Command performed the extremely difficult mission of organizing our largest Army in an amazingly short time and at the same time training another 1,100,000 men to replace casualties. The Ground Forces headquarters has just completed a cycle in its operations. It began with the organization and training of the divisions, then deployment of the Ground Forces overseas and replacement of their casualties. Finally, in June of this year the Ground Forces began receiving the first of these divisions back under its control after the victory in Europe.

The tasks of the Army Service Forces have been difficult and complex beyond description. The efforts of this organization are only vaguely appreciated by the public, or even by the rank and file of the Army itself. The requirements for the support of the Army and the great oversea operations impinge frequently on conditions at home, giving rise to a succession of criticisms, largely unjustified in my opinion, since the critics seldom are aware of the salient facts and basic requirements. With thousands of miles of communications between the United States and the battlefronts, the necessity for reserve stocks here and abroad and the sudden rapid changes of requirements in various theaters have made it necessary for the Service Forces to be prepared for the unexpected. A minute change at the center of the circle usually results in miles of alterations along the circumference.

One consideration in particular is often ignored by the civilian in judging a condition which interferes or restricts with the daily life of America. The burden of supplying the fighting man at the place and at the time of his requirement rests squarely on a responsible officer. Excuses and explanations are not acceptable to the soldier and would not be tolerated by the political leaders, however inconsistent with the previous pressures on the home front which may have been in a measure responsible for the shortcomings.

The Service Forces have accomplished a prodigious task during the past two years in the supply of food, clothing, munitions, transportation, including the operation of a fleet of 1,537 ships; in the handling of pay and allowances amounting to 22.4 billion dollars;

in the processing of approximately 75 billion dollars in contracts; in the management of 3,700 post or cantonment installations in continental United States; in the operation of great base port organizations centered in Boston, New York, Hampton Roads, New Orleans, Los Angeles, San Francisco, and Seattle, in handling 7,370,000 men and 101,750,000 measurement tons of cargo; in the administration of the medical service which has treated 9,083,000 hospital cases and operated 791,000 hospital beds; in the direction of post exchanges now doing a monthly business of 90 million dollars and the organization and management of entertainment and educational opportunities; in the conduct of the administration of the Army and finally in the enormous tasks of redeployment and demobilization.

In the midst of handling this problem we have the constantly increasing pressure of families of the men for their release from the service. This has proved particularly vexatious in the case of high-point men on duty in the installations at home which must at this time bear the triple burden of supplying the requirements of the Pacific war, carrying out the regroupment and redeployment of troops in the United States, and accomplishing the demobilization of thousands of men daily. For the actual discharge of men, the required time for the preparation of papers, records, and accounts, and final payments has been reduced from approximately the 12 days of World War I to a minimum of 2 days, but even so the slightest increase over the minimum period produces a storm of protest. These reactions would ordinarily be accepted as normal to America but at this particular time they are bound to have a very disturbing effect on the morale of the forces overseas.

Almost as complex as the administrative management of these tremendous fighting forces has been the strategic direction of our global operations by the Joint Chiefs of Staff. Without the endless effort and the clear thinking of the officers in the various special groups or agencies attached directly to the Joint Chiefs of Staff to assist them in planning our operations and allocating our resources correctly, the great victories to which we are becoming accustomed would have been impossible.

I wish to make official acknowledgment of the support given me by the War Department General and Special Staffs, which has been beyond all praise in the understanding and handling of the countless problems of global warfare. Denied both public appreciation of their work and the desired opportunity for command in the field, these officers have made a great and selfless contribution to the war effort. The duration of the war has permitted a number of these officers to be given overseas assignments and at the same time, veterans of the fighting could be recalled to duty in the War Department.

No comment is necessary here to inform the public of the leadership given the American Armies by the Commanders-in-Chief in the theaters of operations. Their work has been, in my opinion, well nigh faultless considering the hazards and unexpected developments of war on the vast scale in which it has been conducted. I am sure that in years to come our people will take constantly increasing pride in the splendid contribution of these officers to the prestige of America and the best interests of the world generally.

To the Members of Congress I wish to express my thanks for the complete support given the Army by their willingness to provide the huge sums of money and the necessary legislative authorizations requested by the War Department for the prosecution of the war.

During the past two years the Secretary of War has supported the Army with a courage and a singular integrity of purpose to a degree rarely evidenced in public officials.

I cherish a feeling of deepest gratitude for the confidence President Roosevelt gave me and for the stern resolution with which he met the critical periods of our operations. It might be considered an interesting historical fact to record that during the landing in Normandy he made no request at any time for information other than that furnished him as a matter of routine and that he did not put a single question to me or General Eisenhower during the critical moments of the Battle of the Bulge in the Ardennes. The confidence he gave to the management of the Army was a tremendous source of assurance to the officers of the War Department.

To my new Commander-in-Chief I am indebted for the strong support he gave immediately on assuming office to the efforts of the Army to bring the War in Europe and the Pacific to an early and successful conclusion.

Demobilization

The Army is now involved in the process of demobilizing the tremendous forces it gathered to win the victory. This requires the return of millions of troops to the United States and the processing of their discharge. It means the cessation of the munitions production which has absorbed most of our energies and resources during the last five years.

The demobilization, like the mobilization, affects every phase of national life. Until such time as the authorized governmental agencies determine the policy which will regulate demobilization, the War Department must proceed under existing legislation and policy to carry on this process in an orderly manner. The disturbance to our national economy must be kept to the minimum.

We hope during the twelve months immediately following the cessation of hostilities to have discharged from the Army at least 5,000,000 men and officers. The determining factor throughout this period will be transportation. Soon thereafter, however, legislation must determine the strength of the Army for the immediate future.

The demobilization first got underway with the German surrender. It began simultaneously with the projected full scale redeployment for the final operations in the Pacific which we had planned in the event the Japanese resisted to a suicidal end. In this period first priority on our available shipping had to go for the redeployment—the scheduled movement of men and materiel to the Pacific directly from Europe or via the United States.

The day Japan capitulated orders were issued from the War Department suspending the redeployment operation throughout the world. Theater commanders were immediately directed to devote all facilities not required for the movement of occupational troops into Japan and elsewhere in the Far East to the demobilization.

The citizen Army had been recruited by selection of men on the basis of individual fitness for military duty and comparative essentiality in the Nation's economy. Accordingly, it was decided to discharge men individually rather than by units. An Army-wide survey was conducted to determine the consensus among the enlisted men as to the basis for determining discharge. The opinion was that those who have served longest, fought the hardest, and who have children should be permitted to leave the Army first. As a result the point system of returning men for discharge wherever they are on duty was established.

This system gives credit for length of Army service, overseas service, certain decorations, battle stars and not to exceed three dependent children under 18. The points are computed from 16 September 1940. Originally a minimum requirement of 85 points was established. Now the point system is revised to keep the demobilization steady and orderly.

The selection of soldiers eligible for discharge was made the responsibility of the various overseas commanders. As troops return they are sent to disposition centers near the embarkation ports and then move on in groups to Army stations near their homes. Here they receive a final screening and the separation center should usually be able to accomplish their discharge within 48 hours. In this final administrative procedure the soldier receives his mustering-out pay, his uniform, his discharge certificate, his lapel button, a separation record which summarizes his military service and qualifications, and his fare home. He also receives a pamphlet on veteran rights and benefits and advice regarding the agencies which can assist him in locating a job. Nothing is overlooked which will help the returning veteran to help himself.

Soldiers whose health or fitness has been impaired in the service of the country will not be discharged until everything possible to modern medical science has been done for their rehabilitation.

The War Department has now projected its demobilization schedules as far as it can under existing legislation and policies. The next moves and the next objectives are political more than military. They require decisions on that level. The War Department can only submit recommendations and await further instructions.

Our present national policies require us to: Maintain occupation forces in Europe and the Pacific; prepare for a possible contribution of forces to a world security organization; maintain national security while the world remains unstable and later on a more permanent or stable basis.

These policies require manpower. Yet at the same time it is the policy of the nation to completely demobilize the wartime army as rapidly as possible. Unless hundreds of thousands of men of the wartime forces are to remain in service at home and overseas, more permanent decisions must be made.

The War Department recommends that the occupation forces and the U. S. complement in the International security force be composed as much as possible of volunteers. This can be accomplished by establishing now a new permanent basis for the regular military establishment. If this recommendation and those which I will now discuss in detail for establishing a peacetime security policy are now adopted by the Congress, demobilization can proceed uninterrupted until all men now in temporary service have returned to their homes.

FOR THE COMMON DEFENSE

To fulfill its responsibility for protecting this Nation against foreign enemies, the Army must project its planning beyond the immediate future. In this connection I feel that I have a duty, a responsibility, to present publicly at this time my conception, from a military point of view, of what is required to prevent another international catastrophe.

For years men have been concerned with individual security. Modern nations have given considerable study and effort to the establishment of social security systems for those unable or unwise enough to provide for themselves. But effective insurance against the disasters which have slaughtered millions of people and leveled their homes is long overdue.

We finish each bloody war with a feeling of acute revulsion against this savage form of human behavior, and yet on each occasion we confuse military preparedness with the causes of war and then drift almost deliberately into another catastrophe. This error of judgment was defined long ago by Washington. He proposed to endow this Nation at the outset with a policy which should have been a reasonable guarantee of our security for centuries. The cost of refusing his guidance is recorded in the sacrifice of life and in the accumulation of mountainous debts. We have continued impractical. We have ignored the hard realities of world affairs. We have been purely idealistic.

We must start, I think, with a correction of the tragic misunderstanding that a security policy is a war policy. War has been defined by a people who have thought a lot about it—the Germans. They have started most of the recent ones. The German soldier-philosopher Clausewitz described war as a special violent form of political action. Frederic of Prussia, who left Germany the belligerent legacy which has now destroyed her, viewed war as a device to enforce his will whether he was right or wrong. He held that with an invincible offensive military force he could win any political argument. This is the doctrine Hitler carried to the verge of complete success. It is the doctrine of Japan. It is a criminal doctrine, and like other forms of crime, it has cropped up again and again since man began to live with his neighbors in communities and nations. There has long been an effort to outlaw war for exactly the same reason that man has outlawed murder. But the law prohibiting murder does not of itself prevent murder. It must be enforced. The enforcing power, however, must be maintained on a strictly democratic basis. There must not be a large standing army subject to the behest of a group of schemers. The citizen-soldier is the guarantee against such a misuse of power.

In order to establish an international system for preventing wars, peace-loving peoples of the world are demonstrating an eagerness to send their representatives to such conferences as those at Dumbarton Oaks and San Francisco with the fervent hope that they may find a practical solution. Yet, until it is proved that such a solution has been found to prevent wars, a rich nation which lays down its arms as we have done after every war in our history, will court disaster. The existence of the complex and fearful instruments of destruction now available make this a simple truth which is, in my opinion, undebatable.

So far as their ability to defend themselves and their institutions was concerned, the great democracies were sick nations when Hitler openly massed his forces to impose his will on the world. As sick as any was the United States of America. We had no field army. There were the bare skeletons of three and one-half divisions scattered in small pieces over the entire United States. It was impossible to train even these few combat troops as divisions because motor transportation and other facilities were lacking and funds for adequate maneuvers were not appropriated. The

Air Forces consisted of a few partially equipped squadrons serving continental United States, Panama, Hawaii, and the Philippines; their planes were largely obsolescent and could hardly have survived a single day of modern aerial combat. We lacked modern arms and equipment. When President Roosevelt proclaimed, on 8 September 1939, that a limited emergency existed for the United States we were, in terms of available strength, not even a third-rate military power. Some collegians had been informing the world and evidently convincing the Japanese that the young men of America would refuse to fight in defense of their country.

The German armies swept over Europe at the very moment we sought to avoid war by assuring ourselves that there could be no war. The security of the United States of America was saved by sea distances, by Allies, and by the errors of a prepared enemy. For probably the last time in the history of warfare those ocean distances were a vital factor in our defense. We may elect again to depend on others and the whim and error of potential enemies, but if we do we will be carrying the treasure and freedom of this great Nation in a paper bag.

Returning from France after the last war, with General Pershing, I participated in his endeavors to persuade the Nation to establish and maintain a sound defense policy. Had his recommendations been accepted, they might have saved this country the hundreds of billions of dollars and the more than a million casualties it has cost us again to restore the peace. We might even have been spared this present world tragedy. General Pershing was asked against whom do we prepare. Obviously that question could not be answered specifically until nearly 20 years later when Adolf Hitler led the replenished armies of defeated Germany back into world conflict. Even as late as 1940 I was asked very much the same question before a committee of Congress. Not even then could I say definitely exactly where we might have to fight, but I did recall that in past wars the United States forces had fought in Latin America, in France, in Belgium, in Germany, in Russia, in Siberia, in Africa, in the Philippines, and in China, but I did not anticipate that in the near future American soldiers would fight in the heat of Burma and in the islands of the vast Pacific, and would be garrisoning areas across the entire land and water masses of the earth. From this lesson there is no alternative but that this Nation must be prepared to defend its interest against any nation or combination of nations which might sometime feel powerful enough to attempt the settlement of political arguments or gain resources or territory by force of arms.

Twice in recent history the factories and farms and people of the United States have foiled aggressor nations; conspirators against the peace would not give us a third opportunity.

Between Germany and America in 1914 and again in 1939 stood Great Britain and the USSR, France, Poland, and the other countries of Europe. Because the technique of destruction had not progressed to its present peak, these nations had to be eliminated and the Atlantic Ocean crossed by ships before our factories could be brought within the range of the enemy guns. At the close of the German war in Europe they were just on the outer fringes of the range of fire from an enemy in Europe. Goering stated after his capture that it was a certainty the eastern American cities would have been under rocket bombardment had Germany remained undefeated for two more years. The first attacks would have started much sooner. The technique of war has brought the United States, its homes and factories into the front line of world conflict. They escaped destructive bombardment in the second World War. They would not in a third.

It no longer appears practical to continue what we once conceived as hemispheric defense as a satisfactory basis for our security. We are now concerned with the peace of the entire world. And the peace can only be maintained by the strong.

What then must we do to remain strong and still not bankrupt ourselves on military expenditures to maintain a prohibitively expensive professional army even if one could be recruited? President Washington answered that question in recommendations to the first Congress to convene under the United States Constitution. He proposed a program for the peacetime training of a citizen army. At that time the conception of a large professional Regular Army was considered dangerous to the liberties of the Nation. It is still so today. But the determining factor in solving this problem will inevitably be the relation between the maintenance of military power and the cost in annual appropriations. No system, even if actually adopted in the near future, can survive the political pressure to reduce the military budget if the costs are high—and professional armies are very costly.

There is now another disadvantage to a large professional standing army. Wars in the twentieth century are fought with the total resources, economic, scientific, and human of entire nations. Every specialized field of human knowledge is employed. Modern war requires the skills and knowledge of the individuals of a nation.

Obviously we cannot all put on uniforms and stand ready to repel invasion. The greatest energy in peacetime of any successful nation must be devoted to productive and gainful labor. But all Americans can, in the next generations, prepare themselves to serve their country in maintaining the peace or against the tragic hour when peace is broken, if such a misfortune again overtakes us. This is what is meant by Universal Military *Training*. It is not universal military *service*—the actual induction of men into the combatant

forces. Such forces would be composed during peacetime of volunteers. The trainees would be in separate organizations maintained for training purposes only. Once trained, young men would be freed from further connection with the Army unless they chose, as they now may, to enroll in the National Guard or an organized reserve unit, or to volunteer for service in the small professional army. When the Nation is in jeopardy they could be called, just as men are now called, by a committee of local neighbors, in an order of priority and under such conditions as directed at that time by the Congress.

The concept of universal military training is not founded, as some may believe on the principle of a mass Army. The Army has been accused of rigidly holding to this doctrine in the face of modern developments. Nothing, I think, could be farther from the fact, as the record of the mobilization for this war demonstrates. Earlier in this report I explained how we had allocated manpower to exploit American technology. Out of our entire military mobilization of 14,000,000 men, the number of infantry troops was less than 1,500,000 Army and Marine.

The remainder of our armed forces, sea, air, and ground, was largely fighting a war of machinery. Counting those engaged in war production there were probably 75 to 80,000,000 Americans directly involved in prosecution of the war. To technological warfare we devoted 98 percent of our entire effort.

Nor is it proposed now to abandon this formula which has been so amazingly successful. The harnessing of the basic power of the universe will further spur our efforts to use brain for brawn in safeguarding the United States of America.

However, technology does not eliminate the need for men in war. The Air Forces, which were the highest developed technologically of any of our armed forces in this war, required millions of men to do their job. Every B-29 that winged over Japan was dependent on the efforts of 12 officers and 73 men in the immediate combat area alone.

The number of men that were involved in the delivery of the atomic bomb on Hiroshima was tremendous. First we had to have the base in the Marianas from which the plane took off. This first required preliminary operations across the vast Pacific, thousands of ships, millions of tons of supply, the heroic efforts of hundreds of thousands of men. Further, we needed the B-20's and their fighter escort which gave us control of the air over Japan. This was the result of thousands of hours of training and preparation in the U. S., and the energies of hundreds of thousands of men.

The effective technology on the military structure is identical to its effect on the national economy. Just as the automobile replaced the horse and made work for millions of Americans, the atomic explosives will require the services of millions of men if we are compelled to employ them in fighting our battles.

This war has made it clear that the security of the Nation, when challenged by an armed enemy, requires the services of virtually all able-bodied male citizens within the effective military age group.

In war the Nation cannot depend on the numbers of men willing to volunteer for active service; nor can our security in peace.

In another national emergency, the existence of a substantial portion of the Nation's young manpower already trained or in process of training, would make it possible to fill out immediately the peacetime ranks of the Navy, the Regular Army, the National Guard, and the Organized Reserve. As a result our Armed Forces would be ready for almost immediate deployment to counter initial hostile moves, ready to prevent an enemy from gaining footholds from which he could launch destructive attacks against our industries and our homes. By this method we would establish, for the generations to come, a national military policy: (1) which is entirely within the financial capabilities of our peacetime economy and is absolutely democratic in its nature, and (2) which places the military world and therefore the political world on notice that this vast power, linked to our tremendous resources, wealth, and production, is immediately available. There can be no question that all the nations of the world will respect our views accordingly, creating at least a probability of peace on earth and of good will among men rather than disaster upon disaster in a tormented world where the very processes of civilization itself are constantly threatened.

The decision in this matter is so grave in consequences that it demands complete frankness on my part. Therefore I must say that many of the objections which have been made to Universal Military Training appear to be influenced by ulterior motives, or to ignore completely the tragedies of the past and present which we are seeking to avoid for the future. They often seem to give undue importance to restrictions on our freedom of life, trivial in comparison with the awful tragedies we are seeking to avoid and the great blessings we hope to secure for succeeding generations.

The timing of our decision on the question of Universal Military Training is urgent. The officials of the State Department have been strongly of the opinion that a decision in this matter prior to the final peace negotiations would greatly strengthen the hand of the United States in securing acceptance of a genuine organization to handle international differences.

The terms of the final peace settlement will provide a basis for determining the strength of the regular or permanent postwar military forces of the United States, air, ground, and naval, but they cannot, in my opinion, alter the necessity for a system of Universal Military Training.

The yardstick by which the size of the permanent force must be measured is maximum security with minimum cost in men, materiel, and maintenance. So far as they can foresee world conditions a decade from now, War Department planners, who have taken every conceivable factor into consideration, believe that our position will be sound if we set up machinery which will permit the mobilization of an Army of 4,000,000 men within a period of 1 year following any international crisis resulting in a national emergency for the United States.

The Regular Army must be comprised largely of a strategic force, heavy in air power, partially deployed in the Pacific and the Caribbean ready to protect the Nation against a sudden hostile thrust and immediately available for emergency action wherever required. It is obvious that another war would start with a lightning attack to take us unaware. The pace of the attack would be at supersonic speeds of rocket weapons closely followed by a striking force which would seek to exploit the initial and critical advantage. We must be suffciently prepared against such a threat to hold the enemy at a distance until we can rapidly mobilize our strength. The Regular Army, and the National Guard, must be prepared to meet such a crisis.

Another mission of the Regular Army is to provide the security garrisons for the outlying bases. We quickly lost the Philippines, Guam, and Wake Islands at the beginning of this war and are still expending lives and wealth in recovering them.

The third mission of the permanent Army is to furnish the overhead, the higher headquarters which must keep the machine and the plans up to date for whatever national emergency we may face in the future. This overhead includes the War Department, the War College, the service schools, and the headquarters of the military areas into which continental United States is subdivided to facilitate decentralized command and coordination of the peacetime military machine. This was about all we had on the eve of this war, planners and a small number of men who had little to handle in practice but sound ideas on how to employ the wartime hosts that would be gathered in the storm. Had it not been for the time the British Empire and the Soviets bought us, those plans and ideas would have been of little use.

The fourth and probably the most important mission of the Regular Army is to provide the knowledge, the expert personnel, and the installations for training the citizen-soldier upon whom, in my view, the future peace of the world largely depends.

Of the citizen-Army, the National Guard is in the first category of importance. It must be healthy and strong, ready to take its place in the first line of defense in the first weeks of an emergency, and not dependent upon a year or more of training before it can be conditioned to take the field against a trained enemy. It is not feasible under the conditions of peace for the National Guard within itself to provide the basic, the fundamental training which is an imperative requirement for its mission. Therefore, in my opinion, based on a long and intimate experience with the Guard from 1907 until 1941, the essential requirement for such a system under modern conditions is Universal Military Training from which to draw the volunteers for the ranks of the Guard. Without such a firm foundation, I am clearly of the opinion that a sufficiently dependable force for our postwar needs cannot be maintained.

The second important component of the Citizen Army is the Organized Reserve through which full mobilization of the Nation's resources to war footing is accomplished. At the start of the present war, the Reserve was almost entirely an officer corps, the regimental and divisional groups lacking a practical basis for mobilization. The contribution of this component was therefore largely one of individuals, but of wide extent and great importance. The depleted officer ranks of the Regular Army were filled by the Reserve, the countless new staffs and organizations were mainly composed of Reserve officers, the great training camps for men inducted through the Selective Service System drew in the beginning on the officer strength of the Reserve Corps. The Officer candidate schools from which our present Army acquired its vital small unit leadership were staffed by Reserve officers. These officers were largely veterans of World War I and graduates of the Reserve Officers' Training Corps. Pitifully small appropriations had limited training to a brief period once in every 3 or 4 years and so few numbers of troops that the limited training the Reserve officers received had little relation to actual battle.

This lack of troops with which Reserve officers could acquire practical experience in command and staff work was the most critical limitation. There was no enlisted strength in the Reserve force. There was little connection and understanding between the Officers' Reserve Corps and the National Guard—which had an enlisted strength—and the number of enlisted men in the Regular Army was so small that it was impossible to qualify Reserve officers by training with Regulars. Especially in the dense centers of population there were few Regular troops. Yet here were located the largest groups of Reserve officers. Even had funds for transportation to the areas where Regular troops were stationed been available, and they were not, the few troops on the Regular roles would have been completely submerged under a deluge of Reserve officers. For example, the strength of

the Officers' Reserve Corps in 1938 was more than double the number of Regular soldiers in combat units in the continental United States.

Only by universal military training can full vigor and life be instilled into the Reserve system. It creates a pool of well-trained men and officers from which the National Guard and the Organized Reserve can draw volunteers; it provides opportunities for the Guard and Reserve units to participate in corps and Army maneuvers, which are vital preparations to success in military campaigns. Without these trained men and officers, without such opportunities to develop skill through actual practice in realistic maneuvers, neither the Regular Army, the National Guard, nor the Reserve can hope to bring high efficiency to their vital missions.

Though ROTC graduates composed 12 percent of the war officers, its most important contribution was the immediate availability of its product. Just what we could have done in the first phases of our mobilization and training without these men I do not know. I do know that our plans would have had to be greatly curtailed and the cessation of hostilities on the European front would have been delayed accordingly. We must enlarge and strengthen the system. It must be established on a higher level, comparable to the academic levels of college education in which the young men of the ROTC are engaged. All this is made easily possible if the student has participated in universal military training, and at the same time the length of the course can be shortened by 1 year. He would enter the ROTC as far advanced as his predecessors were after 2½ years of the original 3-years' course. He would have completed his elementary training—the military equivalent of his grammar school and high school courses—and would be prepared for college work, that is for training as an officer, a prospective leader of men. The product of such an ROTC would provide the National Guard and the Organized Reserve with an officer corps of exceptional character.

An unbroken period of 1 year's training appears essential to the success of a sound security plan based on the concept of a citizen army.

It is possible to train individual soldiers as replacements for veteran divisions and air groups as we now do in a comparatively short period of time. The training of the unit itself cannot be accomplished at best in less than a year; air units require even more time. The principle is identical to that of coaching a football team. A halfback can learn quickly how to run with the ball, but it takes time and much practice and long hours of team scrimmage before he is proficient at carrying the ball through an opposing team, utilizing the aid of the ten other men on the team. So it is with an army division or combat air group. Men learn to fire a rifle or machine gun quickly, but it takes long hours of scrimmage, which the army calls maneuver, before the firing of the rifle is coordinated with the activities of more than 14,000 other men on the team.

All men who might someday have to fight for their Nation must have this team training. The seasoned soldiers of our present superb divisions will have lived beyond the age of military usefulness. The situation will be similar in the peacetime army to that which obtained when we began to mobilize for this war and all men had to have at least a year of unit training before we had divisions even fit for shipment overseas.

The training program would be according to the standards which have made the American soldier in this war the equal of the finest fighting men. It would be kept abreast of technical developments and the resulting modifications of tactics.

Throughout the training a strenuous program of instruction would have to be followed, but it would not be possible in peace to carry on the work under the tremendous pressure we now follow in wartime. Athletics, recreational opportunities, short weekends, and other vacational opportunities such as at Christmas time, would, of course, be necessary. However, if the Government is to be justified in the expenditure of the funds involved, a vigorous schedule should be enforced; otherwise we would produce a half-baked product which would fail to command the respectful attention of the nations of the world, and therefore negate the primary purpose of the entire system.

To those who fear the Army might militarize our young men and indoctrinate them with dangerous conceptions, to those who express doubts of the Army's capacity to do the job, I submit the evidence of our present armies. The troops have been trained sufficiently to defeat a first-class enemy. Their minds have not been warped—quite the contrary. The American people are satisfied, I am confident, that their Armies are, in fact, armies of democracy. They know that the men composing those Armies are far better physically than they otherwise would have been, that their general health has been better than at home, except for those serving in the tropical jungles. The officers who trained our Armies were largely citizen-soldiers. They did have the initial guidance of Regular officers, but only 2 percent of the entire officer corps was professional. Only slightly more were of the National Guard; 25 percent were products of the Officers' Reserve Corps, 12 percent more were men commissioned direct from civil life because of certain professional qualifications. The great majority of the officers came up from the ranks, 59 percent of the total, which guaranteed the democracy of the Army.

To those who consider the introduction of a system of universal military training an imposition on democracy, I would reply that in my opinion it would be the most democratic expression of our national life.

Whatever my limitations may be in judging this matter, I submit the evidence of the proposal of our first President.

Washington's program provided for universal training of all men arriving at the age of 17. The citizen-militia was to be divided into three classes, men from 17 to 21, known as the advance corps, men 21 to 46, known as the main corps, and men from 46 to 61, known as the reserve corps. All of the peacetime training would have been concentrated in the advance corps, but eventually all members of main and reserve corps would have been graduates of the training program. The militia bill was first introduced in the Third Session of the First Congress. It was considered in the House on 5 March 1792, and as finally enacted contained no element of any of Washington's recommendations. It was so emasculated when finally adopted that the representative who introduced the bill himself voted against its passage.

It appears probable that had the bill been approved by Congress, the United States might have avoided much of the war making that has filled its brief history. The impressment of American seamen would not have been regarded as a harmless pastime in the early 1800's, nor would the Kaiser have been so easily disposed to avenge the death of the Archduke Franz Ferdinand in 1914 with a world war, nor Adolf Hitler have been quite so quick to break the peace, if over these years the United States had been recognized by the war mongers as a Nation immediately to be reckoned with.

The peacetime army must not only be prepared for immediate mobilization of an effective war army, but it must have in reserve the weapons needed for the first months of the fighting and clear-cut plans for immediately producing the tremendous additional quantities of matériel necessary in total war. We must never again face a great national crisis with ammunition lacking to serve our guns, few guns to fire, and no decisive procedures for procuring vital arms in sufficient quantities.

The necessity for continuous research into the military ramifications of man's scientific advance is now clear to all and it should not be too difficult to obtain the necessary appropriations for this purpose during peacetime. There is, however, always much reluctance to expenditure of funds for improvement of war-making instruments, particularly where there is no peacetime usefulness in the product.

The development of combat airplanes is closely allied with development of civil aeronautics; the prototypes of many of our present transport planes and those soon to come were originally bombers. Many of the aeronautical principles that helped give this Nation the greatest air force in the world grew out of commercial development and our production know-how at the start of this war was partially the fruit of peacetime commercial enterprise. Since many vital types of weapons have no commercial counterpart, the peacetime development of these weapons has been grossly neglected. Antiaircraft weapons are a good example. The highly efficient antiaircraft of today did not materialize until long after the fighting began. The consequent cost in time, life, and money of this failure to spend the necessary sums on such activity in peacetime has been appalling.

There is another phase of scientific research which I think has been somewhat ignored—the development of expeditious methods for the mass production of war matériel. This is of great importance since it determines how quickly we can mobilize our resources if war comes and how large and costly our reserve stocks of war matériel must be. Serious thought and planning along this line can save millions of tax dollars.

We can be certain that the next war, if there is one, will be even more total than this one. The nature of war is such that once it now begins it can end only as this one is ending, in the destruction of the vanquished, and it should be assumed that another reconversion from peace to war production will take place initially under enemy distant bombardment. Industrial mobilization plans must be founded on these assumptions and so organized that they will meet them and any other situation that may develop. Yet they must in no way retard or inhibit the course of peacetime production.

If this Nation is to remain great it must bear in mind now and in the future that war is not the choice of those who wish passionately for peace. It is the choice of those who are willing to resort to violence for political advantage. We can fortify ourselves against disaster, I am convinced, by the measures I have here outlined. In these protections we can face the future with a reasonable hope for the best and with quiet assurance that even though the worst may come, we are prepared for it.

As President Washington said in his message to Congress of 3 December 1793:

I cannot recommend to your notice measures for the fulfillment of our duties to the rest of the world, without again pressing upon you the necessity of placing ourselves in a position of complete defense, and of exacting from them the fulfillment of the duties towards us. The United States ought not to indulge a persuasion, that contrary to the order of human efforts, they will forever keep at a distance those painful appeals to arms, with which the history of every other nation abounds. There is a rank due to the United States among nations, which will be withheld, if not absolutely lost, by the reputation of weakness—if we desire to avoid insult we must be ready to repel it; if we desire to secure peace, one of the most powerful institutions of our rising prosperity, it must be known that we are at all times ready for war.

Washington, D. C.
1 September 1945

Chief of Staff